Graphic Surf

Decals, Patches, Stickers

Ben Marcus

With Forewords by Pete Noble, Cary Weiss, & Keith Eshelman

Schiffer Publishing Ltd

4880 Lower Valley Road, Atglen, PA 19310

Schiffer Books are available at special discounts for bulk purchases for sales promotions or premiums. Special editions, including personalized covers, corporate imprints, and excerpts can be created in large quantities for special needs. For more information contact the publisher:

Published by Schiffer Publishing Ltd.
4880 Lower Valley Road
Atglen, PA 19310
Phone: (610) 593-1777; Fax: (610) 593-2002
E-mail: Info@schifferbooks.com

For the largest selection of fine reference books on this and related subjects, please visit our web site at **www.schifferbooks.com**
We are always looking for people to write books on new and related subjects. If you have an idea for a book please contact us at the above address.

This book may be purchased from the publisher.
Include $3.95 for shipping.
Please try your bookstore first.
You may write for a free catalog.

In Europe, Schiffer books are distributed by
Bushwood Books
6 Marksbury Ave.
Kew Gardens
Surrey TW9 4JF England
Phone: 44 (0) 20 8392-8585; Fax: 44 (0) 20 8392-9876
E-mail: info@bushwoodbooks.co.uk
Website: www.bushwoodbooks.co.uk
Free postage in the U.K., Europe; air mail at cost.

Library of Congress Control Number: 2007940376

Designed by Ro Shillingford
Type set in Zurich BT

ISBN: 978-0-7643-2948-7
Printed in China

CONTENTS

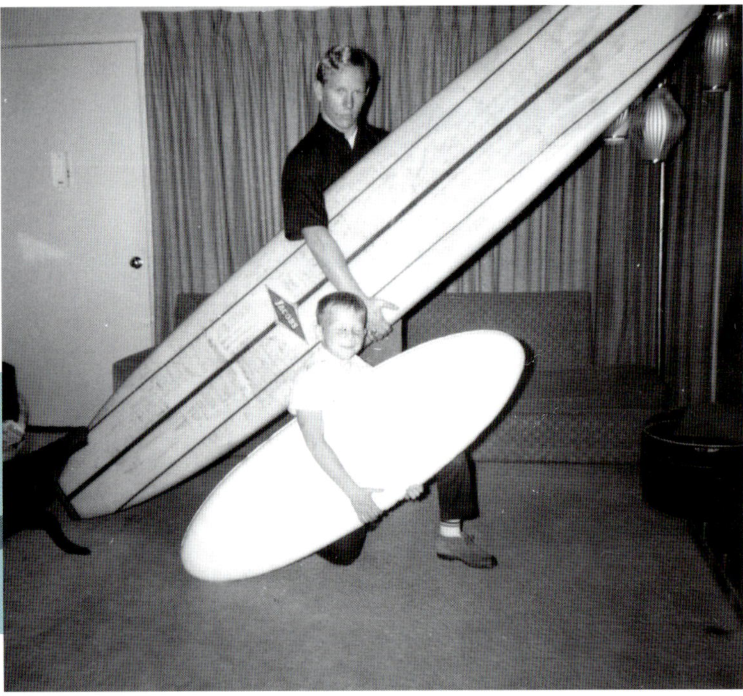

Pete Noble at 15 years old, in the back, embracing his Jacobs modern machine. That is Tommy Noble, eight years old, learning from big brother.

FOREWORDS

PETE NOBLE

As you read this book, jog your memory and try to remember how many of these items you wasted as a kid. How many times did your Dad yell at you for putting them on the car, the bathroom, and/or your bedroom. What do you think? What do these precious items make you think of?

In the summer of 1963, as a 13-year-old, I walked into swim practice in Hayward, California, and most of the guys had surfboard company T-shirts on. They all told me that the only way you could get one of these cool T-shirts and/or decals was to own one of these surfboards. They were cool so I believed them and I told them I was a surfer. Well I was a pretty good athlete, but they let me know not so! Well, if it were not for my longtime friend Rick "Frosty" Hesson, who first took me surfing in Santa Cruz (he refused to let me buy an O'Neill's Surf Shop T-Shirt), I would not have realized how cool surfing was or how cool all the other stuff was. Most important I would have not lived my lifelong passion/lifestyle: surfing!

In 1974 I broke my neck playing rugby. My late brother, Tommy Noble – founder of Toes on the Nose and Newport Surf & Sport – bought me a brand new Steve Colleta, nine foot surfboard for Christmas. I was the guy in the way every summer between coaching and rugby, but Tommy rekindled my desire to surf full time. It was a great surfboard, but I could still turn a head on my old 9' 8" Jacobs. I was hooked again! But longboarding was not revived!

Just for the heck of it I started to research the old surf shops and board makers. They were not all still around but people had bought their shops/names and wanted to get some money out of this stuff. The O'Neills threw away a ton of decals before I could rescue them. I would send a $10 check and they would send me 20 to 50 decals and/or patches. They were happy for the money and glad to get rid of this old stuff. Most people thought I was crazy!

Well not everyone. Barney Langner, the old Portola Surf Shop owner, asked me to line the upper part of his showcase with old decals. I did, and then I thought

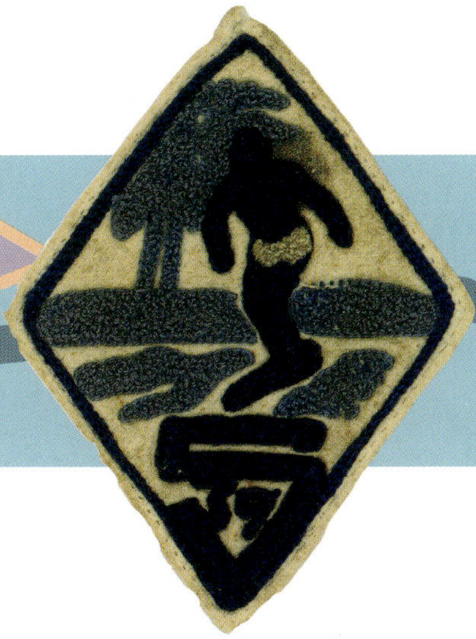

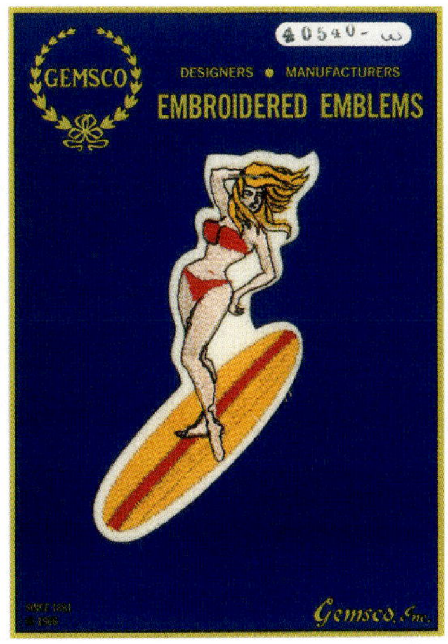

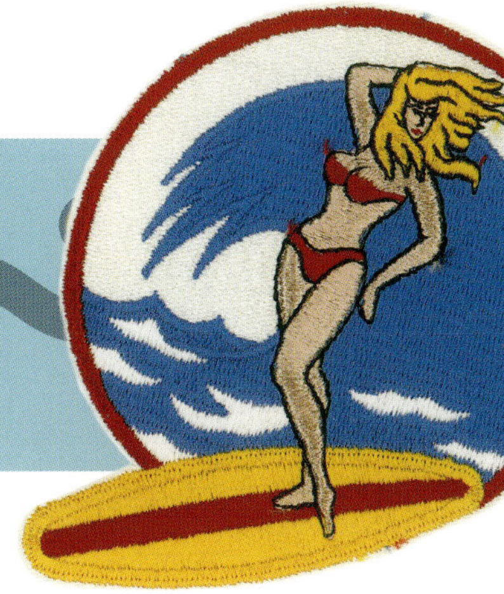

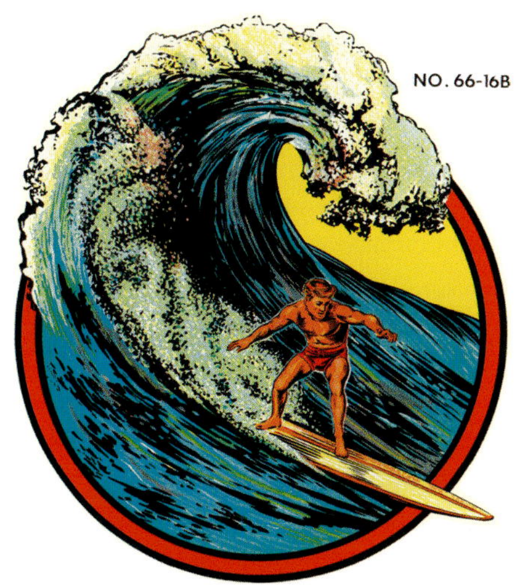

it would be fun to cover a beer refrigerator in the garage with surf decals. It was pretty easy. Then I thought it would be great to turn my old friends back onto the past! The old Portola Surf Shop was the beginning of this fine collection.

I must mention a cool piece of history. My collection really became somewhat complete when I met the late Con Colburn in the mid-eighties. Con was a character. He would send fictitious letters to manufacturers with a quarter to check prices. He would use a kid's address. When I met Con he gave me, and also sold me, a drawer full of pricelists, decals, and business cards. Con wanted a profit for his quarter and four cent stamp! Con was very funny. It had to be cash. A true classic, he would ask for a $1 and a piece of junk, then he would feel sorry for me and give me some. We developed a close friendship before his death.

Who would have thought all these things would be so valuable some day. Well you've all got me off the hook!

I hope this book brings you, your families, and your friends as much fun as it has to collect these great things. Always remember the worst day of surfing is better than the best day at work. This book will for sure help you cure that bad work day, enjoy!

Keep surfing,

Pete Noble, President
Santa Cruz Longboard Union

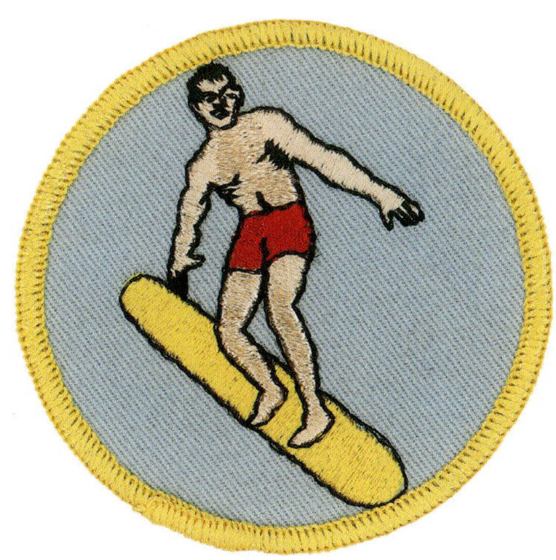

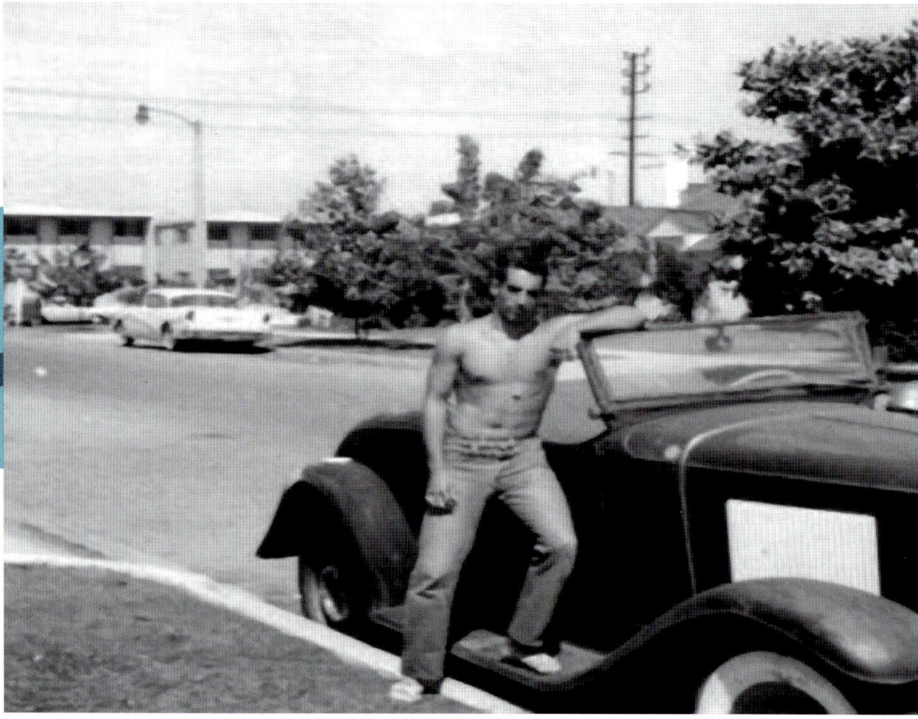

Cary Weiss in 1960 with his surf jalopy. Photo courtesy Cary Weiss.

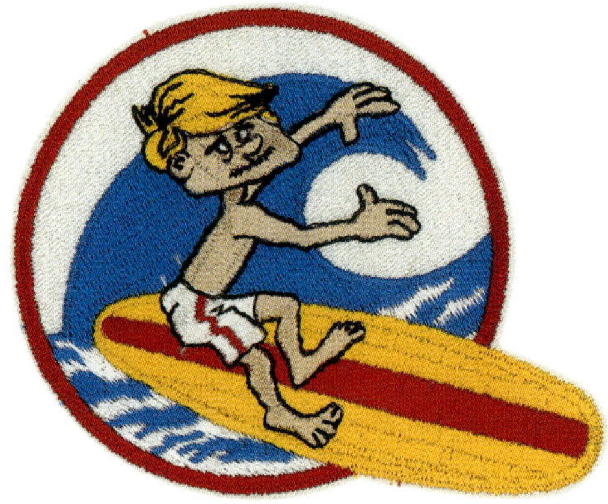

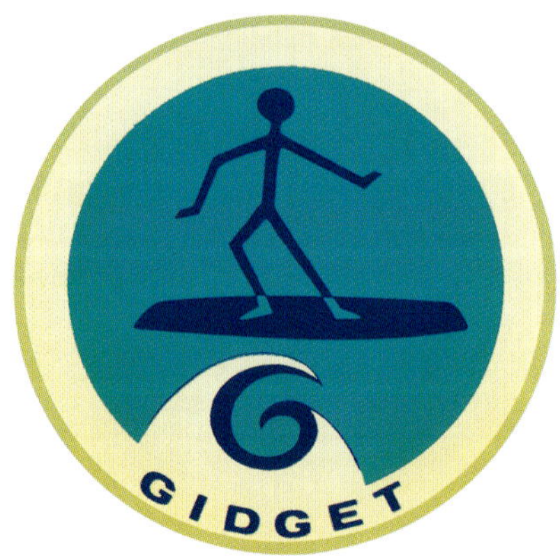

CARY WEISS

As a kid in the mid-50s (I am 64 now, in case you're curious), I would ride my bike down to the beach and the boardwalk. I happened upon this old cement block building. The scent of resin, wood, and foam could be detected blocks away. It was Velzy's shop on Pacific in Venice – my first contact with anything to do with surfing. They gave me some decals and fliers – I was stoked. Soon after that I learned to surf back in the dark ages – around 1958 – when my next door neighbor, who was making Plastic Mart kit boards in his garage, asked me if I wanted to go down to Bay Street in Santa Monica to test ride his new board. I was hooked the minute I lifted the nose of the 30 pound beast and dragged it down to the water!

I kept everything having to do with surfing. When I went to Cal in 1961, I boxed everything up, put two of three boards in the rafters and left home with one board. My parents were kind enough not to throw all this stuff out, as they threatened to do many times.

Collecting just became a part of the stoke of surfing – the search, the find, the trigger of memories, the perpetuation of our surfing culture and history. My first board and first Velzy and Velzy/Jacobs decal still stoke the fire in me today.

Cary Weiss,
Santa Monica, California

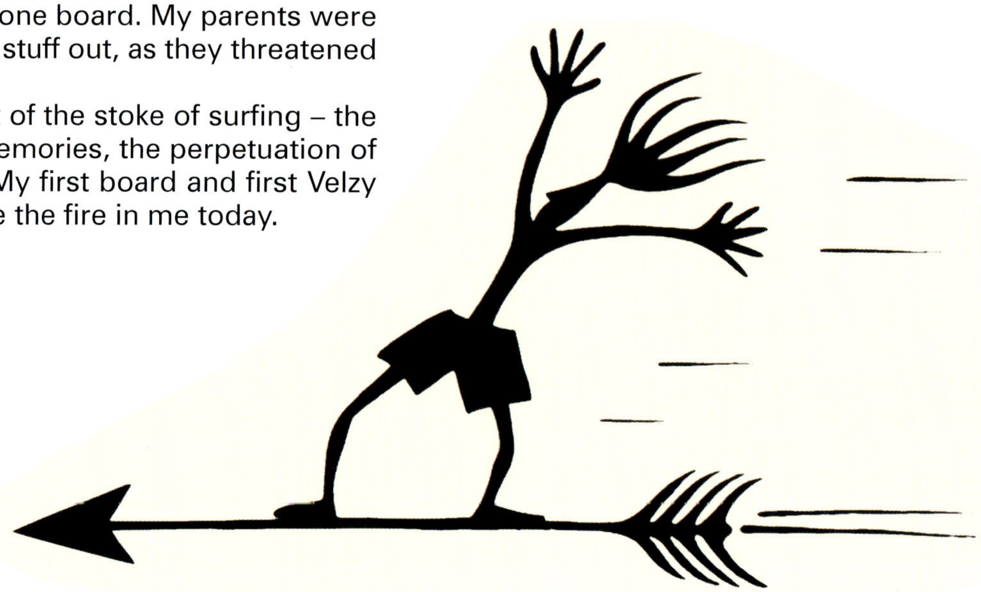

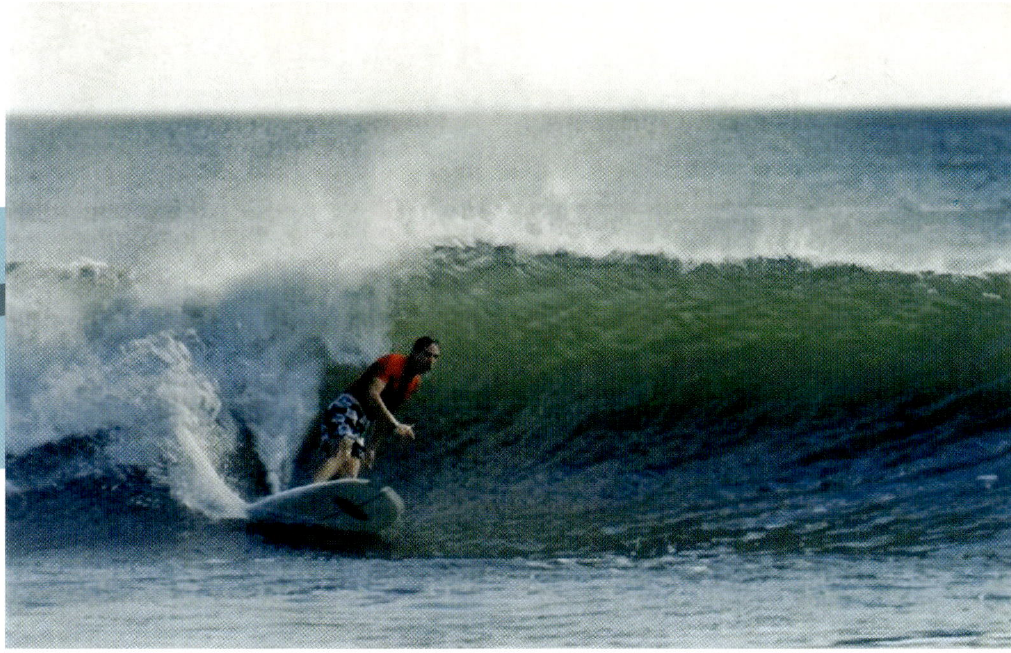

Keith Eshelman at Costa Rica. Courtesy keith Eshelman.

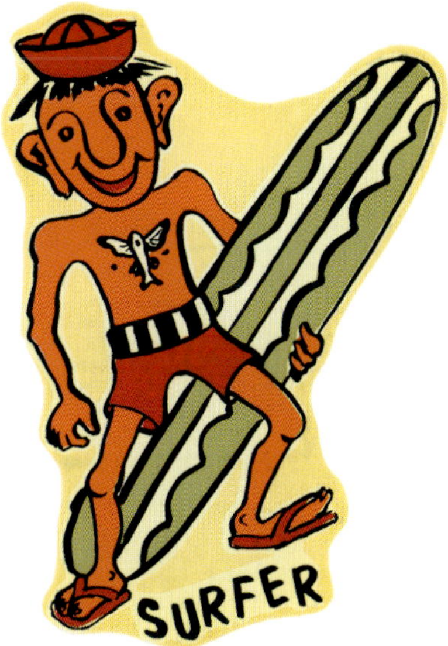

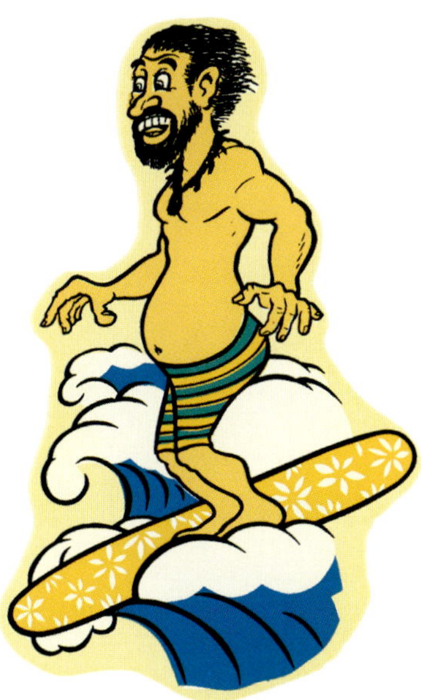

KEITH MAYNARD ESHELMAN

I grew up in Palos Verdes during the surfing explosion in southern California. The popularity of surfing was being spread by Gidget, the music by Dick Dale and the Beach Boys, and the lame Hollywood beach party movies. Back then, you were cool if you were a surfer and wore your Huarache sandals, Levi jeans, and Pendleton shirt, and had bushy blond hair. I have great memories during this period of learning to surf at the Portuguese Bend Club, the Cove, and Rat Beach. I was fortunate to go to Pier Avenue Junior High School and see surf movies personally narrated by John Severson, Bruce Brown, and Greg MacGillivray. I was also at the Santa Monica Civic Auditorium to see Robert August and Mike Hynson surf the perfect waves at Cape St. Francis in Bruce Brown's movie debut of *The Endless Summer*.

My surf collecting began in 1960. I still have my first couple issues of *Reef Magazine* and *Surfer Magazine*. I also kept a few surf movie posters, ticket stubs, decals, and patches. For the past 25 years, I've been buying, selling, and trading with friends and other collectors. In the late 90s, I created a website of my surf movie poster collection called the "Gallery of Surf Classics" (surfclassics.com). Today the site is a virtual museum with over 250 surf movie posters. One of the greatest rewards of collecting has been the friends that I've made throughout the world. It's great to share the same passion for surfing with other collectors.

Today, when I see a Surfboards by Jacobs decal, it takes me back to 1960 at the Jacobs Surf Shop in Hermosa Beach when my dad ordered my first custom surfboard. In those days, you would find surf shops of Bing, Rick, Greg Noll, Dewey Weber, and Jacobs on a two mile stretch of Pacific Coast Highway. It is great to reflect back to a time in my life when I became stoked on surfing and to see how, today, the passion has been kept alive by collecting surf memorabilia and paddling out for that next great ride.

Keith Maynard Eshelman,
San Diego, California

CHAPTER ONE

PLAIN PLANKS

Why Didn't Hawaiians Decorate Their Surfboards? From Old Owyhee to Duke Kahanamoku

The Hawaiians did not decorate their surfboards. The Polynesians had a lot of time on their hands and they tended to ornately decorate everything they put their hands to – including their hands - but that did not include surfboards. We can guess at why and it's hard to know how far back into Polynesian history that goes, but the lack of ornamentation on Hawaiian surfboards was standard as the surfboard evolved as Polynesia's gift to the world, through the 18th, 19th, and well into the 20th centuries.

The surfboard in old Hawaii was an expression of individual freedom and also a symbol of a surfer's place in society. Hawaiian *ali'i* (royalty) rode the longer *olo* surfboards, while the common people stood up on shorter *alai'a* boards or bellyboarded on *paipo* boards. Regardless of class, Hawaiian surfers did not ornament their boards.

A possible explanation of this may have to do with the fact that surfboards in old Hawaii were, as Greg Noll said: "a bugger to make," as the pre-contact Hawaiians had only stone adzes and coral to work very hard hardwoods like *koa* and *wili wili.* Maybe by the time they were done with hundreds of hours of cutting, shaping, and scraping, they just wanted to ride the things and not spend another hundred hours decorating them.

The Hawaiian Islands are the land of milk and honey, a perfect climate requiring minimal shelter and clothing, where food grows in abundance on land and swims in the sea. The Hawaiians had a lot of time on their hands and their culture decorated almost everything they put their hand to, from the tattoos on their hands to fish hooks to floral leis to feather headdresses to the traditional Hawaiian tiki.

In the modern world, tattoos are considered low class and vulgar. In old Hawaii, tattoos had meaning and status. According to the www.indianchild.com website:

> "The literal translation of the word for tattoo in Hawaiian is *uhi,* meaning a covering... The symbolism of tattoos was as a benchmark of privilege whereby the quantity and intricacy of the design indicated one's status... The detailed tattoos were done by the highly skilled artists; an exclusive preserve for the chiefs and their families while the rest of the population and women got it done by the apprentices. The tattoos of women were less extensive being limited to the hand, arms, feet, ears and lips... Tattoo designs were also done during auspicious occasions and in many cases the individual's *aumakua*, the family or personal god was tattooed for protection. Patterns such as reeds or other natural forms, graced men's arms, legs, torso and face. Women were generally tattooed on the hand, fingers, wrists and sometimes on their tongue... there is a marked difference between those done before the Hawaiians came into contact with the Europeans. In this period, the designs were geometric with liberal use of lines, circles etc, whereas after the arrival of the Europeans the influence displayed itself in depiction of pictorial objects such as goats, guns etc."

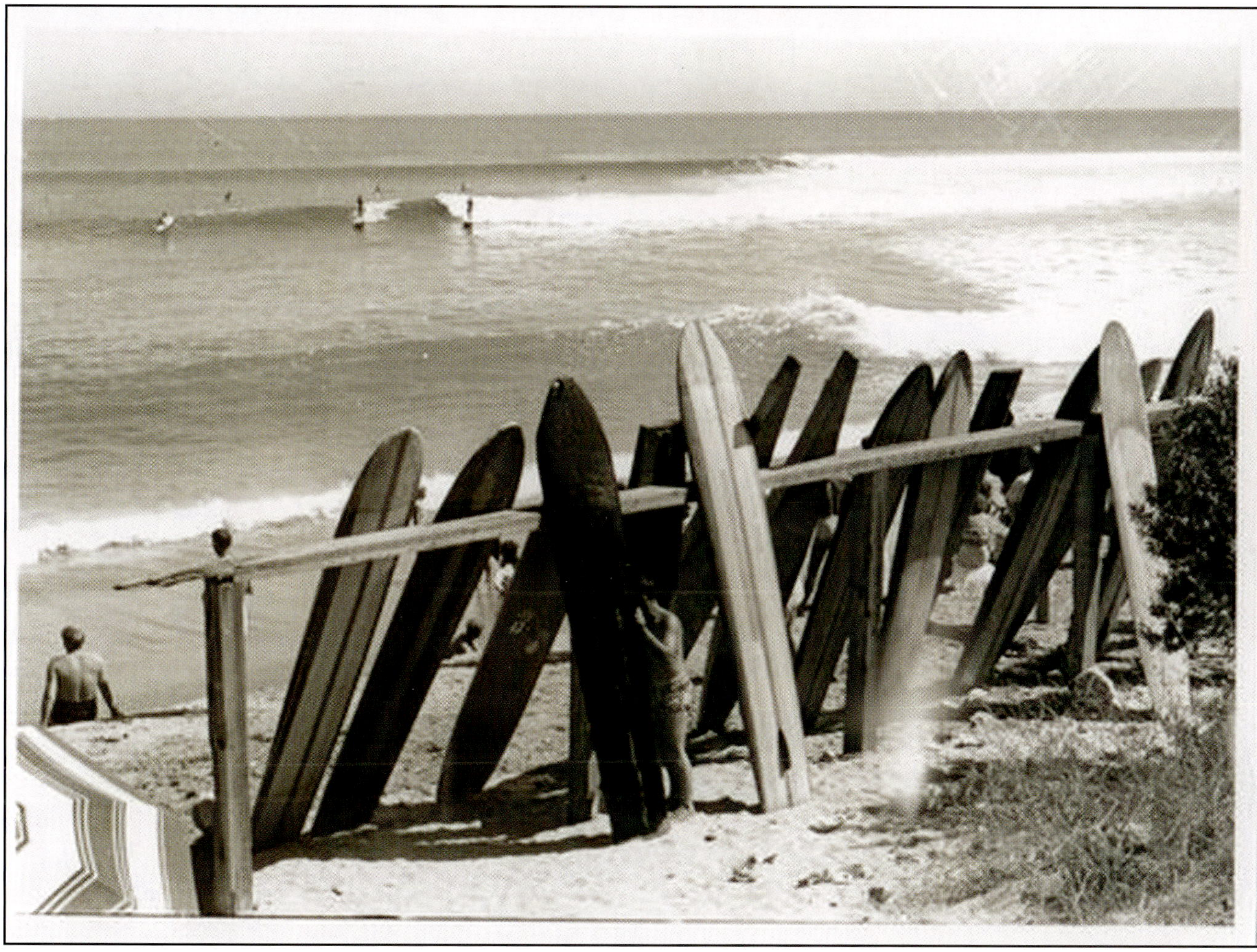

Life just prior to WWII, at Malibu, circa 1939. After 1941, Malibu was fenced off by the Coast Guard and available only to military personnel, but since every able-bodied man or woman was in the military, there were plenty of takers for some R and R. Photo courtesy Cary Weiss collection.

Hawaiians spent countless hours ornamenting functional tools and fun toys. but that elaborate ornamentation seemed to stop at the water's edge. The Hawaiians were an ocean-dependent people with a deep understanding and respect for the seas. Apparently form followed function when it came to designing and decorating the craft they used to ride on the water.

Think of a Hawaiian canoe and you might come up with an image of an ornately decorated ocean-going craft, but the reality is that the Hawaiians did not decorate their canoes, large or small, either before contact with Cook or after. That could be a clue to the lack of ornamentation of surfboards. According to Veronica S Schweitzer in her article "A Legacy of Paddling" on the www.coffeetimes.com website: "The most distinctive feature of the Hawaiian canoe is the absence of any ornamentation or decoration. No fancy carvings, no extra wood. The furious Hawaiian waters and the pounding surf demanded a clean, streamlined shape, and just as the functions created the god in Hawaii, function also created the form."

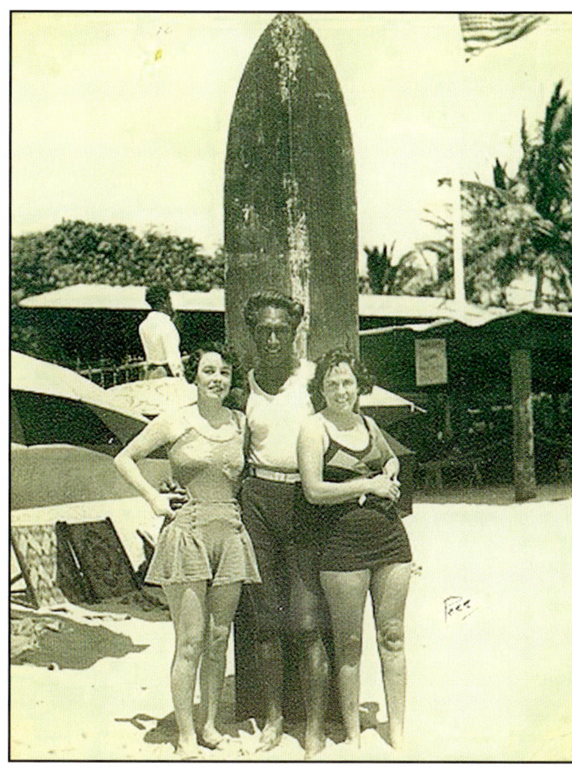

Two girls for every full-blooded Hawaiian Olympic hero: Duke, in Waikiki, circa the 1930s. Photo courtesy Cary Weiss collection.

This argument was supported by Herb Kawainui Kane in his article "Evolution of the Hawaiian Canoe": "It's been argued by Tommy Holmes (*The Hawaiian Canoe*, p. 71) and others that the absence of ornament on Hawaiian canoes (by comparison with South Pacific canoes) may be attributed to the rough Hawaiian waters, an environment in which no carving or inlay that might weaken or burden the canoe could be tolerated. Be that as it may, accounts of Maori canoes in the rough waters off New Zealand, riding 'like ducks' under sail or paddles, leave no doubt about their seaworthiness and structural integrity despite the elaborate carving of their end pieces and gunwales. Quite possibly, esthetics in Hawai'i simply took a different turn, inspired by some long forgotten designer who saw clean, flowing simple lines as the most beautiful as well as functional. Form follows function, but, as architects and automobile designers know very well, form is also shaped by esthetics."

So it could be as simple as that. The Hawaiians did not decorate their canoes because their canoes were built with a respect for life and death. And so they regarded their surfboards in the same way: No nonsense. Form follows function.

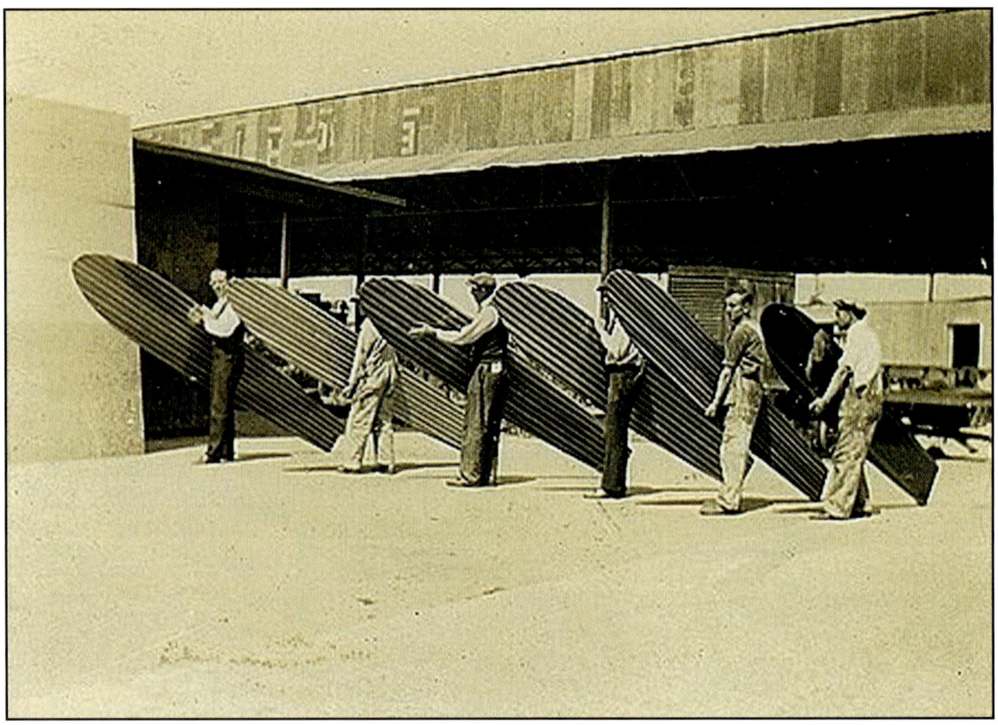

Just like Model T's rolling off the Ford assembly line in 1914, pre-packaged homebuilder Pacific System Homes mass-produced surfboards in the 1930s. And they came in more than one color, mixing up balsa, pine, redwood and other hardwoods into functional works of art that are prized by collectors today. Photo courtesy Cary Weiss collection.

Visit the Bishop Museum in Hawaii and get permission to go down into the tombs or up into the photo archive and you will see hardwood relics of old Hawaii and also countless photos of surfboards going back to the contact with Captain Cook. Down in the tombs at the Bishop you will find the personal *alaia* of Princess Ka'iulani, the surfer girl who would have been queen. Ka'iulani was "the daughter of a double race" according to Robert Louis Stevenson, the child of a Hawaiian royal and a Scottish businessman. She was equally comfortable picking *opihi* off the rocks or cucumber sandwiches off fine china, and she was also a dedicated surfer. Her *alaia* board at the Bishop is the board of an *ali'i,* and yet there is nothing on it to suggest the status of the owner.

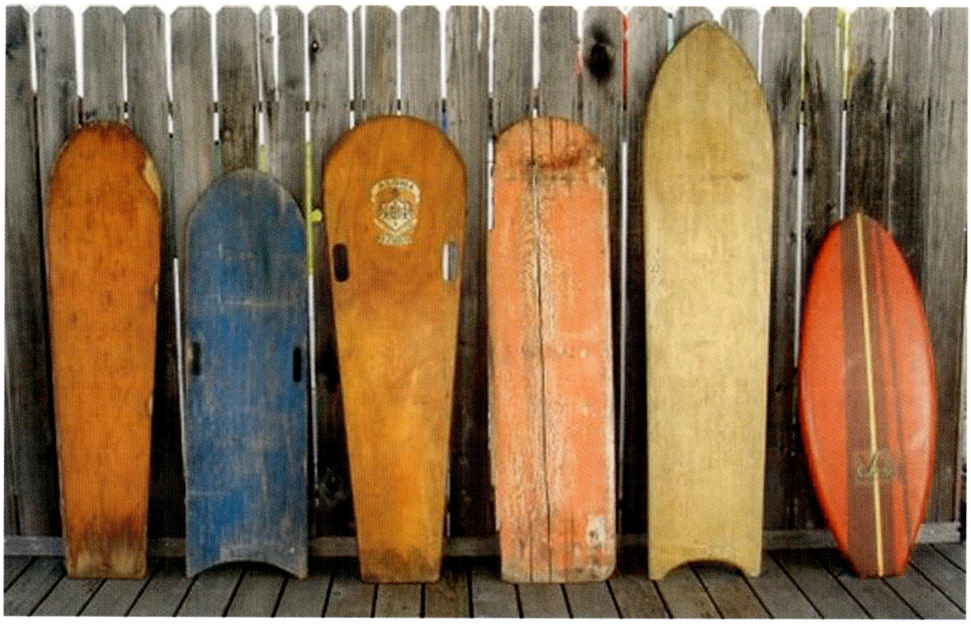

In Hawaiian times, the royalty rode standing up on the 12-foot long *olo* boards, while commoners rode the shorter *alaia*. *Paipo* boards were the old Hawaiian version of body-boards, and everyone had a blast on them, from Kings to kids. This is an array of *paipo* from the 20s to the 60s. Photo courtesy Cary Weiss collection.

Go upstairs into the library and photo archive of the Bishop Museum and you will find hundreds and hundreds of images of Hawaiian surfboards, going back to a carving of Captain Cook arriving in Kealakekua Bay in 1786. In that etching there is a figure paddling on a surfboard, but there is not enough detail to determine if the board was detailed. From the late 1700s to the turn of the 19th century into the 20th there are many etchings, illustrations, and, then, photos and moving images of Hawaiian natives and visiting *haole* with surfboards. They are standing with them and riding on them, but what all the photos have in common is that same cleanliness. There might be a name here and there on the nose, or a piece of art, but for the most part, the fine grain of the polished boards was the only esthetic.

The arrival of Captain Cook in the Hawaiian islands in the 1780s was to the Hawaiians what a visit by Martians would be to the modern world. The Hawaiians figured they were alone in the universe, and then along came men with giant ships, tools, medicine, and new Gods. Of course the Hawaiians were swayed to these new, powerful Gods and Hawaiian culture was changed forever.

History likes to blame the Puritan missionaries for killing off the heathen practice of *he'e nalu* in the Hawaiian Islands, but the truth is, over the next 100 years, surfing died off in Hawaii because the Hawaiians died off. The population of Hawaii is estimated at between 400,000 and 800,000 when Captain Cook arrived, but within 100 years the population of native Hawaiians was less than 40,000. This was more of a cultural genocide than a deliberate massacre – the effect of alcohol, new diseases, new ways and the depression of a proud people exposed to a more sophisticated, overpowering culture. Surfing became less popular because the Hawaiian *kapu* system crumbled in 1820, a year before

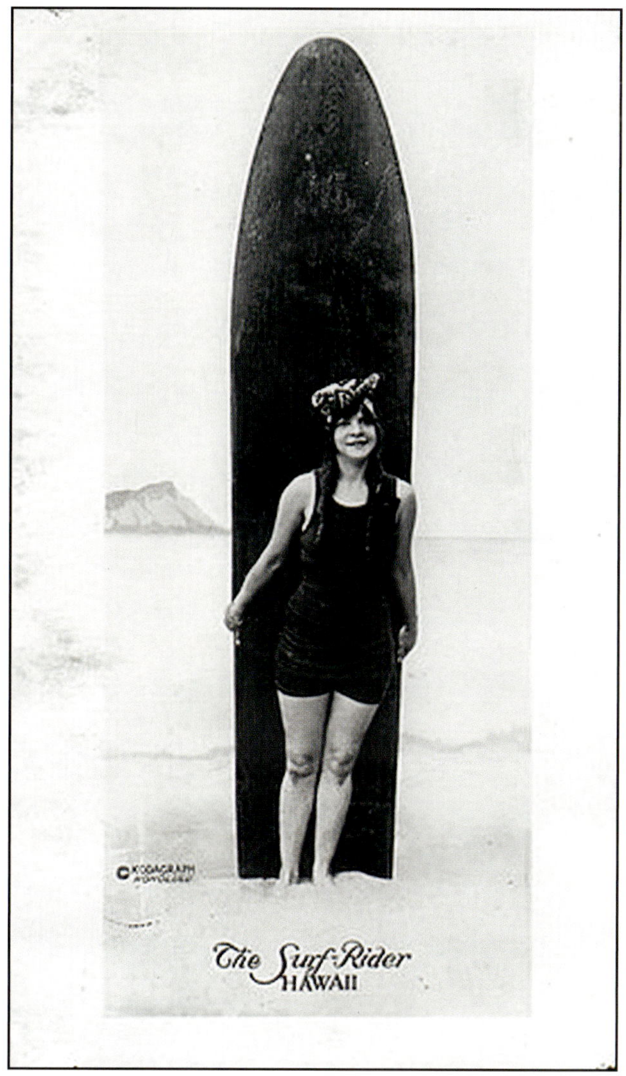

At the turn of the century, the Hawaiian Islands were one of the most remote places on earth, and one of the most exotic vacation spots on earth. Surf riding was part of the allure. Photo courtesy Cary Weiss collection.

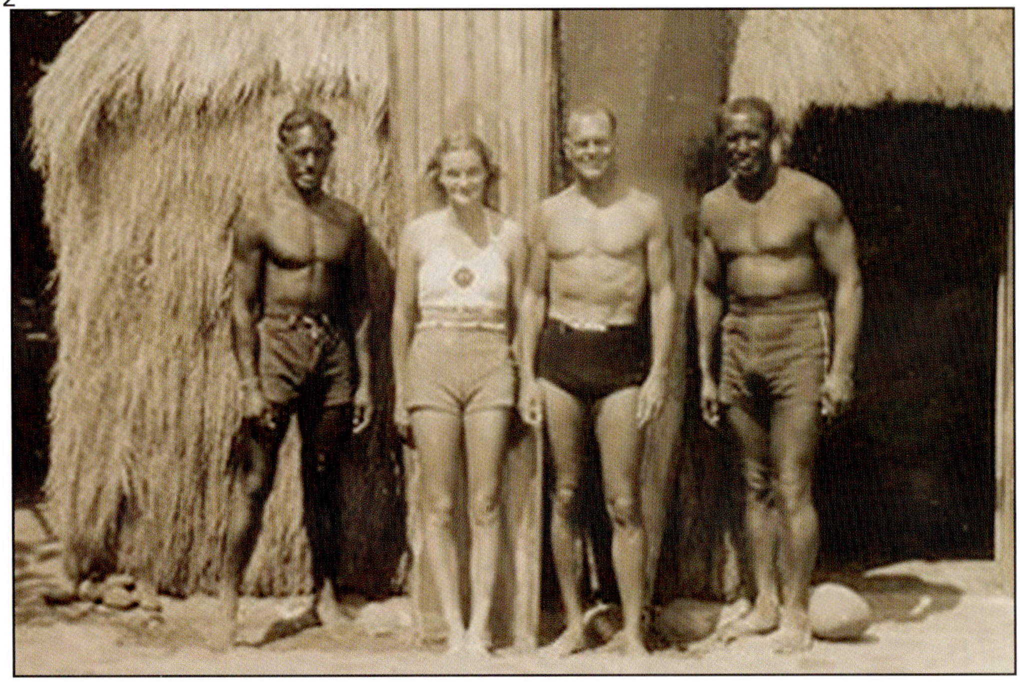

Doris Duke was kind of the Paris Hilton of the first half of the 20th Century. She inherited her father's fortune in 1925 and became "the richest girl in the world." A smart, athletic, adventurous woman, Doris Duke loved the healthy life and had the time and money and leisure to do what was off limits to the masses. Doris was close friends with the Kahanamoku brothers. That is Duke, with Doris Duke, her husband James Cromwell and either Sam or Sargent Kahanamoku circa 1935-1937. Photo courtesy Cary Weiss collection.

the Puritans arrived in Hawaii. Surfing had religious significance in the festivals and rituals of Hawaiian life, but as the Hawaiians were swayed by the Christian Gods and the *kapu* system was replaced by the Biblical codes, surfing lost that significance.

Hawaiian art was dramatically changed by the introduction of European fashions and tools, but going by the photos available in the Bishop Museum, the influence of the West on surfboards waited until the turn of the 19th century into the 20th. It is around the turn of the century that surfboards start having some decoration, usually a piece of Hawaiian art on the nose, or sometimes the symbol of an organization or sometimes the name of the surfer who owns the board.

The most famous name on the nose of a surfboard in the first 20 years of the 20th century was Duke Kahanamoku. A multi-gold medal hero at the 1912 Olympics in Oslo, Duke became world famous as the noble savage from a small dot in the middle of the Pacific, who swam like a brown barracuda, sped up by flashes of gold. Duke was an all-around waterman who grew up surfing Waikiki. He was smarter than people suspected and became sophisticated through all his travel, but he was Hawaiian to the bone and that included the ability to make his own surfboards with whatever tools and wood were around.

Every day of the year where the water is 76, day and night, and the waves roll high, I take my sled, without runners, and coast down the face of the big waves that roll in at Waikiki.

— Duke Kahanamoku

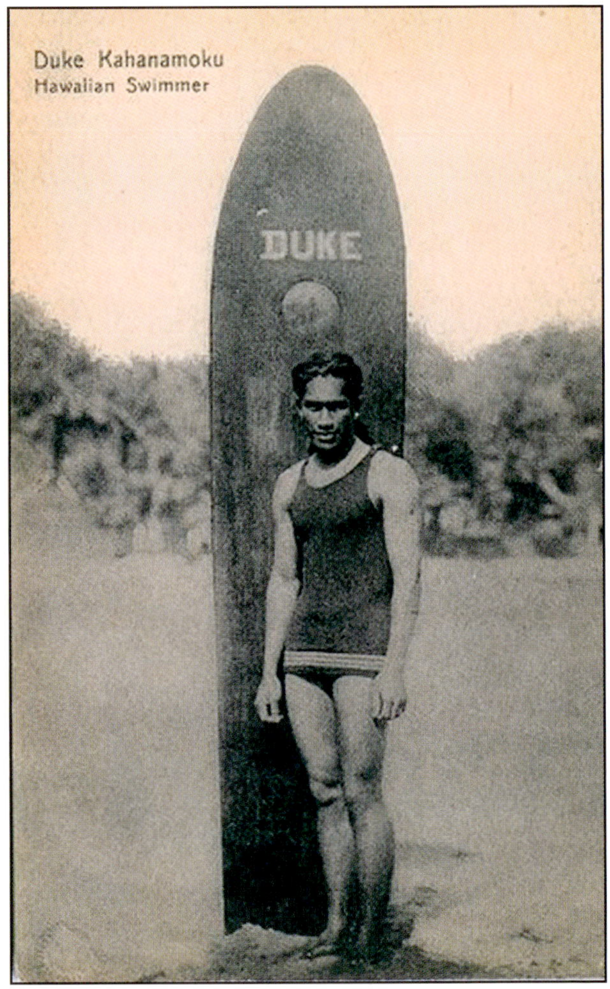

The man, the Olympic swimmer, the legendary Godfather of Modern Surfing. Duke Kahanamoku was the Tiger Woods of his day, an internationally famous athlete who spread the love of surfing around the world. A soft-spoken, modest Hawaiian, Duke wasn't bragging when he put his name on his board. That was just the fashion during the 1910s and 1920s. Photo courtesy Cary Weiss collection.

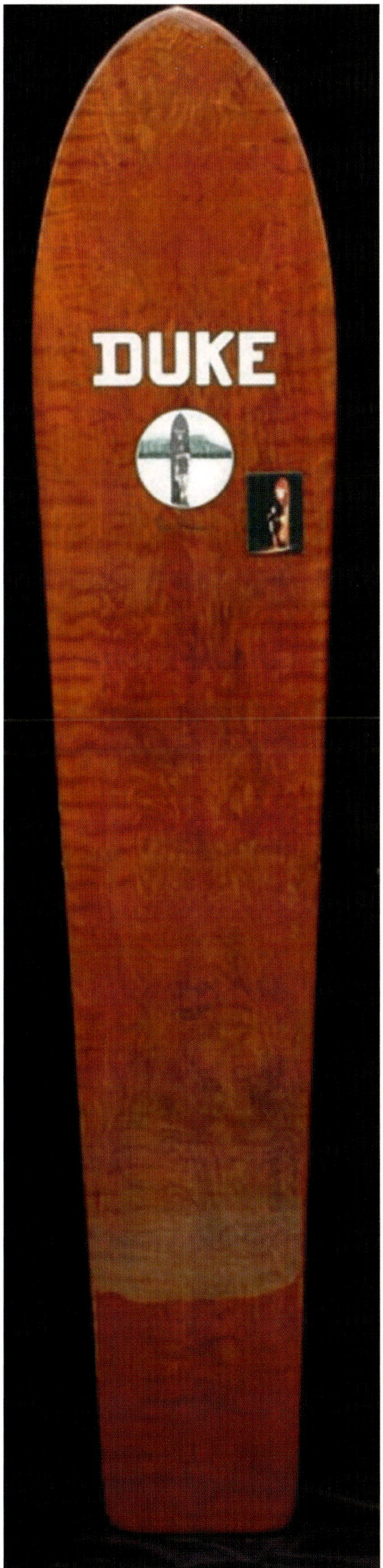

A Greg Noll recreation of Duke Kahanamoku's Hawaiian plank, circa 1905. Photo: Juliana Morais. Courtesy Fernando Aguerre and Voyageur Press.

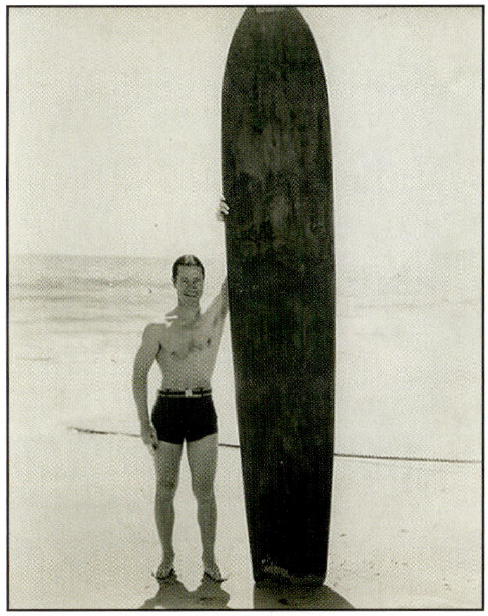

During the 1930s, Joe E. Brown was one of Hollywood's top comedians, kind of the Adam Sandler of his day. Like Sandler now, Brown liked to go surfing when he wasn't shooting. Photo courtesy Cary Weiss collection.

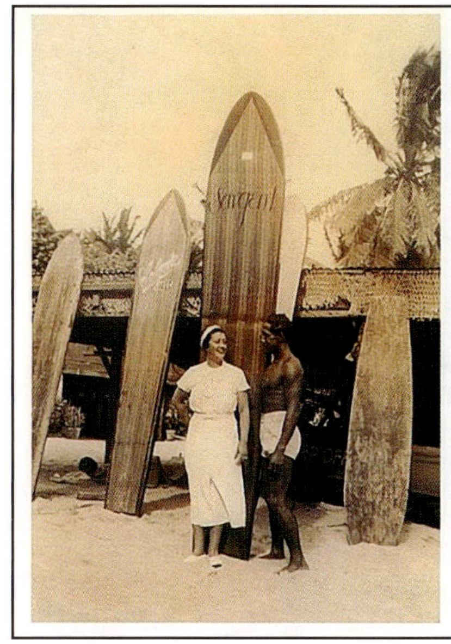

Sargent Kahanamoku was one of Duke's six brothers, who all worked as beach boys at Waikiki, taking tourists out surfing and canoeing. Because of Olympic rules, Duke was not allowed to be paid to be in the water in any way, so he could not follow his brothers into the profession. So while Duke got the Gold and the glory, his brothers got the *wahine*. Photo courtesy Cary Weiss collection.

In 1914, Duke was invited to Australia by the New South Wales Swimming Association. He left Honolulu aboard the *RMS Ventura* on November 30, 1914, and crossed the equator without one of his Hawaiian surfboards, because Duke was thinking about on-land pool swimming on this trip, and didn't know what Australia offered in the way of rideable waves.

Duke landed in Sydney, looked around, saw surf and most likely regretted leaving his board back in Hawaii. He had a week to kill with no official duties, so he was accommodated at the Boomerang Camp at Freshwater Beach, where he fell in with the local rogues who knew how to bodysurf but didn't have much of a clue about surfing.

Australians felt that the waves of Sydney were not compatible with board riding, so Duke went to George Hudson's, a Sydney timber firm, and found a good piece of imported sugar pine that was 9 ft long, 2 ft wide and 3" thick. The lumberyard cut out a board to Duke's template and he finished the board with rails, lift in the nose, and – some say – a concave section in the bottom.

Duke's surfing exhibition at Freshwater Beach on the day before Christmas, 1914, started Australia on the road to surfing superpower status. The board Duke made and rode was eight feet long, 23 inches wide and three inches thick. Duke put his name up on the nose but the board also had a little bit extra: a white and purple double pinline that traced the rail. But this board was true to the style of 1914: form still following function.

A Hawaiian plank circa 1920, with the Outrigger Canoe Club logo, which was one of the first repeating brands on a surfboard. Photo: Juliana Morais. Courtesy Fernando Aguerre and Voyageur Press.

Tom Blake did not decorate or brand the custom surf and paddleboards he made by hand, but when Blake licensed some of his designs to the Los Angeles Ladder Company of Los Angeles, they saw logos as good business.

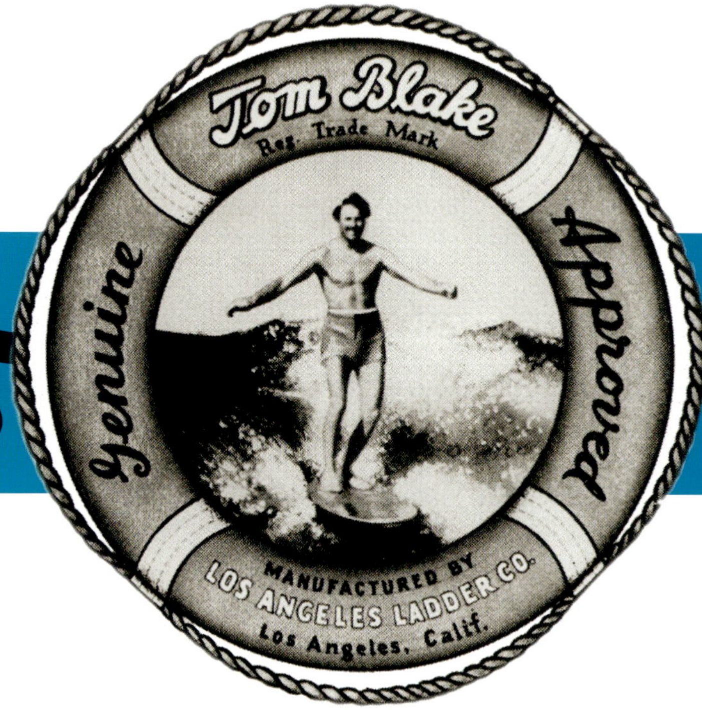

CHAPTER TWO

THE FIRST REICH

Tom Blake, Swastikas and the Beginning of Branding: 1920 to 1952

Walk into the Surfing Heritage Foundation in San Clemente and be amazed by the greatest single collection of surfboards on earth. Spencer Croul and Dick Metz have been collecting a couple hundred years of surfboards for several years and in 2004 they commingled their collections in a 4,000 square foot room that now has 160 boards, from planks to plastics. The collection is lined up chronologically, beginning on the immediate right of the door as you walk in, with a Greg Noll reproduction of a 16- foot Hawaiian *olo* – the ride of the *ali'i*. From there, each board is displayed usually face first, some as tall as 14 feet, sometimes dating back to the 1800s, each with a placard giving the vintage and provenance of each board.

Walking the silent halls in the surfing equivalent of the British Museum, you will see a lot of beautiful boards made of different kinds of hardwoods. The boards move from old Hawaiian *koa, wili wili,* and redwoods from Hawaii, into Tom Blake hollow *olo* paddleboards and surfboards from the 20s and 30s and Pacific System Homes Swastika models. The boards from the turn of the century into the 1940s are big and beautiful, increasingly foiled and finely tuned and as crafted as the best furniture and what they all have in common is an almost complete lack of ornamentation.

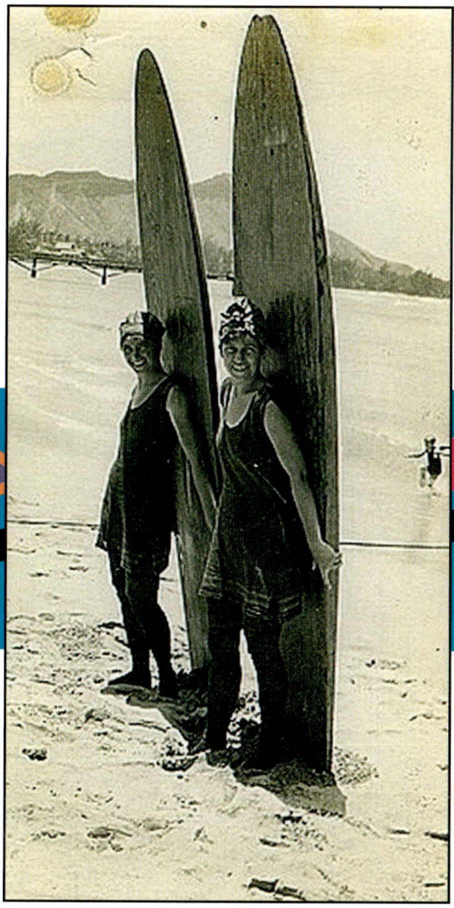

The good life in Hawaii, circa 1912. The boards were hardwood and weighed 80 pounds. The bathing costumes were wool and soaked up nine times their weight in salt water. But these ladies didn't know any different, and they were styling and smiling. Photo courtesy Cary Weiss collection.

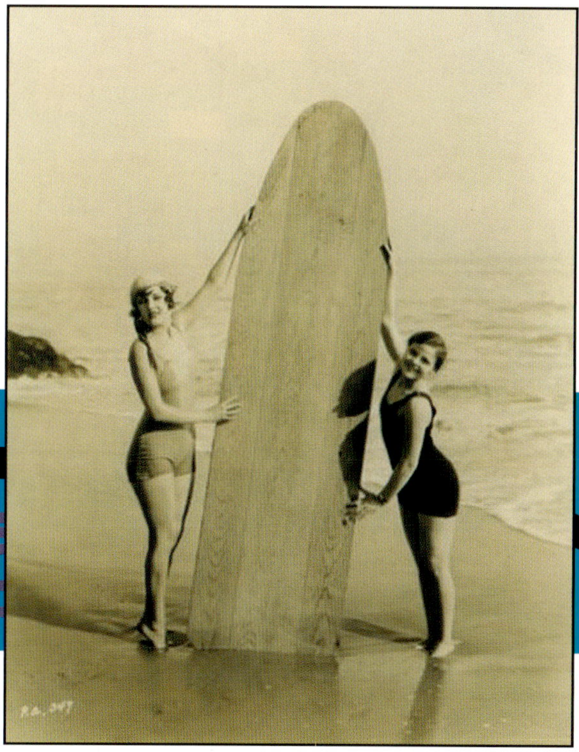

The fashion of the 1920s was a little bit of broadness in the beam, and that went for women, too. These bathing beauties pose with a surfboard that looks like it was cut from the door of a house, but is as unadorned as other boards of the time. Photo courtesy Cary Weiss collection.

The Hawaiian tradition of sleek but plain surfboards crossed into the 20th century and also crossed the Pacific. By 1920, more and more "coast *haole*" were stowing away, paying for passage or otherwise making way to one of the most exotic places on earth, and when they got there, a lot of them saw surfing on the beaches of Waikiki and thought what Jack London thought when he arrived in 1907: "They don't know what they got."

Tom Blake remains the most famous of all the coast *haole*, a kid from Wisconsin whose life was spun into a new direction by a chance meeting with Duke Kahanamoku. They met in Detroit in 1920, when Duke was returning from the Olympic Games in Antwerp, where he won a gold medal in the 100-meter freestyle. By this time, Duke was world famous, and he was crossing the country with a group of swimmers, heading to California and then home to Hawaii.

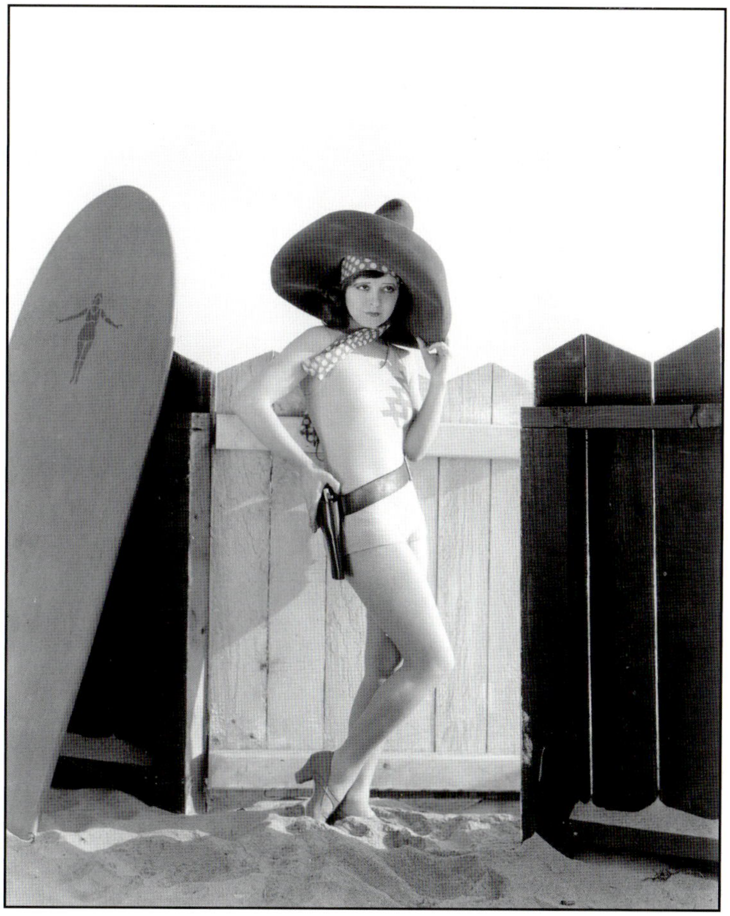

A Roaring Twenties starlet poses with her western kit. Photographer unknown, courtesy Surfing Heritage Foundation.

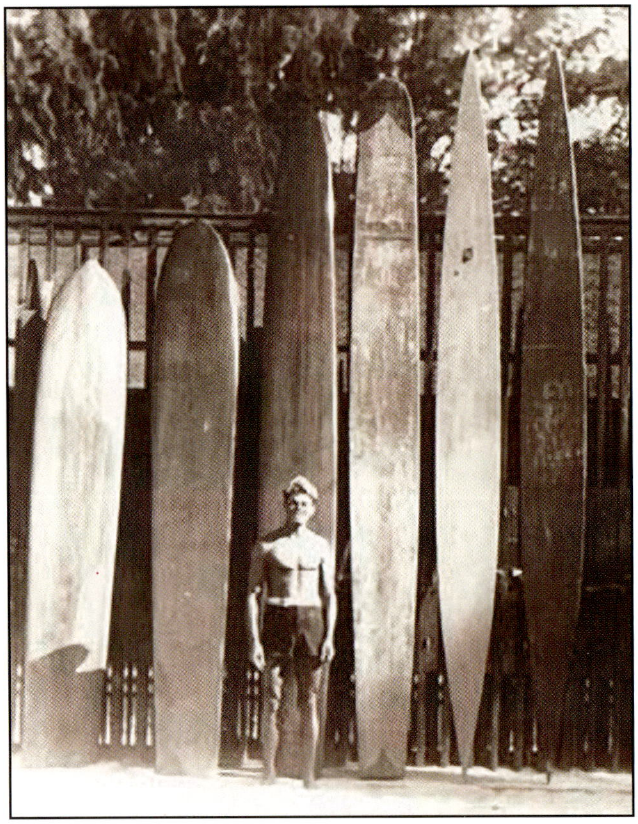

Tom Blake, circa 1930, posing with a thoroughly modern quiver. At a sturdy six feet, Blake was dwarfed by all of these boards, the shortest being an 11′ redwood "riding board" that was 23" wide and 3½" thick. Next to that was a 12-footer made of red cedar that Blake used both for surfing and paddling. The third board in the quiver was one of the hollow *olo* Blake made from boards he had seen in the Bishop Museum. This board was 14′6" and 20" wide and weighed 120 pounds. The fourth board was *Okohola*, the riding version of his hollow *olo*-inspired shapes originally made for paddle racing. The last two boards in the quiver are the two that caused all the fuss. They were identical, hollow 16-footers, the one with the Outrigger Canoe Club logo on the deck a lighter version used for racing, while the sixth board was identical but heavier and used for training. These were the boards Blake used to break records in the Ala Wai Canal, sparking a battle—and changing the surfboards everyone rode for the next eighty years. Surfing Heritage Foundation.

Blake was a wanderer at the time, a young athlete who was too young for World War I and was finding his way in the world. They both ended up in a theater that night to watch a newsreel of the Olympics. "A motion picture newsreel showing the United States swimming team's performance at Antwerp was running at a local theater," Tom Blake was quoted in *Tom Blake: The Uncommon Journey of a Pioneer Waterman* by Gary Lynch.

> "Duke and his fellow Hawaiian teammates came to see themselves in action on the screen. I, too, had come to see the film and I was so impressed when I found myself near this champion that I intercepted him in the theater lobby and asked to shake his hand. 'Sure!' Duke replied, smiling and eager to please, as always. He held out to me his big, soft paw of a hand and gave me a firm, hearty handshake. It made a lasting impression. I felt that somehow he had included an invitation to me to come over to his own Hawaiian Islands."

Blake accepted that invitation and now the world of the surfboard divides itself into Before Blake and After Blake.

Blake tried surfing in California in 1921, but the heavy, redwood planks were big and clunky then and he was more interested in competitive swimming and lifeguarding: "Took it out, tried to ride it," Blake wrote about the experience. "Caught a wave, took a big, mean, nasty pearl dive in a three-foot wave. Got shook up, put the board away and forgot about it for awhile." He tried again in 1924 with a 9′ 10" plank and did little better, then a little better. In 1924 Blake went to Hawaii for the first time, fell in with the beach boys around Waikiki and from that point on Blake's life changed, and changed the surfing world forever.

After 1924 Blake was one of the pioneers of the coast *haole* lifestyle, blazing a path that surfers are still following: Mainland for work, Hawaii for surf: "From those days onward I was fascinated by surfing," Blake wrote in *Duke, As I Knew Him* in 1931.

> "With this came an ever-growing interest in the design and building of surfboards which might make possible greater rides. I went to the Bishop Museum in Honolulu and there began to study the enormous old boards preserved from the days of the ancient Hawaiians, who had been master surf-riders long before the influence of foreign nations took over the life of the Islands. Among these were the long, narrow, giants of the kind called *olo* boards by the natives."

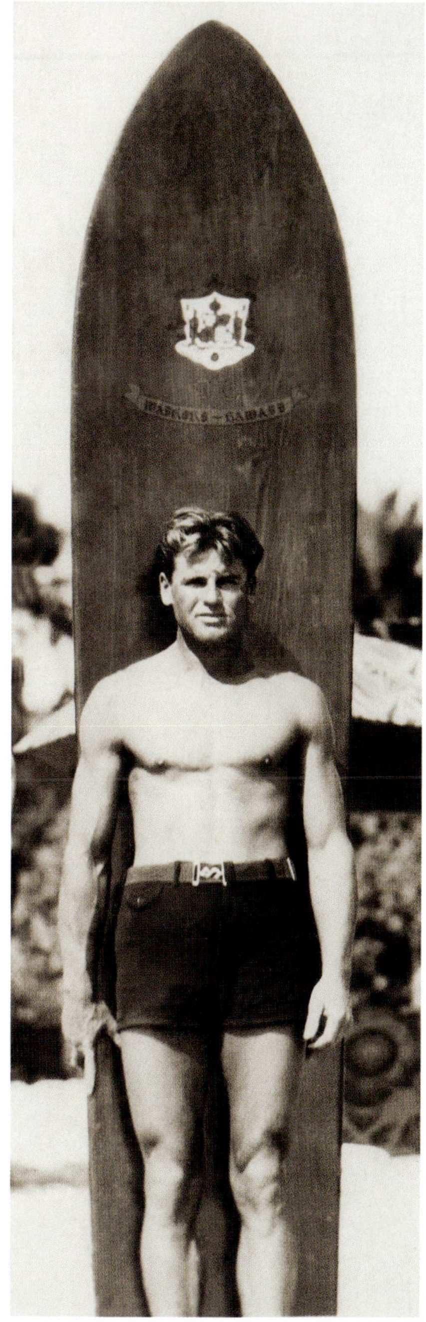

Tom Blake in Hawaii with a traditionally-decorated Hawaiian plank. Photographer unknown, courtesy Surfing Heritage Foundation.

Blake went back to California for a while and became the first man to surf Malibu, with Sam Reid, in 1926. That same year he went back to Hawaii and took an interest in the long, foiled *olo* surfboards on display in the Bishop Museum.

At the Bishop Museum, Blake took an interest in three boards in particular: "Strange as it may seem," Blake wrote in "Surf Riding – The Ancient and Royal Sport" in *Pan Pacific Magazine*,

> "Three old-style Hawaiian surfboards of huge dimensions and weight have hung on the walls of the Bishop Museum in Honolulu for twenty years or more without anyone doing more than wonder how in the world these great boards were used, and were they not too long and heavy to be practicable. Two fine examples of a now extinct design are these two old boards on which Chief Paki once rode the Kalahuewehe [sic] surf at Waikiki."

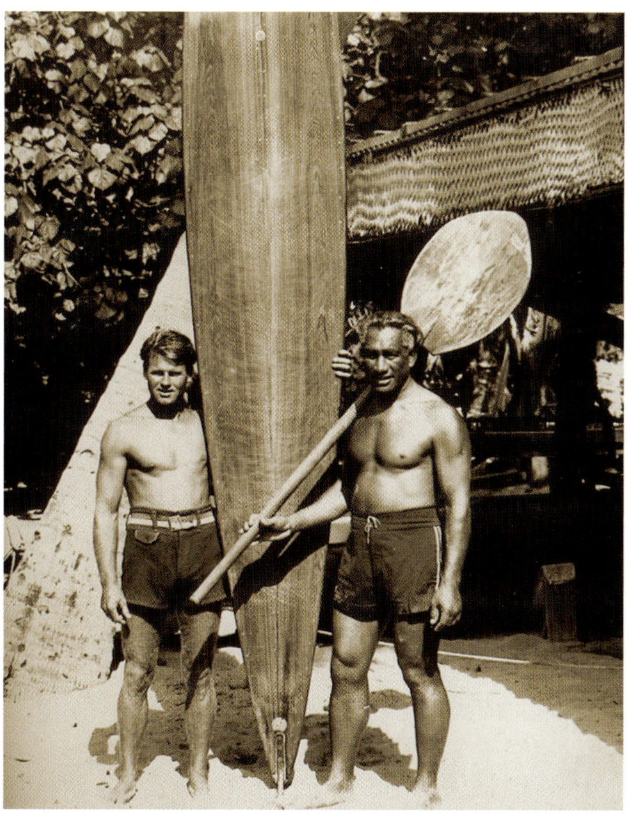

Tom Blake and Duke Kahanamoku together in Hawaii in the late 20s or early 30s. Photographer unknown, courtesy Surfing Heritage Foundation.

After some persistent pestering of Bishop Museum officials, Blake was allowed to restore those *olo* and what Blake felt in his hands he transferred to a modern *olo* as long as 14 feet. Blake revolutionized the world of surfing and paddleboarding with these *olo*, which he eventually made hollow and chambered, like an airplane wing. These *olo* allowed Waikiki surfers access to bigger waves and different kinds of waves and all of the surfboard innovation that followed and continues to this day was inspired by Blake.

Blake's first boards were also traditional in that they were mostly unadorned. Looking at the photo of Blake, taken in 1930, one of his boards has a name – *Okohola* – and one has the Outrigger Canoe Club logo stamped on the nose. Prior to Blake, that Outrigger Canoe Club logo might have been the first or at least the most recurring logo on all the surfboards that came before, but by 1930, surfboards went into mass production, and the first logos were born.

The Depression was bad for America, but good for surfing. Americans figured out pretty quick that ocean energy was free, and a one-time investment in a surfboard bought a lot of good times at the beach.

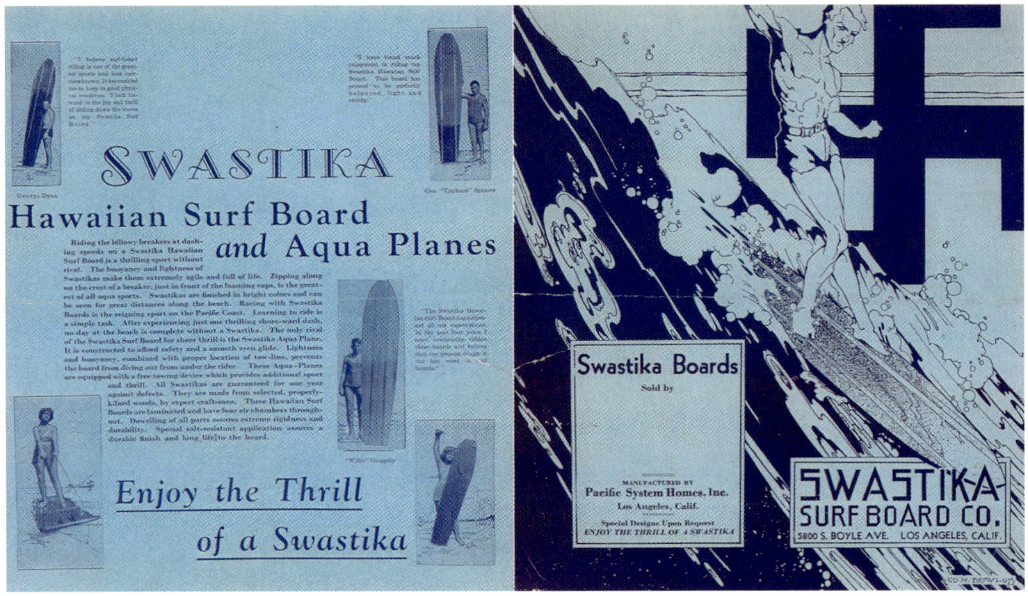

A brochure for the Swastika model board from Pacific System Homes. Although the branding of the surfboards had nothing to do with the Nazi party, that artwork looks like it's Third Reich-approved, and the surfer with that moustache looks like an idealized portrait of You Know Who. Courtesy Surfing Heritage Foundation.

The Depression forced a young Stanford student named Meyers Butte to leave school and return to Los Angeles and the family business. Meyers was the son of William Butte, one of the founders of Pacific System Ready Cut Homes, a fabricator of pre-made homes that was becoming one of the largest in California and the world. Meyers was a wealthy kid who had tried surfing in Waikiki and caught the bug. Out of school, back home, and looking for something to do, Meyers had access to 25 acres of lumber and milling equipment and he saw an opportunity in making quality surfboards out of redwood, balsa, and other hardwoods and selling them to a growing surf scene in California and as far away as Hawaii. "His initial offerings were similar in shape to the basic planks in use at Waikiki Beach," Craig Stecyk wrote in *The Surfer's Journal*.

> "Swastika paddleboards were highly reminiscent of Tom Blake's world record setting shape.... Early boards were of solid redwood construction and had long lag bolts holding them together... Later redwood versions such as those used by notable riders like Typhoon Spencer, Chauncey Granstrom, George Dyna, Willie Grigsby, and Bud Morrissey were routed out in places and many of these types had progressive dowel and biscuit joinery. Contrasting colored pine strips were incorporated into some of their decks. Later versions of this construction featured alternating dark and light colored woods laid up in narrow strips."

Pete Peterson and Lorrin "Whitey" Harrison were among the early California surfers who worked for Pacific System Homes. "Quite a few surfers worked there; this was about 1931," Whitey Harrison said to Malcolm Gault-Williams. "We were shipping sixty boards a month to Hawaii... There was this guy there named 'Dutch' that was notching these swastika symbols in some of the boards, and he couldn't speak a word of English. They called these 'Swastika boards.'

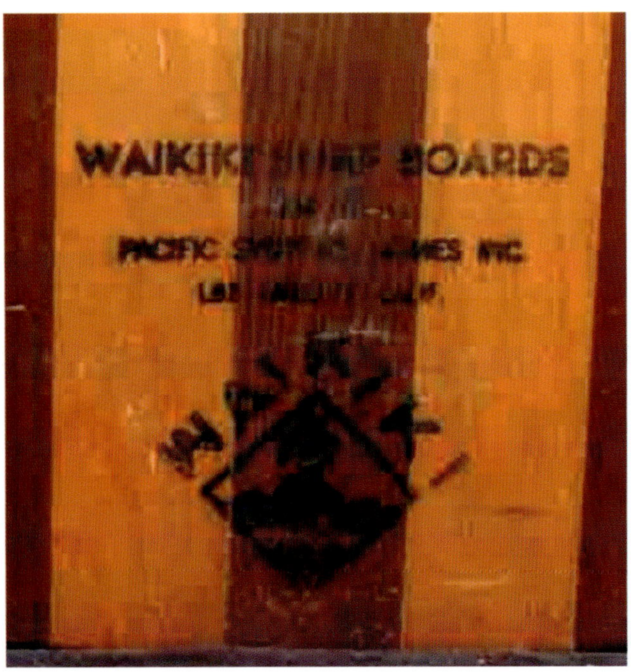

The Waikiki Surf Boards logo on the tail of a redwood/balsa bodyboard, sometime after 1938, when Pacific System Homes dropped the Swastika logo for something more politically correct. Photo: Juliana Morais. Courtesy Fernando Aguerre and Voyageur Press.

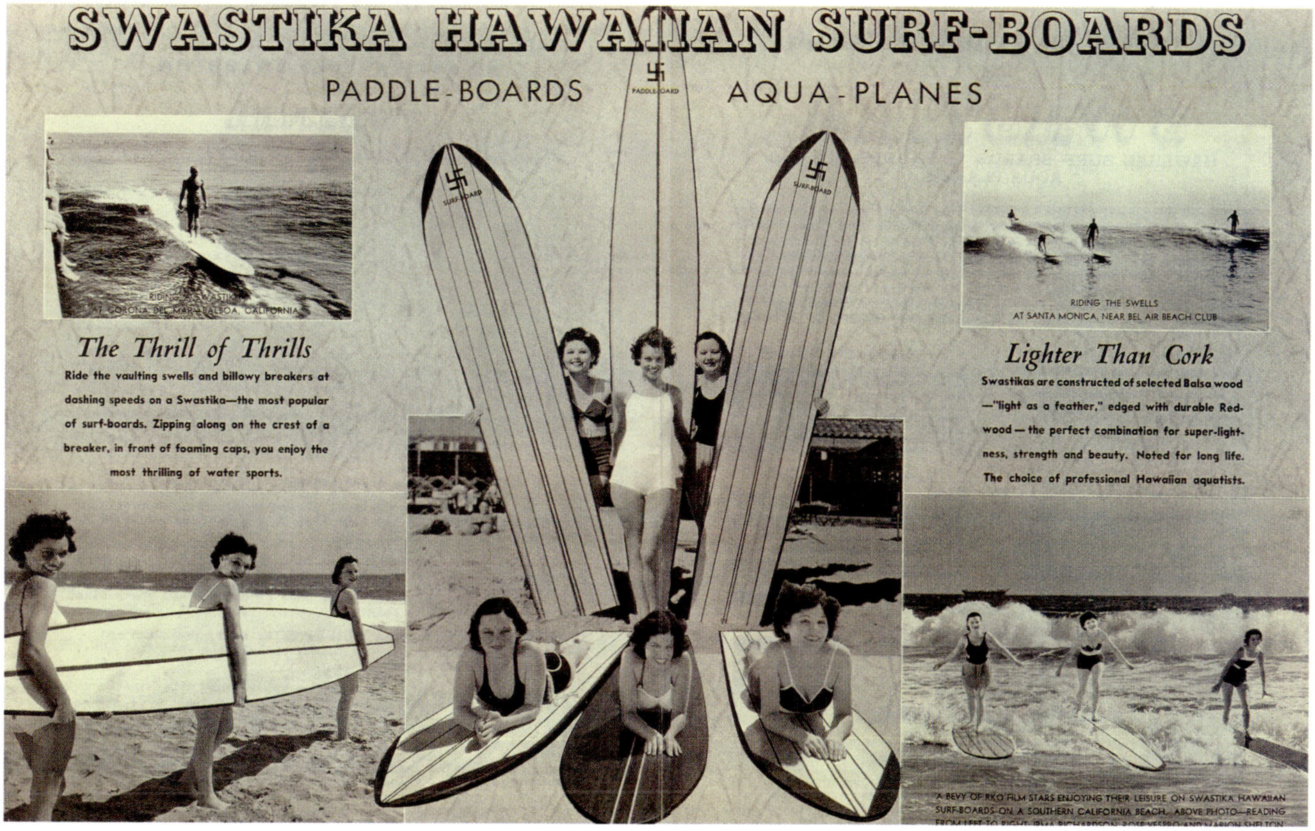

The Swastika surfboard brand suffered the same fate as the AYDS diet plan in the 80s. One was destroyed by German National Socialism. The other by an infectious disease. Courtesy Surfing Heritage Foundation.

The Swastika surfboard brand suffered the same fate as the AYDS diet plan in the 80s. One was destroyed by German National Socialism. The other by an infectious disease.

In 1931, the Swastika was not yet a symbol for German National Socialism. Meyers Butte saw the Swastika as a symbol with "connotations of health and good fortune," according to Wilson Butte, the son of Meyers. What the Germans call the *hakenkreuz* – "hooked cross" – is a symbol found in cultures, continents, and eras from ancient Greece to India, and it usually is a symbol of good and productivity. The word *swastika* is Sanskrit and translates to "the welfare-bringing thing" and that was how the Buttes intended it.

Swastika boards were a brand, with a significant marketing campaign featuring the word and the symbol. The first Swastika boards had the symbol on the nose and then it moved to the tail. The surfboard business had some success through the 1930s, as people found that an investment in a surfboard was good for many hours of health and happiness and fitness on the beaches of California and Hawaii.

Oddly, one of the first surfboard brands also became one of the first victims of the Third Reich: "My father abandoned it to avoid any controversy soon after Hitler began using it," Wilson Butte said. "The Waikiki boards came out around 1938."

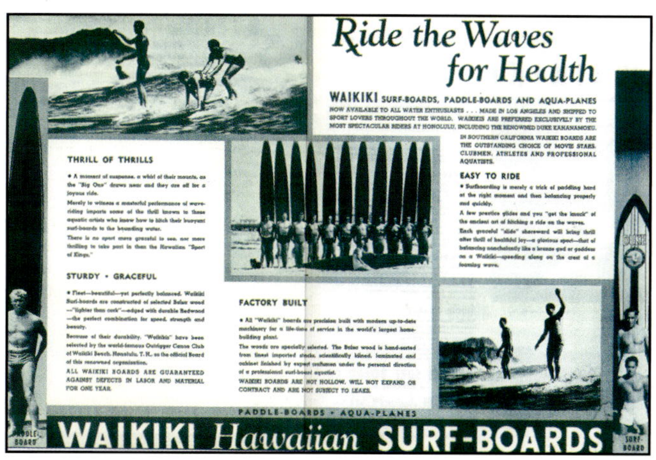

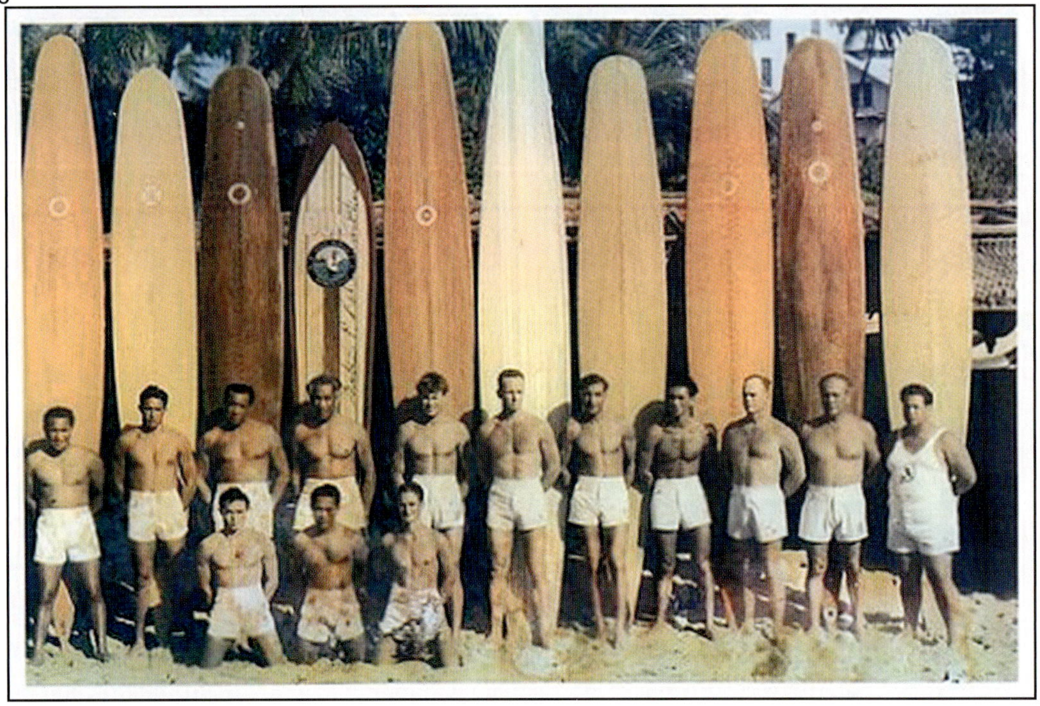

Thirty years before California had the Beach Boys in the 1960s, Hawaii had the beach boys – ocean pros who took tourists safely into the ocean and taught them to swim, sail, paddle and surf. This crew is posing with hollow cigar boards inspired by Tom Blake, and at least one Pacific System Homes solid plank. Photo courtesy Cary Weiss collection.

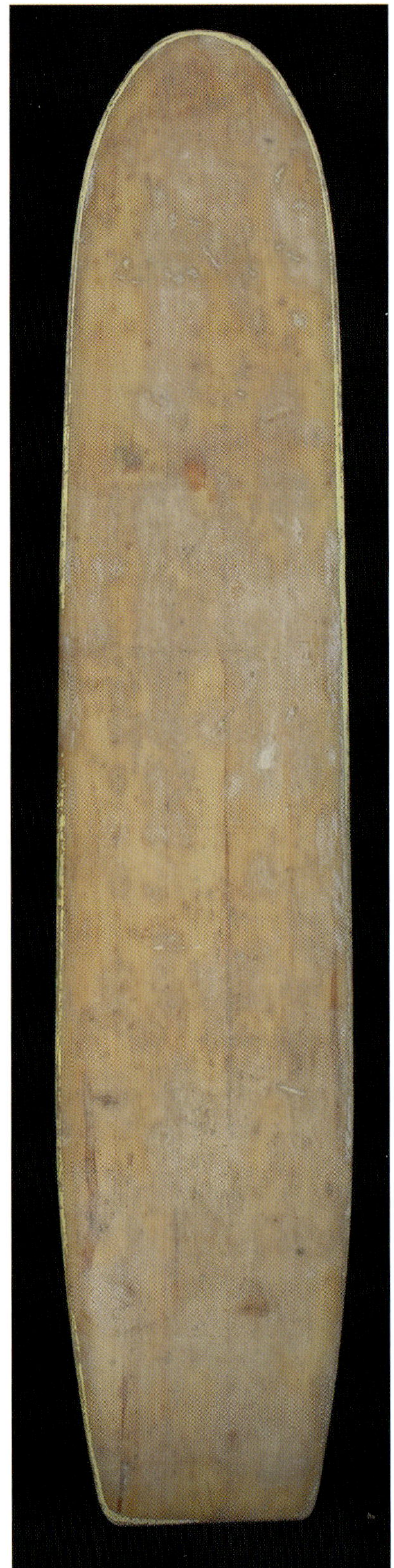

A classic Simmons balsa board, circa late 1940s, without an identifying mark on it. A Simmons surfboard was so distinctive, the creator felt no need for a logo or brand. Photo: Juliana Morais. Courtesy Fernando Aguerre and Voyageur Press.

Walk along the rows of boards at the Surfing Heritage Foundation and you will see the evolution of the surfboard as it changed gradually, out of the 30s, through the war years, and into life after wartime. During this time, innovators like Bob Simmons, Matt Kivlin, and Joe Quigg made increasingly sophisticated boards using wartime materials and ideas, like resin, fiberglass, and planing hull theory. By the late 40s, most surfboards were made of lighter balsawood, and there was some experimentation with Styrofoam – which didn't work – and polyurethane foam – which did.

These are beautiful surfboards, sleek and built for speed and performance in the perfect waves of Malibu, Rincon and Hawaii, and while these boards were made commercially out of shapes around southern California, the shapes and look of the boards were distinct enough that the shapers did not feel the need to brand them in any way. A Simmons dual-finned slot board was so obviously a Simmons, and a Quigg or Kivlin Malibu Chip was so obviously made by those two, that there was no need for a mark or a brand.

As the 40s turned into the 50s, surfing boomed along with post-war prosperity in southern California and the time was right for a guy to come along and lay down the foundation for the modern surf industrial complex.

And then came Velzy.

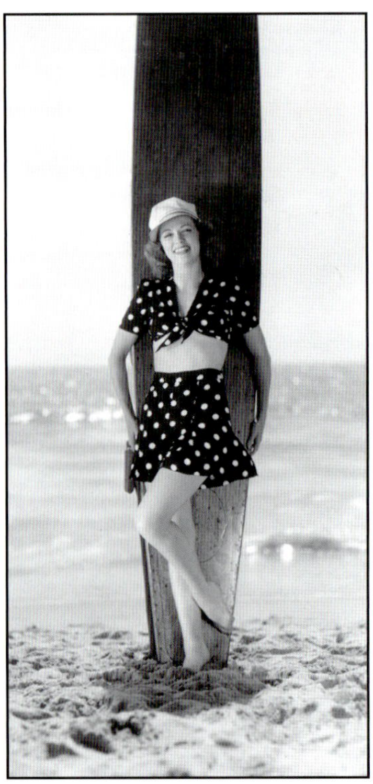

A dancer and actress in the 1940s, Eleanor Powell poses with a plank in front of a seascape that might be a set. Courtesy Surfing Heritage Foundation.

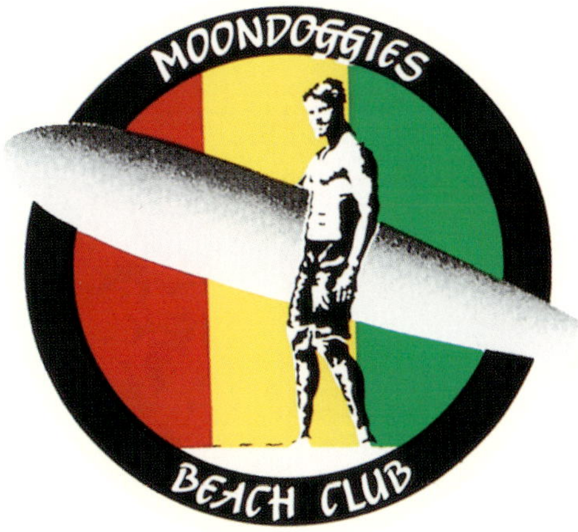
MOONDOGGIES
BEACH CLUB

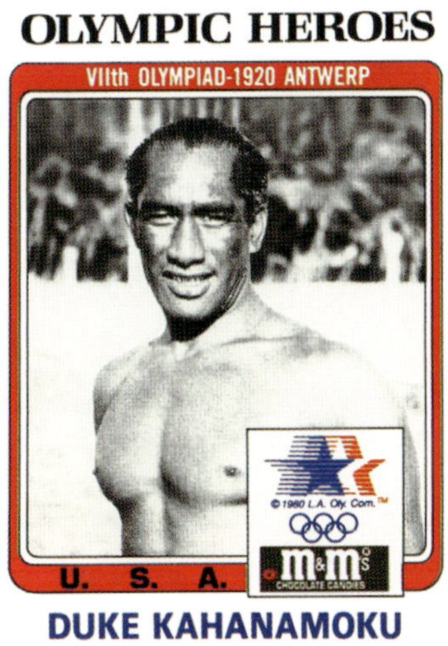
OLYMPIC HEROES
VIIth OLYMPIAD-1920 ANTWERP
U. S. A.
m&m's
DUKE KAHANAMOKU

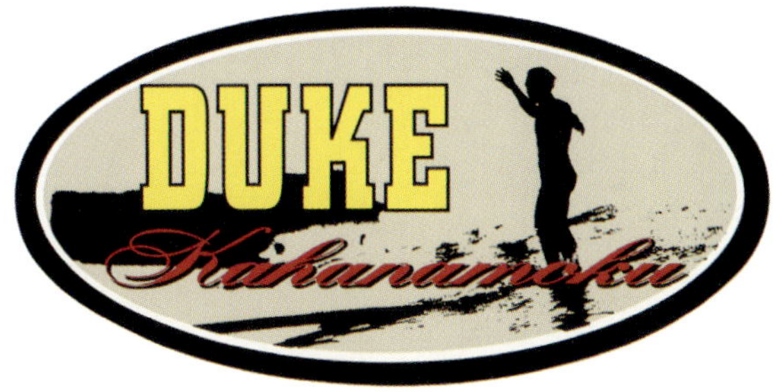
DUKE
Kahanamoku

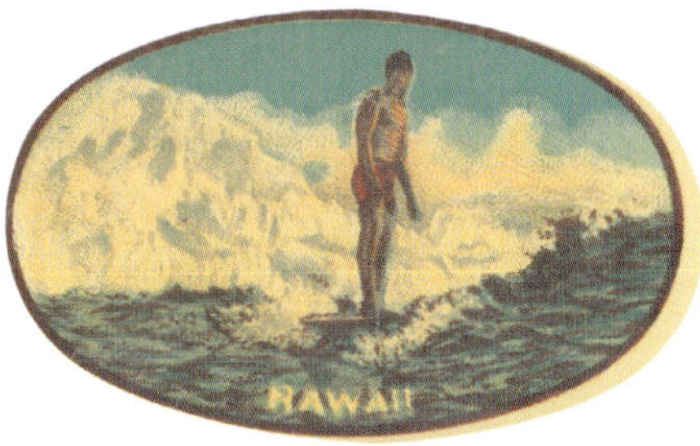
HAWAII

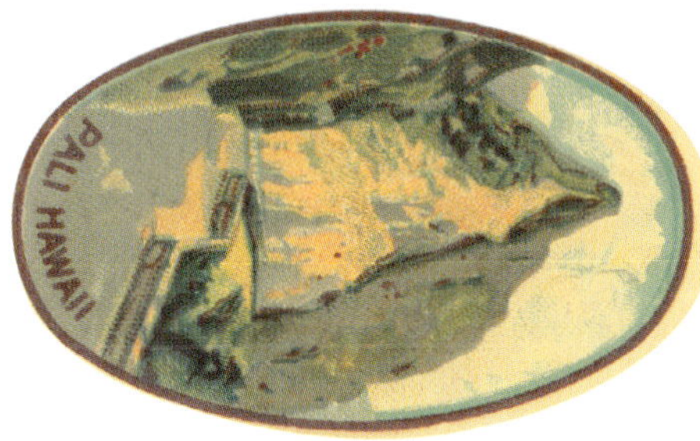
PALI HAWAII

HAWAII

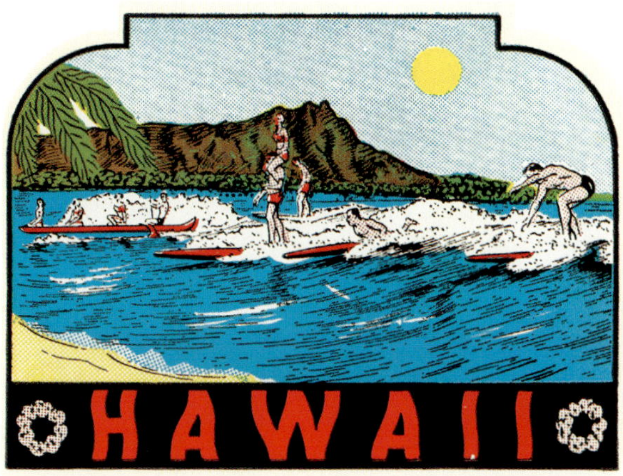
HAWAII

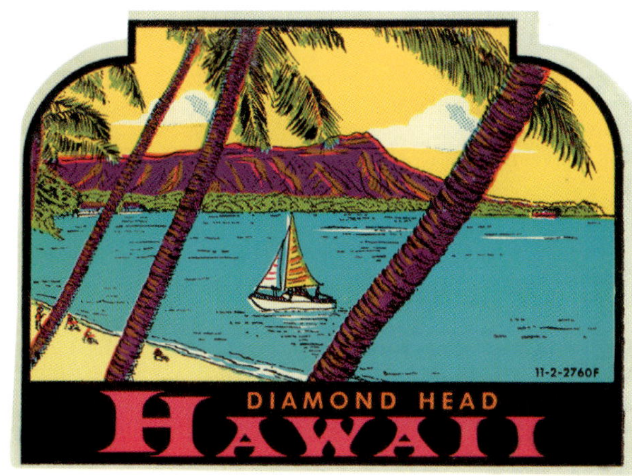
11-2-2760F
DIAMOND HEAD
HAWAII

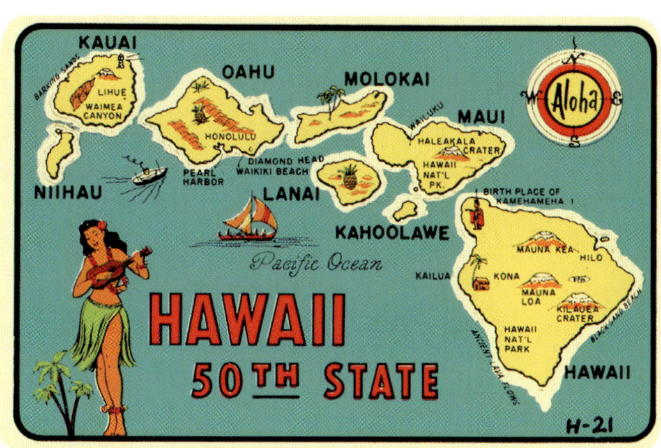
KAUAI
LIHUE
WAIMEA CANYON
OAHU
HONOLULU
DIAMOND HEAD
WAIKIKI BEACH
PEARL HARBOR
MOLOKAI
MAUI
HALEAKALA CRATER
HAWAII NAT'L PK
Aloha
NIIHAU
LANAI
KAHOOLAWE
BIRTH PLACE OF KAMEHAMEHA I
MAUNA KEA
HILO
KAILUA
KONA
MAUNA LOA
KILAUEA CRATER
HAWAII NAT'L PARK
Pacific Ocean
HAWAII
50TH STATE
HAWAII
H-21

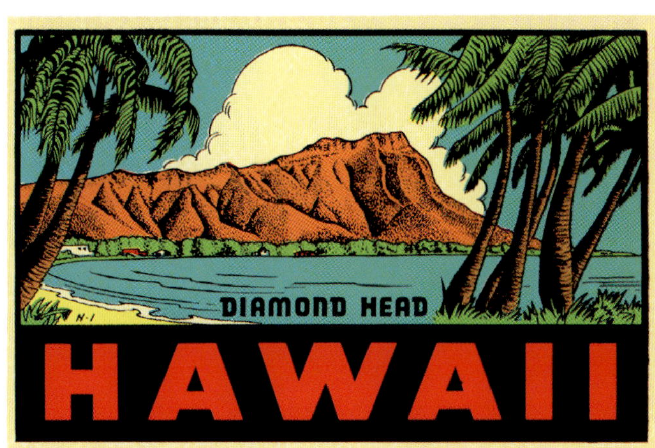
DIAMOND HEAD
HAWAII

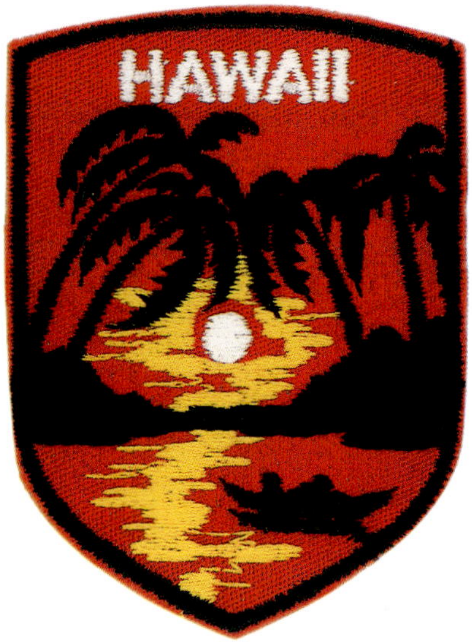
HAWAII

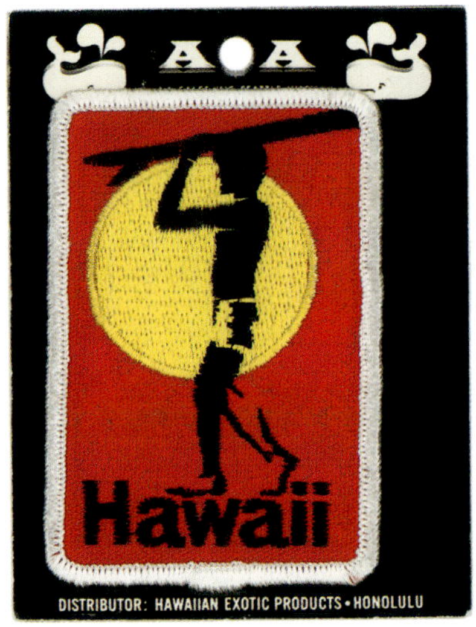
AOA
Hawaii
DISTRIBUTOR: HAWAIIAN EXOTIC PRODUCTS • HONOLULU

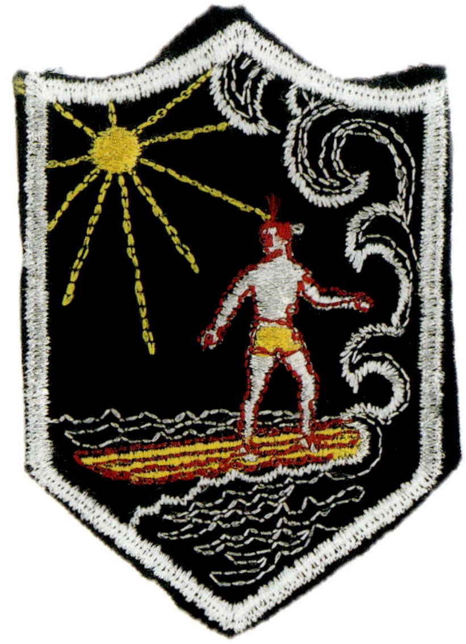

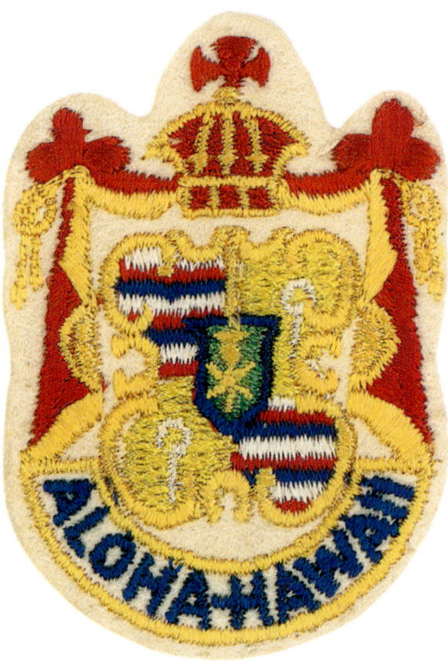
ALOHA-HAWAII

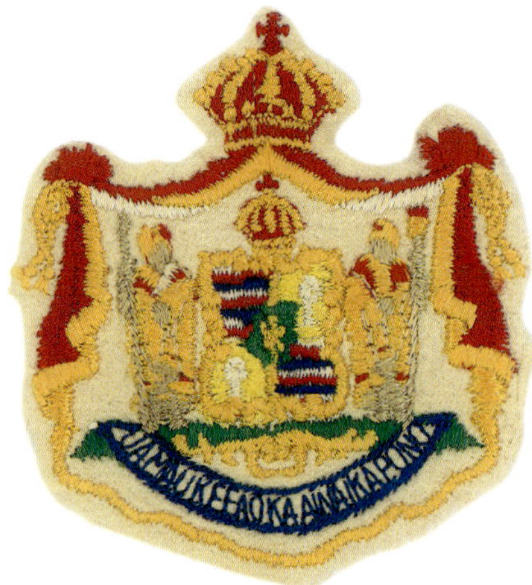

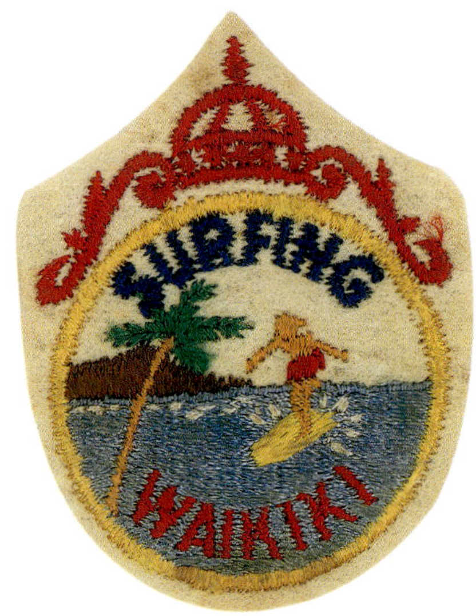
SURFING
WAIKIKI

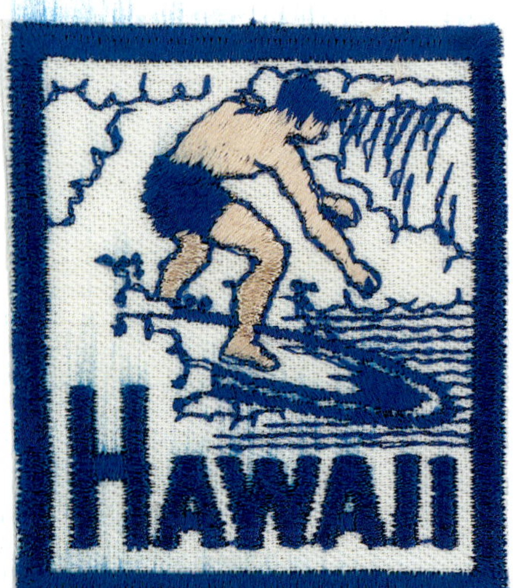
HAWAII

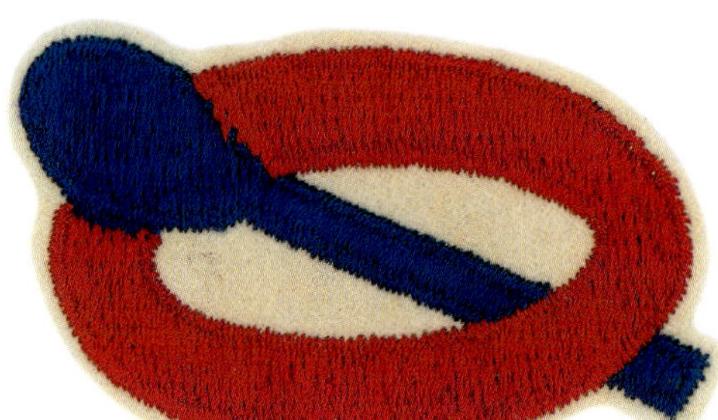

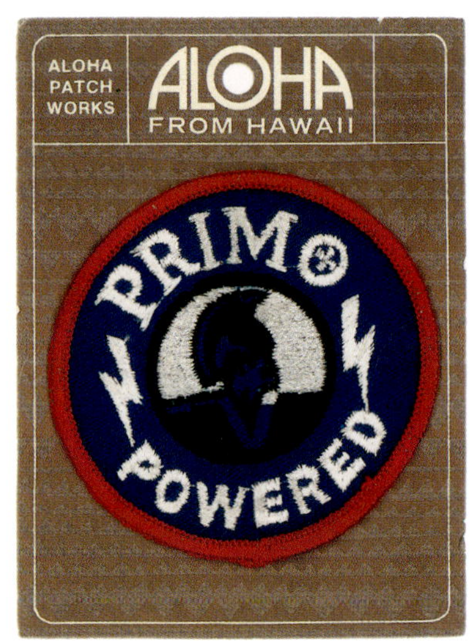
ALOHA PATCH WORKS
ALOHA
FROM HAWAII
PRIMO
POWERED

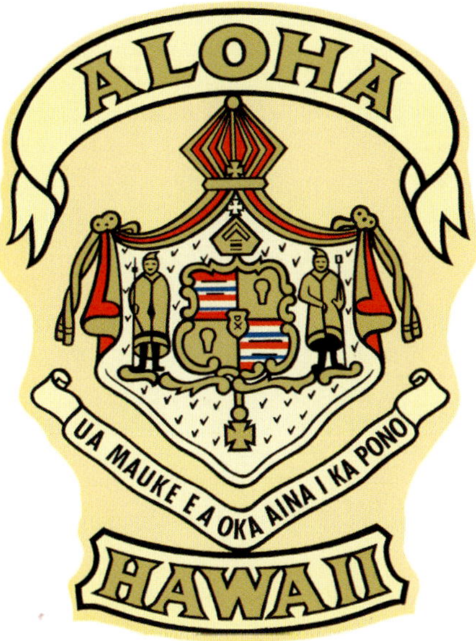
ALOHA
UA MAUKE E A OKA AINA I KA PONO
HAWAII

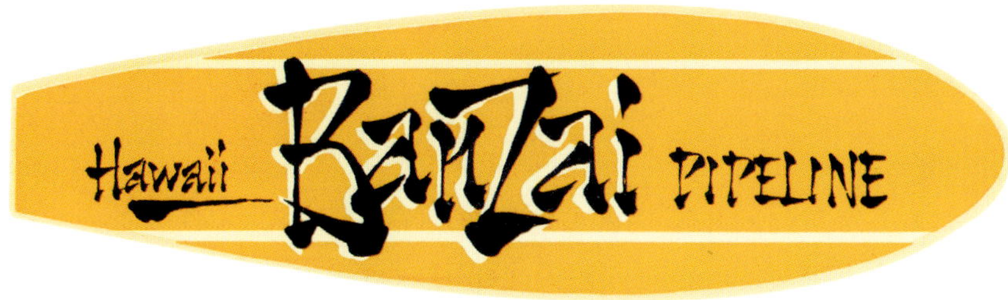
Hawaii Banzai PIPELINE

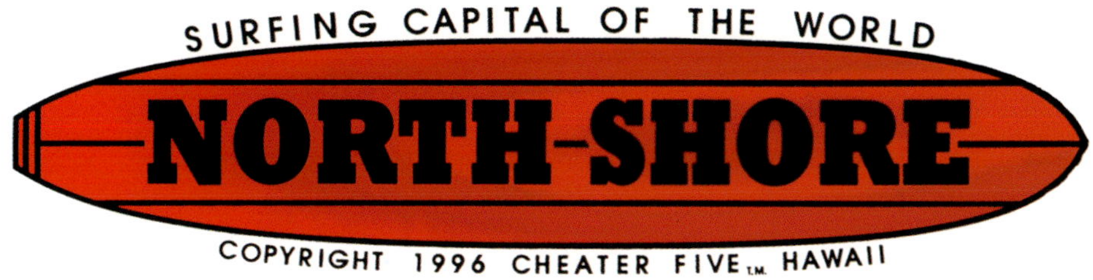
SURFING CAPITAL OF THE WORLD
NORTH-SHORE
COPYRIGHT 1996 CHEATER FIVE T.M. HAWAII

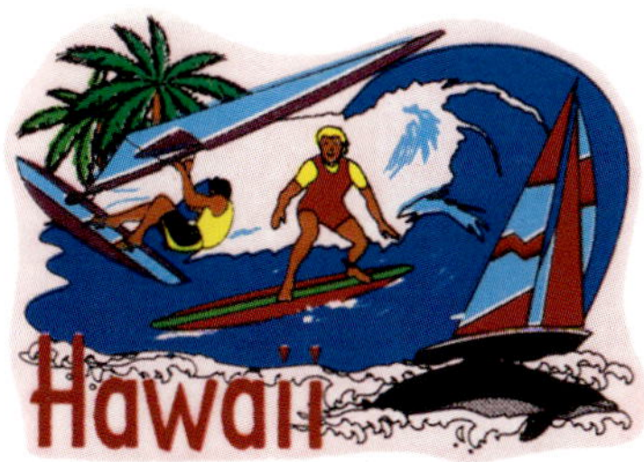
Hawaii

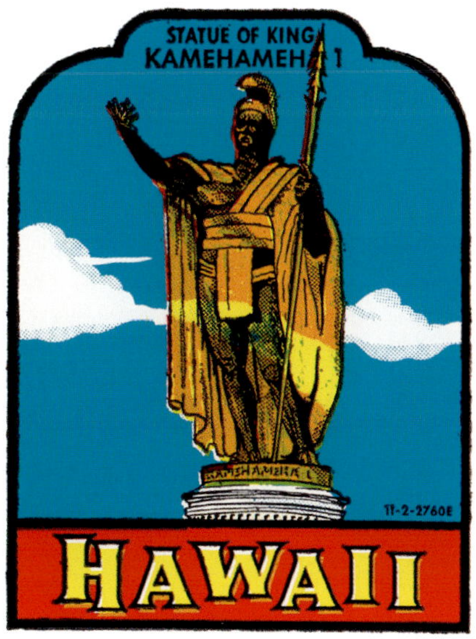
STATUE OF KING
KAMEHAMEH 1
HAWAII

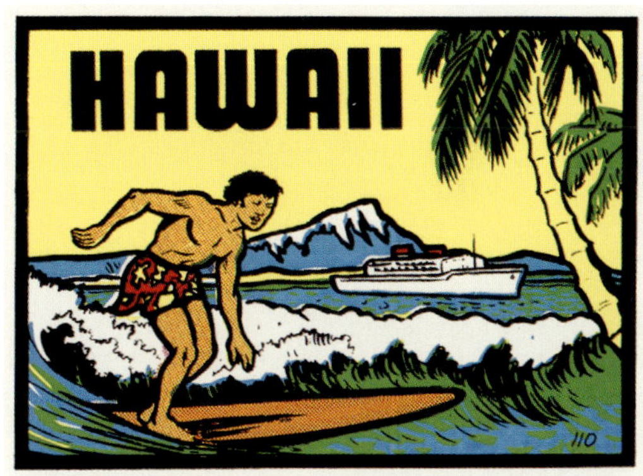
HAWAII
110

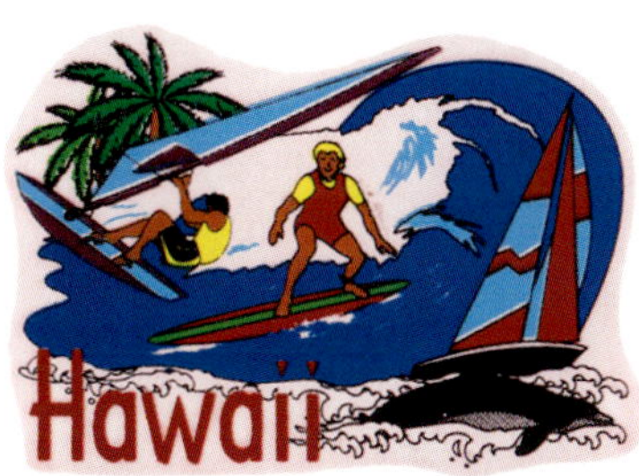
Hawaii

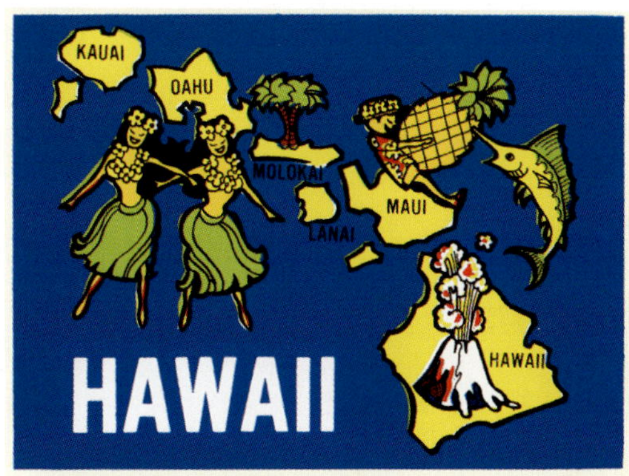
KAUAI
OAHU
MOLOKAI
LANAI
MAUI
HAWAII
HAWAII

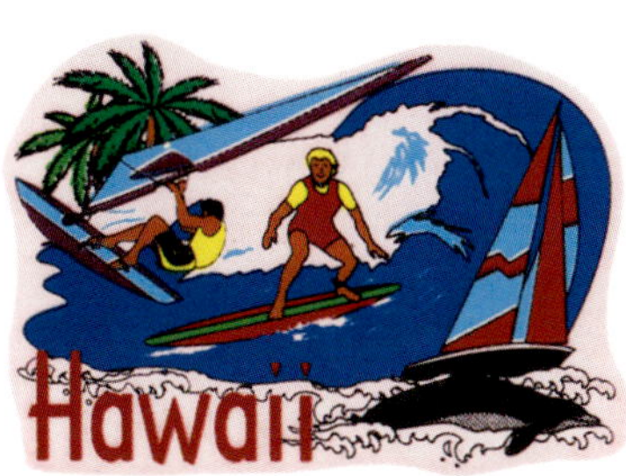
Hawaii

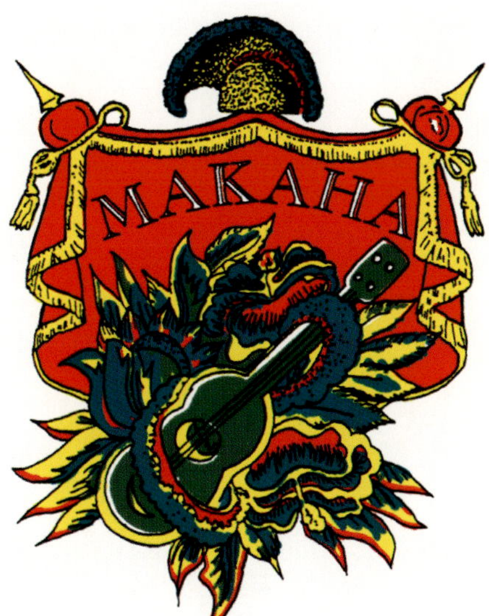
MAKAHA

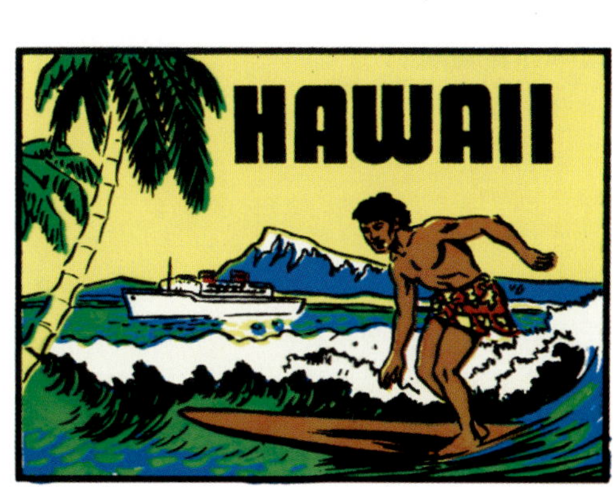
HAWAII

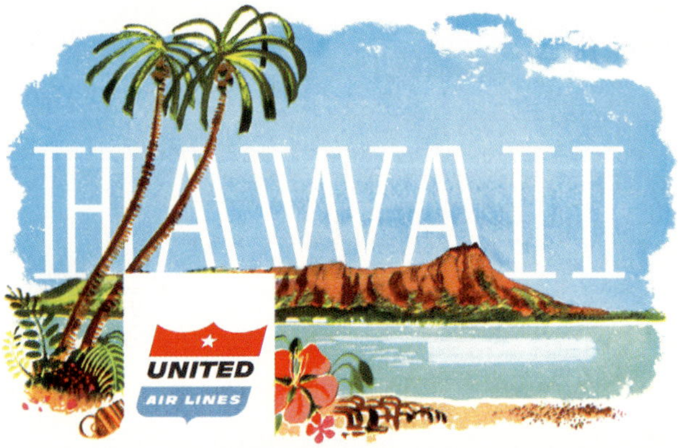
HAWAII
UNITED
AIR LINES

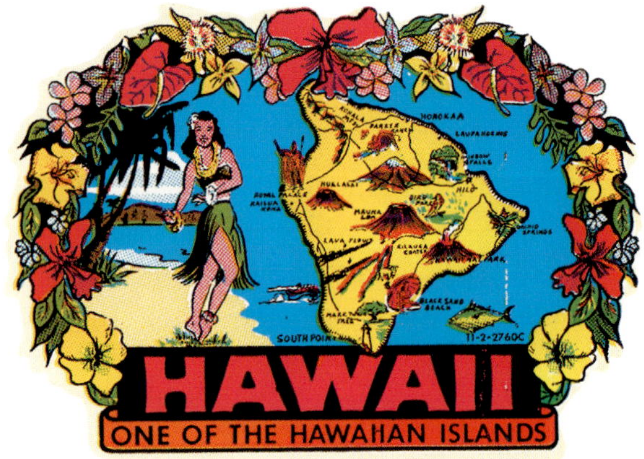
HAWAII
ONE OF THE HAWAIIAN ISLANDS

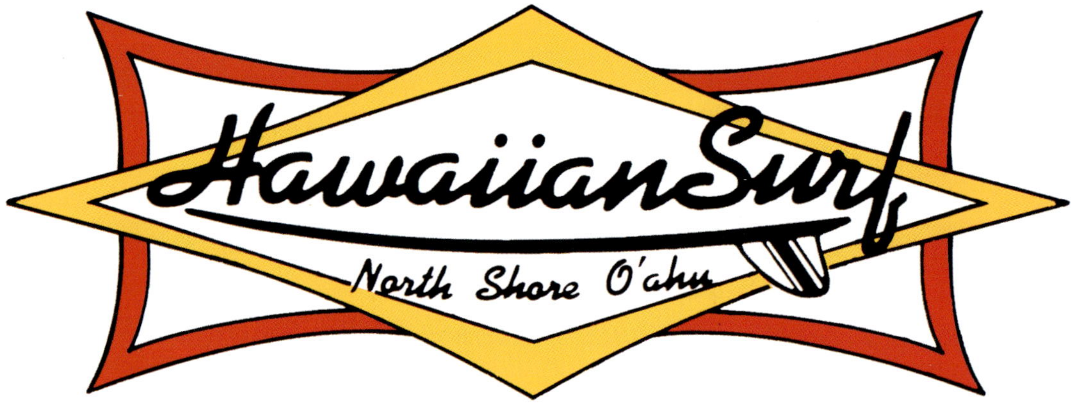
Hawaiian Surf
North Shore O'ahu

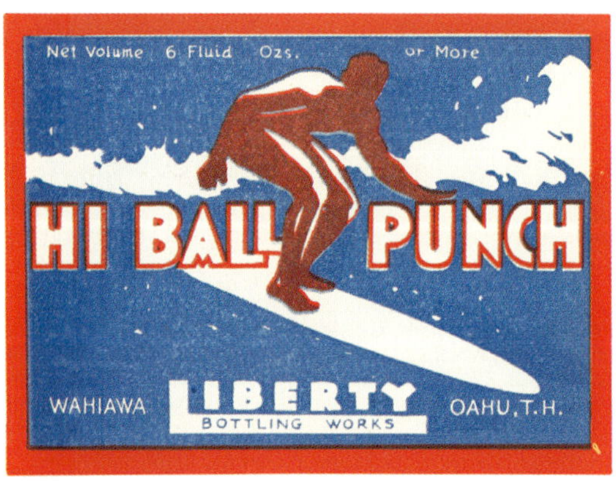
Net Volume 6 Fluid Ozs. or More
HI BALL PUNCH
WAHIAWA LIBERTY OAHU, T.H.
BOTTLING WORKS

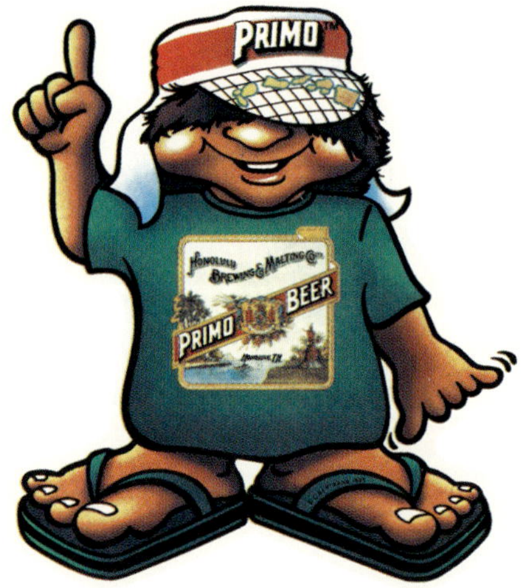
PRIMO
PRIMO BEER

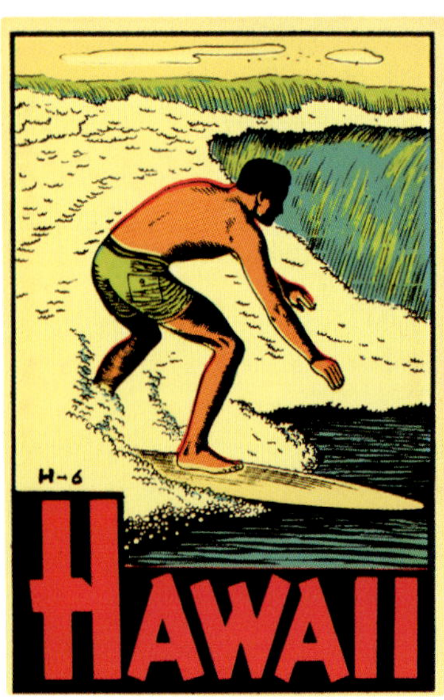
H-6
HAWAII

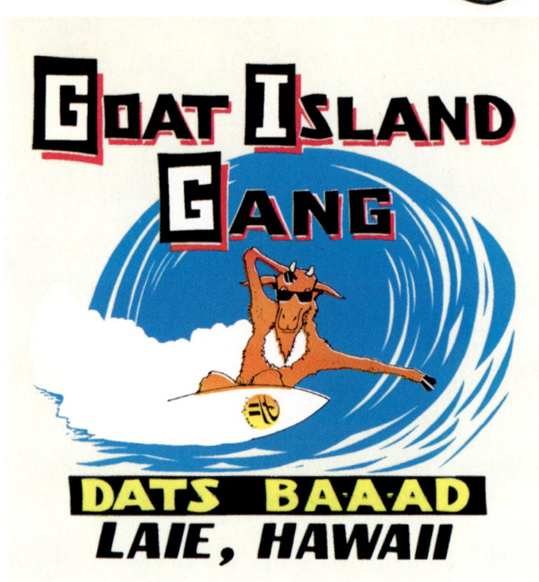
GOAT ISLAND
GANG
DATS BAA-AD
LAIE, HAWAII

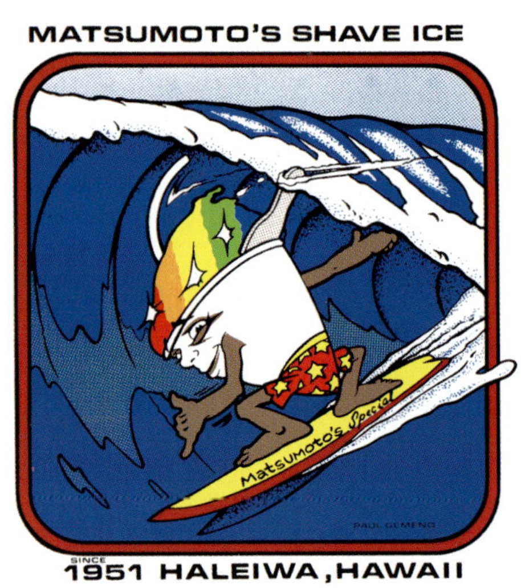
MATSUMOTO'S SHAVE ICE
Matsumoto's Special
SINCE
1951 HALEIWA, HAWAII

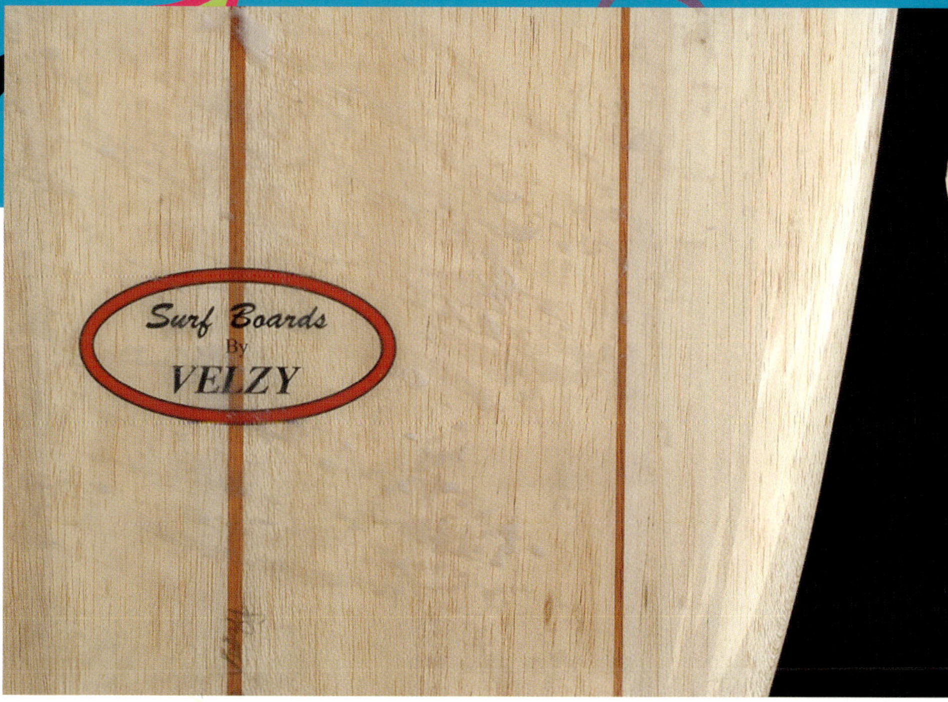

A classic Velzy balsa with the original oval log, on the tail. Photo: Juliana Morais. Courtesy Fernando Aguerre --and Voyageur Publishing.

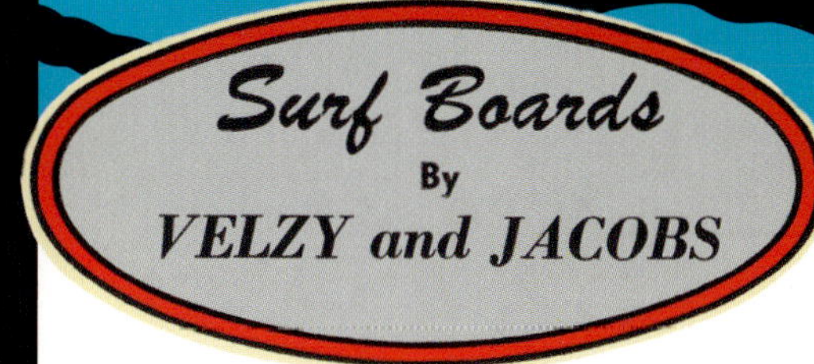

This is the original sticker, one of seven left in the shop before Velzy closed the shop in San Clemente. This guy who was a Woody owner had it because he helped clean the shop as Velzy was closing up. That's strange, because Velzy would rather sell you something, than give it away. The Woody owner guy said he would trade me a Gordie and a Hobie for it. We met in the parking lot of El Patio in Capo Beach at 7:00 in the evening. I sat in the car, it looks like a drug deal, he is a little late. People look at us like we are exchanging heroin or cocaine. And I'm the seller because I am the poor guy. This was probably around 1997 or 1998. – Pete Noble

CHAPTER THREE

WATER SLIDE

Then Came Velzy, From 1952 to Gidget

By 1952, Dale Velzy was 25 years old and had his feet planted as one of the foundations of the surf-industrial complex. Born on the beach in 1927, Velzy began surfing when he was "just a little squirt" on boards cut down by his woodworker father. Velzy began cutting his own boards down at 10 years old: "There were a bunch of us little kids [getting into it]," Velzy said to Paul Holmes for the book *Dale Velzy is Hawk*. "But I had the advantage of cutting my boards down. They were just riding hand-me-downs. They weren't thinning them down and giving them tail rocker. And my boards were lighter. Every time you cut two feet off the tail of one of those planks you were losing 40 pounds!"

Velzy sailed through World War II – literally – as a merchant marine. He went around the world a couple of times, saw what was happening in Hawaii, surfed places in Sumatra that wouldn't be in vogue for decades, and came back to California with a head full of ideas, a fistful of cash, and a lot of ambition perfectly positioned to feed the post-war surfing boom.

Back in the South Bay, Velzy had a great business trimming down the Pacific System Homes and other planks that their forefathers had been riding through the 20s and 30s. And, in 1949, business was so good, he went into business, opening Velzy Surfboards under the Hermosa Beach pier.

Three years later, Velzy began branding every surfboard he made with a decal produced en masse by Art Decal in Long Beach. Velzy was as much into cars and motorcycles as he was into surfing, and it's possible he was inspired by the hot rod world to make that first Velzy decal, if you believe Stanley's Surf Decal Collecting Tips from the www.surfcrazy.com website:

> "Southern California was the surfboard building capitol of the world in the 40's, 50's and 60's. Boards sold in Hawaii and U.S. East Coast at that time were manufactured in So Cal. The majority of decal decorators were located in So Cal. Most Hawaiian decals and laminates from the late 60's through the early 70's were produced in So Cal. Early California hot rod speed part manufacturers spawned the popularity of decals. All hotrodders had to have decals affixed to their cars to display what was under the hood. Hot rod and surfboard decals were printed by the same companies, sometimes on the same sheets, side by side. The advent of mylar and vinyl stickers simplified the decoration process, eliminating the need for water-slide glue, spelling doom for many water-slide decal decorators."

Decal comes from the word decalcomania. According to Wikipedia: "Decalcomania, or décalcomanie, a decorative technique by which engravings and prints may be transferred to other materials, was invented in Russia and introduced into the United States at least as early as 1868.

By 1952, Decalcomania had become decals, which are, also according to Wikipedia: "A decal or transfer is a plastic, cloth, paper, or ceramic substrate that has printed on it a pattern that can be moved to another surface upon contact, usually with the aid of heat or water. The word is short for "decalcomania." Decals are often used on hot rod automobiles and plastic models."

The mania didn't drop entirely from decalcomania, because by the early 50s, hot rod mania was taking over southern California. The term "hot rod" refers to a period between the end of World War II and the beginning of the "muscle car" era of 1965, when cars made before 1942 were modified for speed and customized for looks, inside and out. Part of the protocol of hotrodding was to let the world know what engine, magneto, headers, carburetor, tachometer, cams, motoroil, and rods were running on the inside, what speed shop did the work and what customizer did the outside.

The first decals were called "water slide" or "slip" decals. They were printed face up on an adhesive layer which had a layer of dextrose corn syrup residue between the sticker and a white paper backing. To apply the sticker, it had to be wetted and then "slipped" or "slid" onto glass or metal or plastic. This took a bit of skill, and it still does, but water slide decals are now considered collector's items and are more often put under glass than on it. From the www.surfcrazy.com website:

> "The old ones are almost always water slide decals, They were printed by a handful of printers who printed their mark on the back slider sheet, Art Decal, Color Brite, The Hyalac Co. are a few that come to mind. Always inspect the paper. The old decals were printed with lacquer, they kind of stained the paper, the paper is 30-40 years old so it usually is yellowing. Hang Ten was one of the first surf companies to use R. Stanton Avery's adhesive sticker labels."

By 1952, Velzy was into hot rodding cars and was customizing surfboards, essentially hotrodding the boards of his forefathers, customizing them for speed but not necessarily for looks. Velzy claimed the inspiration did not come from the car world: "I just started drawing out circles and put my name inside it," Velzy was quoted by Brian Gillogly in "Diamonds and Ovals," in *The Surfer's Journal*. "Some people said we borrowed it from Ford, but this was way before Ford's oval. It was just something that was easy to look at. And it looked great in black, silver and red."

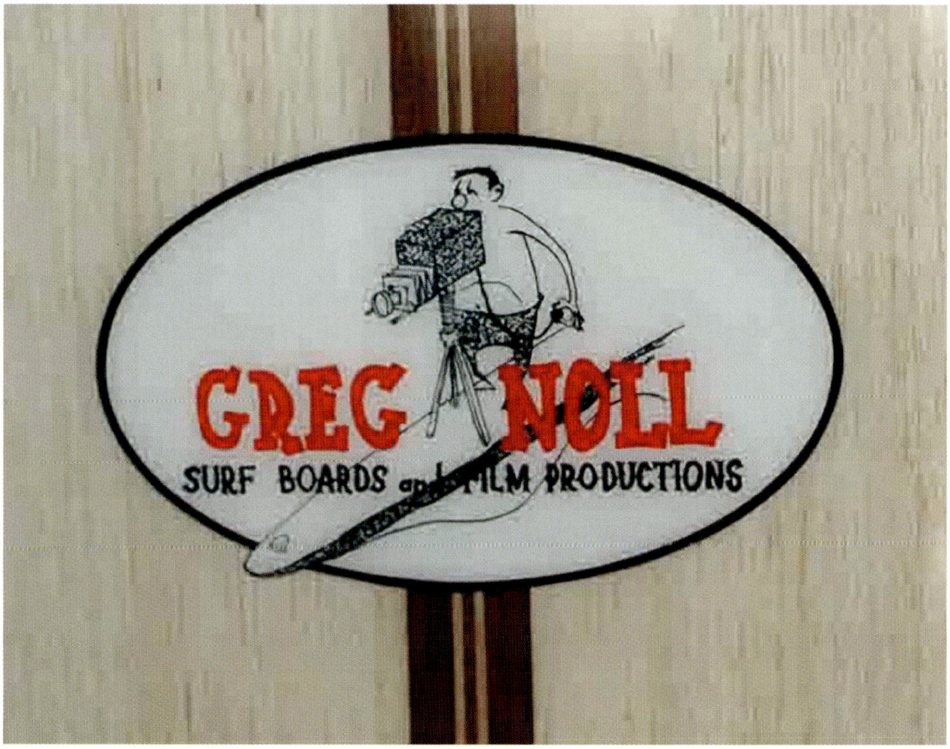

An old-style Greg Noll logo on a modern recreation of one of his balsa/redwoods. Photo: Juliana Morais. Courtesy Fernando Aguerre and Voyageur Press.

CHAPTER 3.1
SURFBOARDS BY...

This first batch of stickers are all by surfboard manufacturers, and while they are presented alphabetically and not by year, era, or location, you will see a lot of stickers inspired by that original Velzy oval and also a tendency toward geometric shapes like diamonds, squares, rectangles.

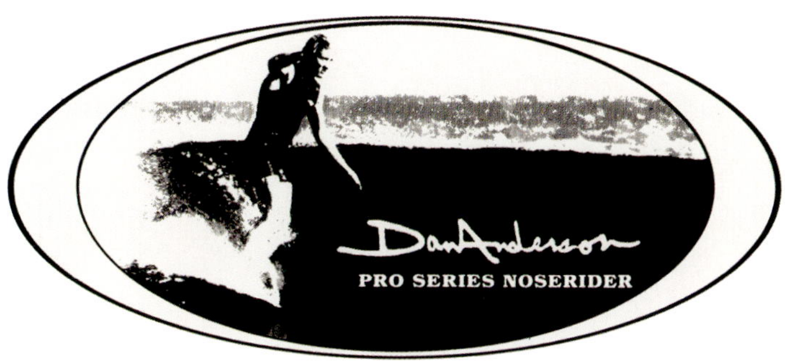

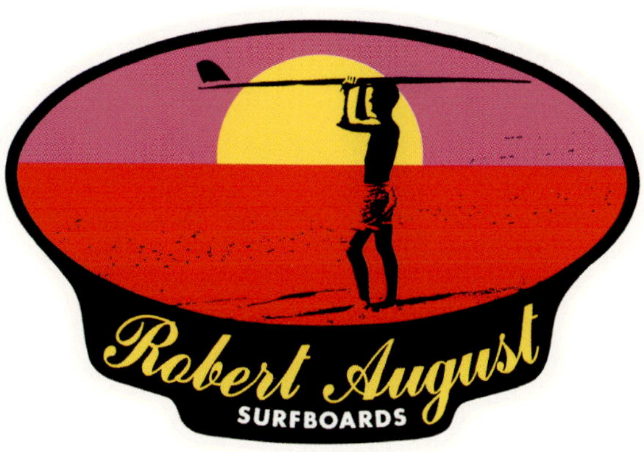

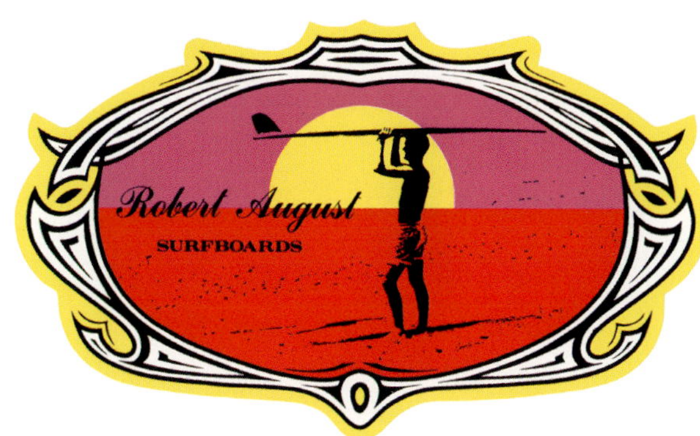

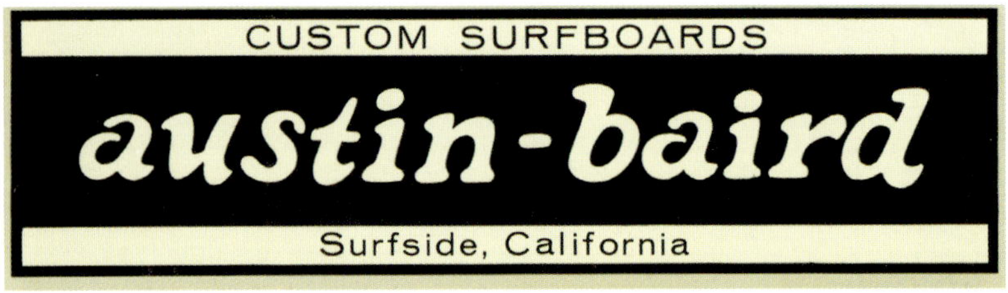
CUSTOM SURFBOARDS
austin-baird
Surfside, California

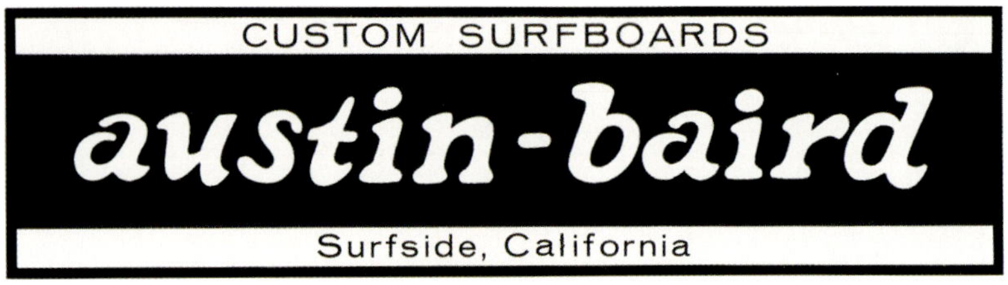
CUSTOM SURFBOARDS
austin-baird
Surfside, California

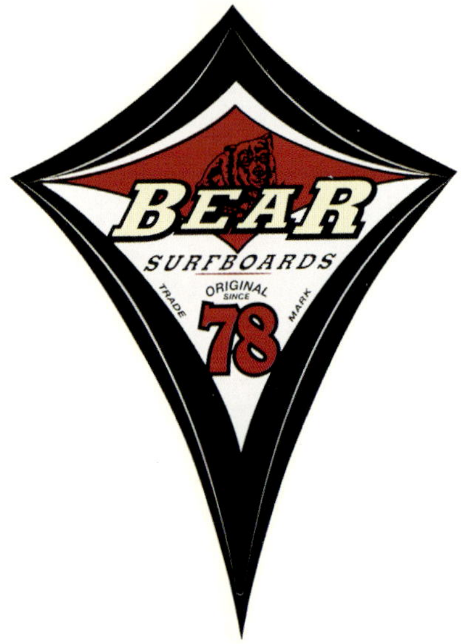
BEAR
SURFBOARDS
ORIGINAL SINCE
TRADE MARK
78

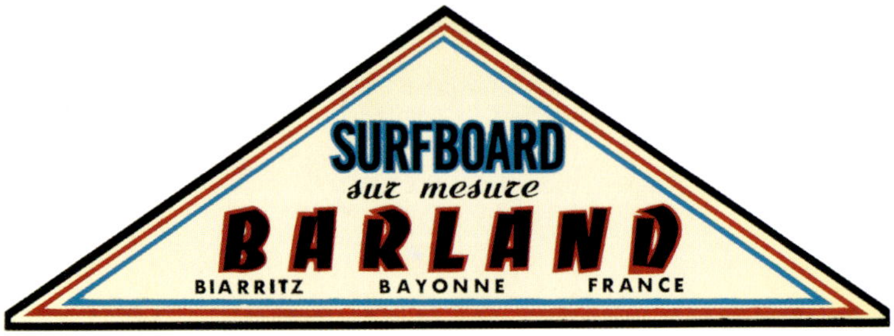
SURFBOARD
sur mesure
BARLAND
BIARRITZ BAYONNE FRANCE

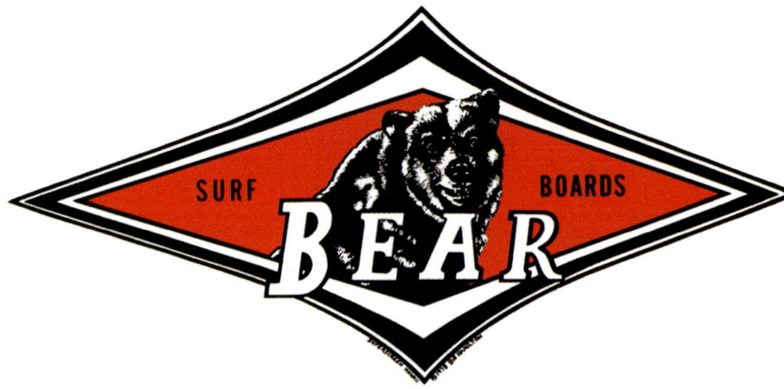
SURF BOARDS
BEAR

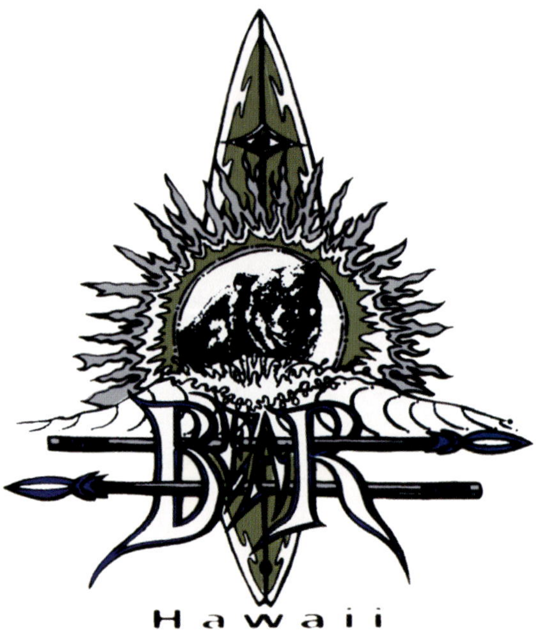
BEAR
Hawaii

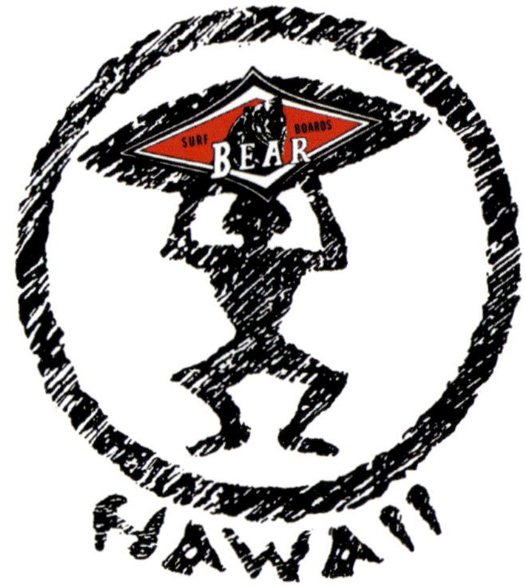
SURF BOARDS
BEAR
HAWAII

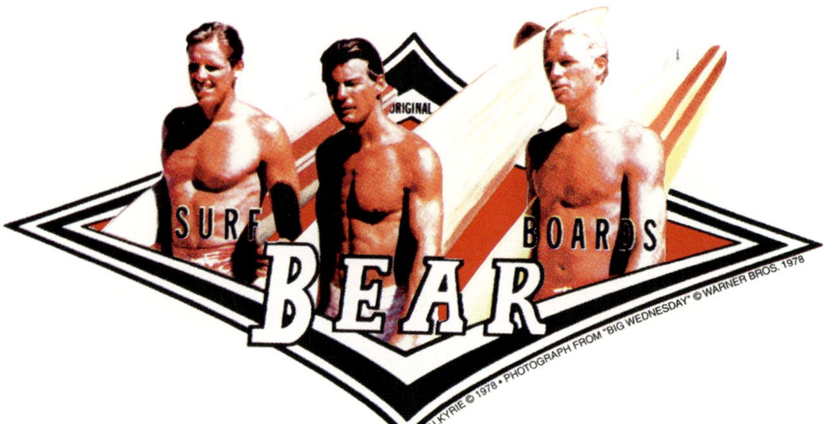
ORIGINAL
SURF BOARDS
BEAR
VALKYRIE © 1978 • PHOTOGRAPH FROM "BIG WEDNESDAY" © WARNER BROS. 1978

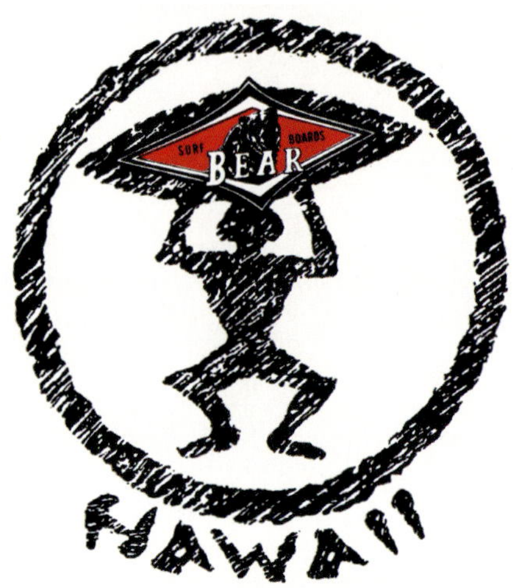
SURF BOARDS
BEAR
HAWAII

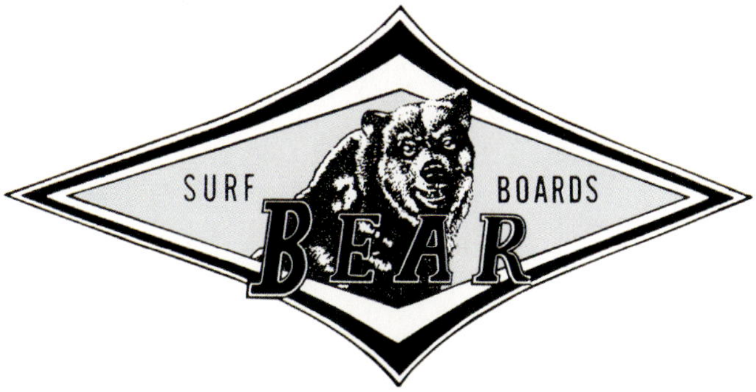

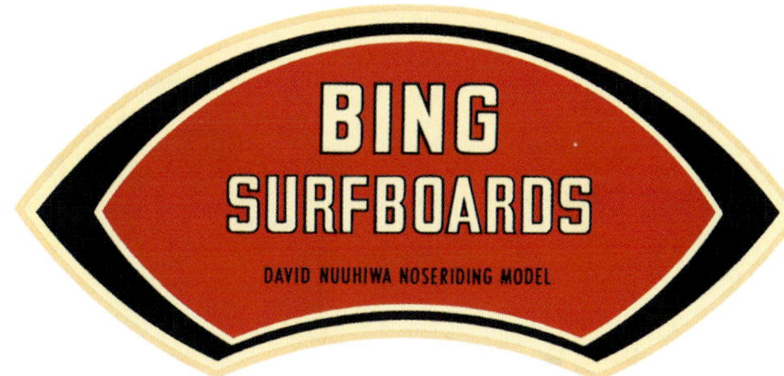

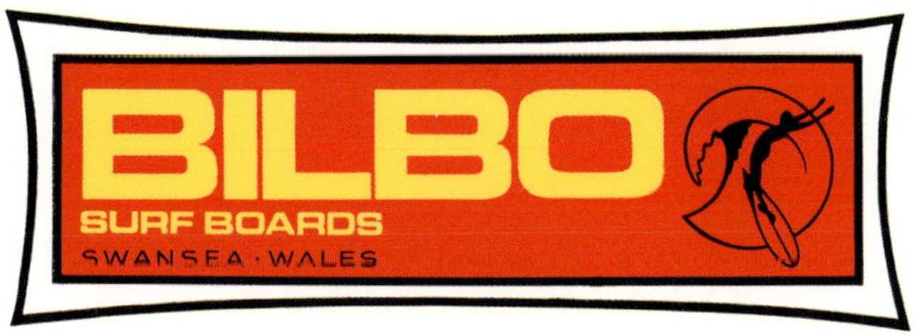

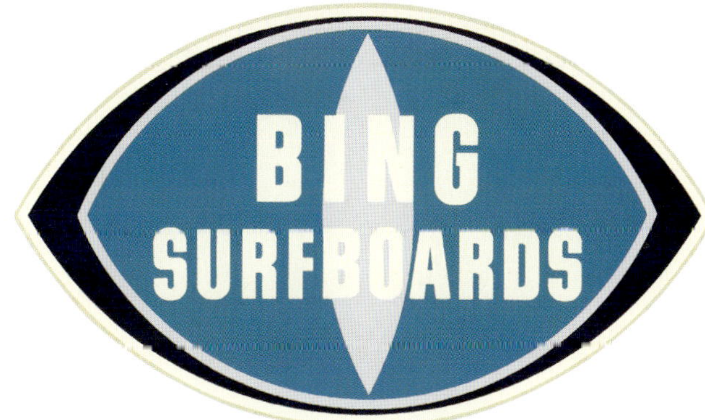

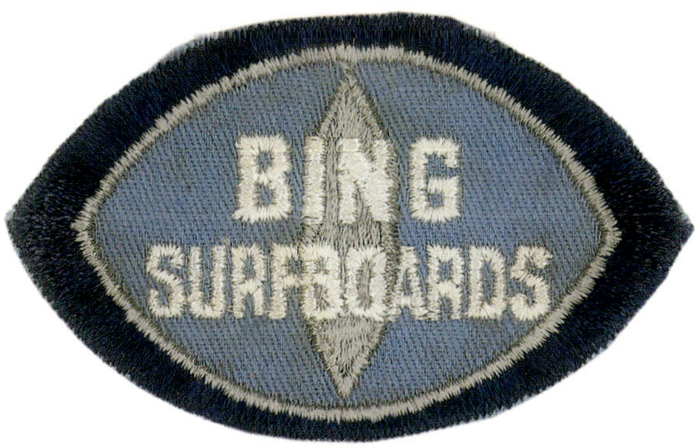

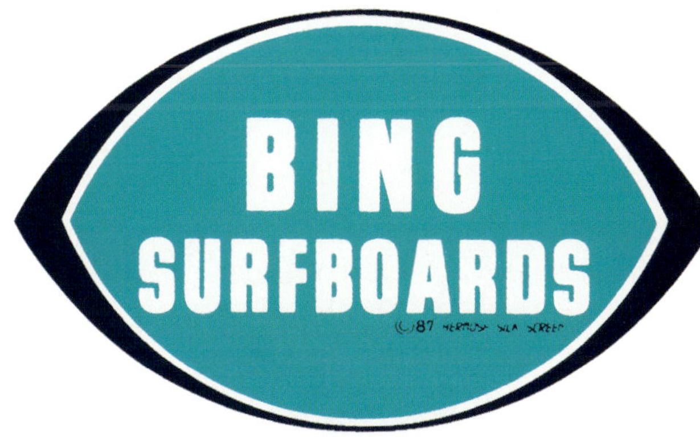

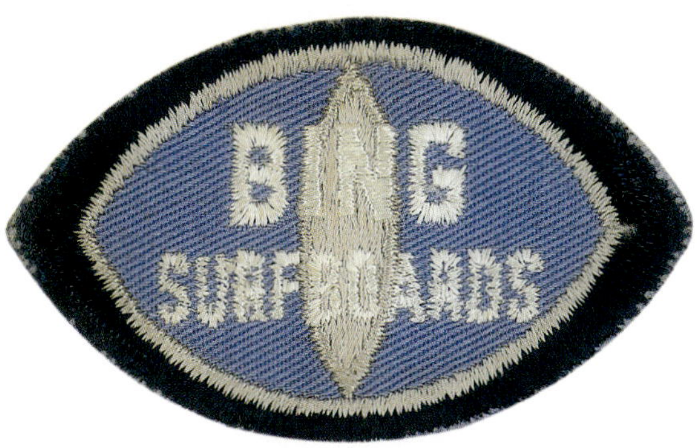

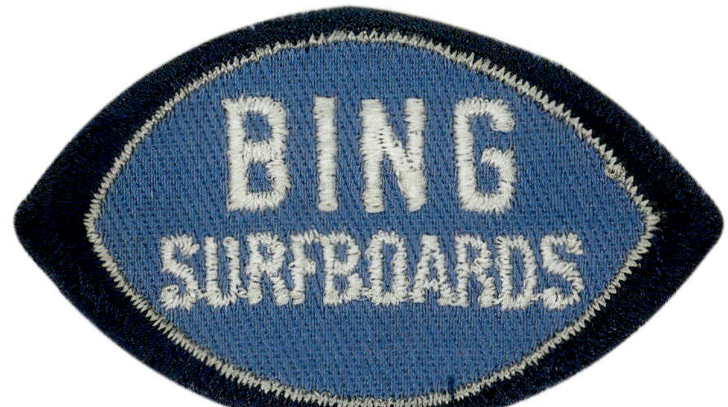

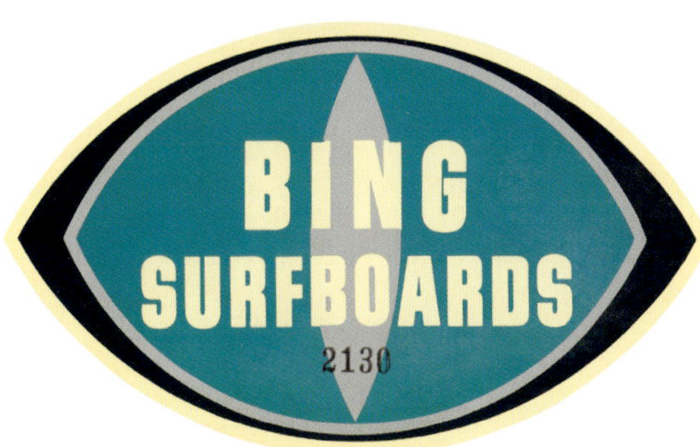

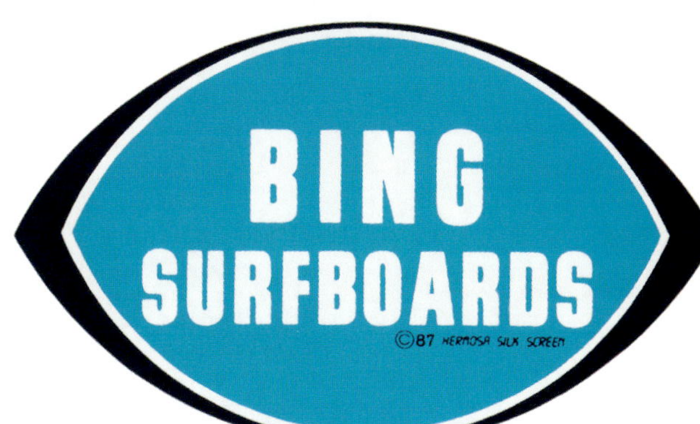

The Bings with ID numbers on them all went on surfboards. I got that from Tom Craig in Cayucos. – Pete Noble

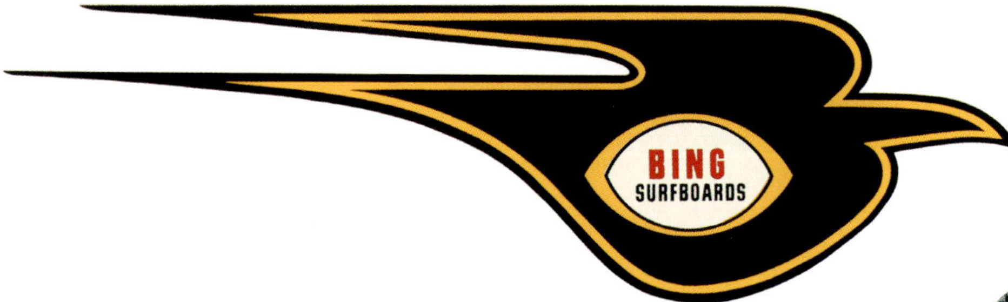
BING
SURFBOARDS

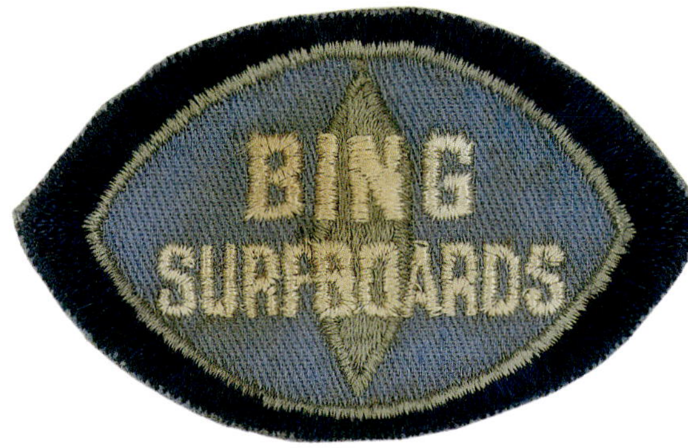
BING
SURFBOARDS

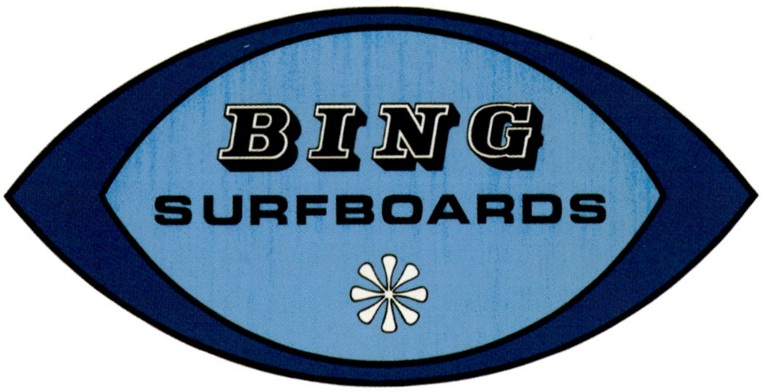
BING
SURFBOARDS

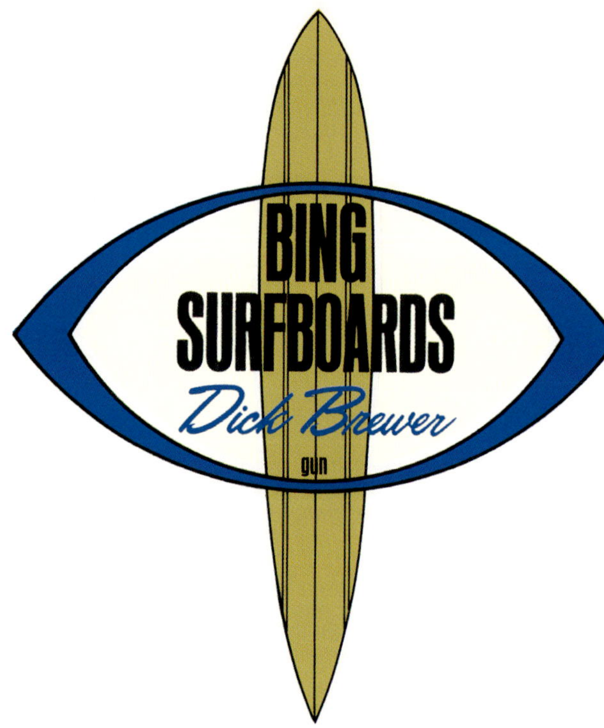
BING
SURFBOARDS
Dick Brewer
gun

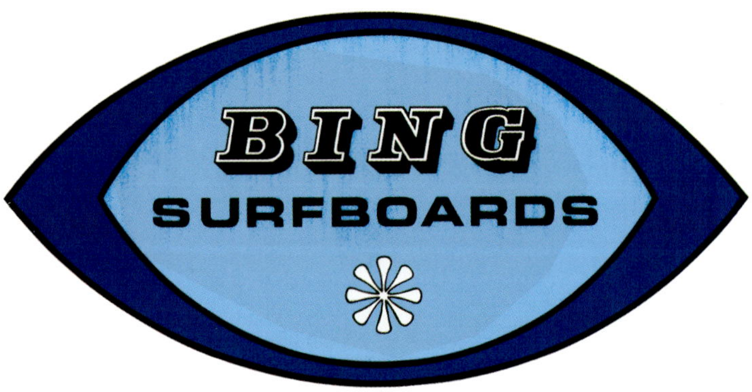
BING
SURFBOARDS

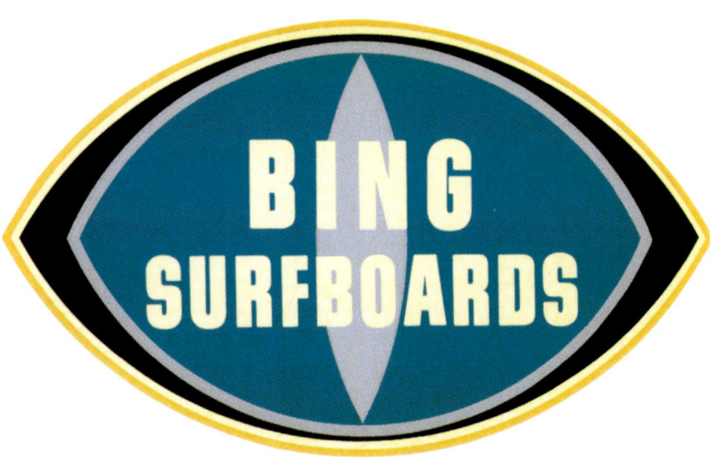
BING
SURFBOARDS

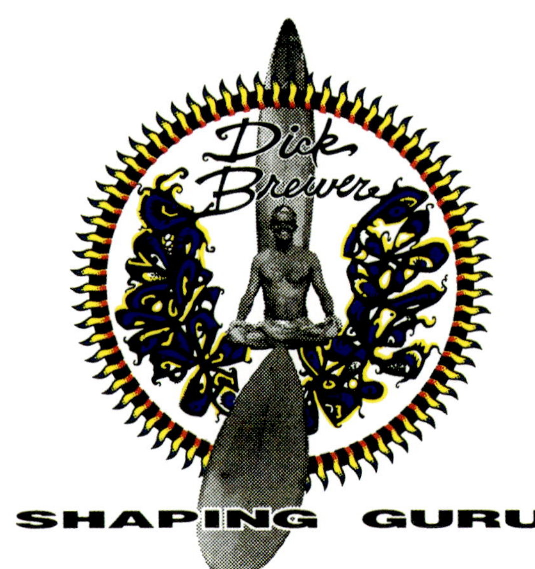
Dick
Brewer
SHAPING GURU

BREWER HAWAII

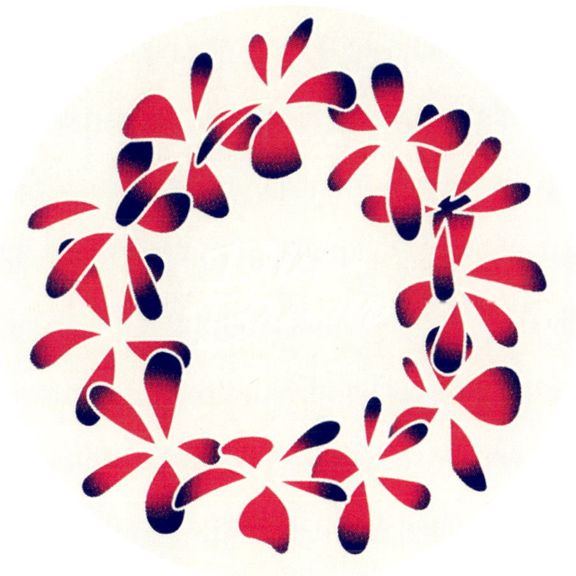

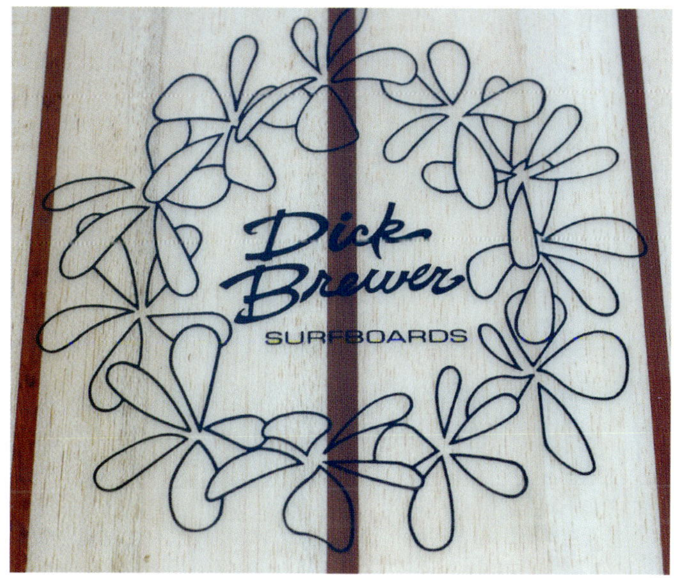

Dick Brewer logo on balsa/redwood re-creations. Photo: Juliana Morais. Courtesy Fernando Aguerre and Voyageur Press.

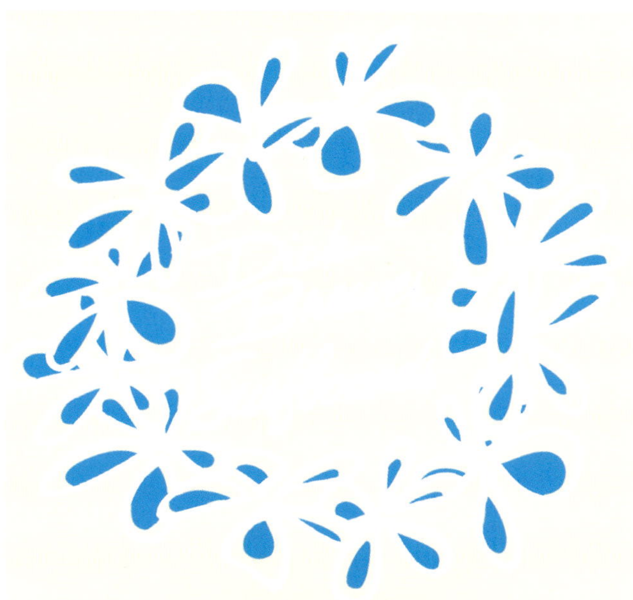

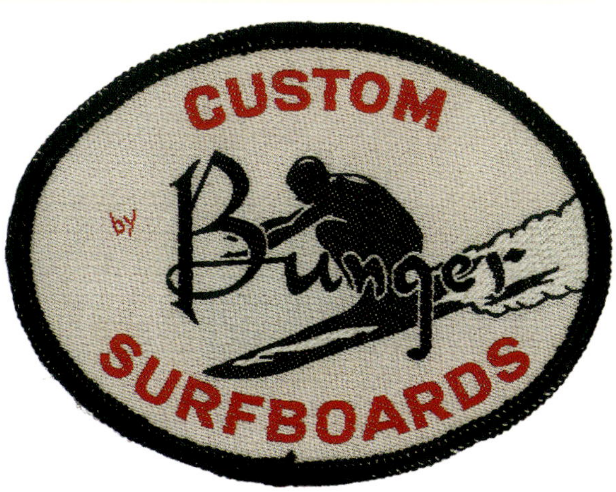

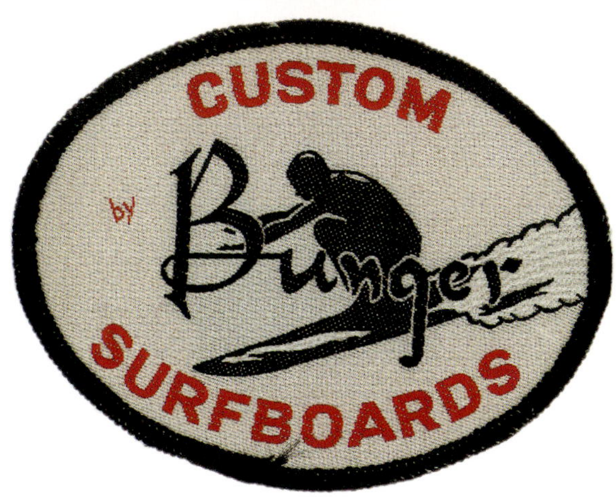

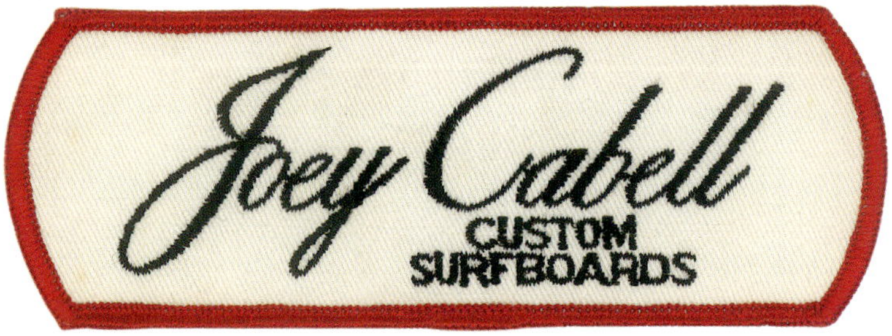
Joey Cabell
CUSTOM
SURFBOARDS

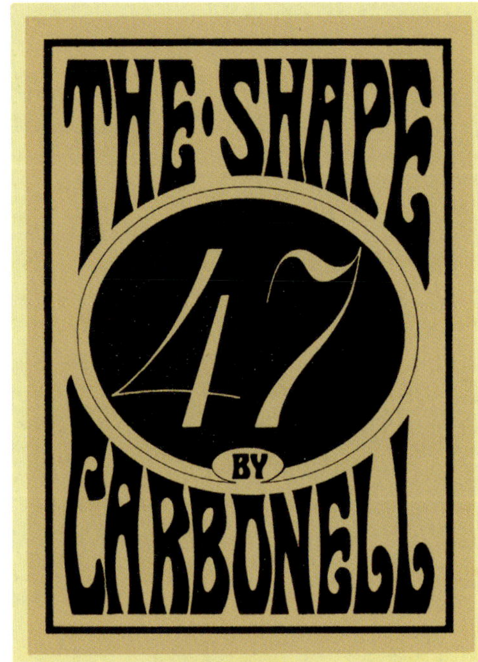
THE SHAPE
47
BY
CARBONELL

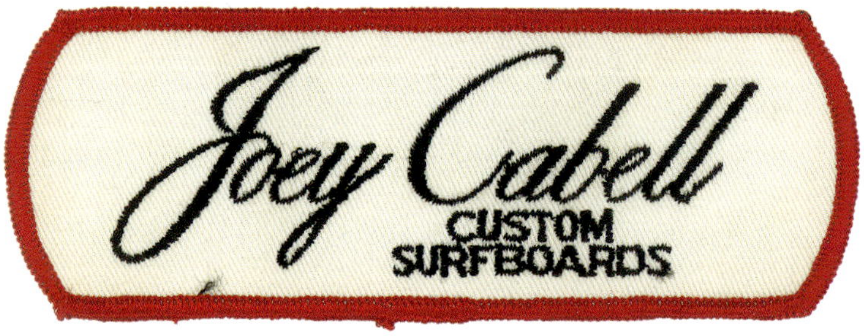
Joey Cabell
CUSTOM
SURFBOARDS

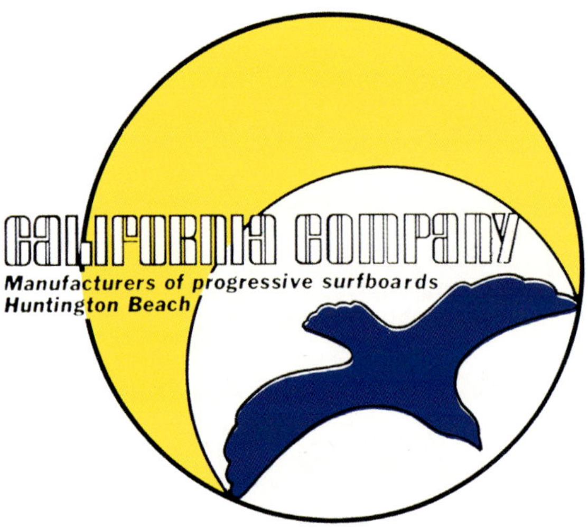
CALIFORNIA COMPANY
Manufacturers of progressive surfboards
Huntington Beach

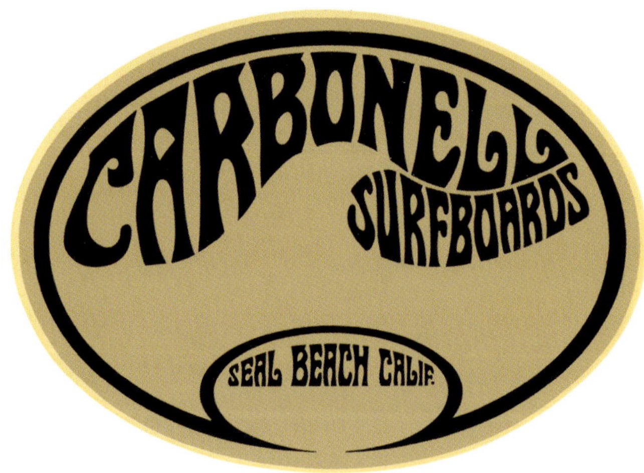
CARBONELL
SURFBOARDS
SEAL BEACH CALIF.

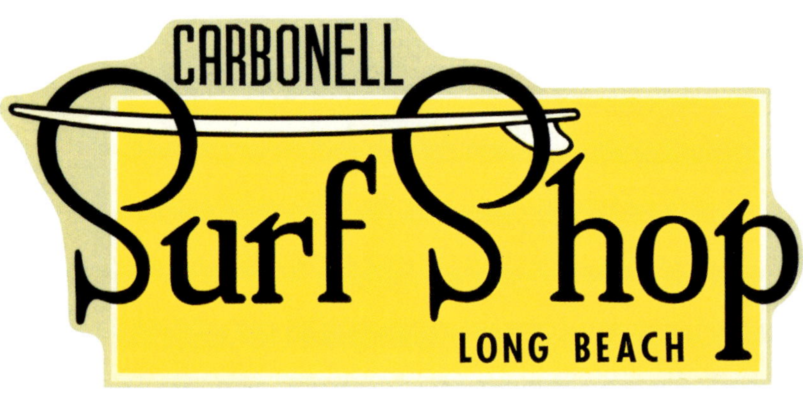
CARBONELL
Surf Shop
LONG BEACH

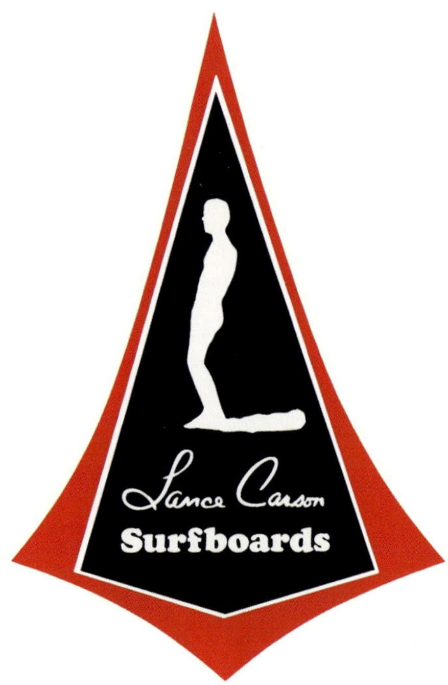
Lance Carson
Surfboards

CUSTOM
NORM CASEY
53 BAY RD. TAREN PT. AUS.

CHANNEL ISLANDS
surfboards
VENTURA-SANTA BARBARA

Caster
SURFBOARDS

Classic Glass
SUNSET CLIFFS CALIFORNIA™

CENTRAL COAST
SURFBOARDS™

C-STREET • RINCON • MALIBU • DANA POINT • STEAMER LANE • SAN ONOFRE
Classic
SURF
© Beele

CCS

SURFBOARDS
BY
CHALLENGER
The Means That Make Good Surfers Great Surfers!

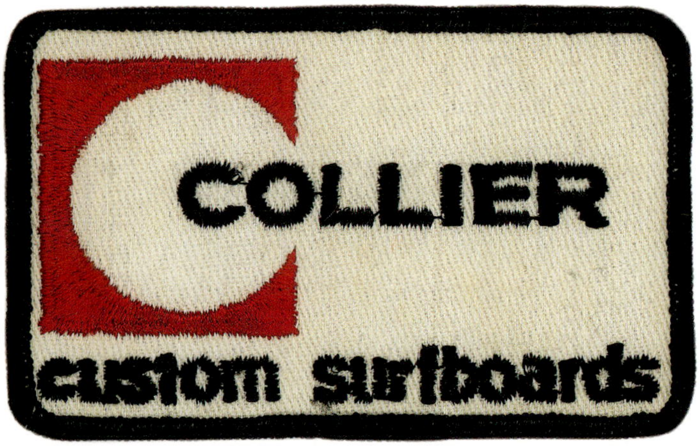
COLLIER
custom surfboards

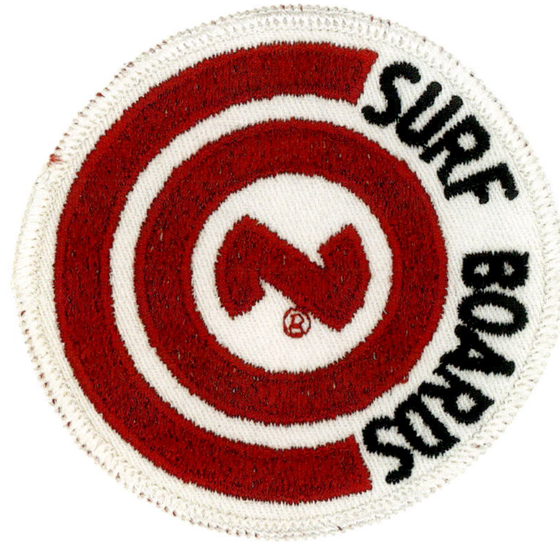
SURF BOARDS

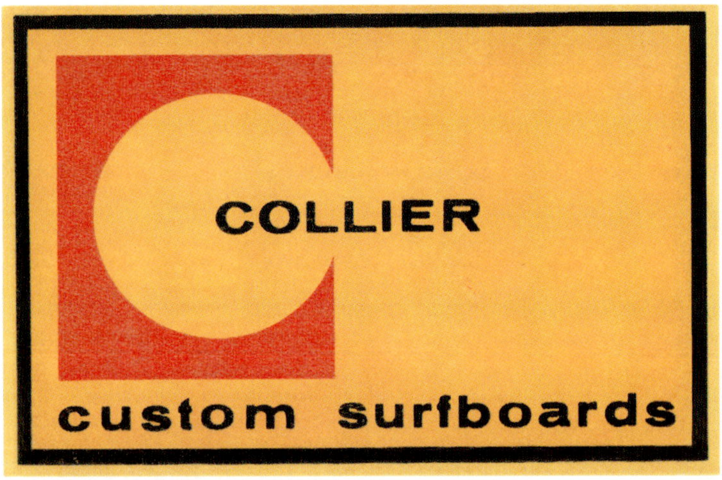
COLLIER
custom surfboards

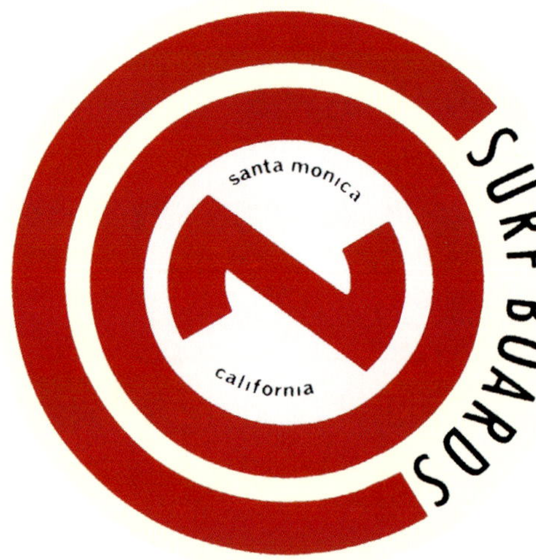
santa monica
california
SURF BOARDS

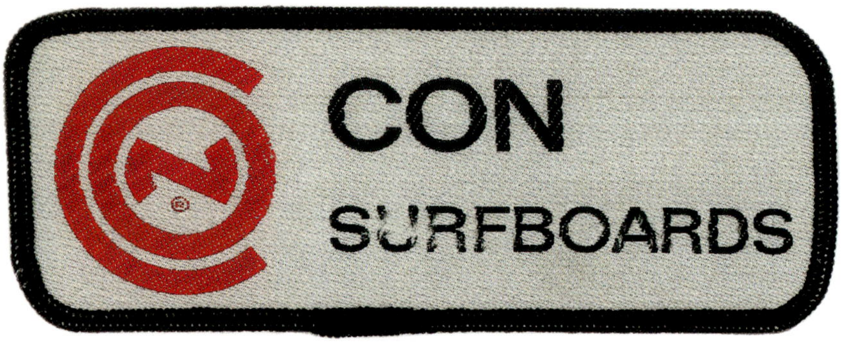
CON
SURFBOARDS

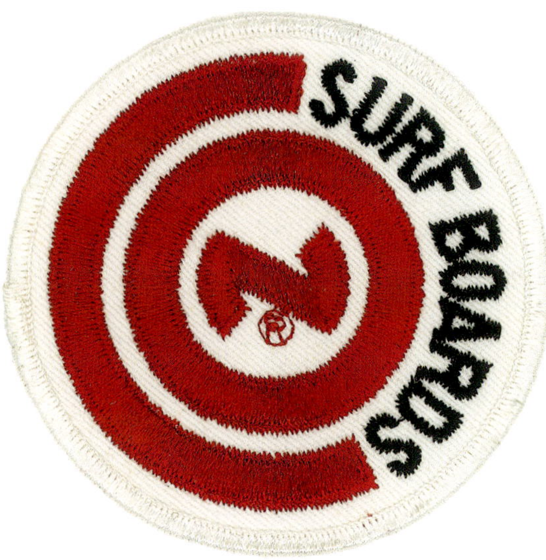
SURF BOARDS

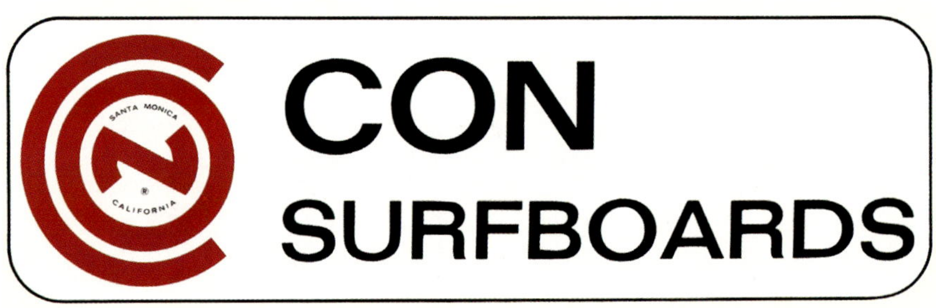
SANTA MONICA
CALIFORNIA
CON
SURFBOARDS

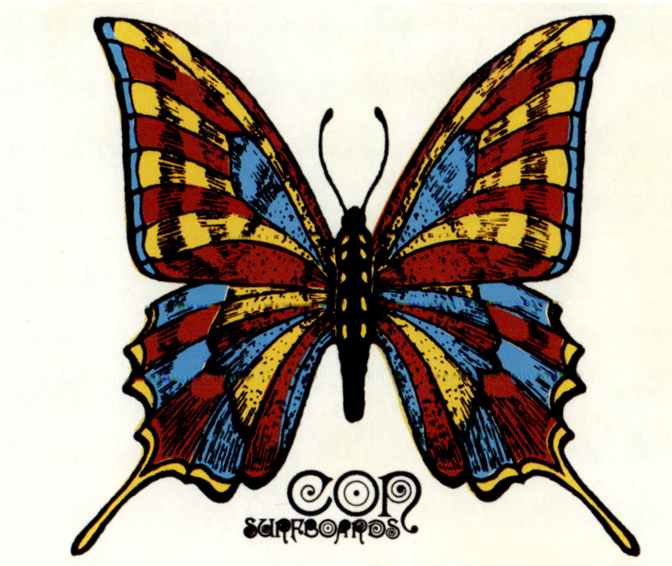
CON
SURFBOARDS

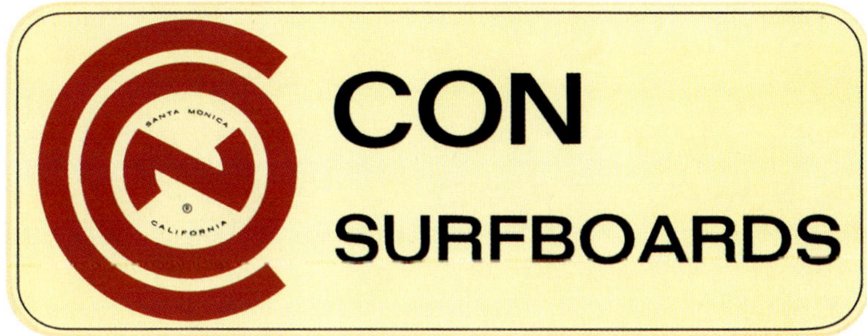
SANTA MONICA
CALIFORNIA
CON
SURFBOARDS

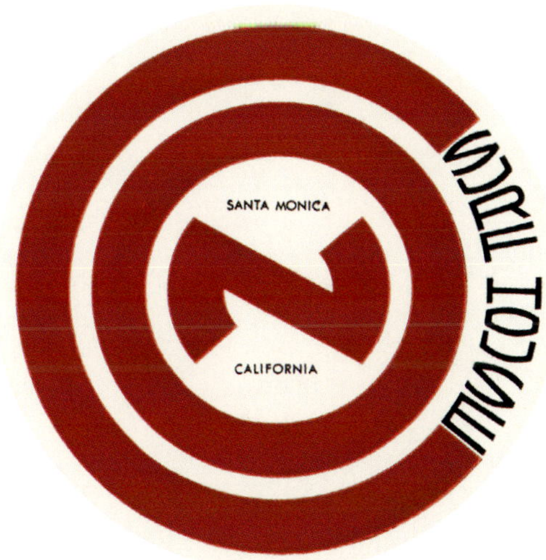
SANTA MONICA
CALIFORNIA

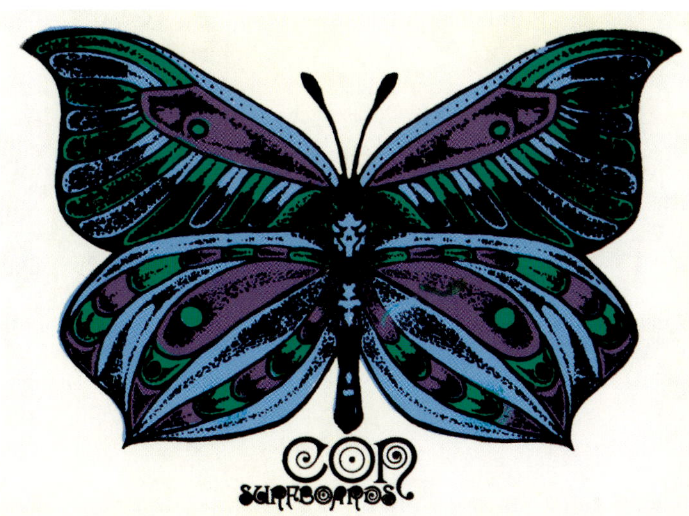
CON
SURFBOARDS

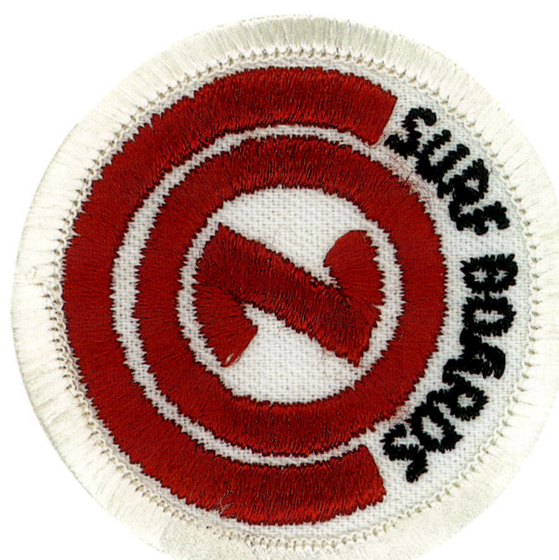
SURF BOARDS

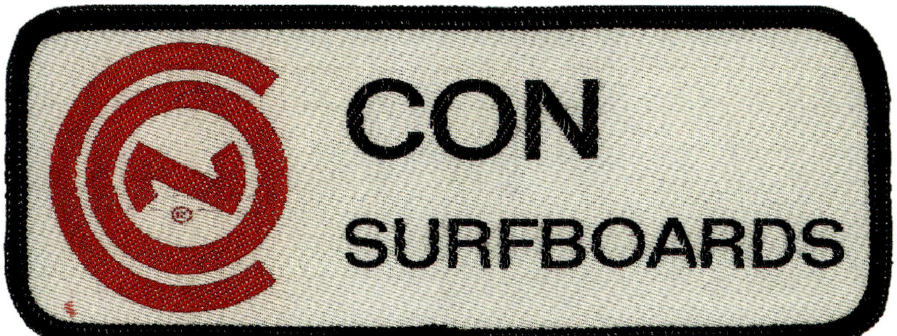
CON
SURFBOARDS

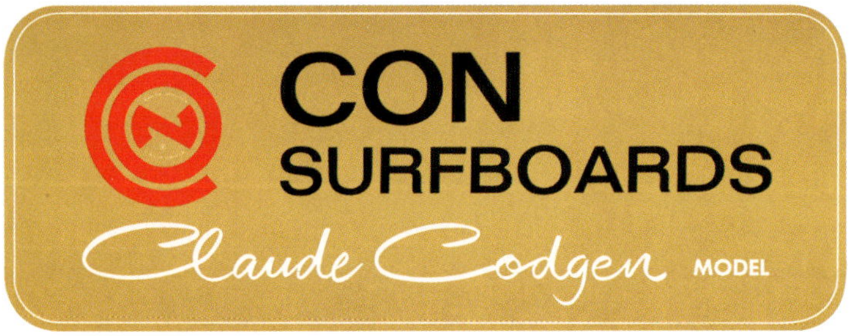

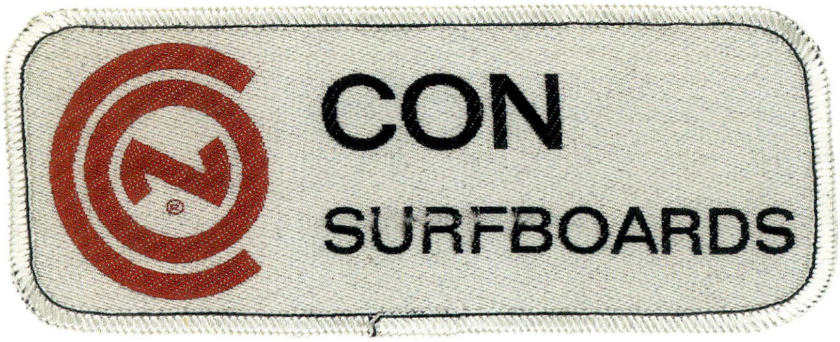

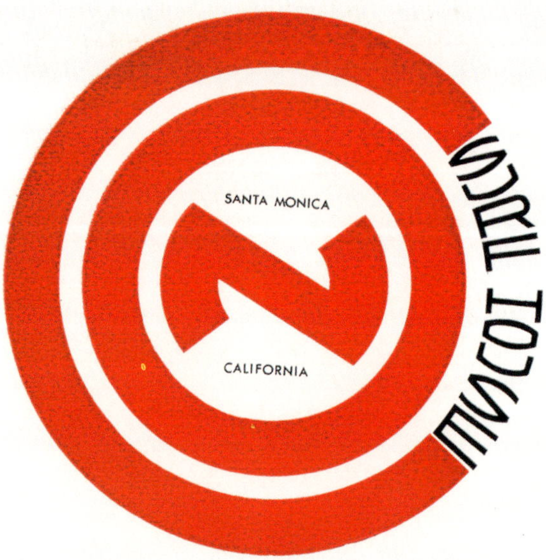

Missing from the collection here is the original Con water slide. It said "Con Surfboard House" or "Con House." Not sure why it isn't in here.
– Pete Noble

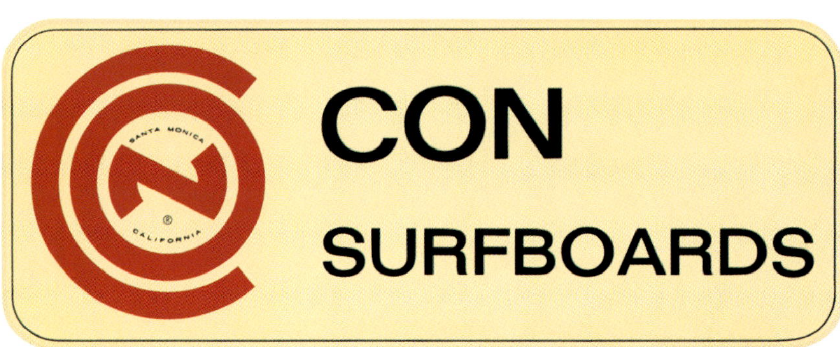

THE Crow SURF BOARD
SURFSIDE • CALIFORNIA

SURF BOARDS by Dewey Weber

Pat Curren
designed and shaped
Guns

DIWAIN
Surfboards, INC.
7719 STATE ST. - LU 96939 - HUNTINGTON PARK, CALIF.

SURFBOARDS
by
JEFFREY DALE
SANTA ANA

dc
DEL CANNON
SURFBOARDS

Hawaiian Pro Designs
Mike Doyle

DYNO
SURFBOARDS

E.T.
SURFBOARDS

E. T. Surfboards
Since 1971

FLAHERTY

Phil Edwards

SURF BOARD
CUSTOM FRY BUILT
COSTA RICA

ENCINITAS
SURFBOARDS

Skip Frye

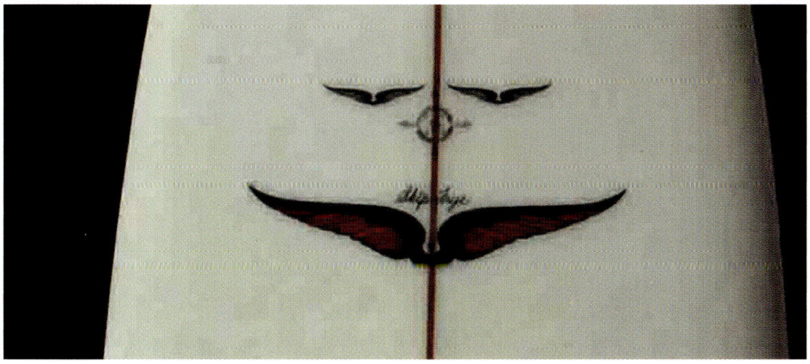

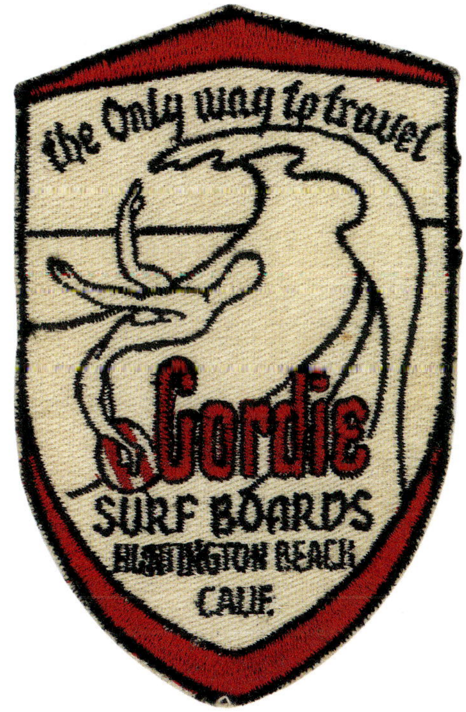

GALT
CUSTOM

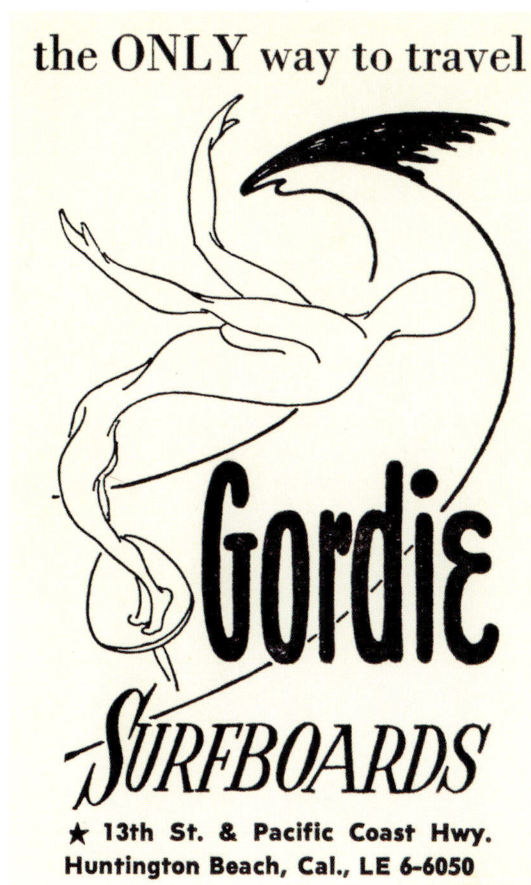

CLIFFORD GEORGE
Surfboards
SANTA BARBARA

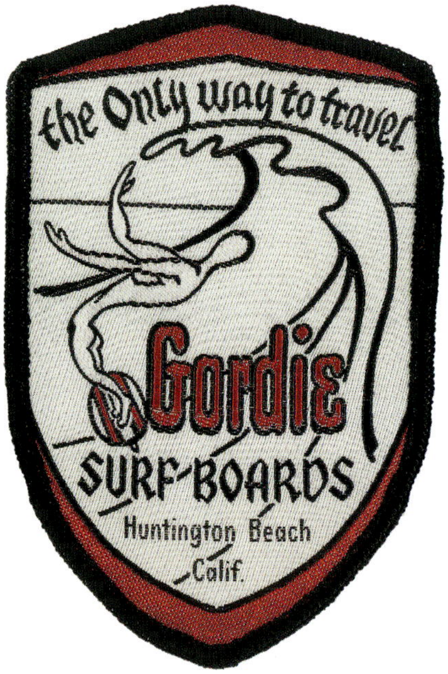
the Only way to travel
Gordie
SURF-BOARDS
Huntington Beach
Calif.

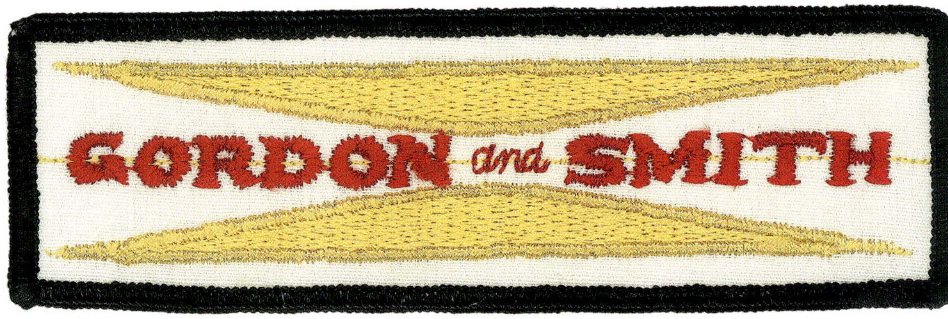
GORDON and SMITH

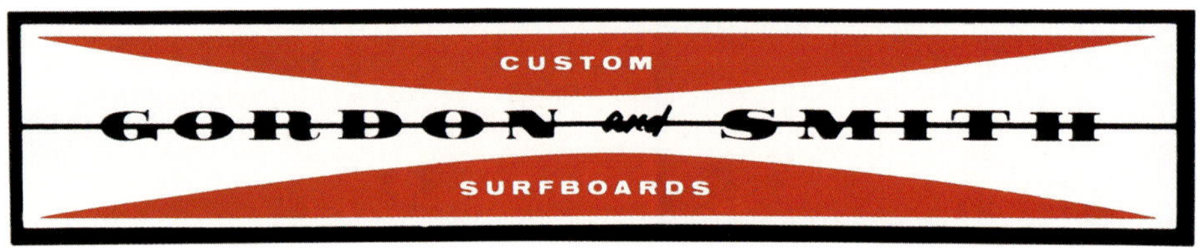
CUSTOM
GORDON and SMITH
SURFBOARDS

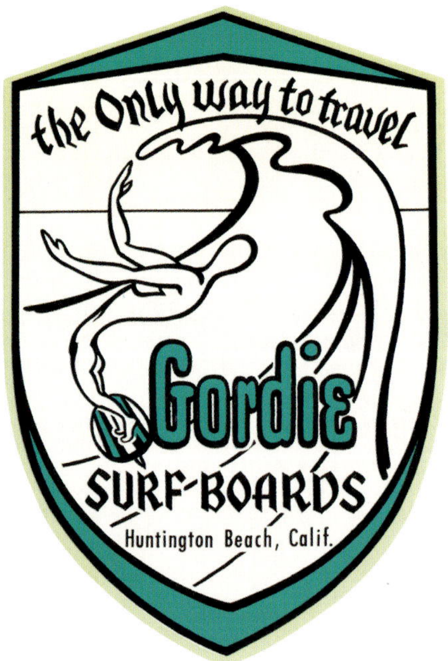
the Only way to travel
Gordie
SURF-BOARDS
Huntington Beach, Calif.

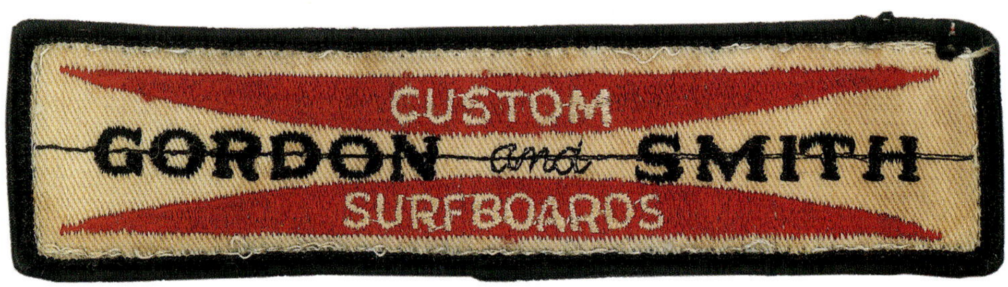
CUSTOM
GORDON and SMITH
SURFBOARDS

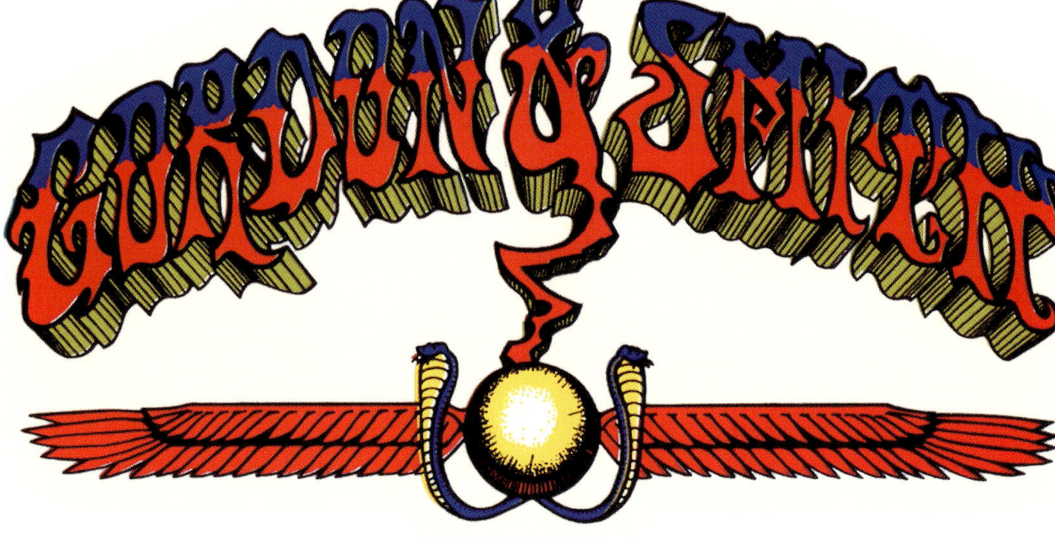

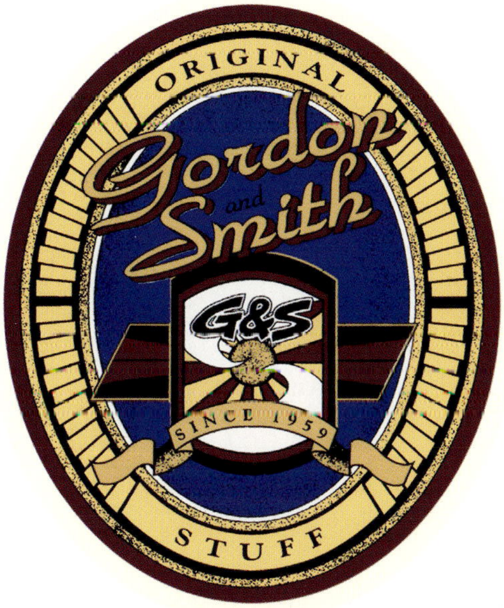
ORIGINAL
Gordon and Smith
G&S
SINCE 1959
STUFF

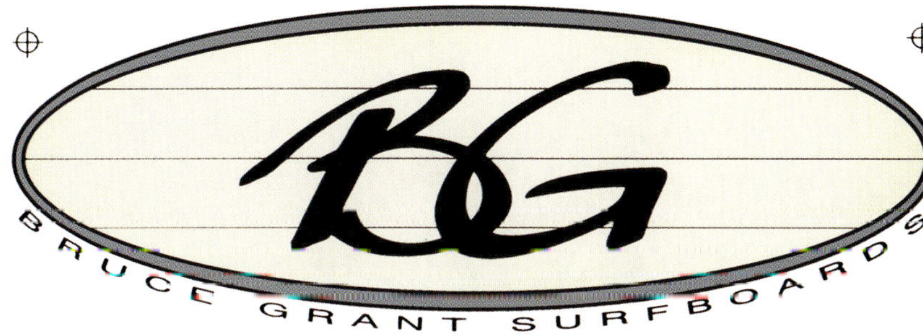
BG
BRUCE GRANT SURFBOARDS

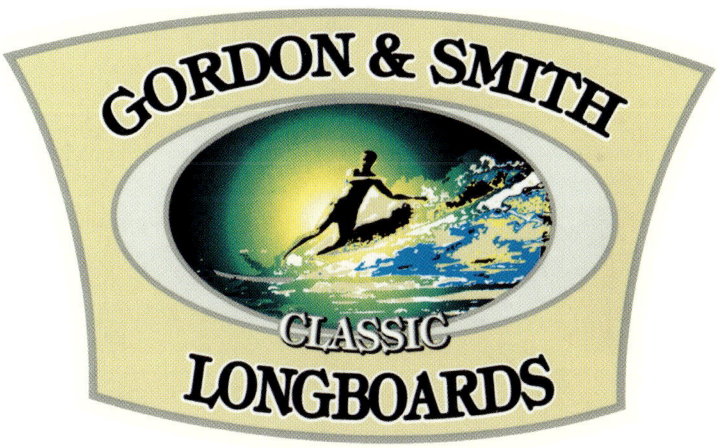
GORDON & SMITH
CLASSIC
LONGBOARDS

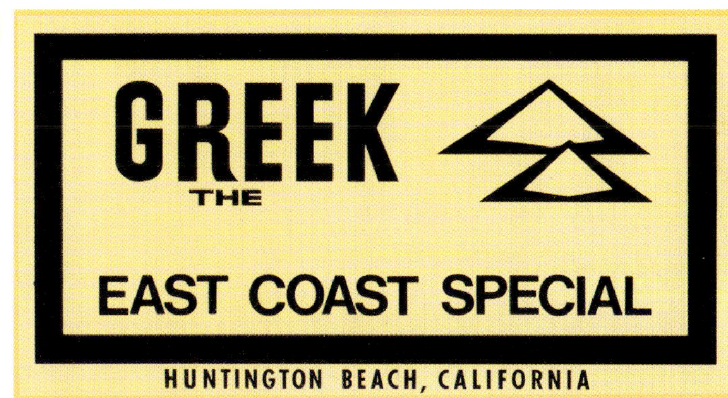
THE GREEK
EAST COAST SPECIAL
HUNTINGTON BEACH, CALIFORNIA

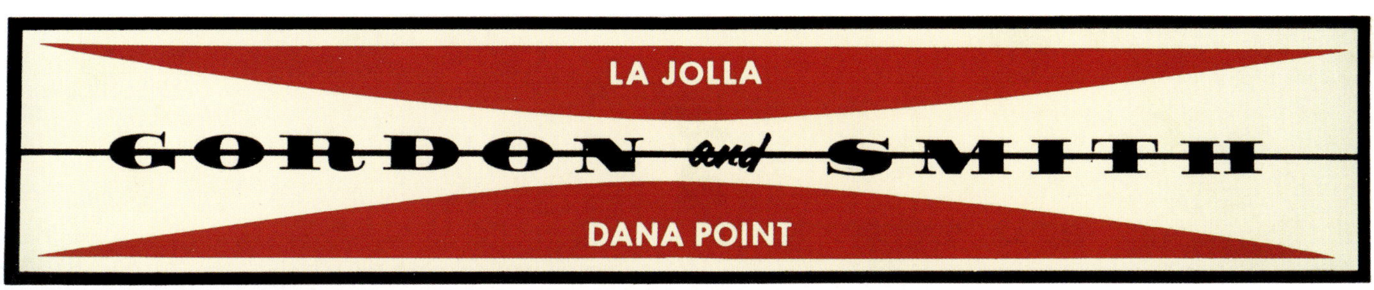
LA JOLLA
GORDON and SMITH
DANA POINT

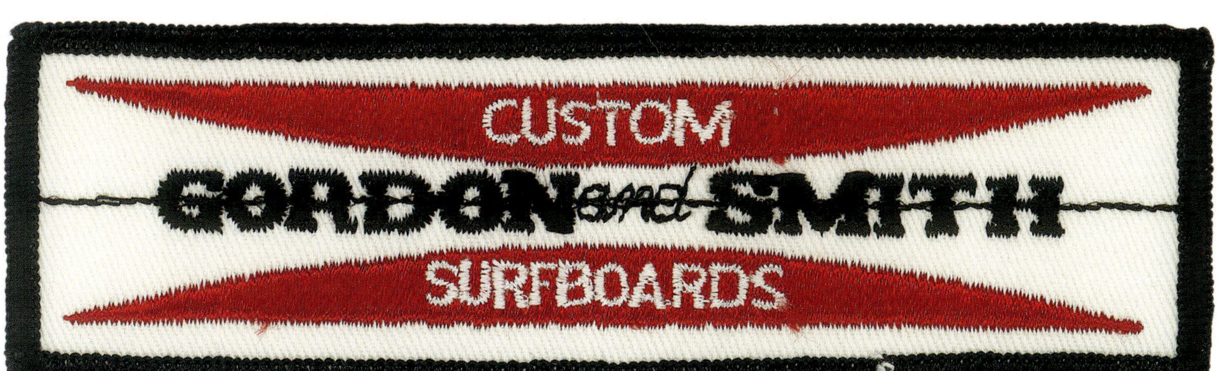
CUSTOM
GORDON and SMITH
SURFBOARDS

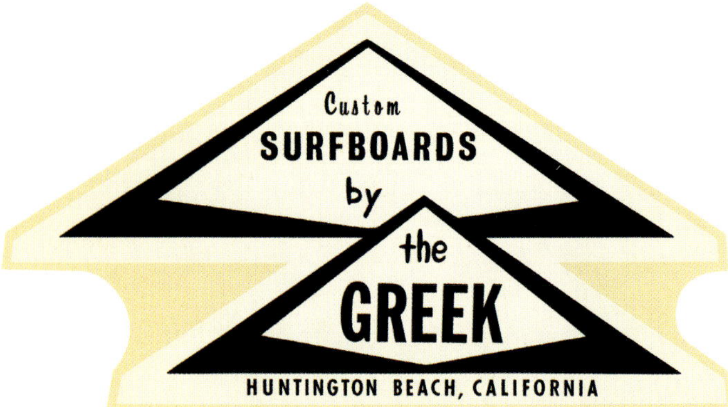
Custom
SURFBOARDS
by
the
GREEK
HUNTINGTON BEACH, CALIFORNIA

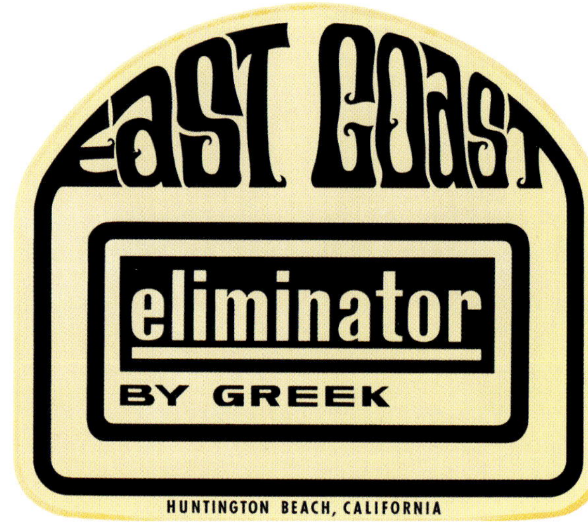
EAST COAST
eliminator
BY GREEK
HUNTINGTON BEACH, CALIFORNIA

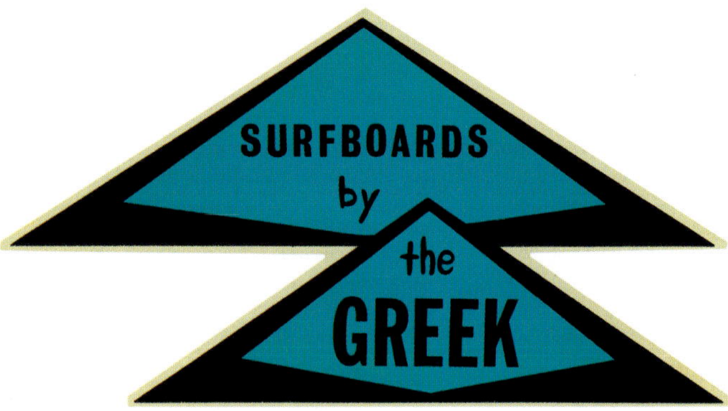
SURFBOARDS
by
the
GREEK

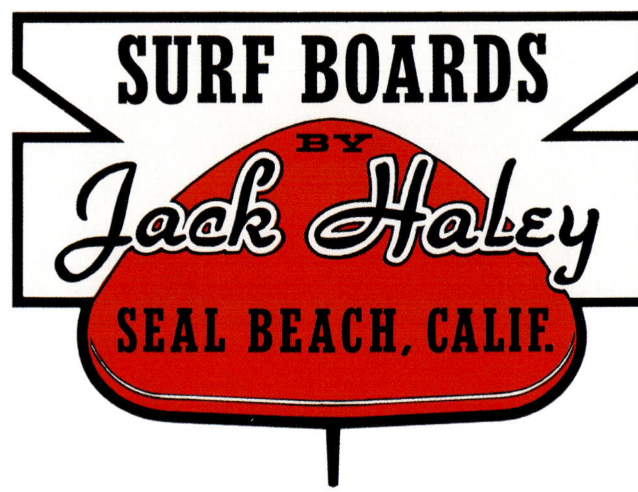
SURF BOARDS
BY
Jack Haley
SEAL BEACH, CALIF.

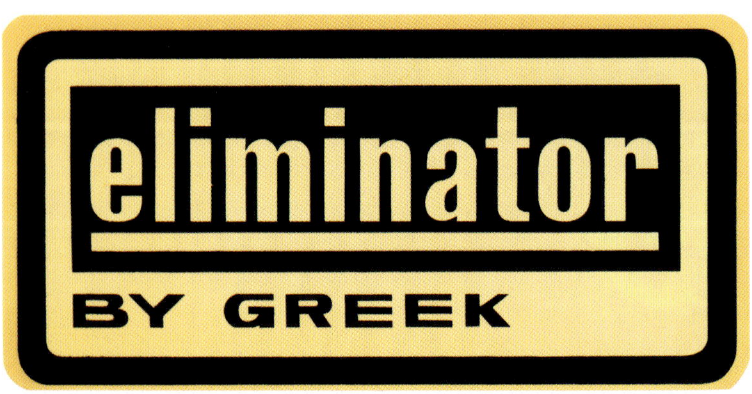
eliminator
BY GREEK

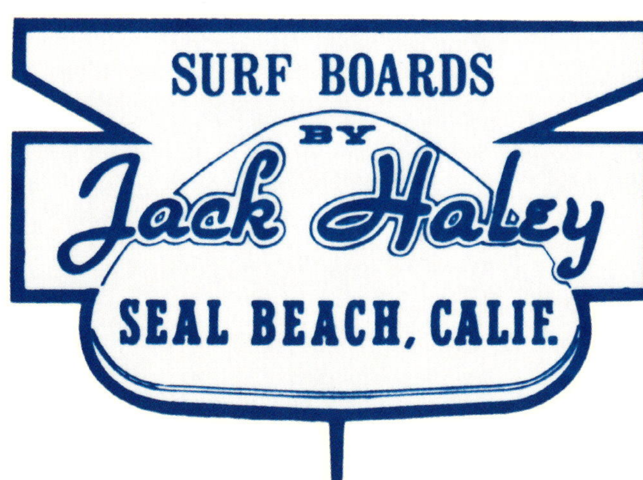
SURF BOARDS
BY
Jack Haley
SEAL BEACH, CALIF.

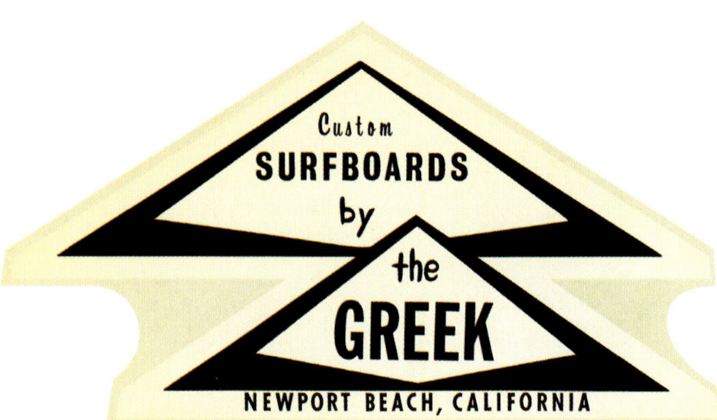
Custom
SURFBOARDS
by
the
GREEK
NEWPORT BEACH, CALIFORNIA

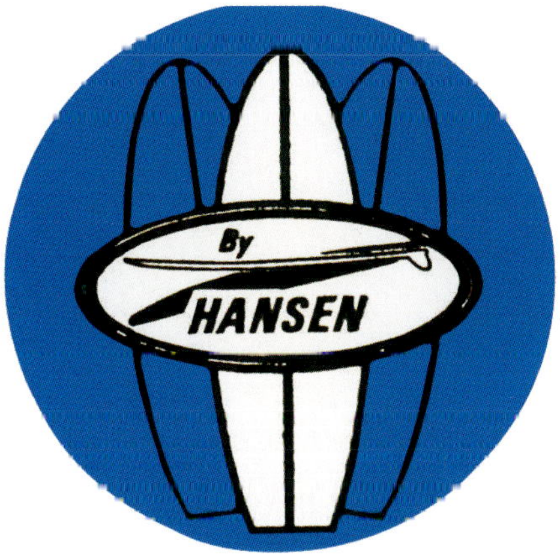
By
HANSEN

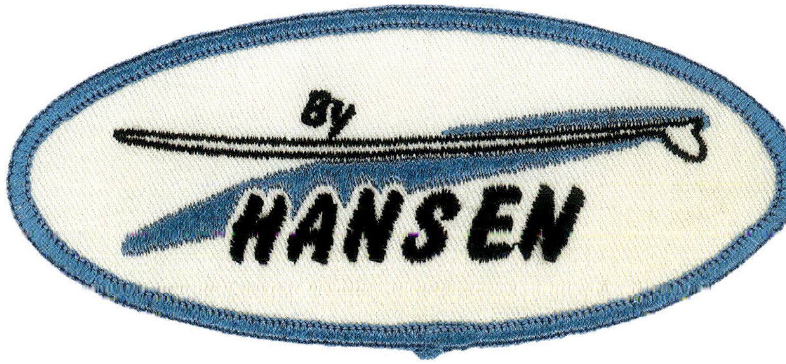
By
HANSEN

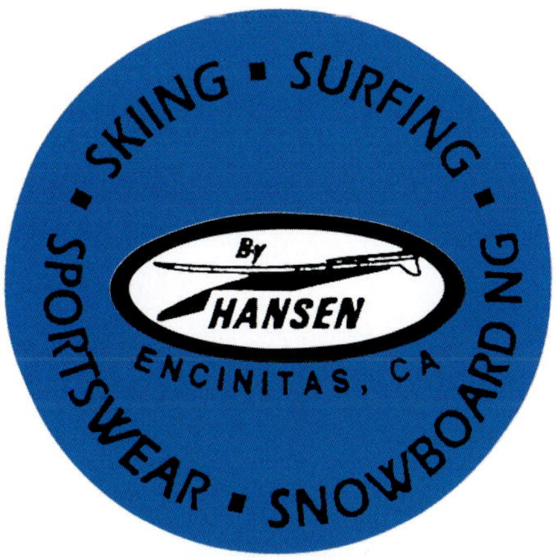
SKIING ▪ SURFING ▪ SNOWBOARDING ▪ SPORTSWEAR
By
HANSEN
ENCINITAS, CA

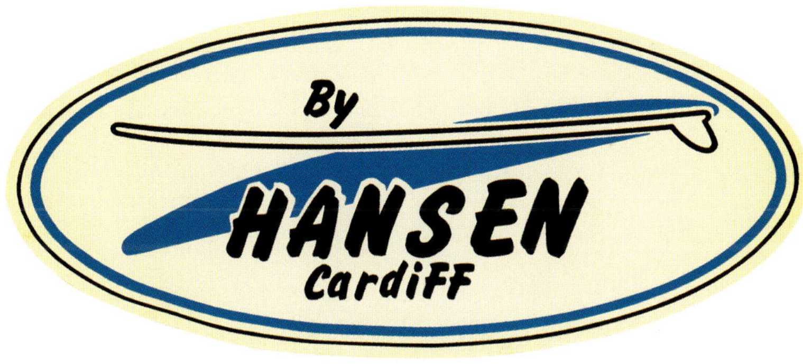
By
HANSEN
Cardiff

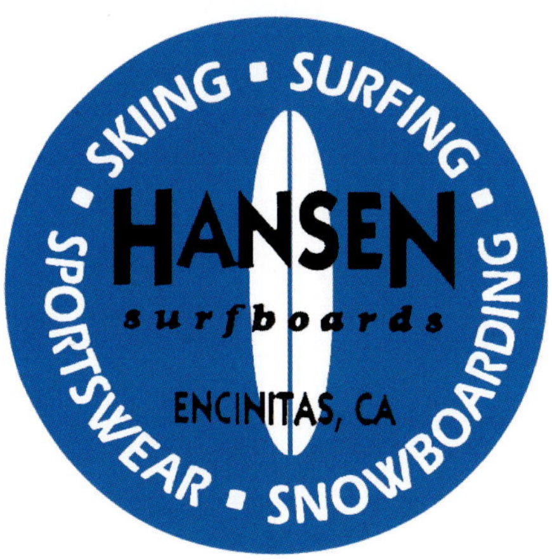
SKIING ▪ SURFING ▪ SNOWBOARDING ▪ SPORTSWEAR
HANSEN
surfboards
ENCINITAS, CA

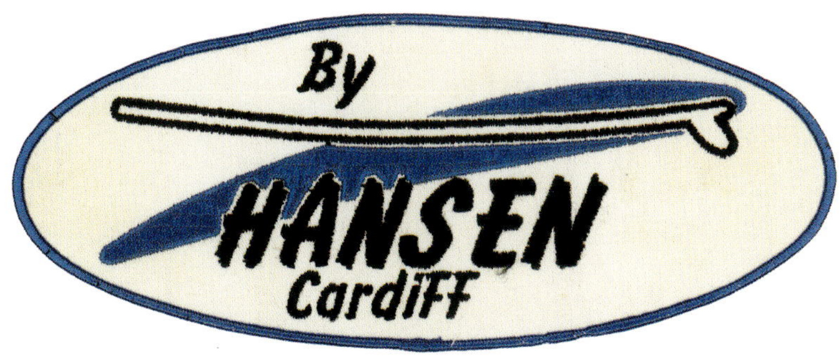
By
HANSEN
Cardiff

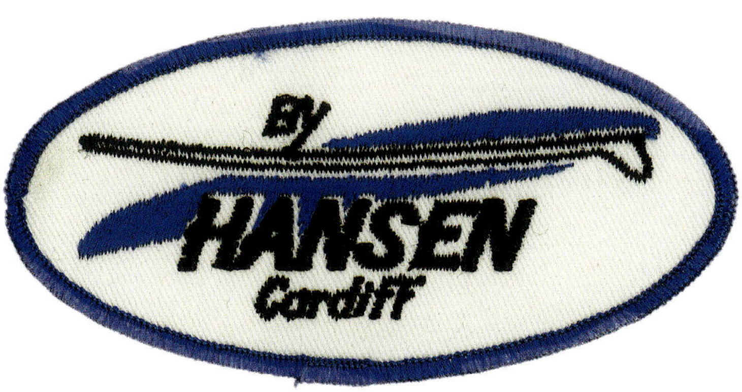
By
HANSEN
Cardiff

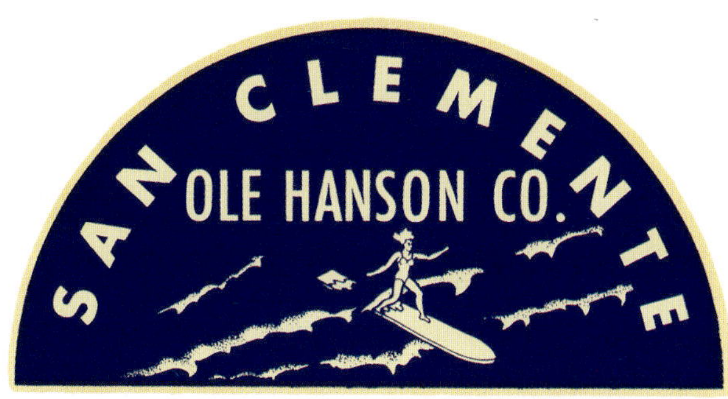
SAN CLEMENTE
OLE HANSON CO.

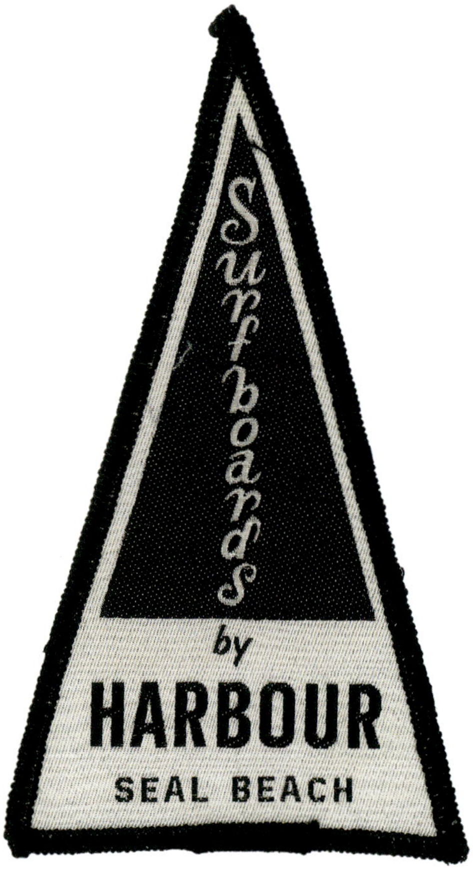
Surfboards
by
HARBOUR
SEAL BEACH

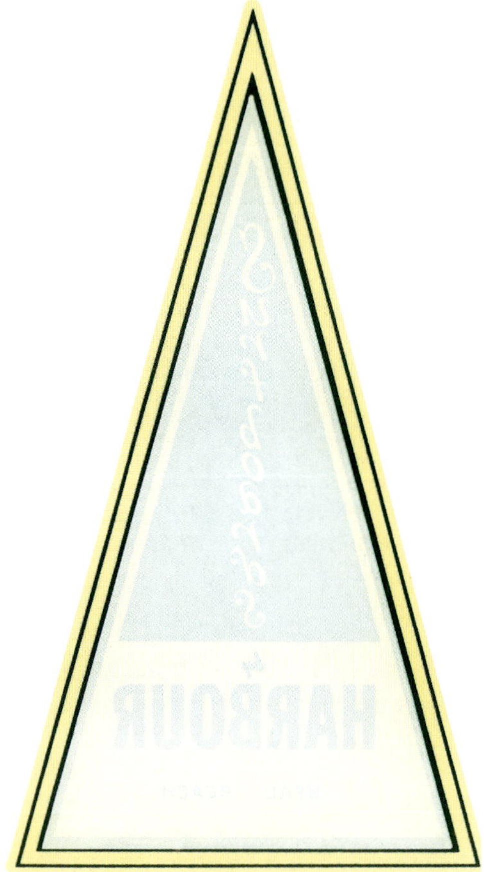

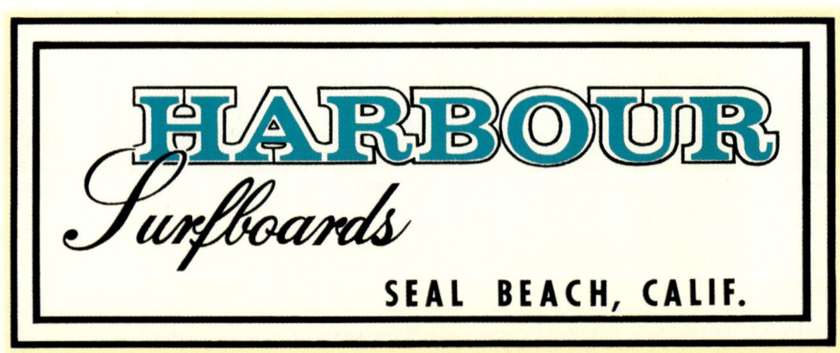
HARBOUR
Surfboards
SEAL BEACH, CALIF.

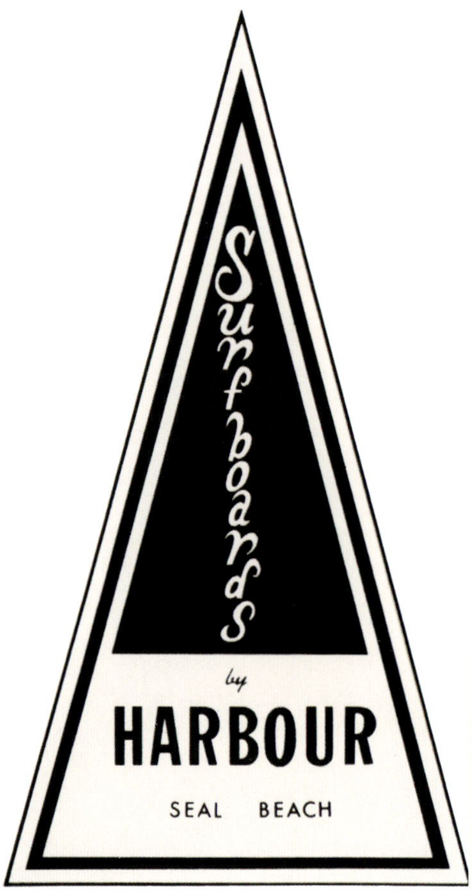
Surfboards
by
HARBOUR
SEAL BEACH

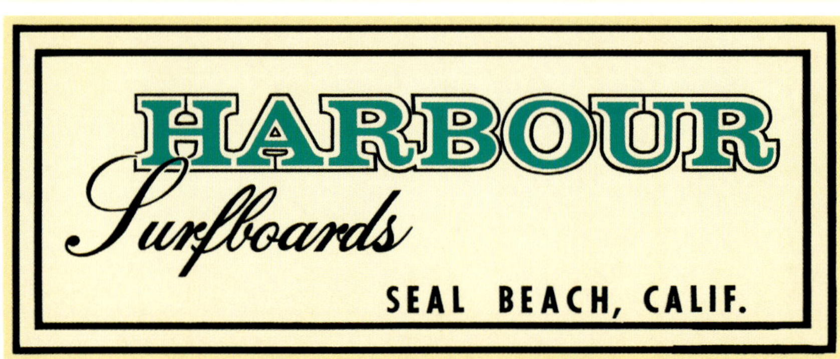
HARBOUR
Surfboards
SEAL BEACH, CALIF.

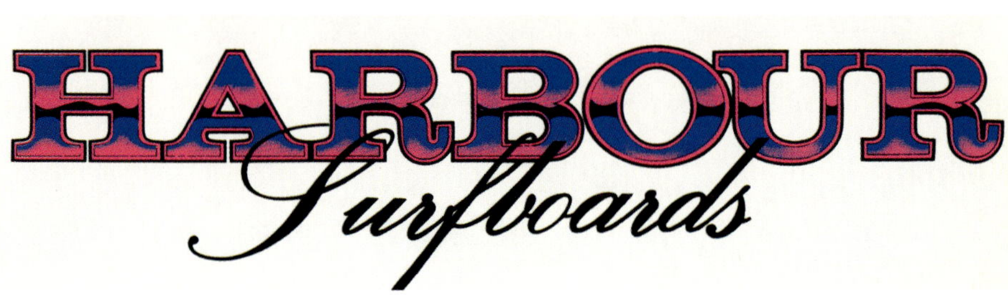
HARBOUR
Surfboards

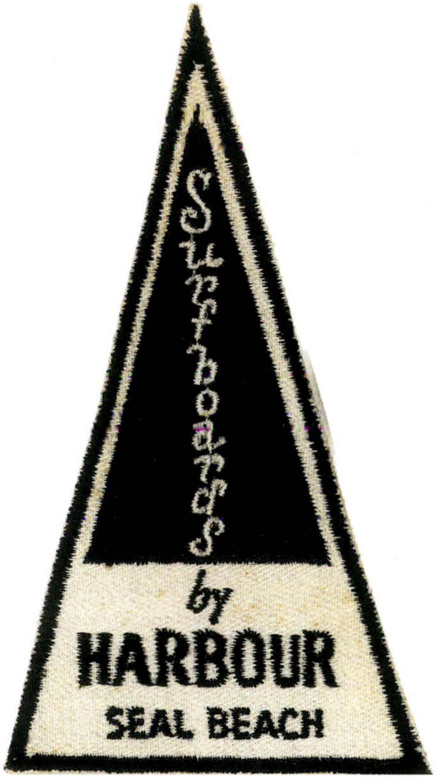
Surfboards
by
HARBOUR
SEAL BEACH

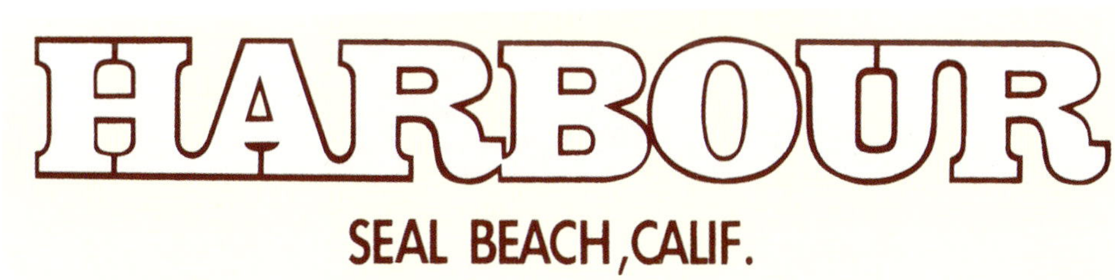
HARBOUR
SEAL BEACH, CALIF.

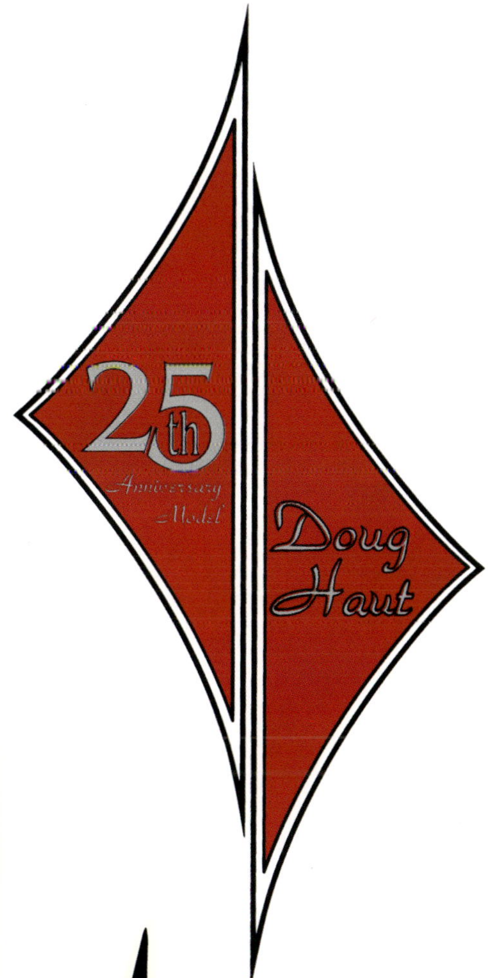
25th
Anniversary
Model
Doug
Haut

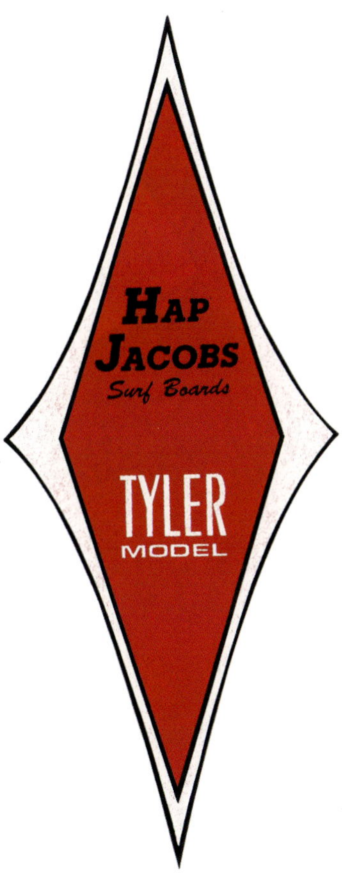
HAP
JACOBS
Surf Boards
TYLER
MODEL

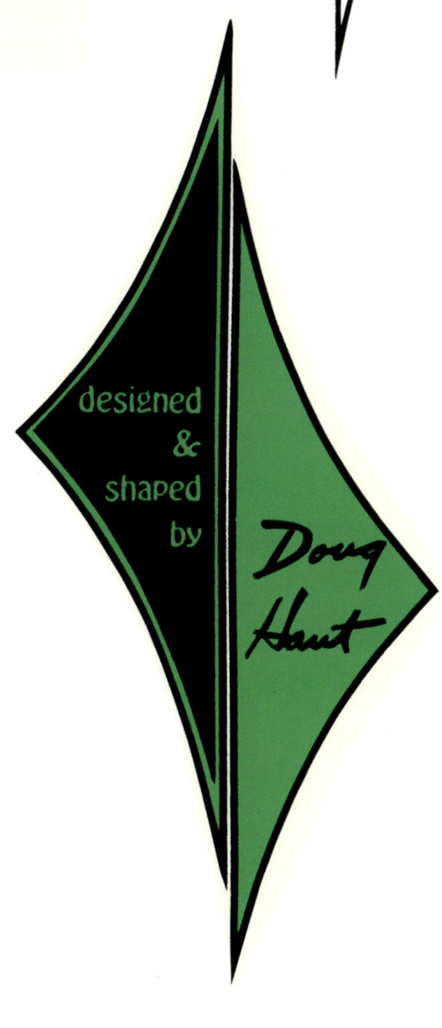
designed
&
shaped
by
Doug
Haut

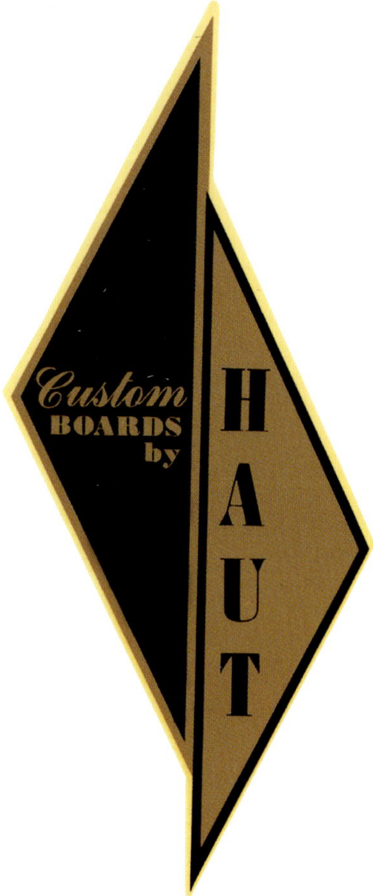
Custom
BOARDS
by
HAUT

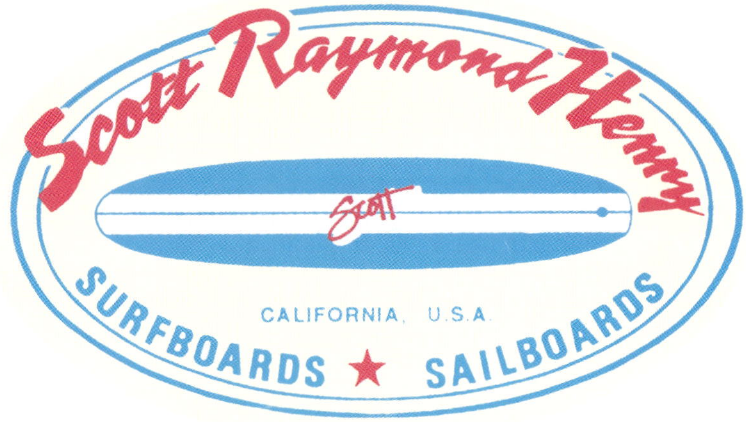
Scott Raymond Henry
SCOTT
CALIFORNIA, U.S.A.
SURFBOARDS ★ SAILBOARDS

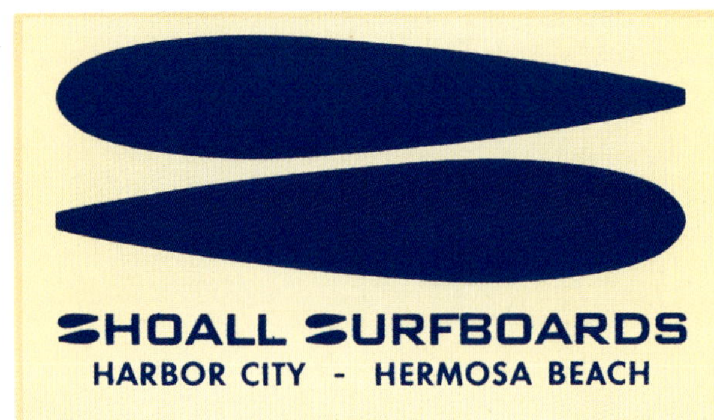
SHOALL SURFBOARDS
HARBOR CITY - HERMOSA BEACH

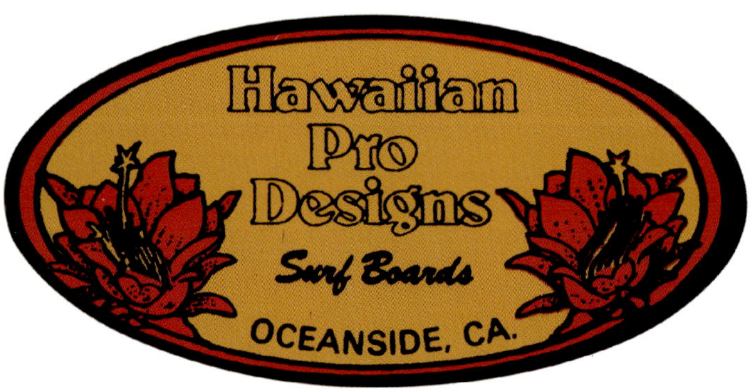
Hawaiian
Pro
Designs
Surf Boards
OCEANSIDE, CA.

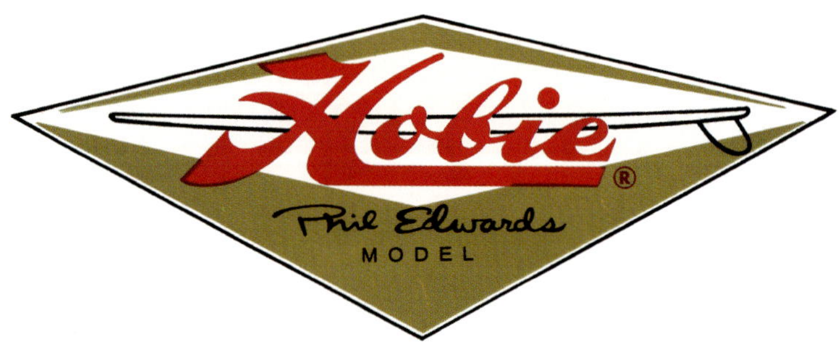
Hobie®
Phil Edwards
MODEL

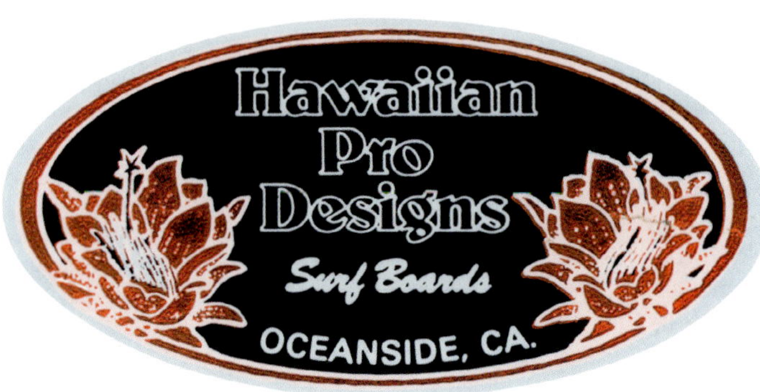
Hawaiian
Pro
Designs
Surf Boards
OCEANSIDE, CA.

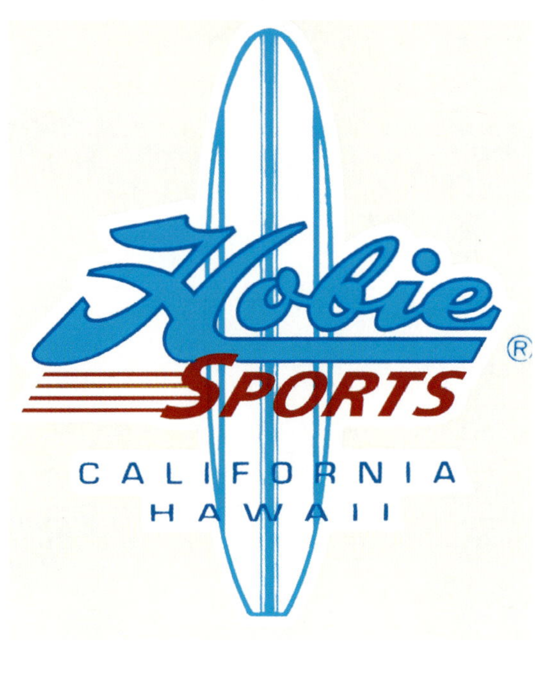
Hobie®
SPORTS
CALIFORNIA
HAWAII

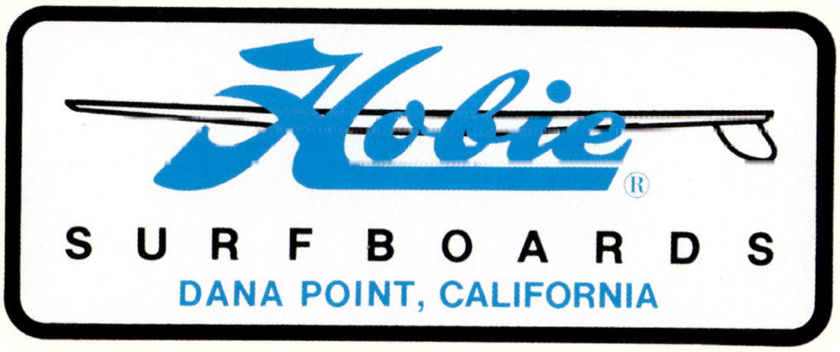
Hobie
SURFBOARDS
DANA POINT, CALIFORNIA

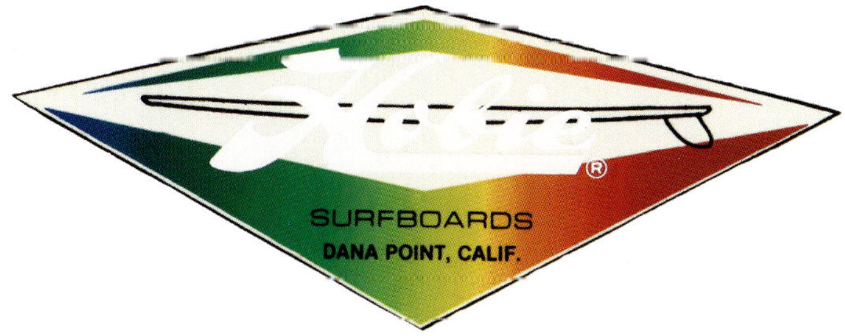
Hobie
SURFBOARDS
DANA POINT, CALIF.

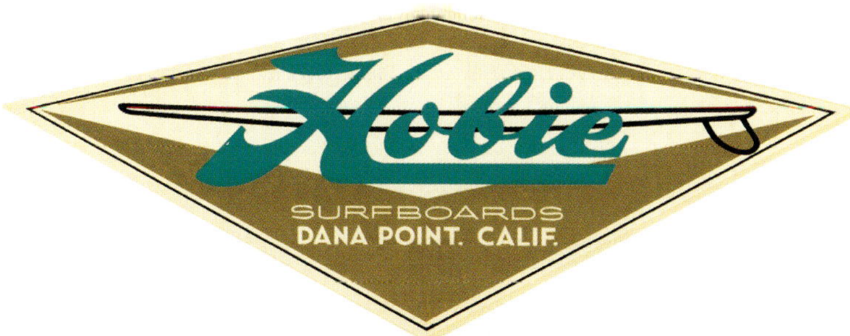
Hobie
SURFBOARDS
DANA POINT. CALIF.

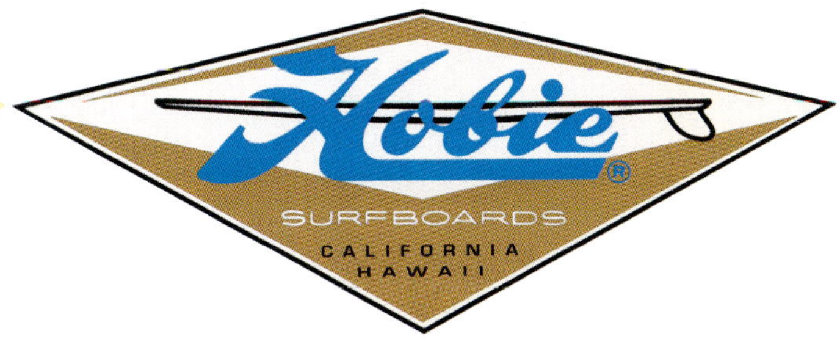
Hobie
SURFBOARDS
CALIFORNIA
HAWAII

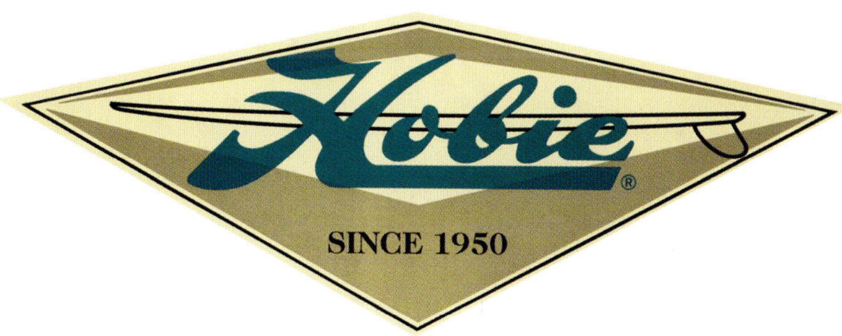
Hobie
SINCE 1950

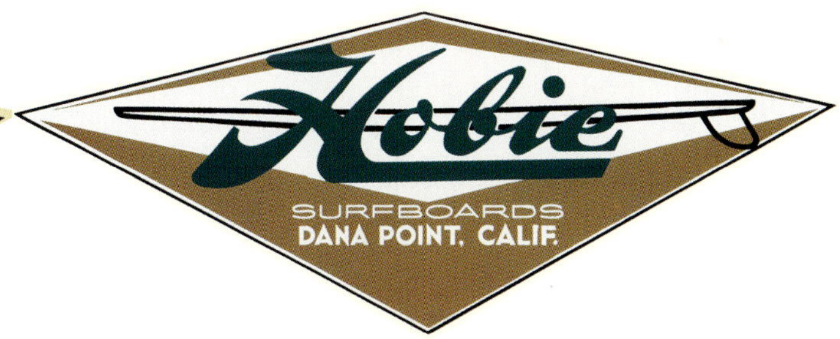
Hobie
SURFBOARDS
DANA POINT. CALIF.

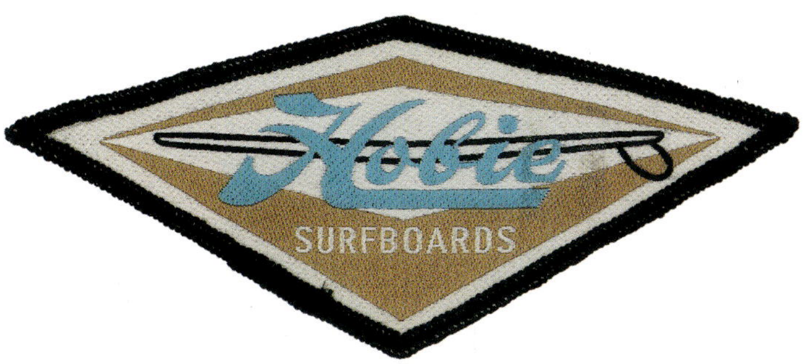
Hobie
SURFBOARDS

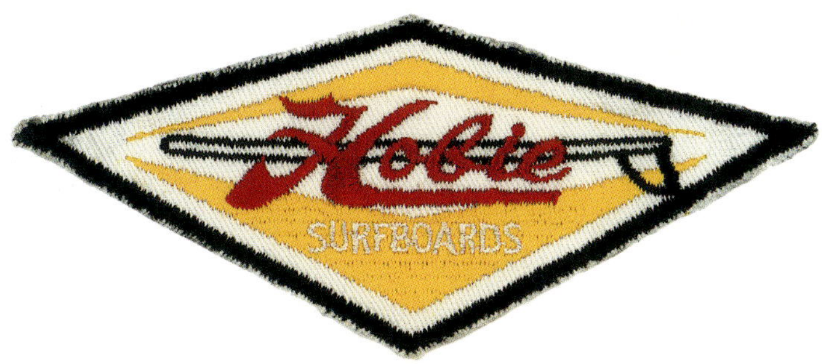
Hobie
SURFBOARDS

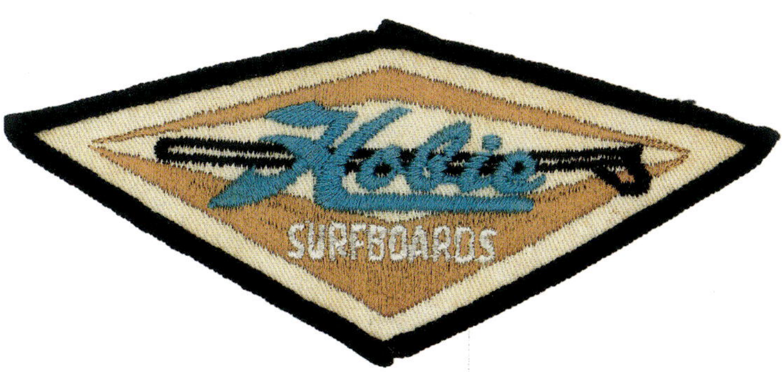
Hobie
SURFBOARDS

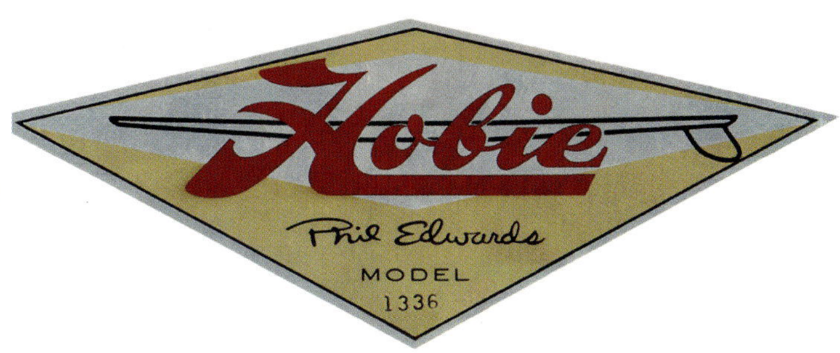
Hobie
Phil Edwards
MODEL
1336

Corky Carroll
MODEL
BY
Hobie

Israel Paskowitz
Hobie
SURFBOARDS
DANA POINT, CALIF.

Hobie
SURFBOARDS
DANA POINT, CALIF.

Corky Carroll
MODEL
BY
Hobie

Gary Propper
MODEL
BY
Hobie

Hobie

Hobie

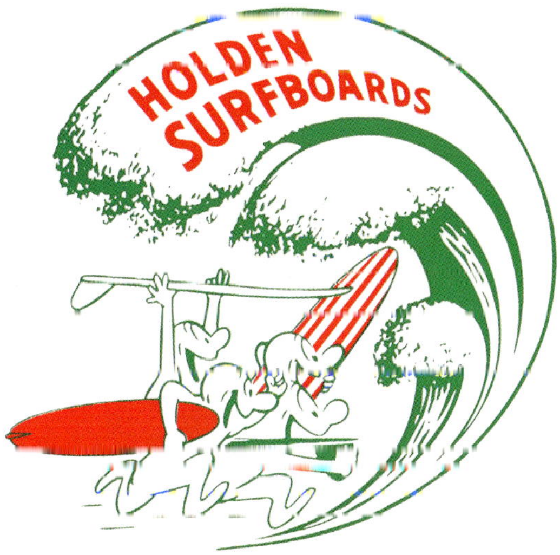
HOLDEN
SURFBOARDS

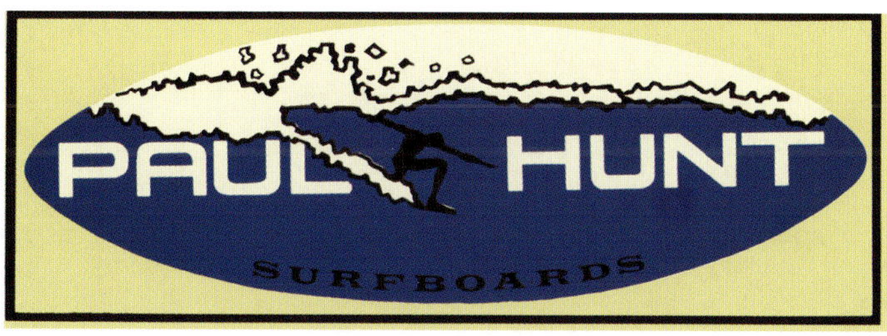
PAUL HUNT
SURFBOARDS

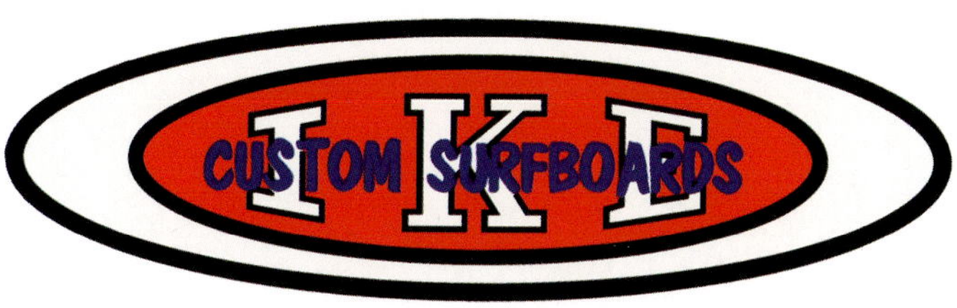
IKE
CUSTOM SURFBOARDS

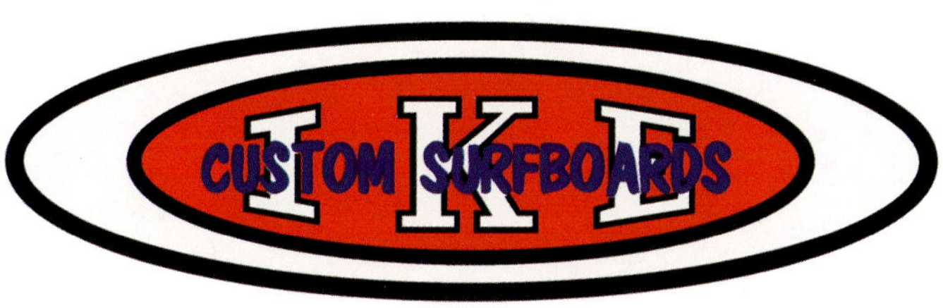
IKE
CUSTOM SURFBOARDS

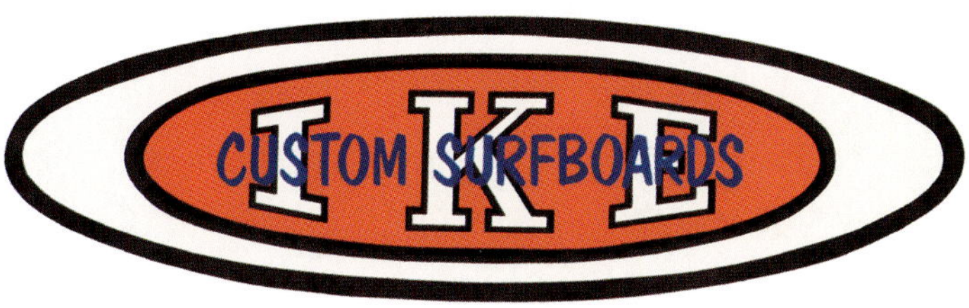
IKE
CUSTOM SURFBOARDS

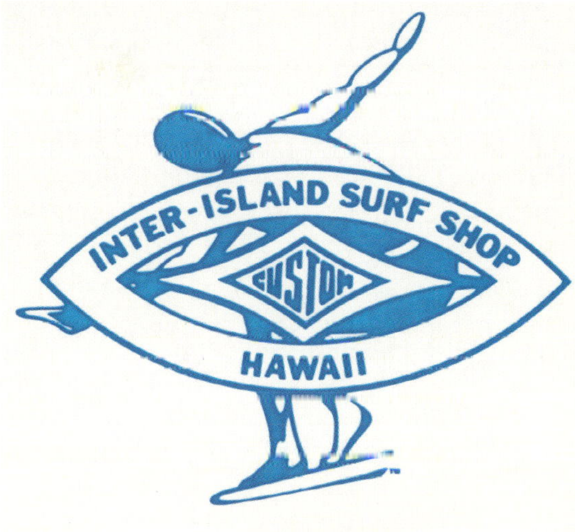
INTER-ISLAND SURF SHOP
CUSTOM
HAWAII

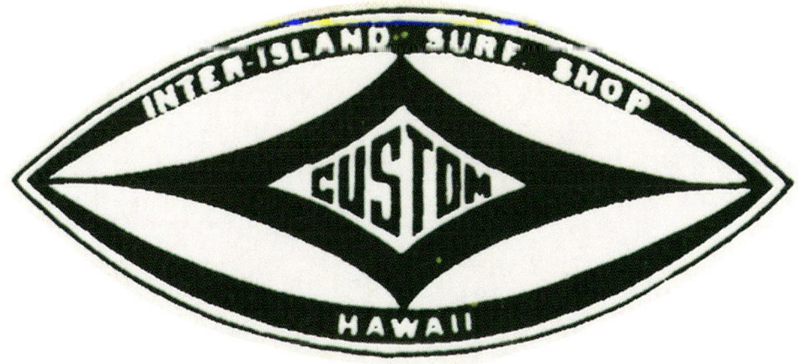
INTER-ISLAND SURF SHOP
CUSTOM
HAWAII

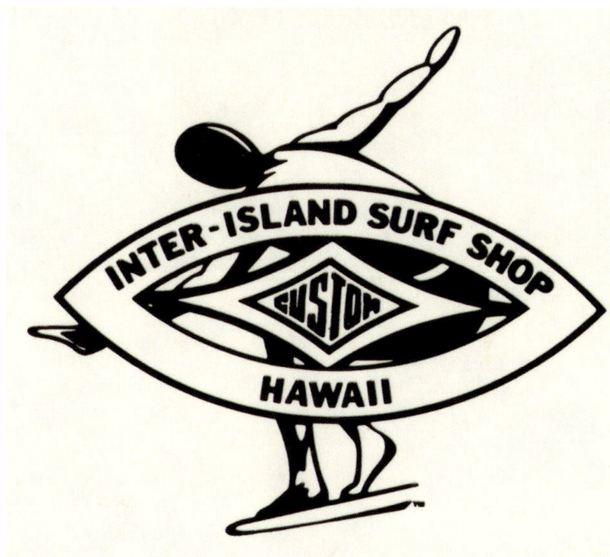
INTER-ISLAND SURF SHOP
CUSTOM
HAWAII

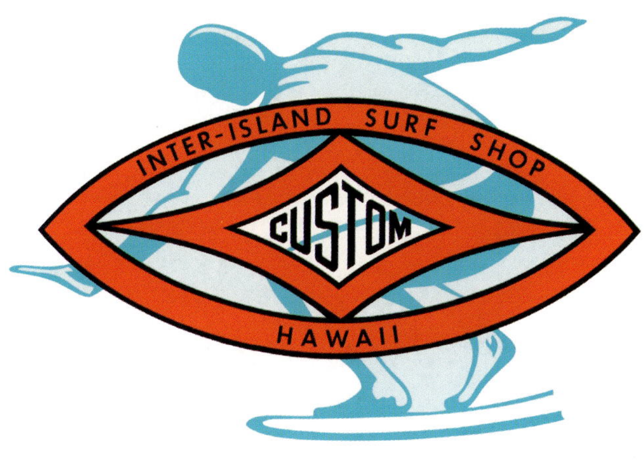
INTER-ISLAND SURF SHOP
CUSTOM
HAWAII

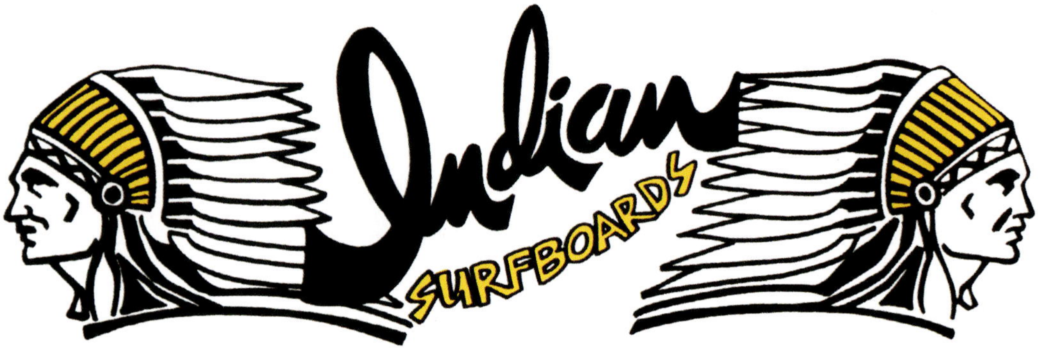
Indian
SURFBOARDS

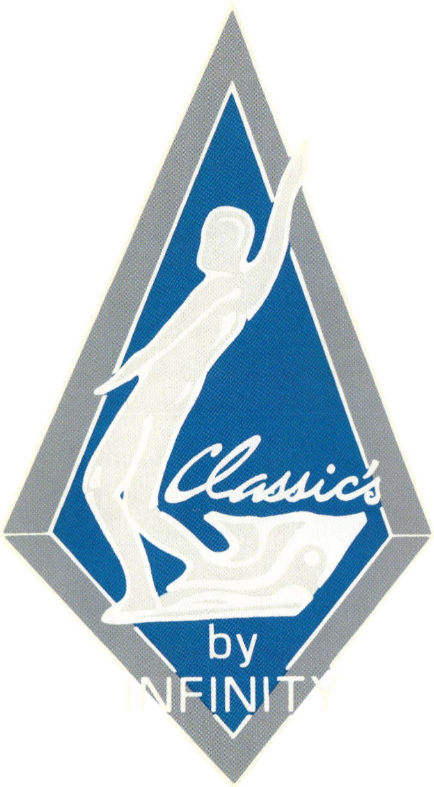
Classic's
by
INFINITY

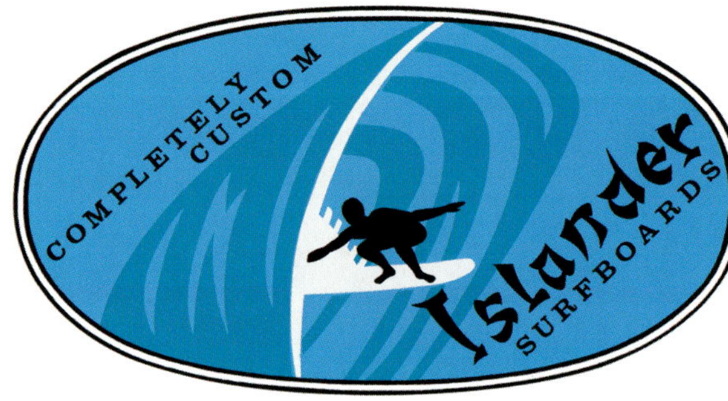
COMPLETELY CUSTOM
Islander
SURFBOARDS

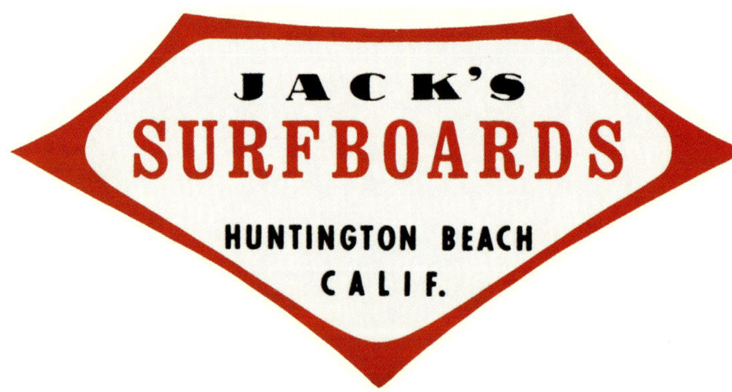
JACK'S
SURFBOARDS
HUNTINGTON BEACH
CALIF.

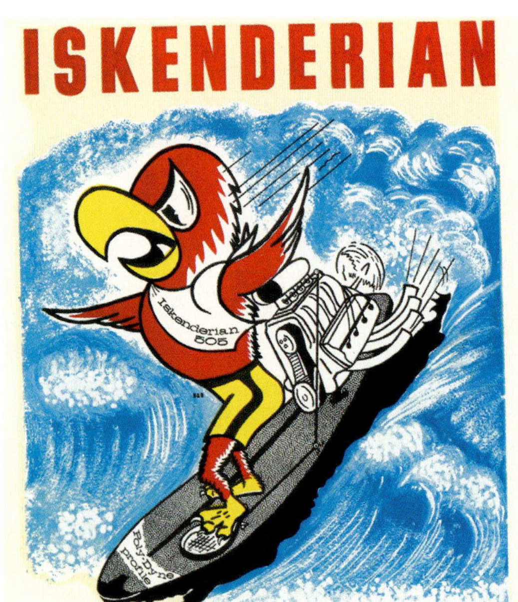
ISKENDERIAN
Iskenderian
505

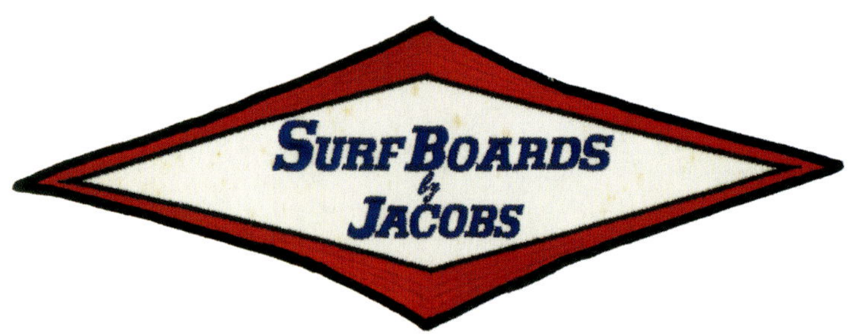
SURF BOARDS
by
JACOBS

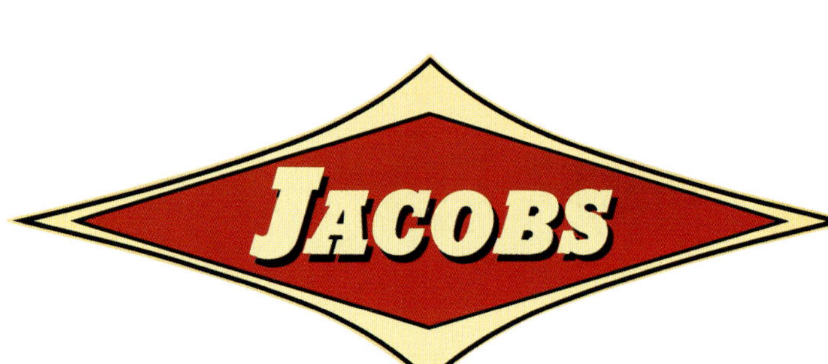
JACOBS

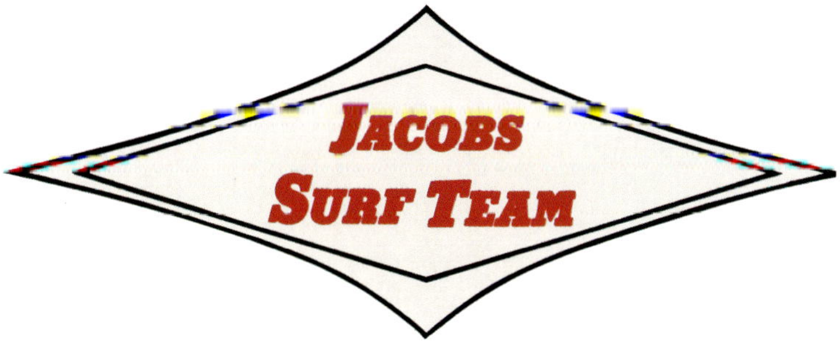
JACOBS
SURF TEAM

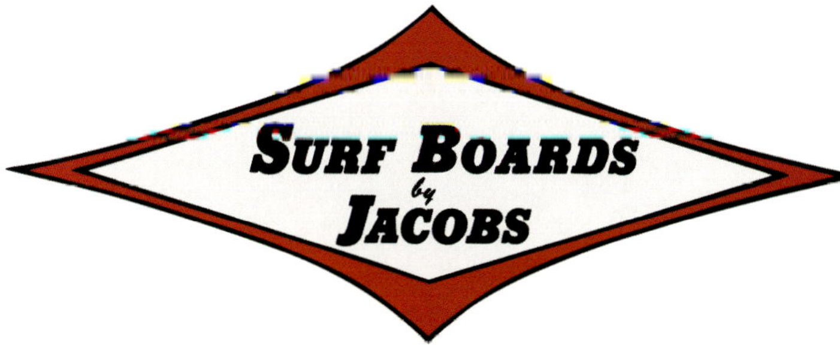
SURF BOARDS
by
JACOBS

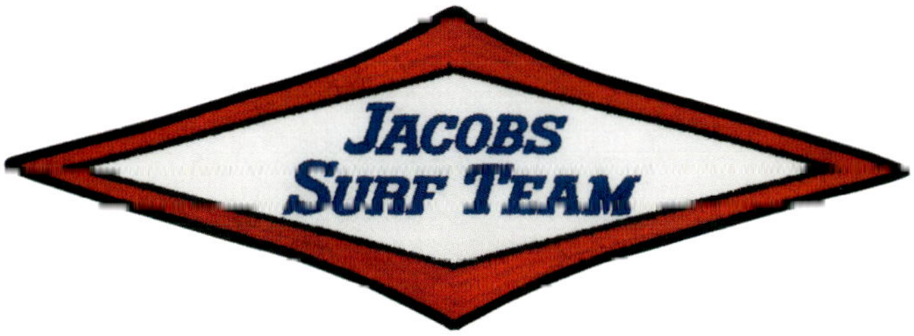
JACOBS
SURF TEAM

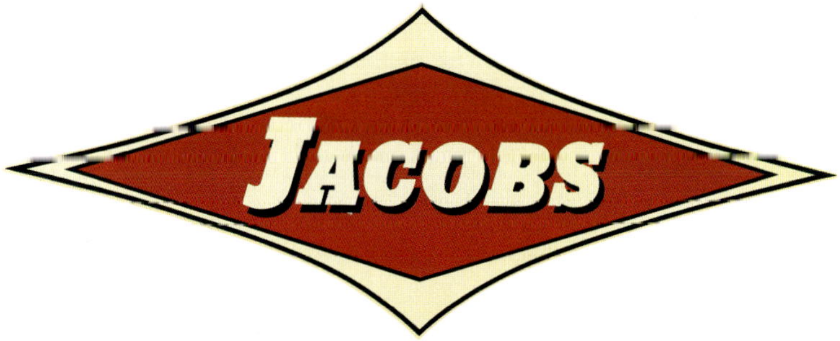
JACOBS

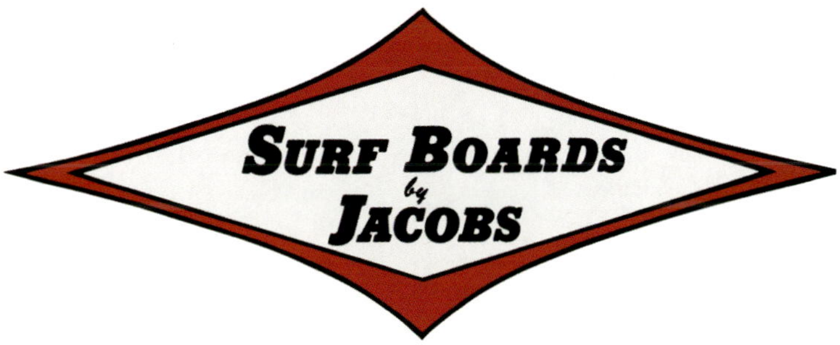
SURF BOARDS
by
JACOBS

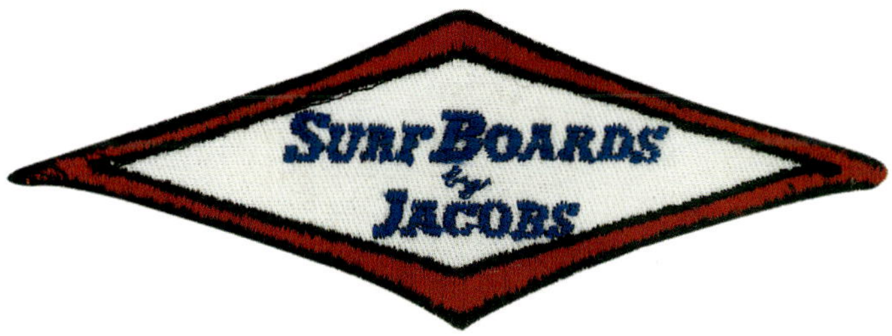
SURF BOARDS
by
JACOBS

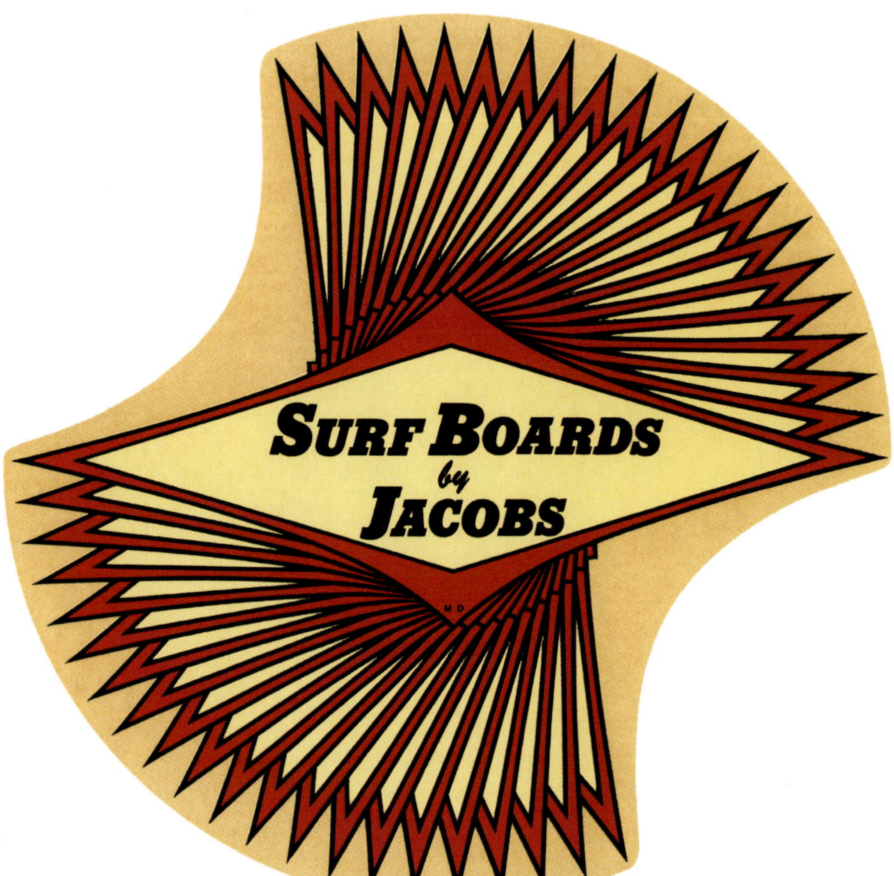
SURF BOARDS
by
JACOBS

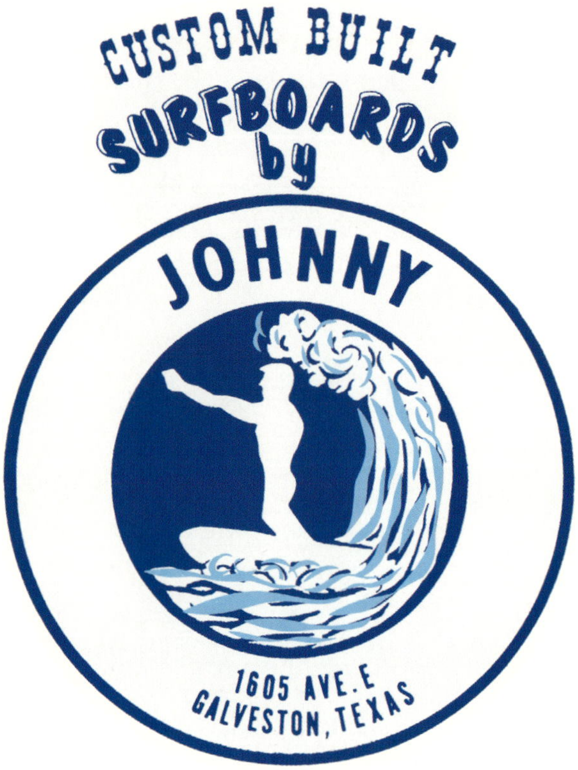

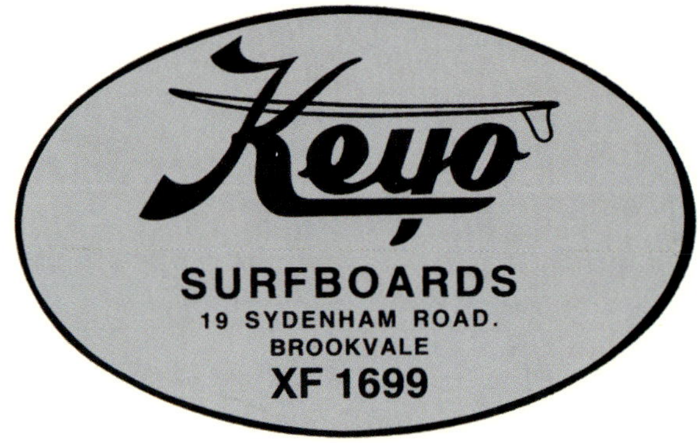

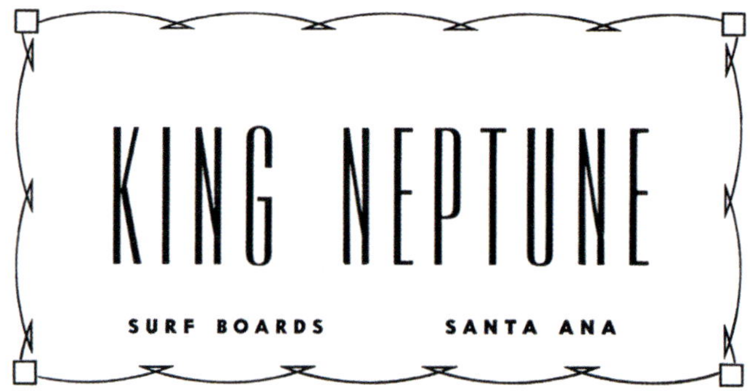

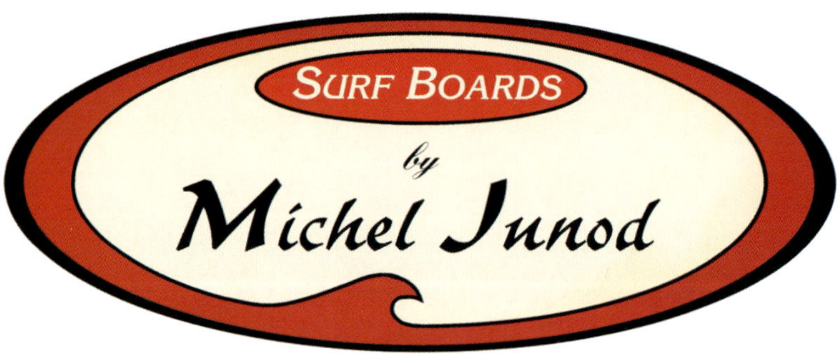

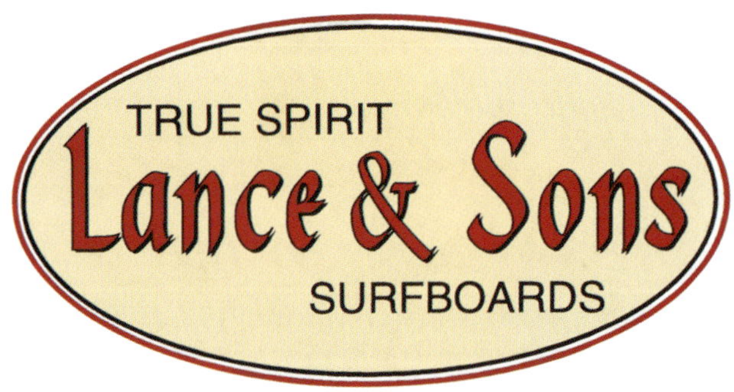

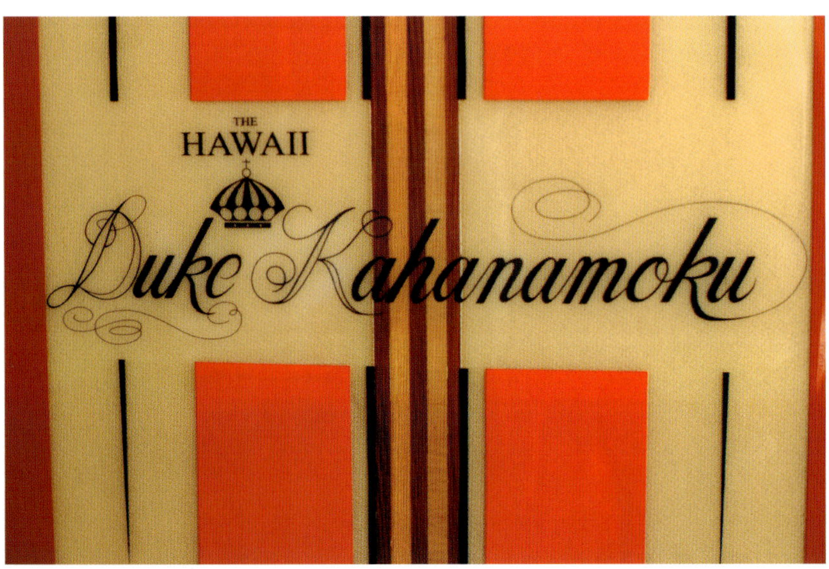

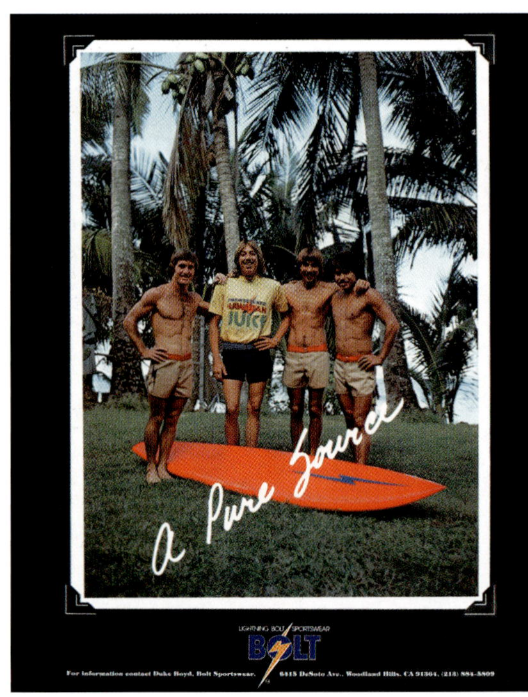

Team Lightning Bolt, lean and mean and ruling Hawaii with the biggest label of the 70s.

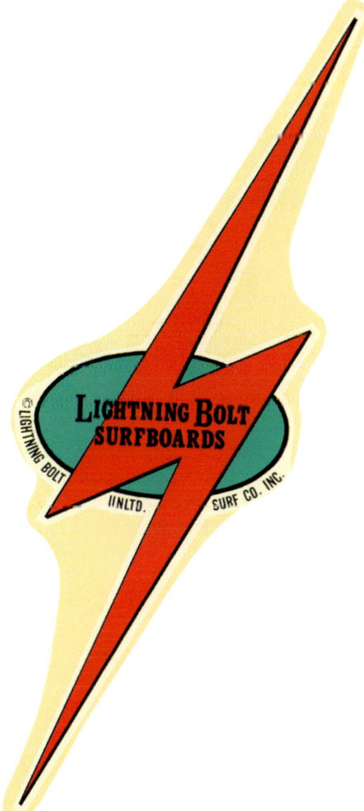
LIGHTNING BOLT
SURFBOARDS
© LIGHTNING BOLT
UNLTD.
SURF CO. INC.

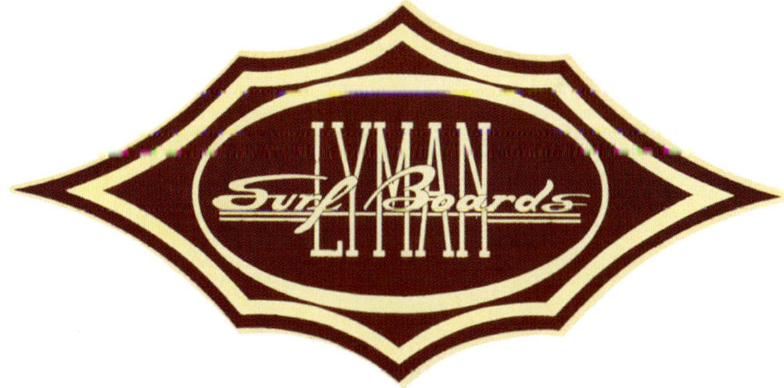
LYMAN
Surf Boards
LYMAN

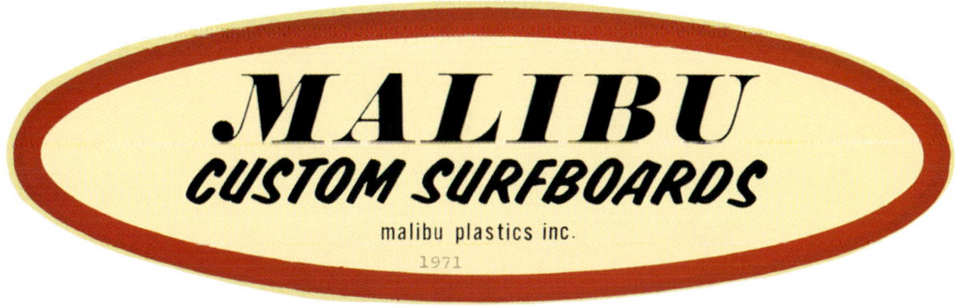
MALIBU
CUSTOM SURFBOARDS
malibu plastics inc.
1971

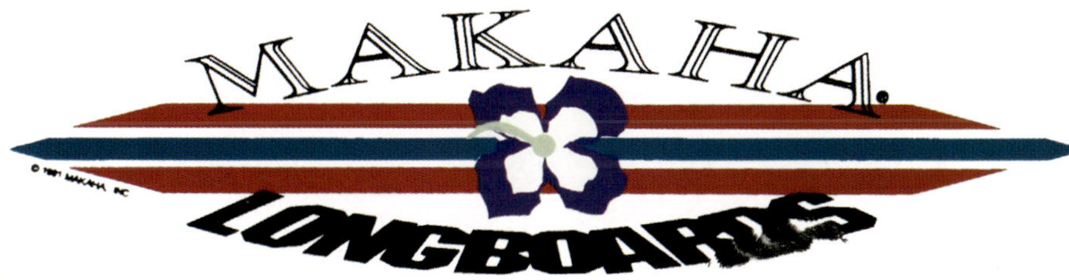
MAKAHA
LONGBOARDS

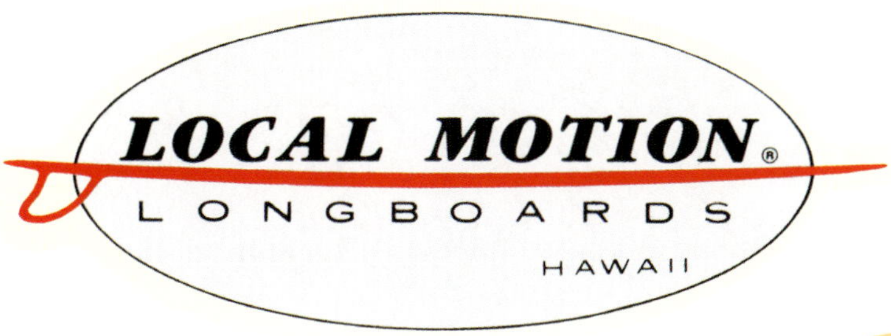
LOCAL MOTION®
LONGBOARDS
HAWAII

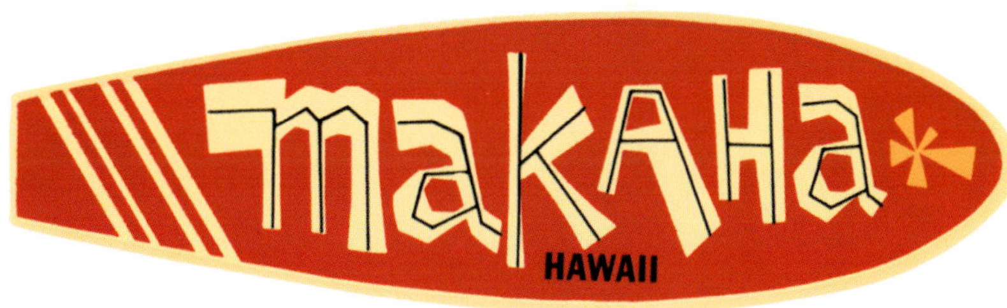
makaha
HAWAII

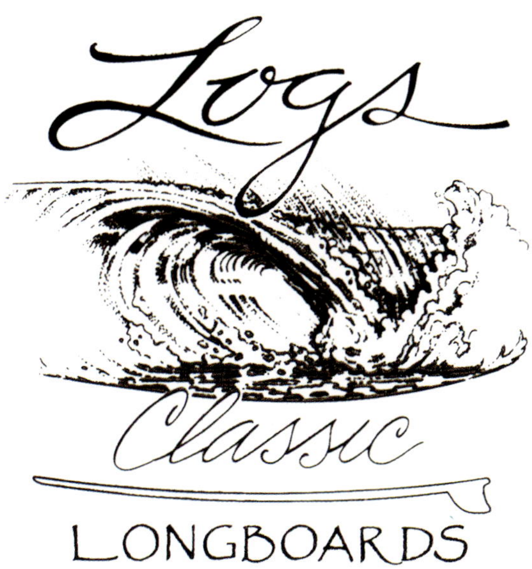
Logs
Classic
LONGBOARDS

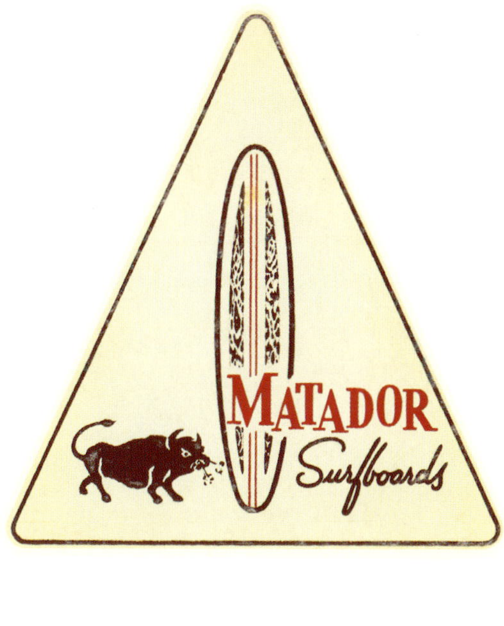
MATADOR
Surfboards

CUSTOM SURFBOARDS
BY MIKE MERRY HAWAII

MOREY-POPE

hanshaped · designed by Tom Morey

Surf Boards by MOSELLE

NATIVE
DART
REG. T.M. CALIF.
L.S. ENTERPRISES - BAKERSFIELD, CALIFORNIA

morey, pope & company

NATIVE
SPEAR
REG. T.M. CALIF.
L.S. ENTERPRISES - BAKERSFIELD, CALIFORNIA

DISTINCTIVE BOARDS
NATIVE
L.S. ENTERPRISES BAKERSFIELD, CALIF.
REG. T.M. CALIF.

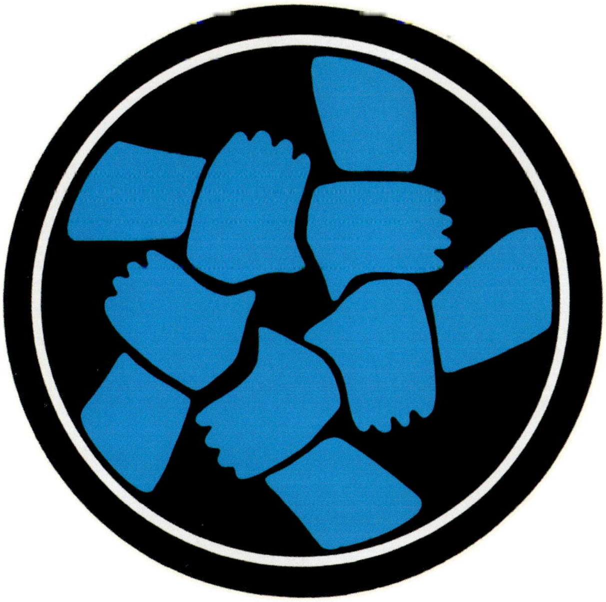

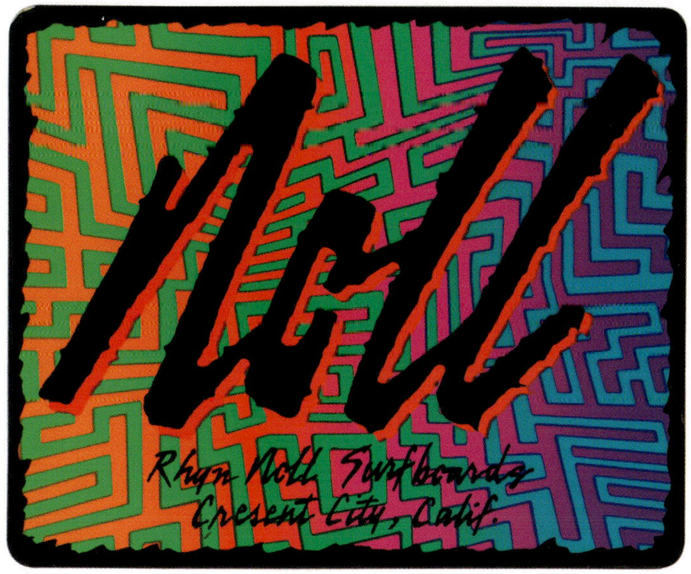
Noll
Rhyn Noll Surfboards
Cresent City, Calif.

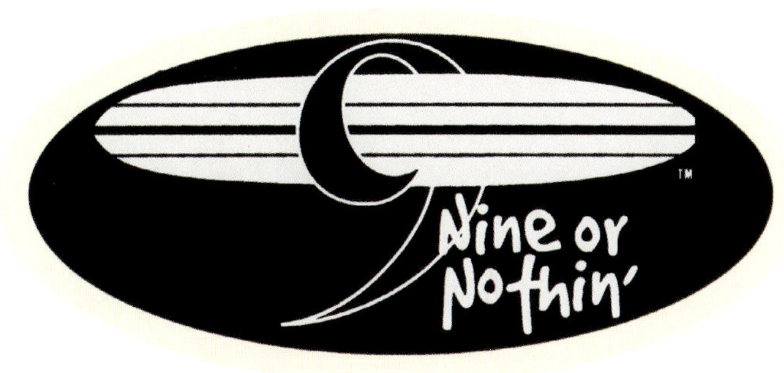
TM
Nine or
Nothin'

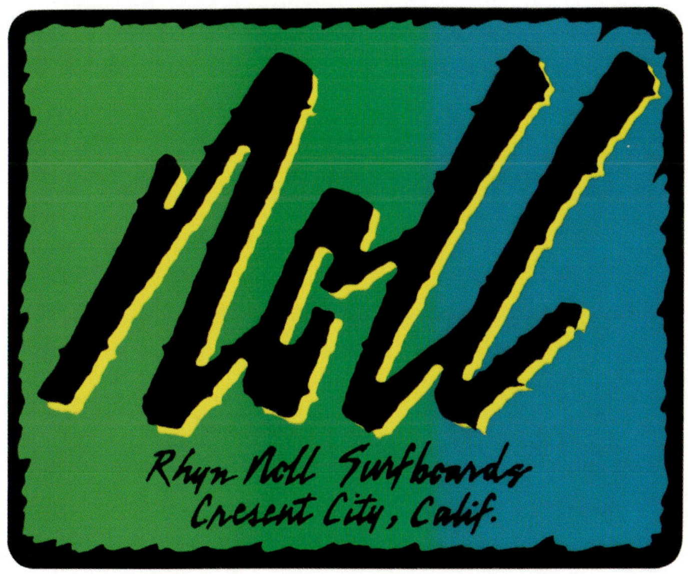
Noll
Rhyn Noll Surfboards
Cresent City, Calif.

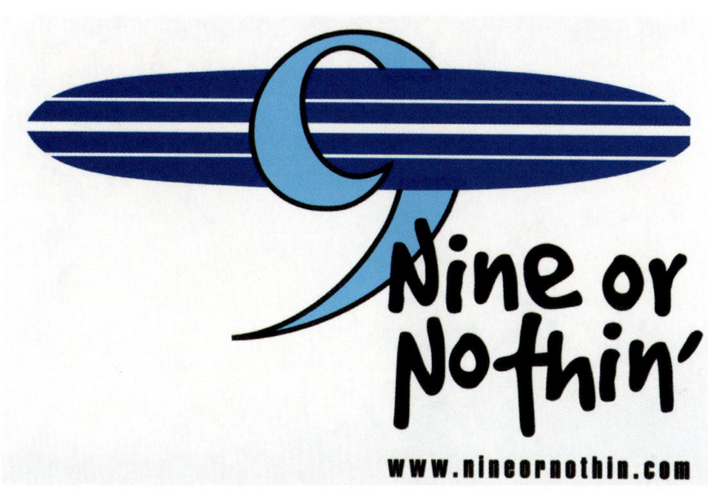
Nine or
Nothin'
www.nineornothin.com

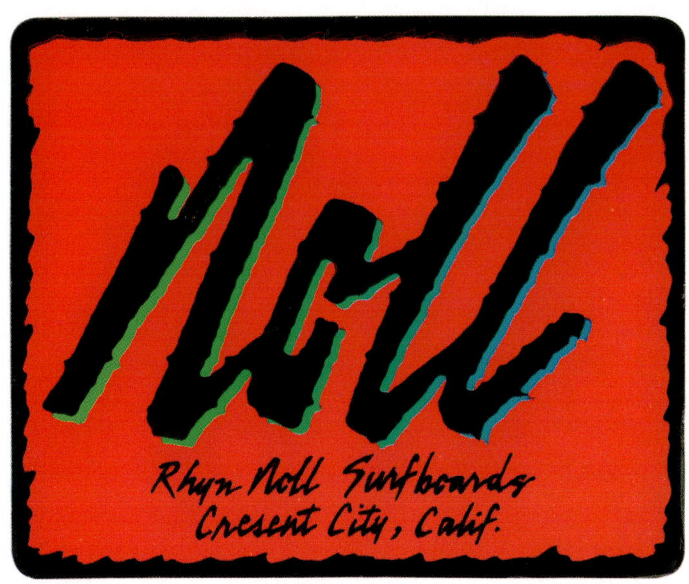
Noll
Rhyn Noll Surfboards
Cresent City, Calif.

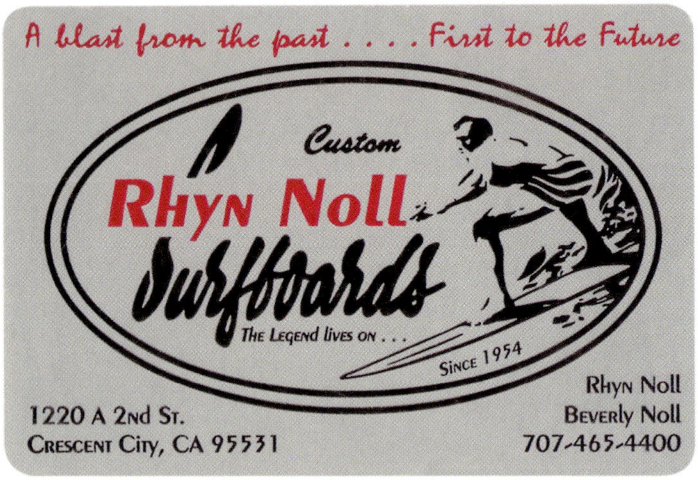

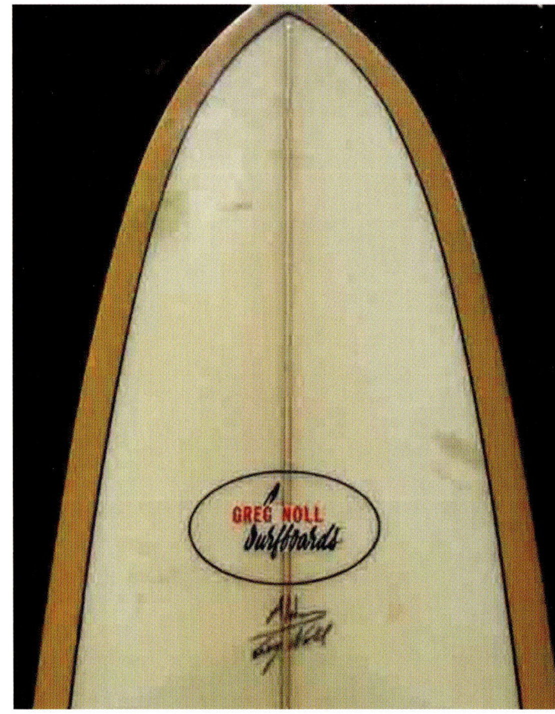

A 60s-era Noll decal. Photo: Juliana Morais. Courtesy Fernando Aguerre and Voyageur Press.

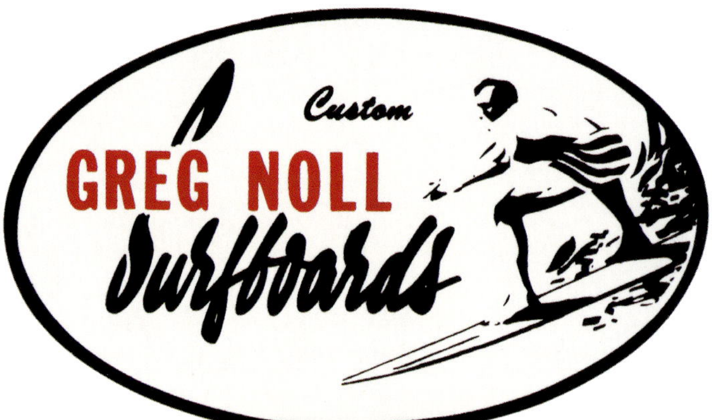

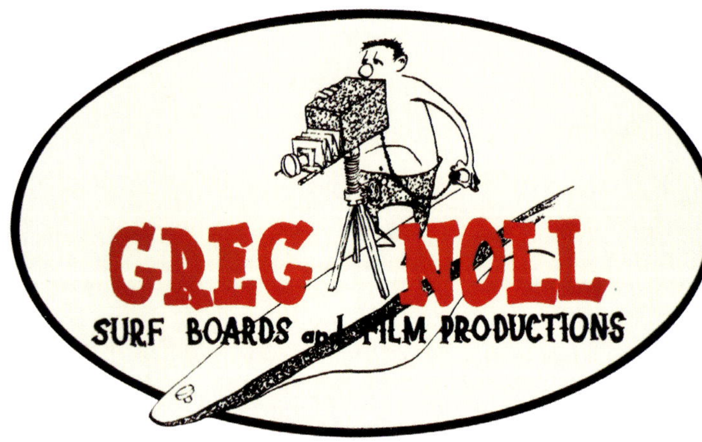

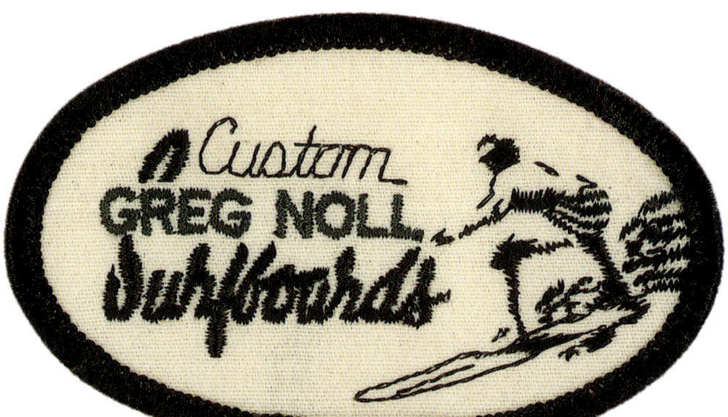

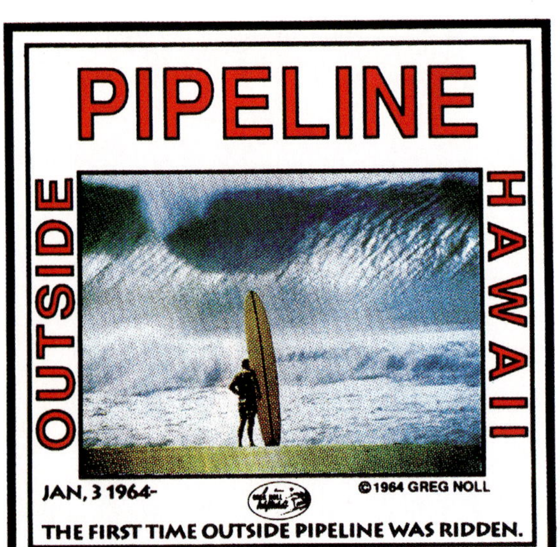

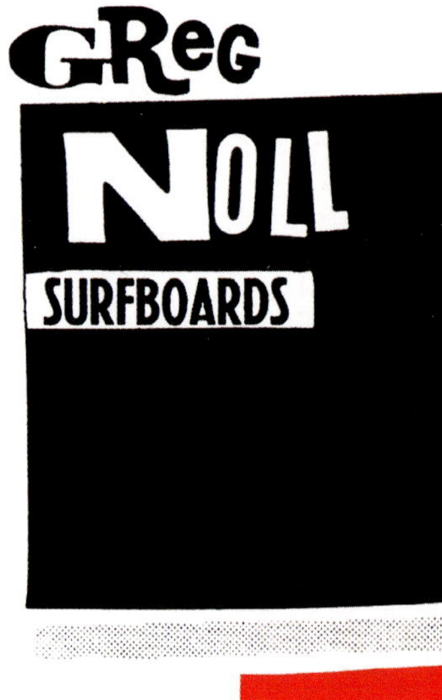

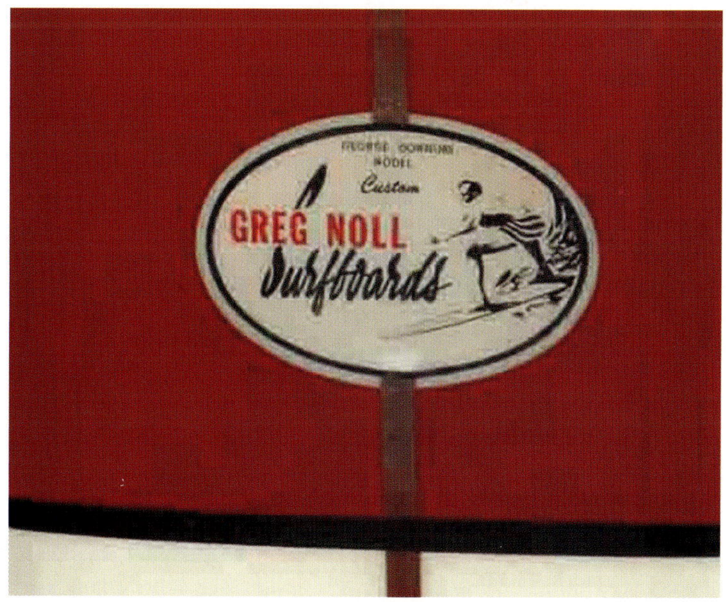

Photo: Juliana Morais. Courtesy Fernando Aguerre and Voyageur Press.

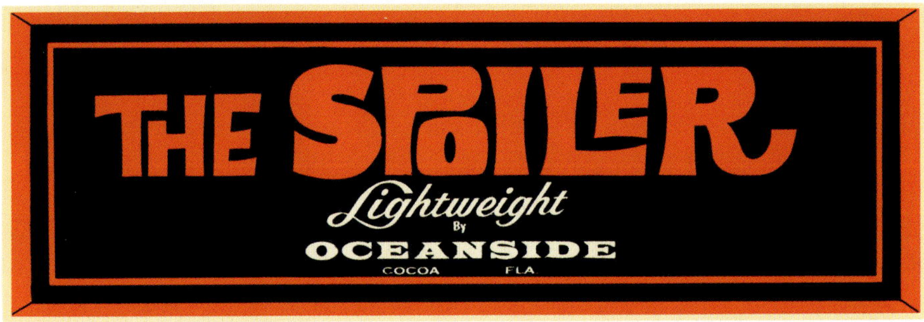
THE SPOILER
Lightweight
By
OCEANSIDE
COCOA FLA

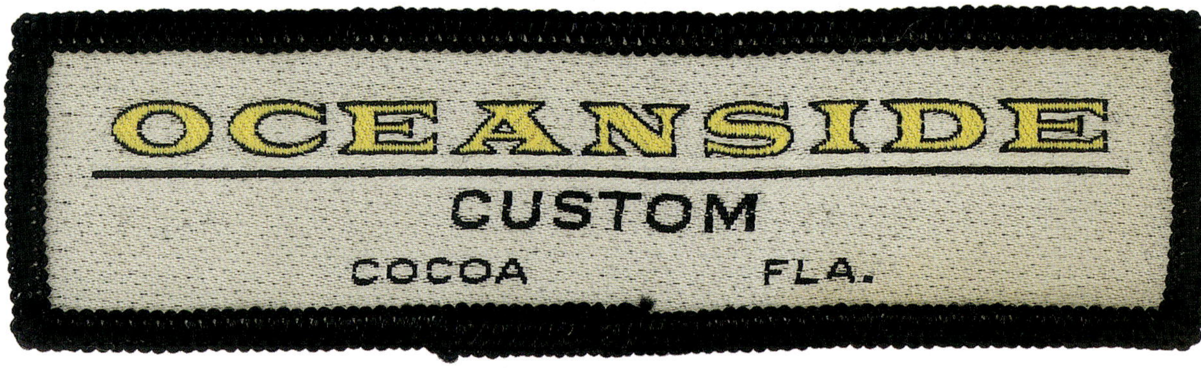
OCEANSIDE
CUSTOM
COCOA FLA.

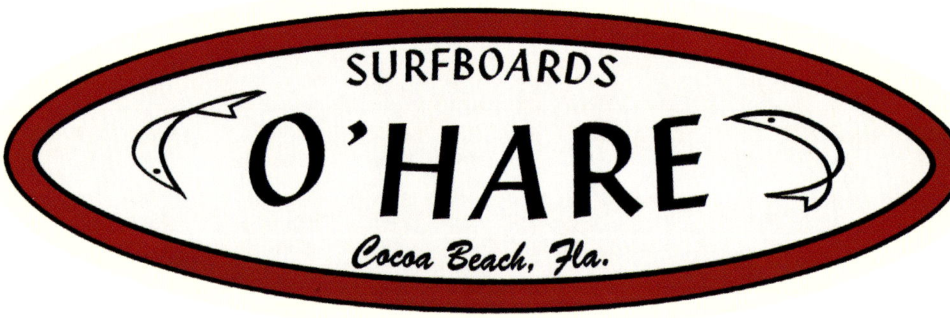
SURFBOARDS
O'HARE
Cocoa Beach, Fla.

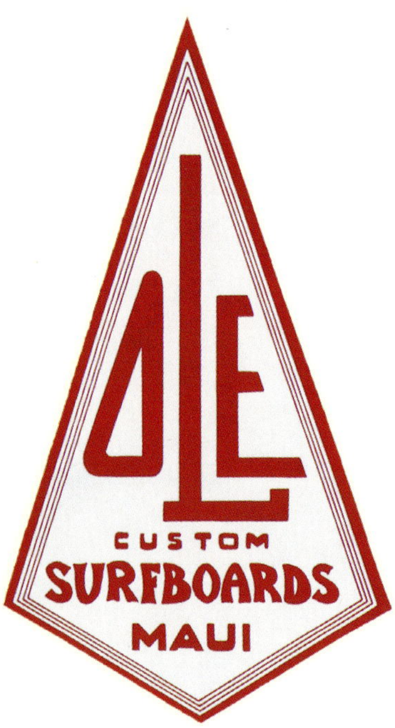
OLE
CUSTOM
SURFBOARDS
MAUI

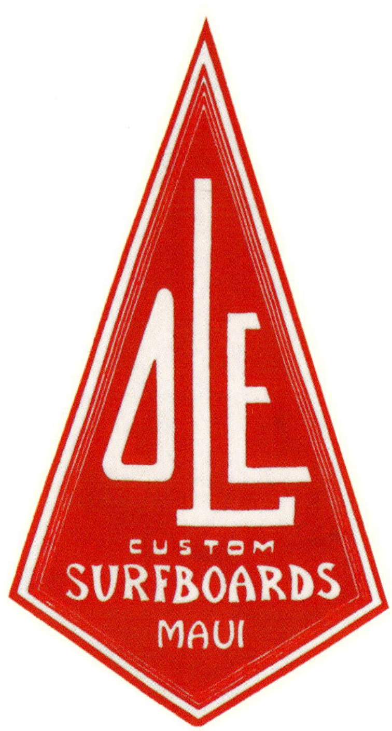
OLE
CUSTOM
SURFBOARDS
MAUI

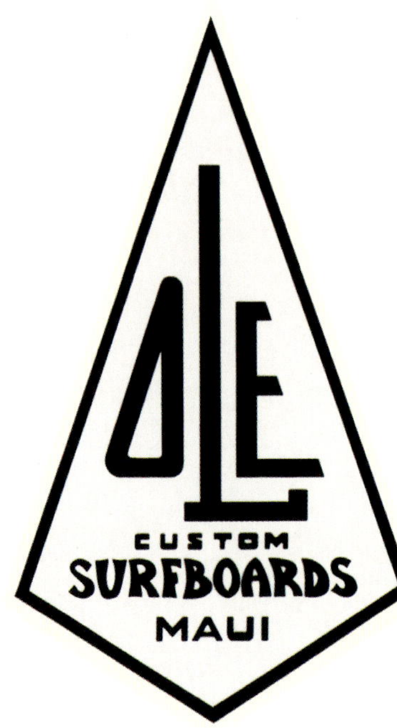
OLE
CUSTOM
SURFBOARDS
MAUI

That was improvised by Jimmy Phillips for George Olson. Jimmy told me this, but that was the used car insignia for Oldsmobile in the 60s. – Pete Noble

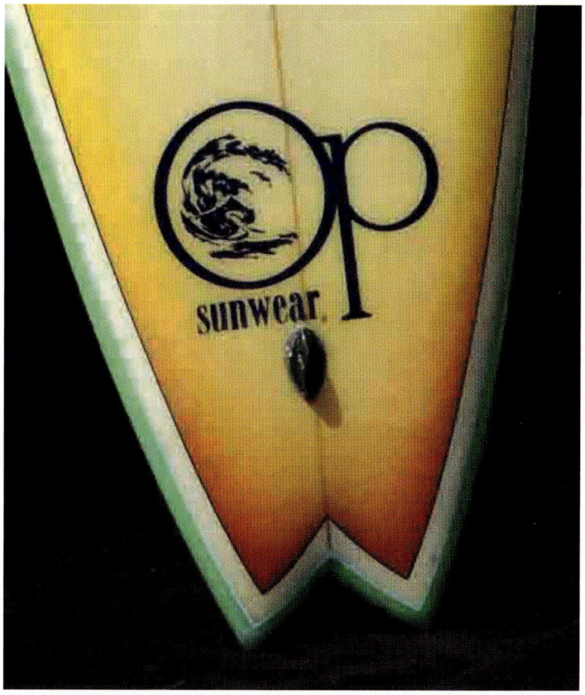

An Op logo from the 80s on a classic swallow-tail. Photo: Juliana Morais. Courtesy Fernando Aguerre and Voyageur Press.

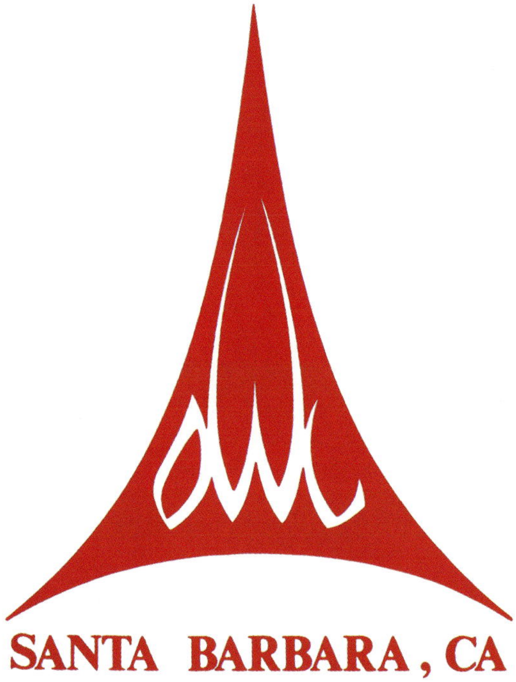
SANTA BARBARA, CA

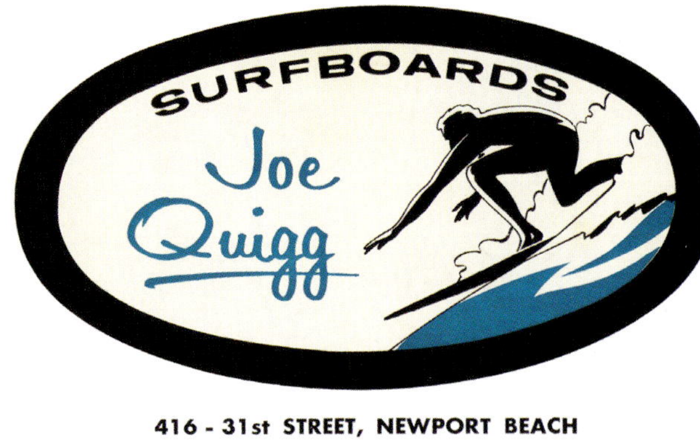
SURFBOARDS
Joe
Quigg
416 - 31st STREET, NEWPORT BEACH

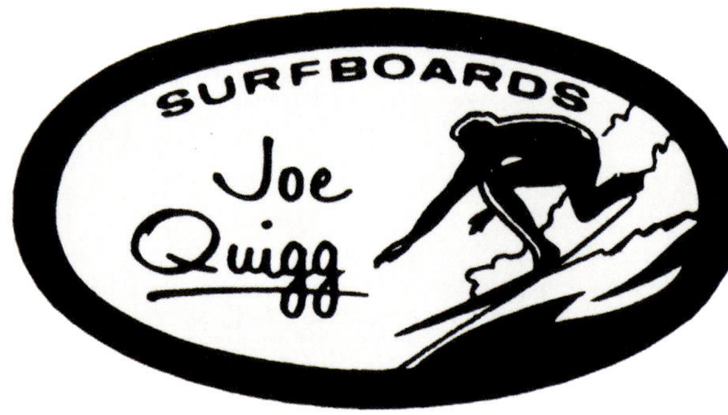
SURFBOARDS
Joe
Quigg

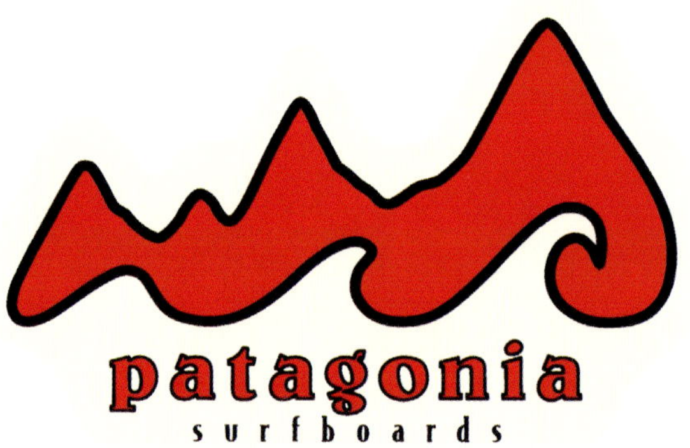
patagonia
surfboards

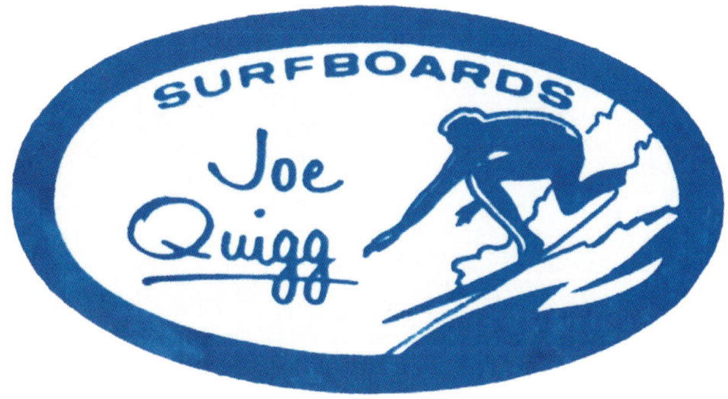
SURFBOARDS
Joe
Quigg

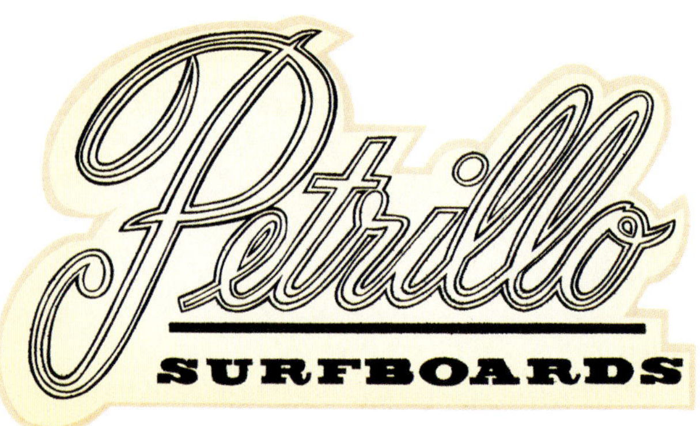
Petrillo
SURFBOARDS

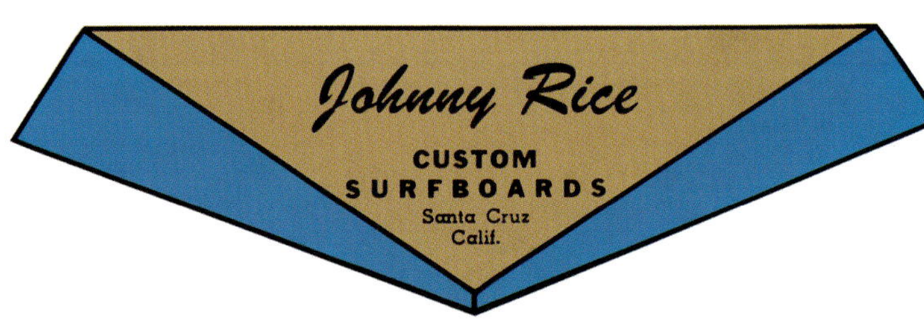
Johnny Rice
CUSTOM
SURFBOARDS
Santa Cruz
Calif.

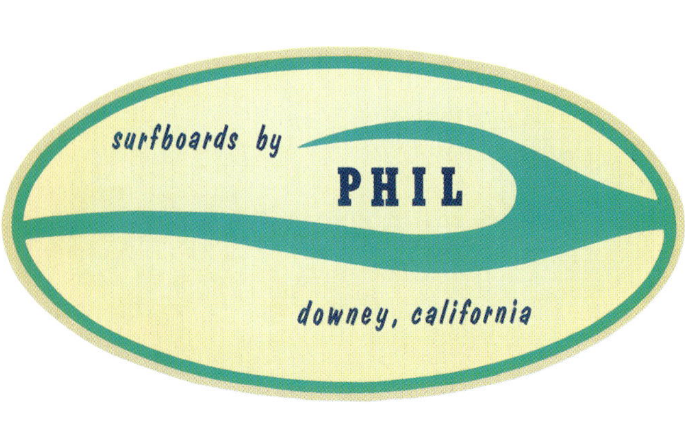
surfboards by
PHIL
downey, california

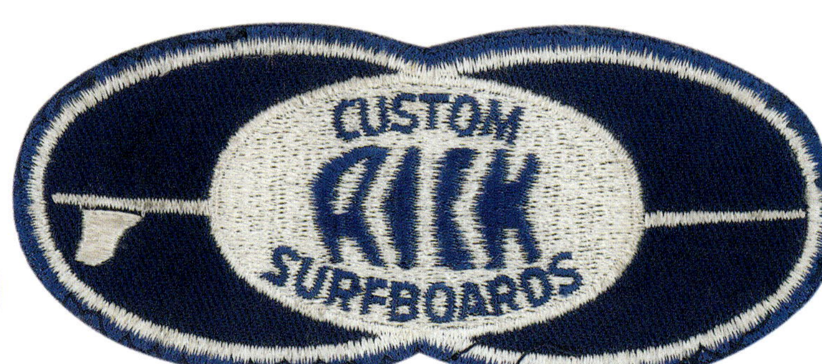
CUSTOM
RICK
SURFBOARDS

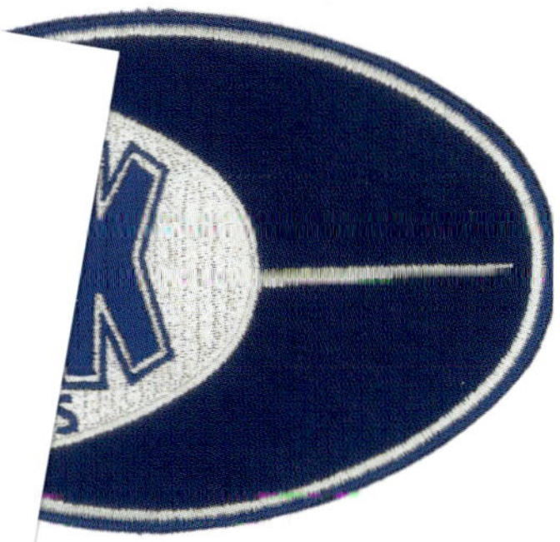

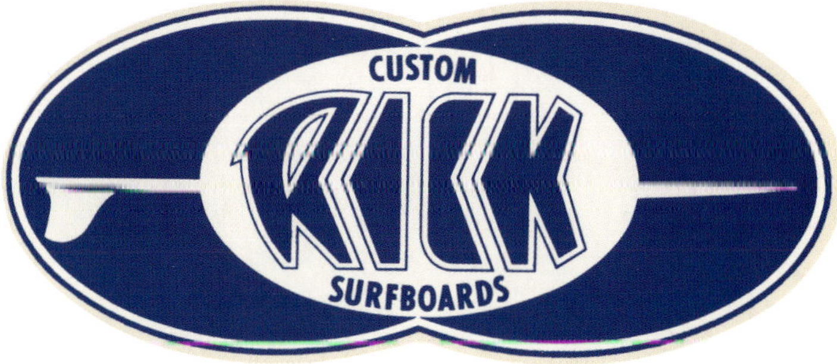

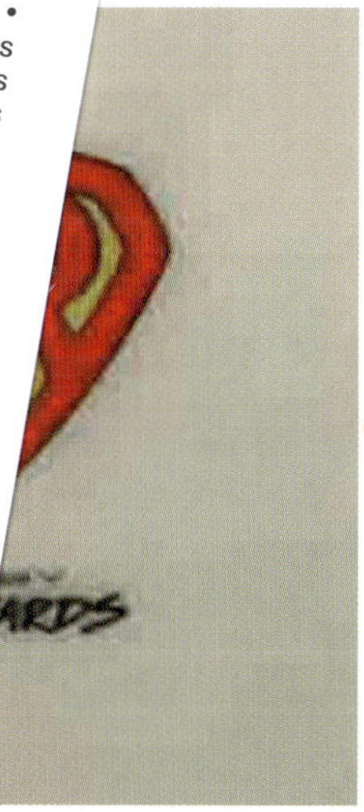

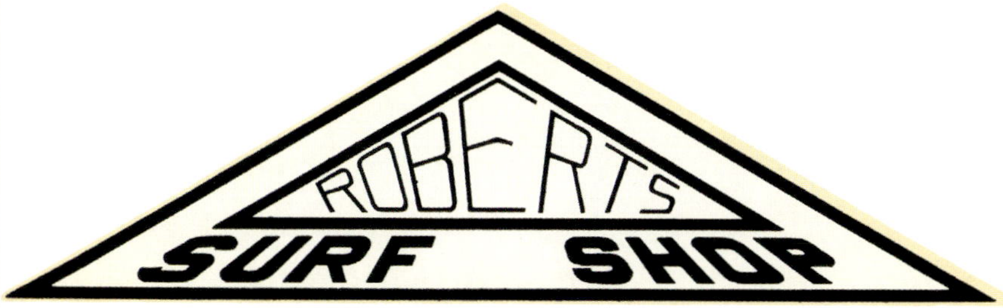

his twin fins. Photo: Ju- … Aguerre and Voyageur

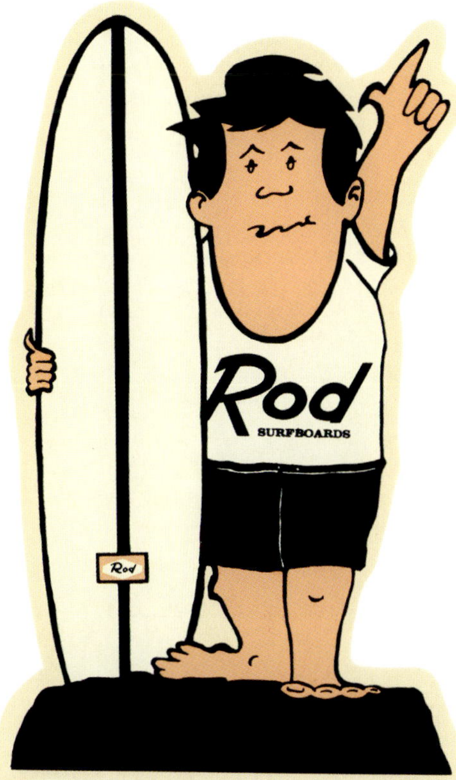

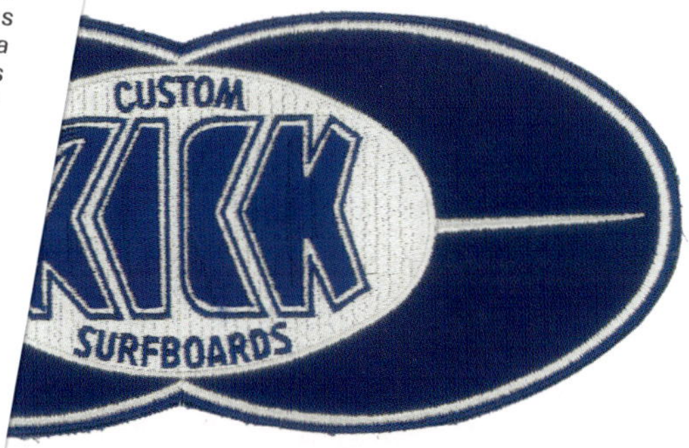

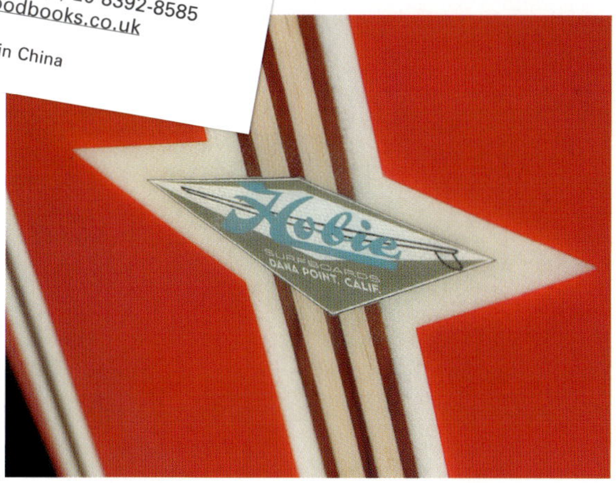

A Hobie logo circa the mid-60s. Photo: Juliana Morais. Courtesy Fernando Aguerre and Voyageur Press.

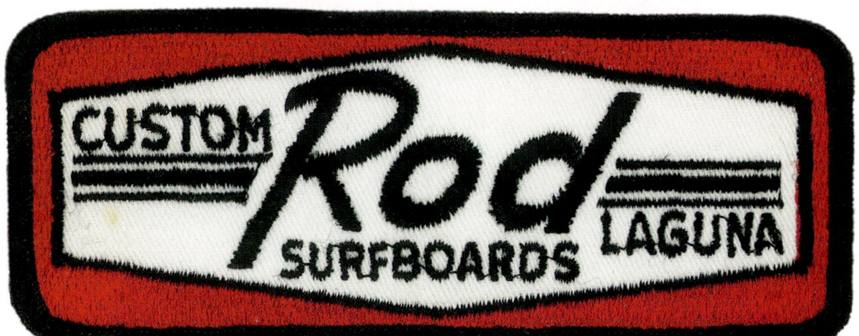

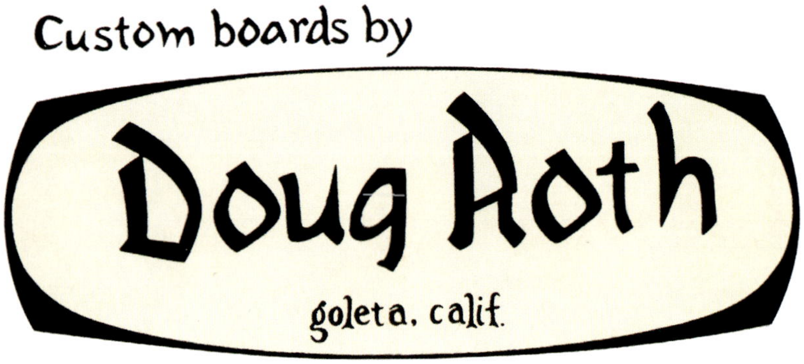

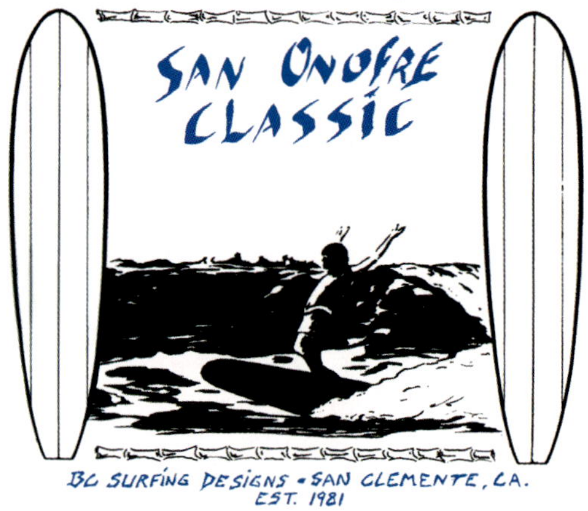

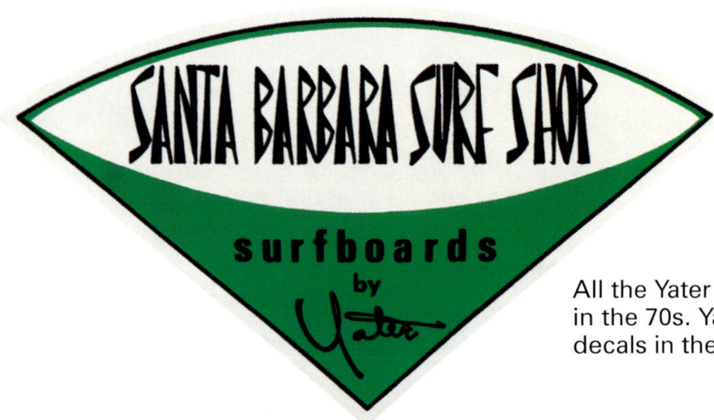

All the Yater decals were made in the 70s. Yater didn't make decals in the 60s. – Pete Noble

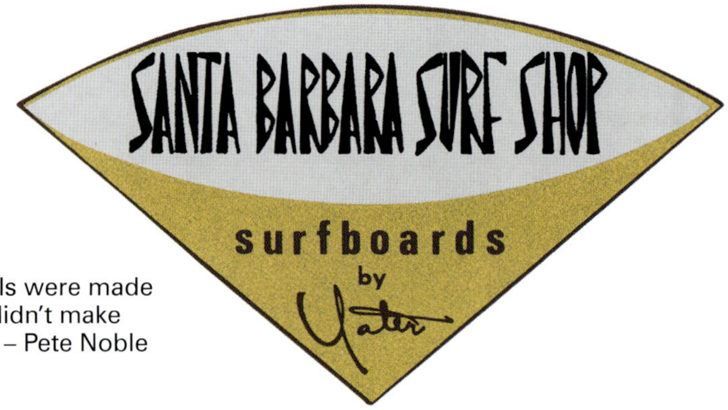

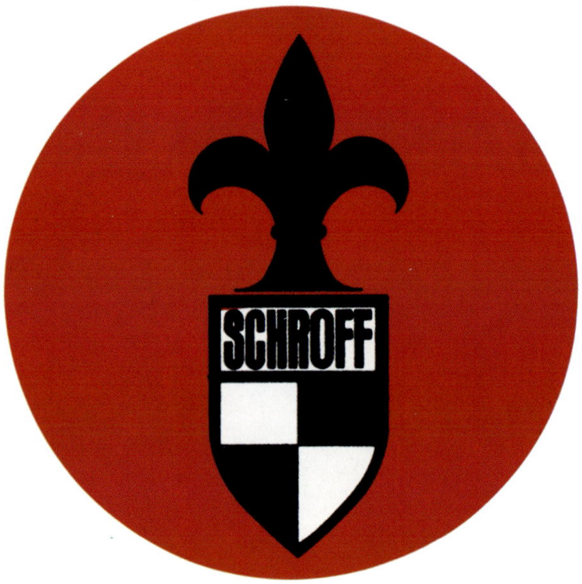

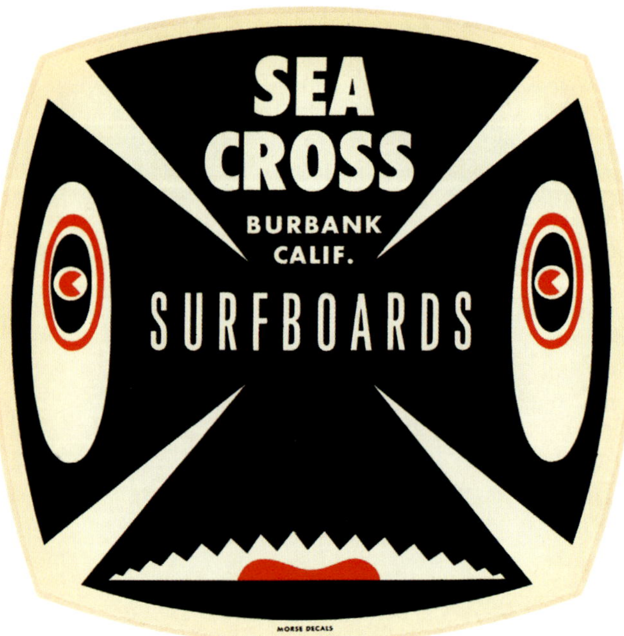

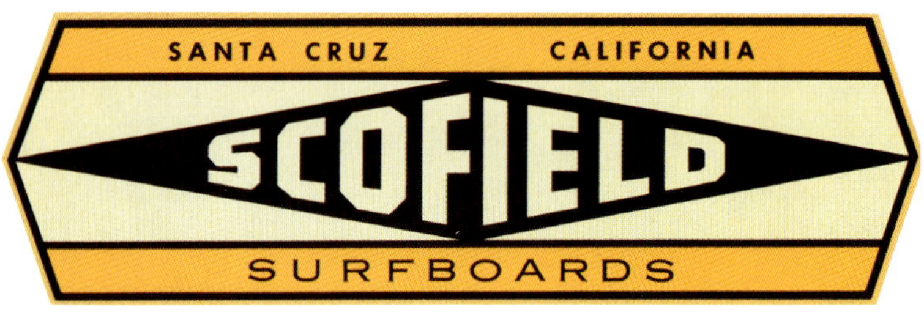

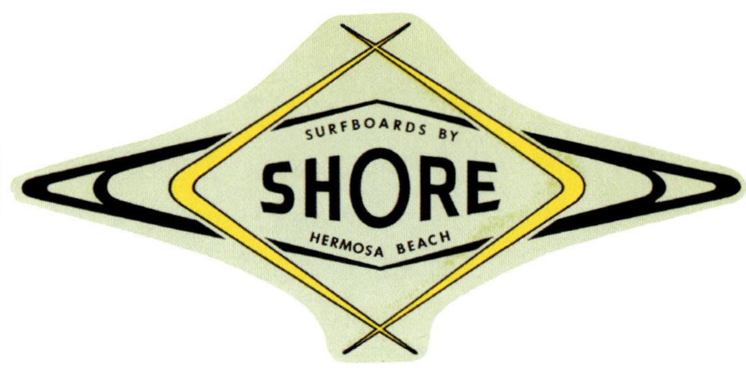

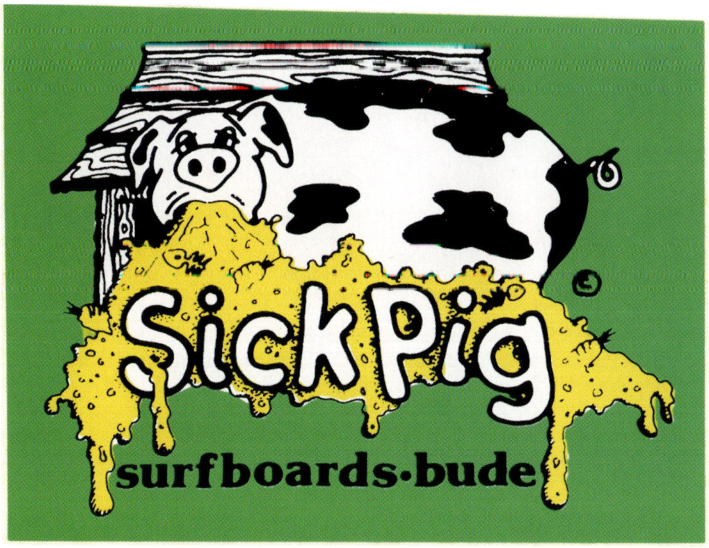
SickPig
surfboards·bude

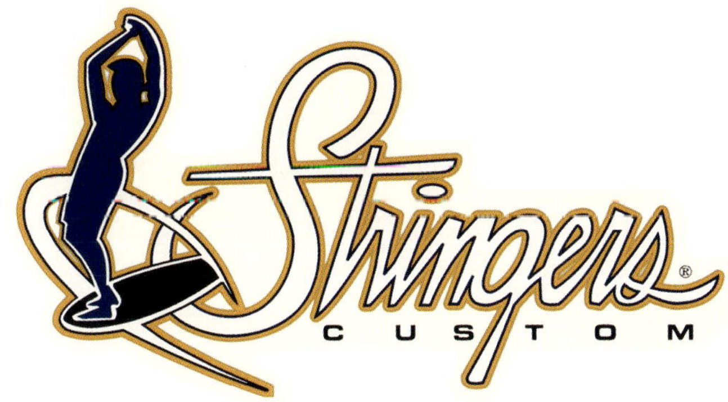
Stringers
CUSTOM

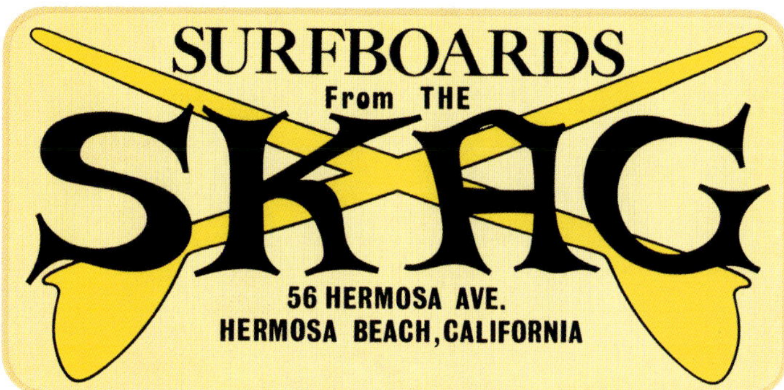
SURFBOARDS
From THE
SKAG
56 HERMOSA AVE.
HERMOSA BEACH, CALIFORNIA

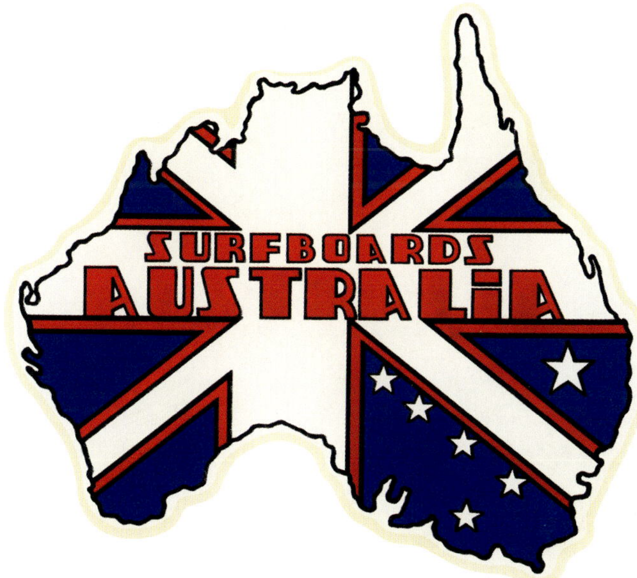
SURFBOARDS
AUSTRALiA

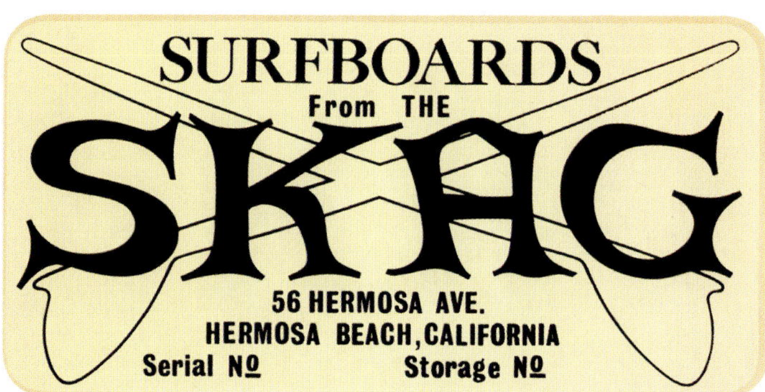
SURFBOARDS
From THE
SKAG
56 HERMOSA AVE.
HERMOSA BEACH, CALIFORNIA
Serial No
Storage No

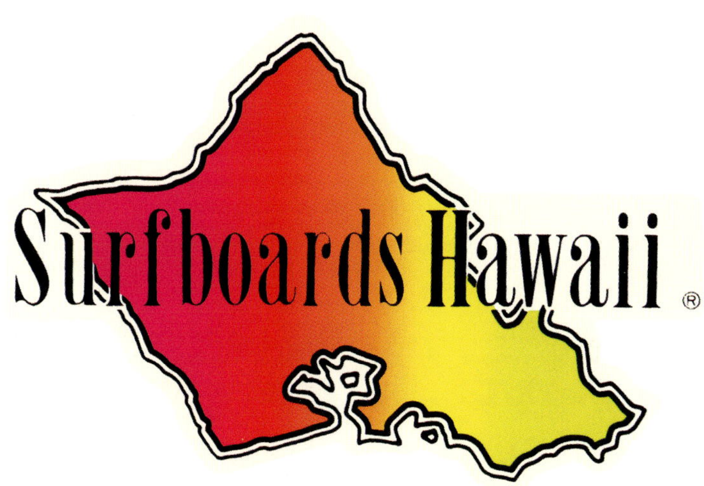
Surfboards Hawaii

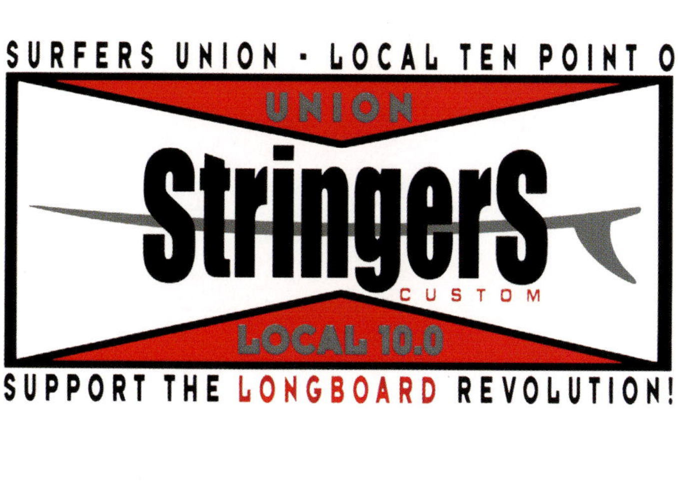
SURFERS UNION - LOCAL TEN POINT O
UNION
StringerS
CUSTOM
LOCAL 10.0
SUPPORT THE LONGBOARD REVOLUTION!

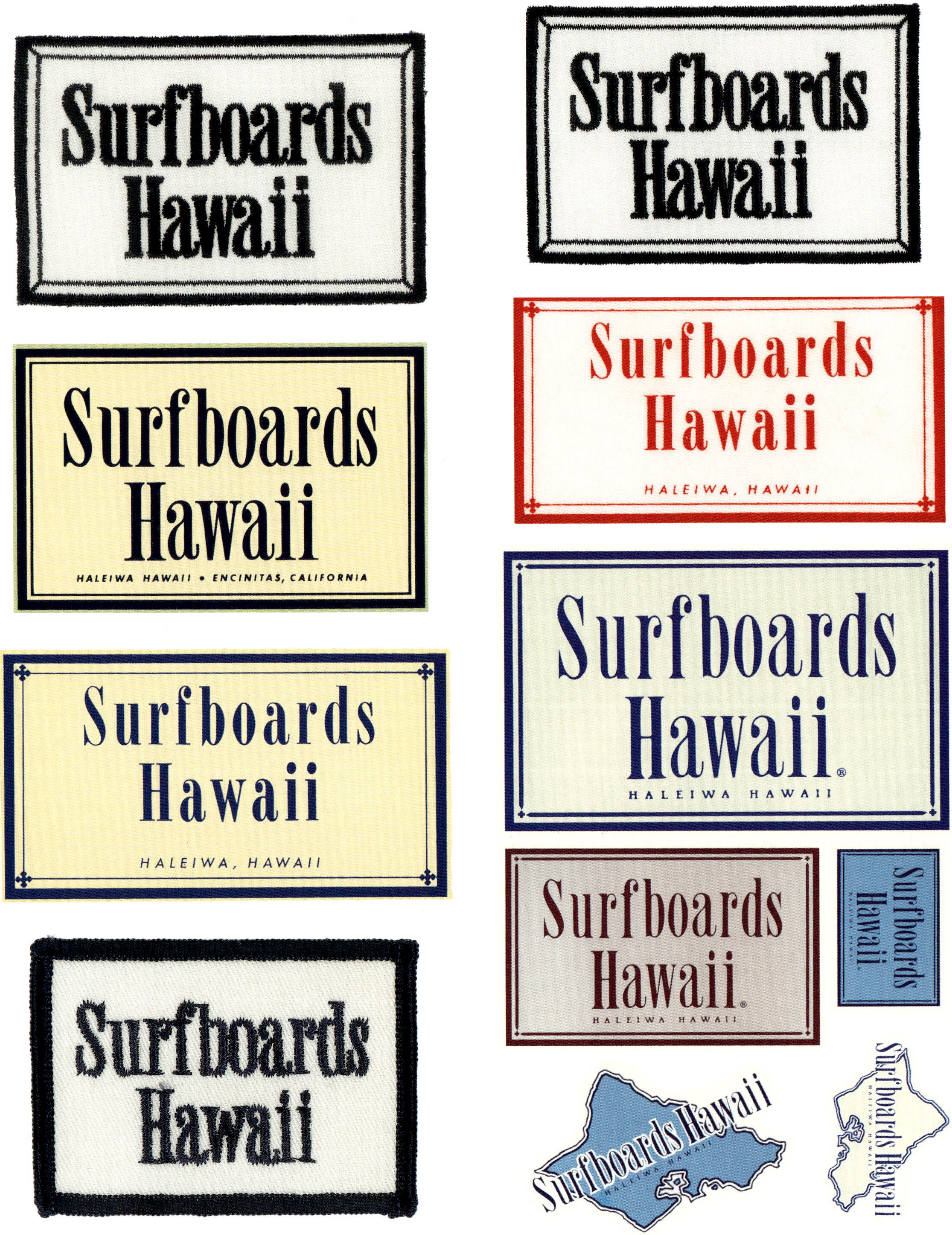
Surfboards Hawaii
Surfboards Hawaii
Surfboards Hawaii
HALEIWA, HAWAII
Surfboards Hawaii
HALEIWA HAWAII • ENCINITAS, CALIFORNIA
Surfboards Hawaii®
HALEIWA HAWAII
Surfboards Hawaii
HALEIWA, HAWAII
Surfboards Hawaii®
HALEIWA HAWAII
Surfboards Hawaii
Surfboards Hawaii
Surfboards Hawaii
HALEIWA HAWAII
Surfboards Hawaii

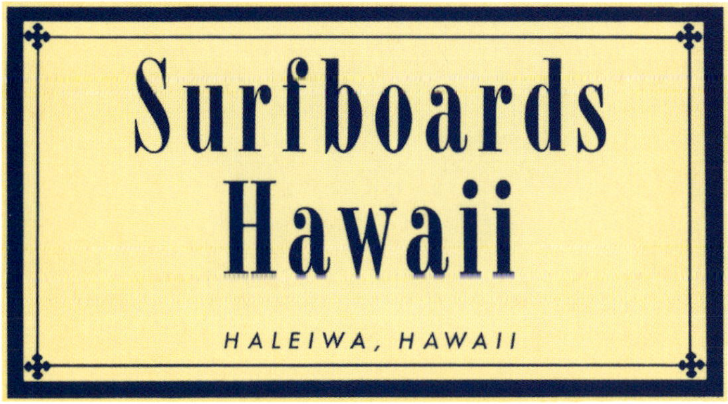
Surfboards
Hawaii
HALEIWA, HAWAII

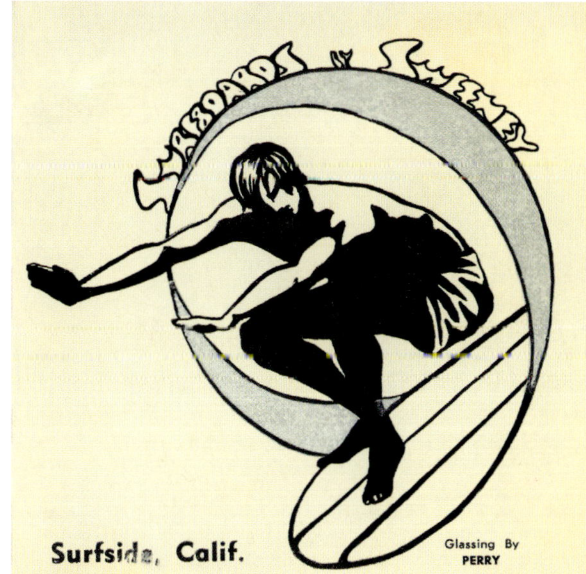
Surfside, Calif.
Glassing By
PERRY

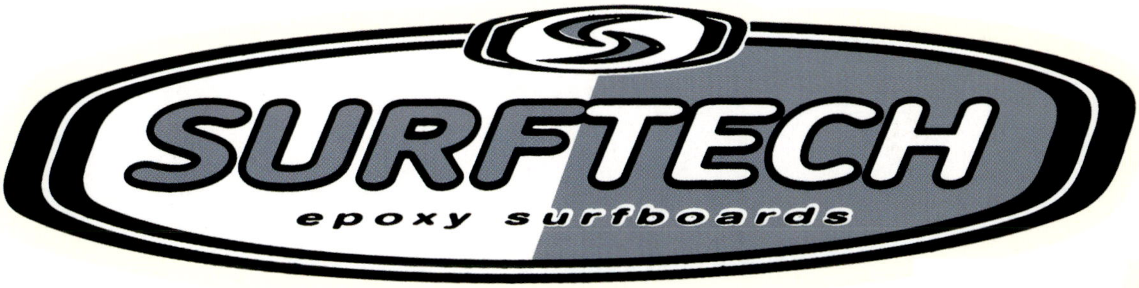
SURFTECH
epoxy surfboards

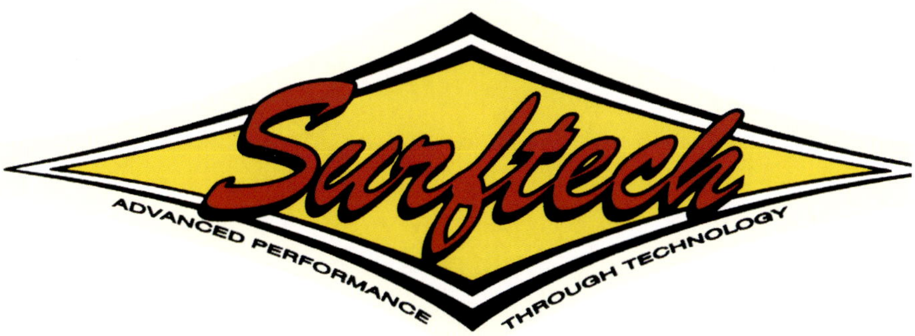
Surftech
ADVANCED PERFORMANCE THROUGH TECHNOLOGY

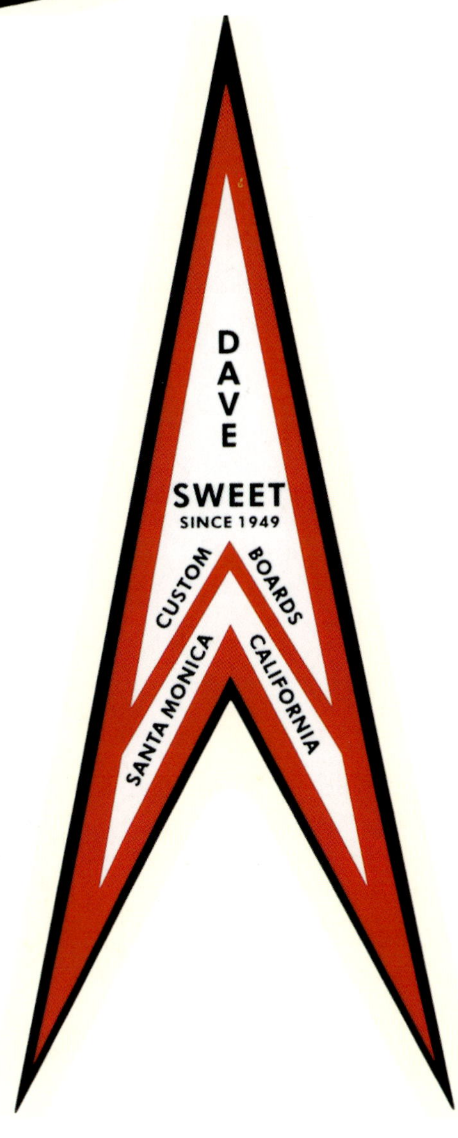
DAVE
SWEET
SINCE 1949
CUSTOM
BOARDS
SANTA MONICA
CALIFORNIA

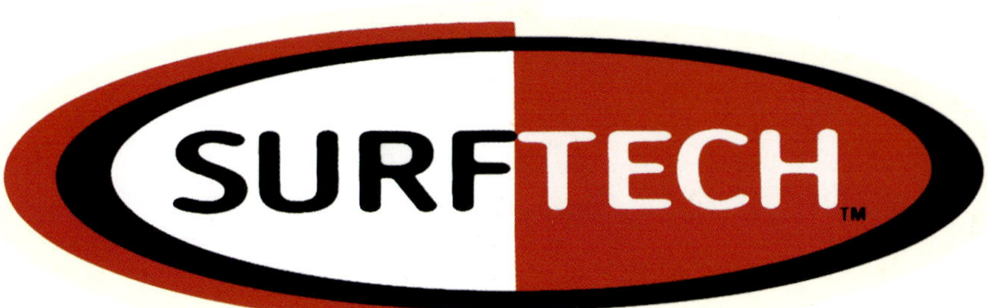
SURFTECH
TM

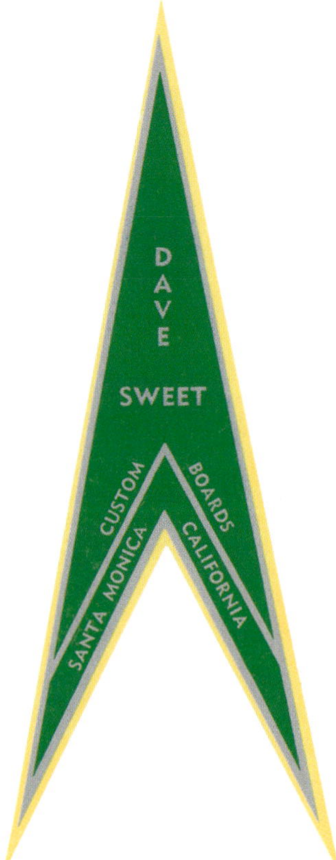
DAVE
SWEET
CUSTOM BOARDS
SANTA MONICA CALIFORNIA

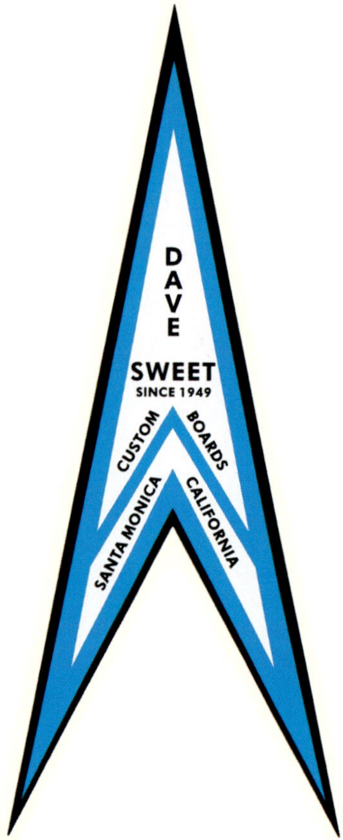
DAVE
SWEET
SINCE 1949
CUSTOM BOARDS
SANTA MONICA CALIFORNIA

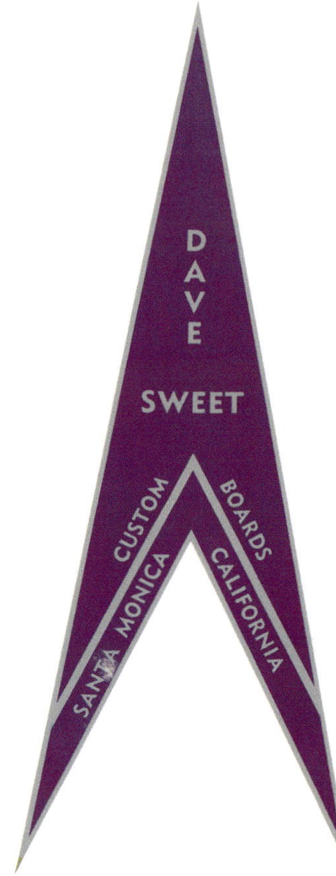
DAVE
SWEET
CUSTOM BOARDS
SANTA MONICA CALIFORNIA

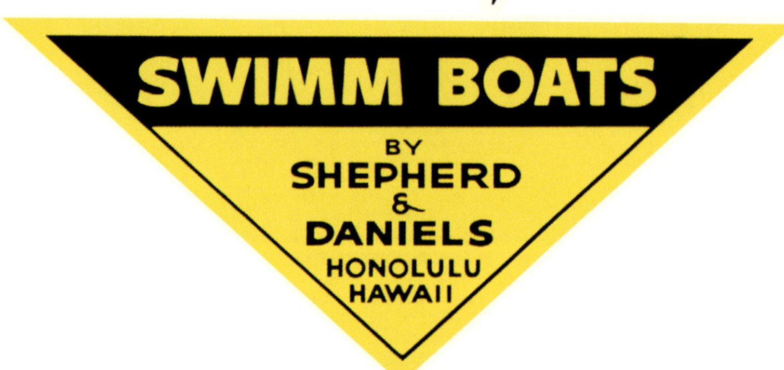
SWIMM BOATS
BY
SHEPHERD
&
DANIELS
HONOLULU
HAWAII

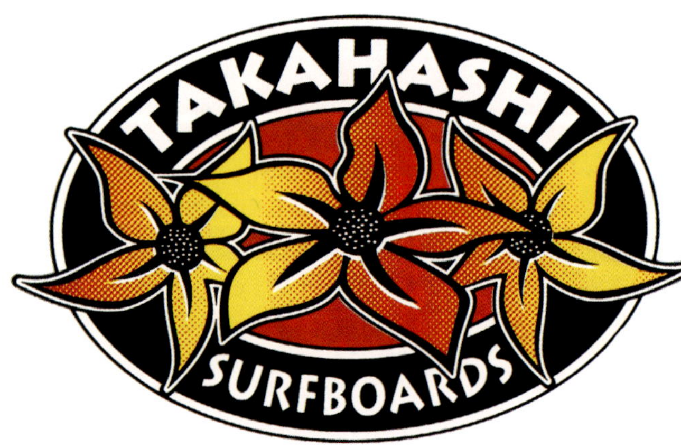
TAKAHASHI
SURFBOARDS

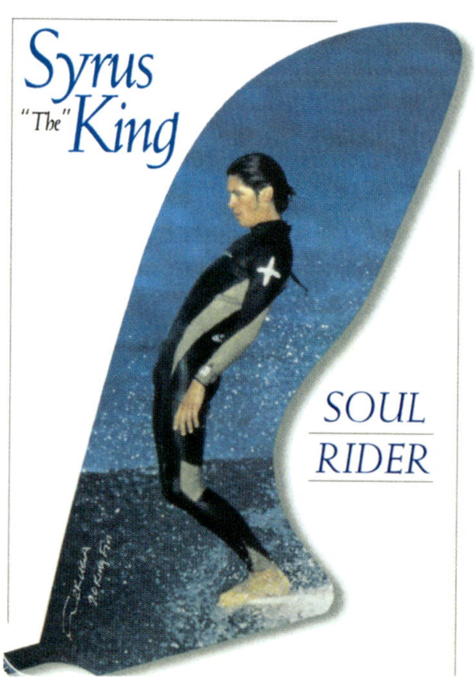
Syrus
"The" King
SOUL
RIDER

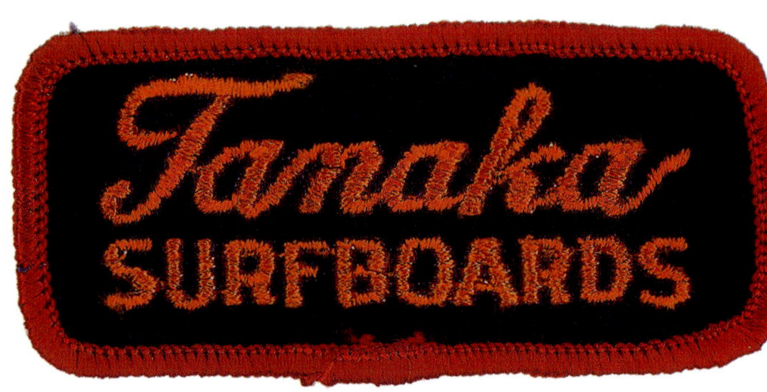
Tanaka
SURFBOARDS

Timpone makes a lot of the tow in surfboards now, but he learned from Gordon Duane. He made a lot of Tommy's boards when he was at Newport Surf and Sport. He said he would make me one but I am still waiting for it. – Pete Noble

THE TRESTLE SPECIAL

VAGABOND
custom
SURFBOARDS

NEWPORT
SURFBOARDS by TUCKER
SURFING
BALBOA ISLAND
CENTER

VARDEMAN
SURFBOARDS

SURFBOARDS by TUCKER
BALBOA ISLAND

SONNY
VARDEMAN
SURFBOARDS

VAGABOND
custom
SURFBOARDS

VARDEMAN
SURFBOARDS

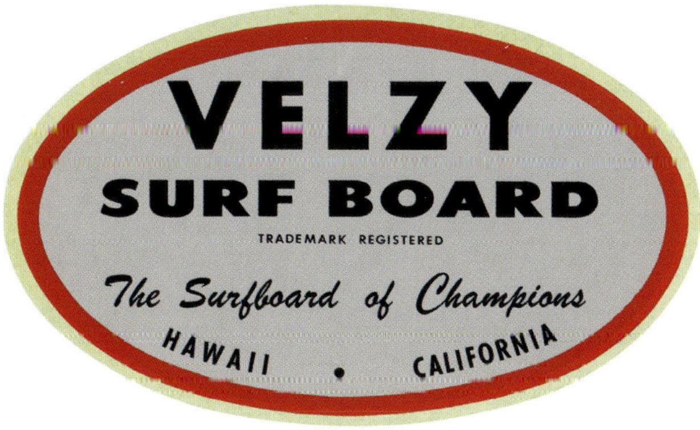
VELZY
SURF BOARD
TRADEMARK REGISTERED
The Surfboard of Champions
HAWAII • CALIFORNIA

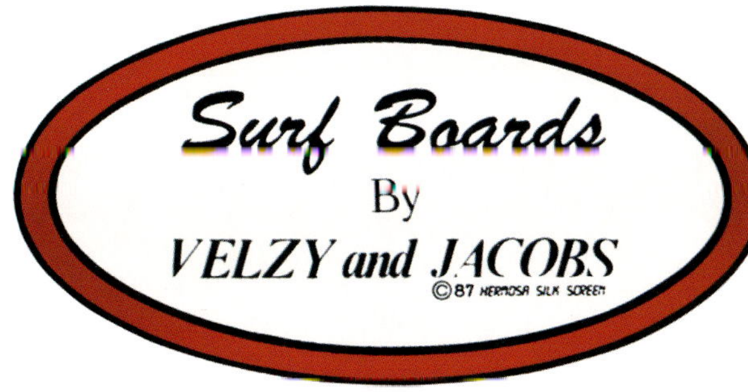
Surf Boards
By
VELZY and JACOBS
©87 HERMOSA SILK SCREEN

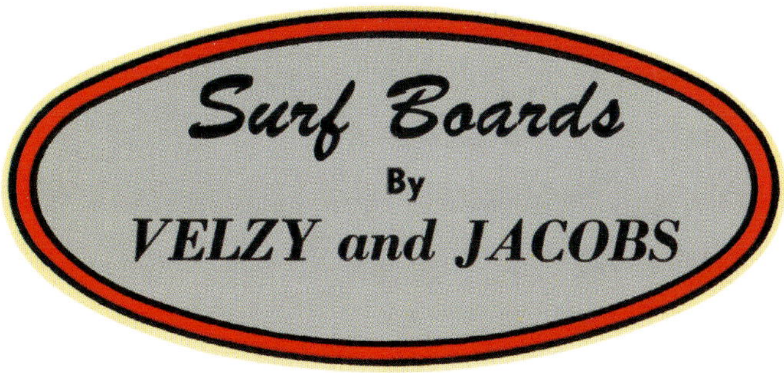
Surf Boards
By
VELZY and JACOBS

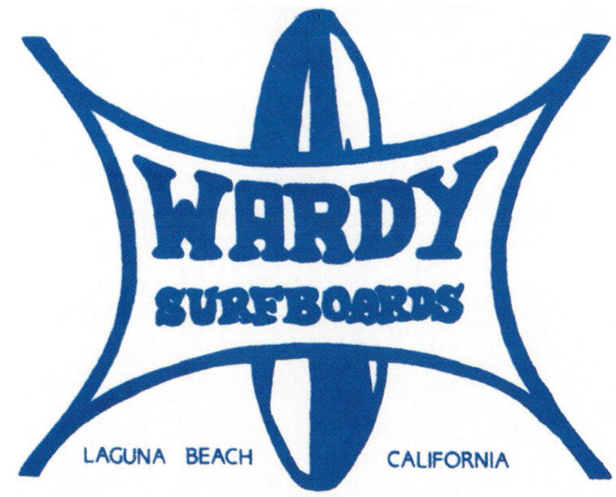
WARDY
SURFBOARDS
LAGUNA BEACH
CALIFORNIA

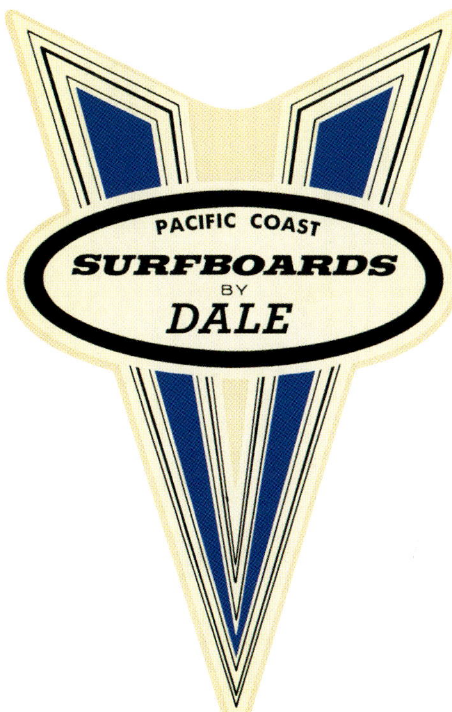
PACIFIC COAST
SURFBOARDS
BY
DALE

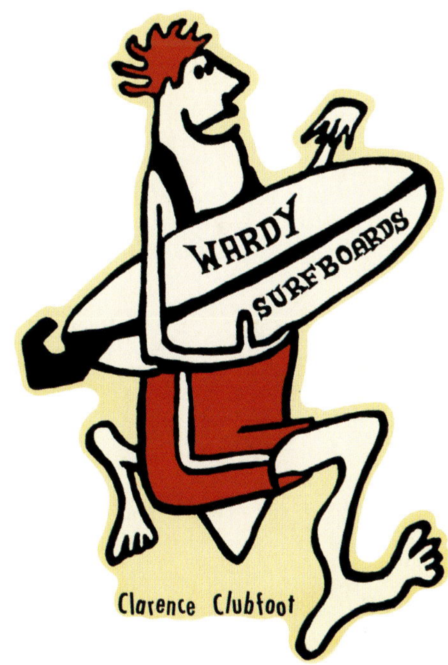
WARDY
SURFBOARDS
Clarence Clubfoot

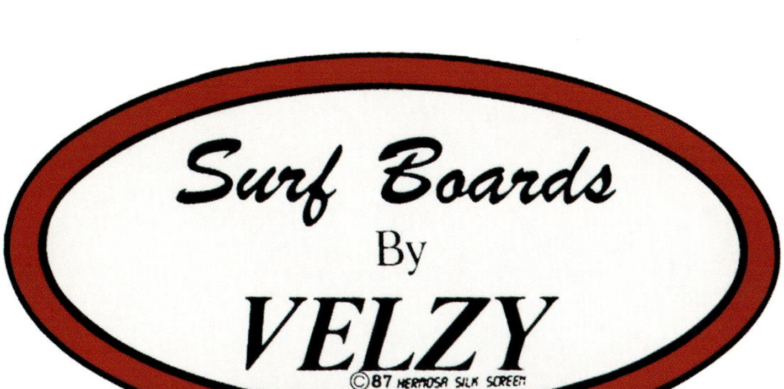
Surf Boards
By
VELZY
©87 HERMOSA SILK SCREEN

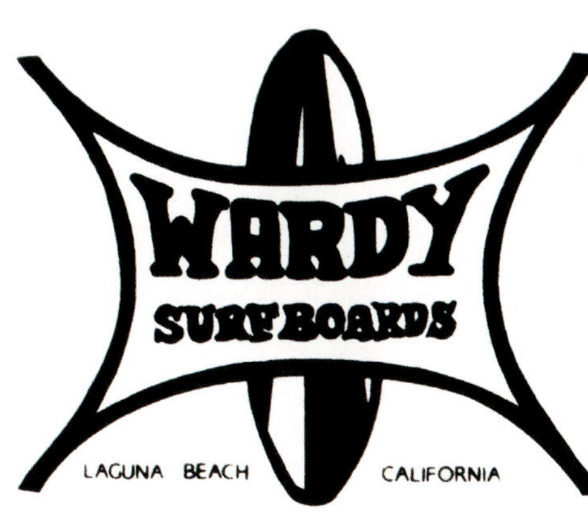
WARDY
SURFBOARDS
LAGUNA BEACH
CALIFORNIA

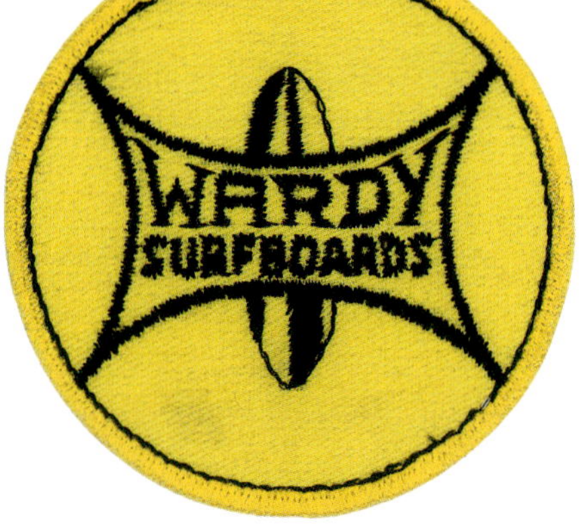
WARDY
SURFBOARDS

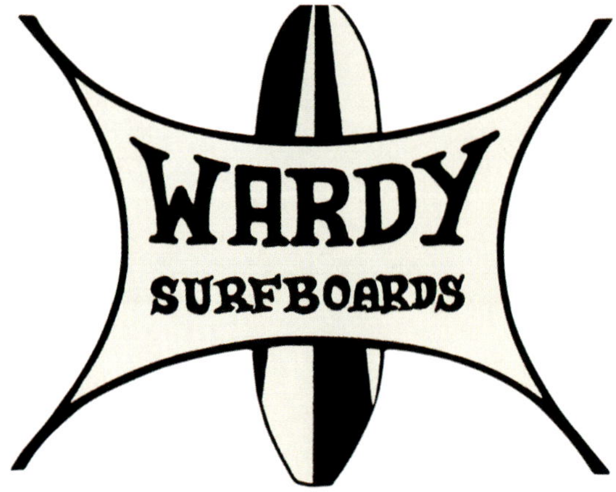
WARDY
SURFBOARDS

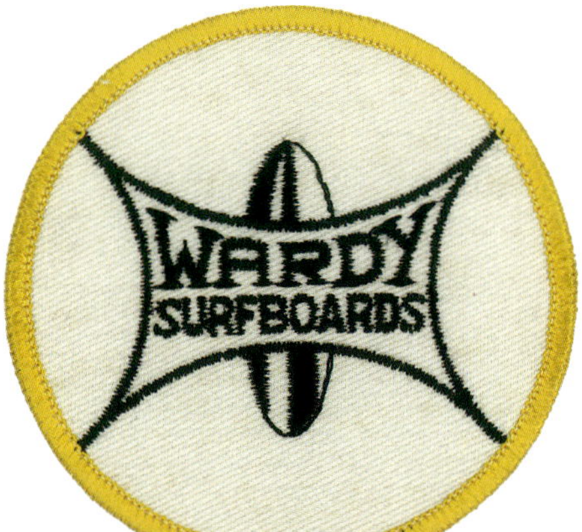
WARDY
SURFBOARDS

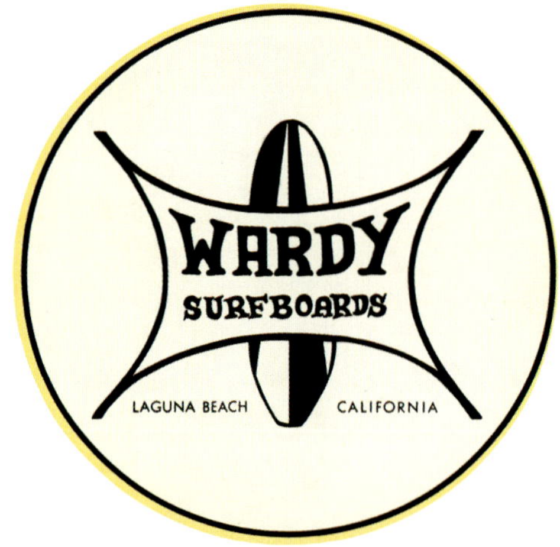
WARDY
SURFBOARDS
LAGUNA BEACH CALIFORNIA

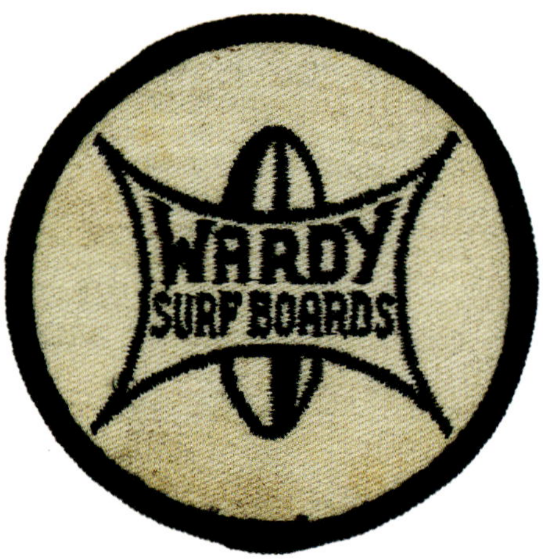
WARDY
SURF BOARDS

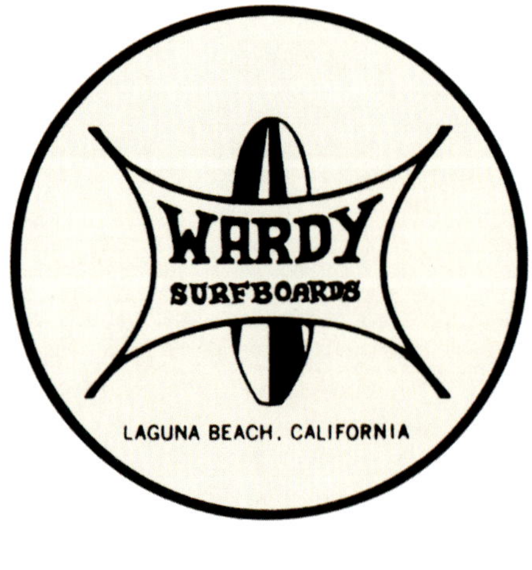
WARDY
SURFBOARDS
LAGUNA BEACH, CALIFORNIA

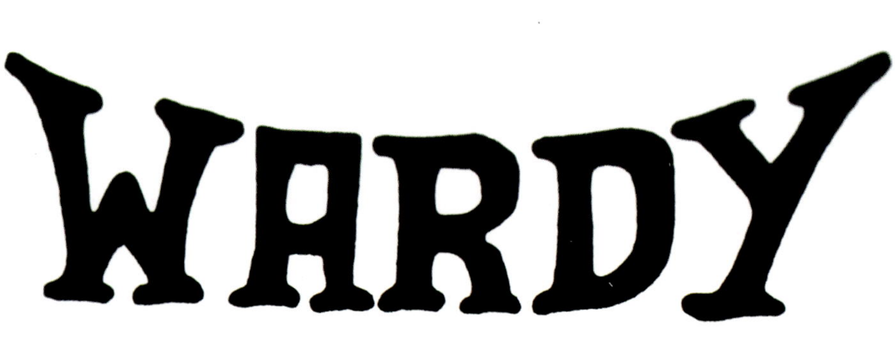
WARDY

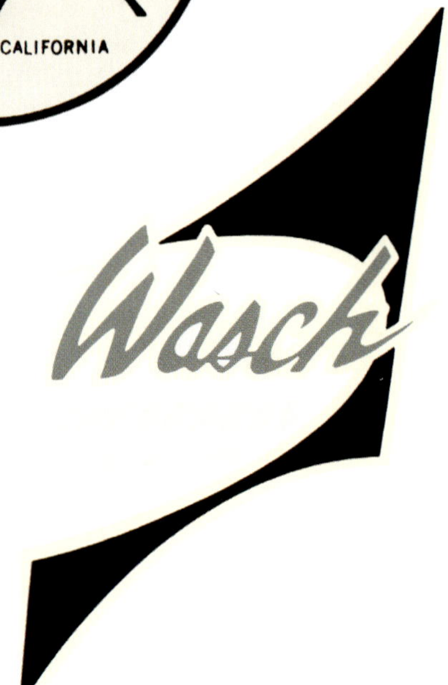
Wasch

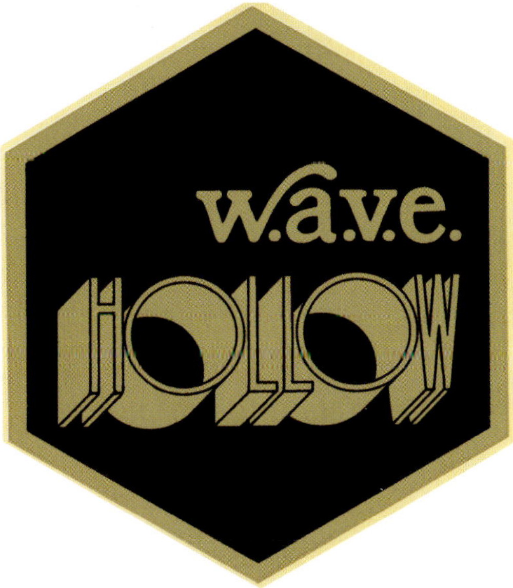

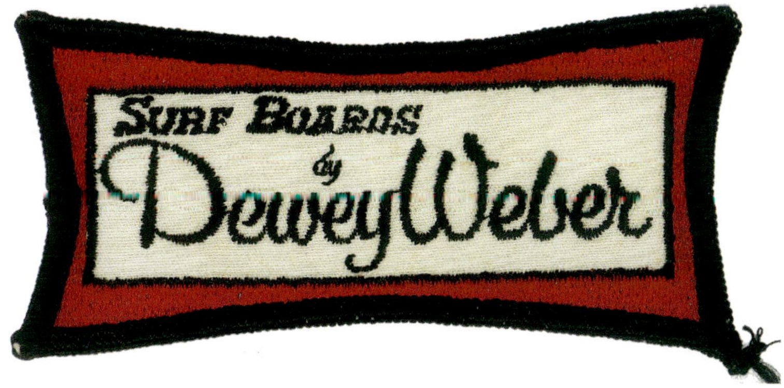

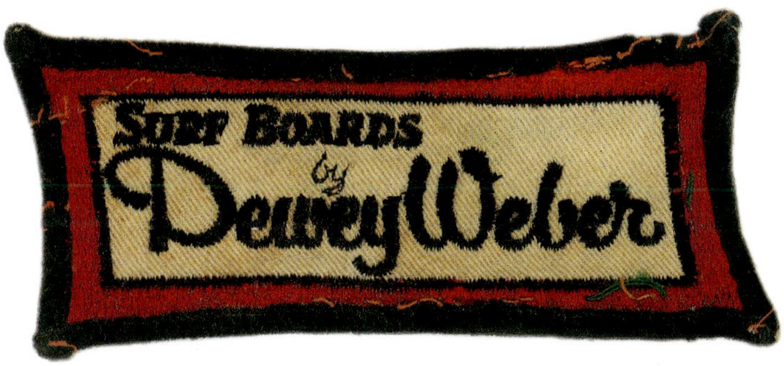

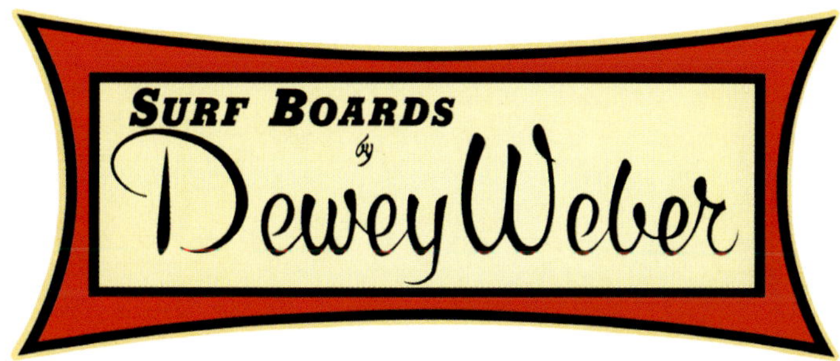

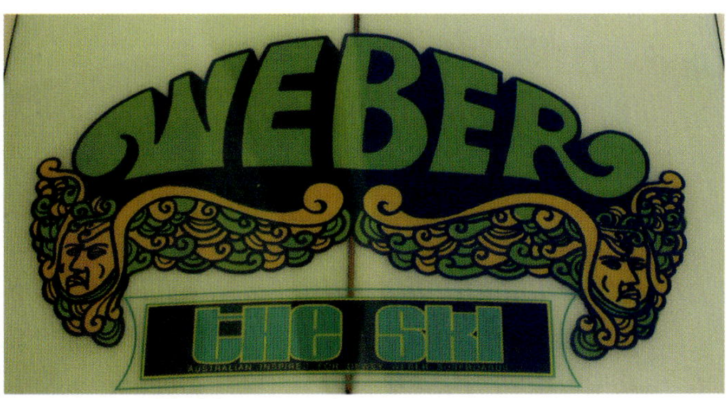

Photo: Juliana Morais. Courtesy Fernando Aguerre and Voyageur Press.

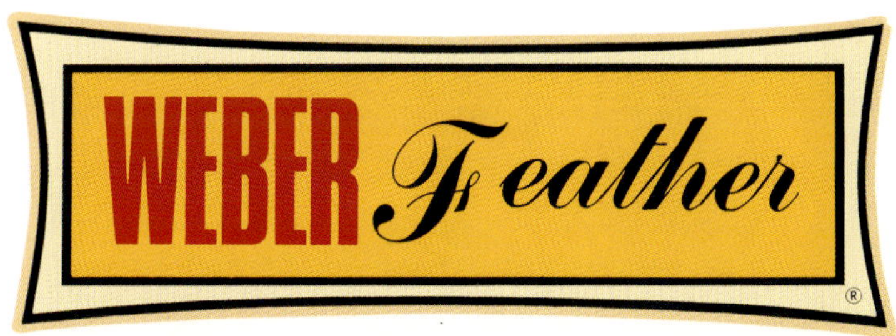

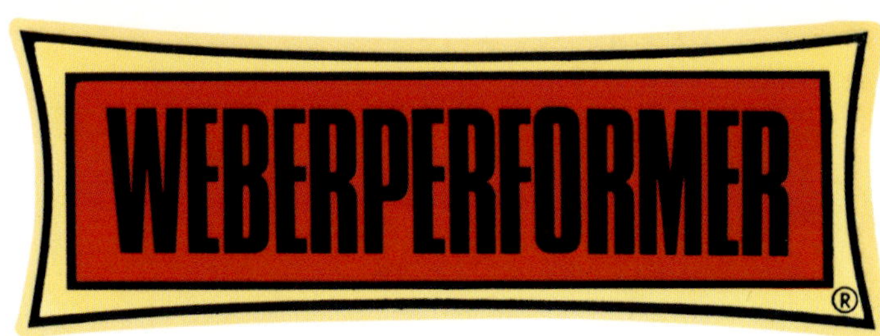

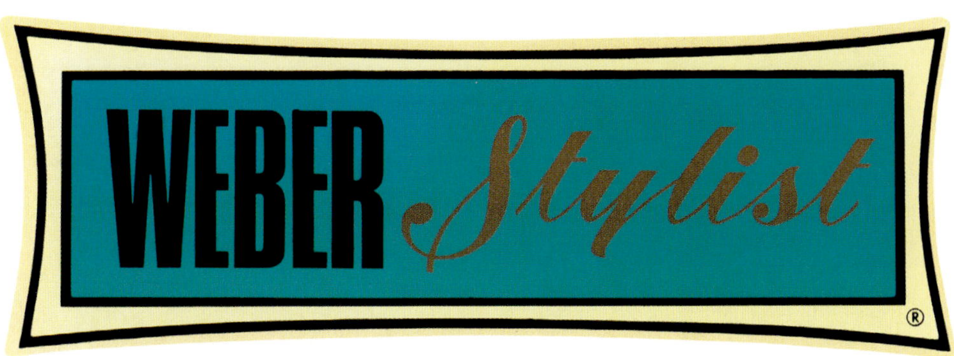

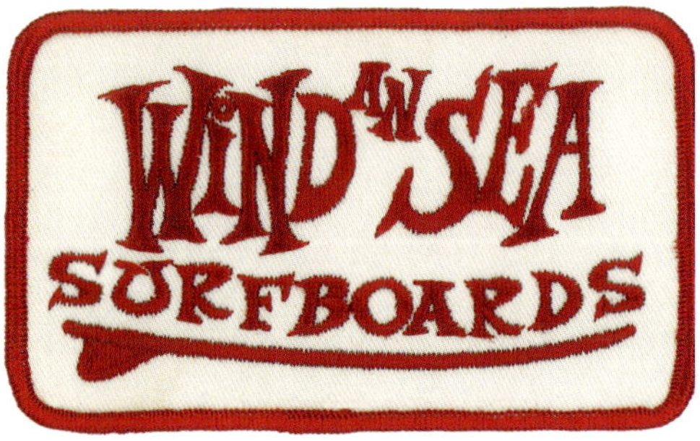
WIND AN SEA
SURFBOARDS

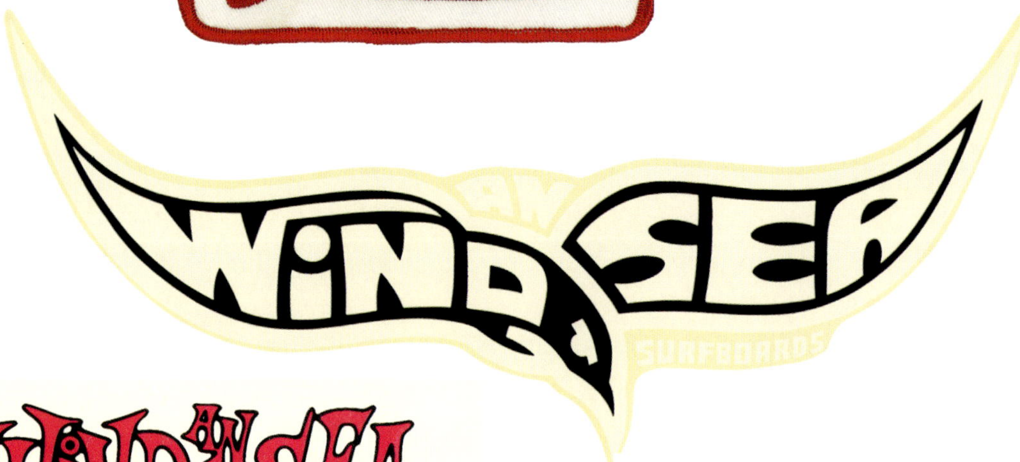
WIND SEA
SURFBOARDS

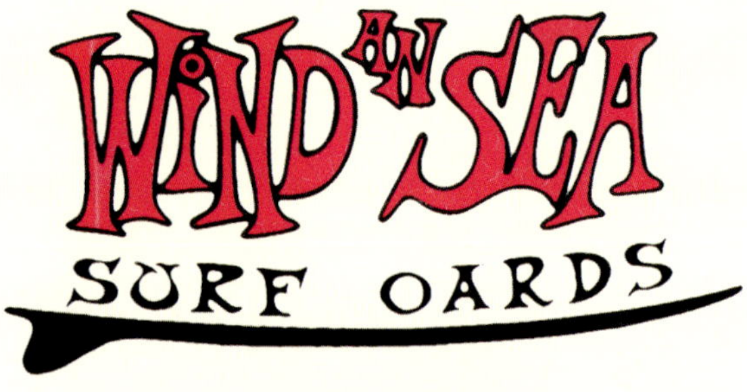
WIND AN SEA
SURF OARDS

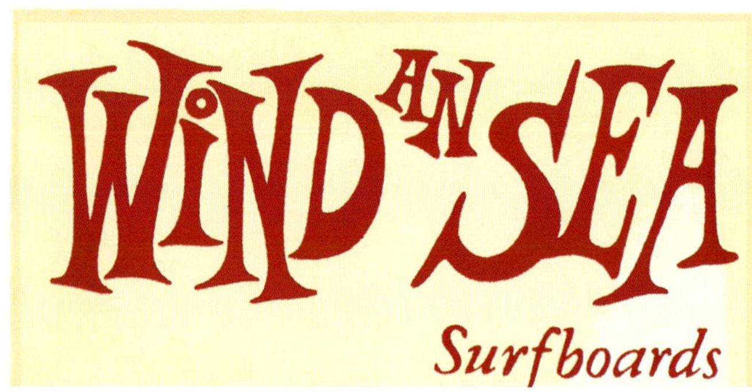
WIND AN SEA
Surfboards

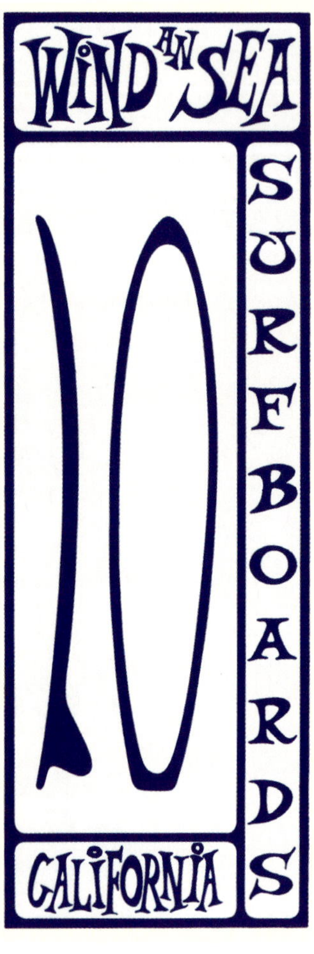
WIND AN SEA
SURFBOARDS
CALIFORNIA

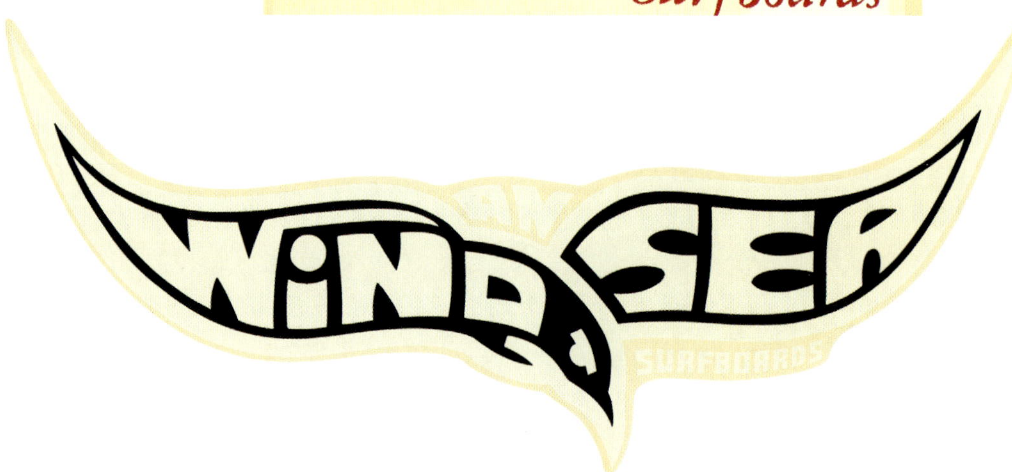
WIND SEA
SURFBOARDS

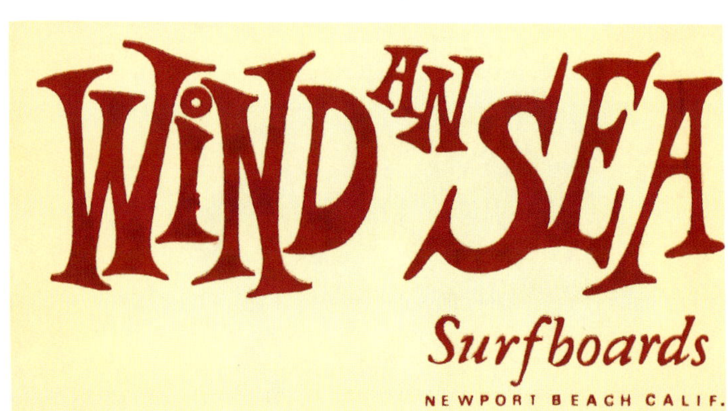
WIND AN SEA
Surfboards
NEWPORT BEACH CALIF.

WINGNUT
M·O·D·E·L

ZUMA JAY SURFBOARDS

CUSTOM SURFBOARDS
Gordon Woods
BROOKVALE SYDNEY

ZUMA
JAY
SURFBOARDS
EST. 1975
MALIBU,CA.

YEAKEL
custom surfboards
CAPISTRANO BEACH, CA

ZUMA JAY
SURFBOARDS
BUDE ENGLAND MALIBU CALIFORNIA

SURFBOARDS
---BY---
YOUNT
SANTA CRUZ

ZUMA JAY
SURFBOARDS
MALIBU, CALIFORNIA.
BUDE, ENGLAND.

CHAPTER FOUR

SURFING USA

The surf music of the early 60s has roots in the rock and roll, doo wop, and country and western music that came out of the 40s and 50s. In 1959, Dick Dale changed the name of his band from Dick Dale and The Rhythm Wranglers to Dick Dale and the Del Tones and started doing regular "surfer stomps" at the Rendezvous Ballroom in Newport Beach.

That same year, a high school student named Brian Wilson got a C for a composition called *Surfin'*. Within four years, "surf music" would be the name for the music craze that launched a hundred hits from Dick Dale, the Beach Boys, Jan and Dean, the Surfaris. and the Trashmen.

This batch of stickers is inspired by some of the surf music songs that were the biggest hits of the 60s.

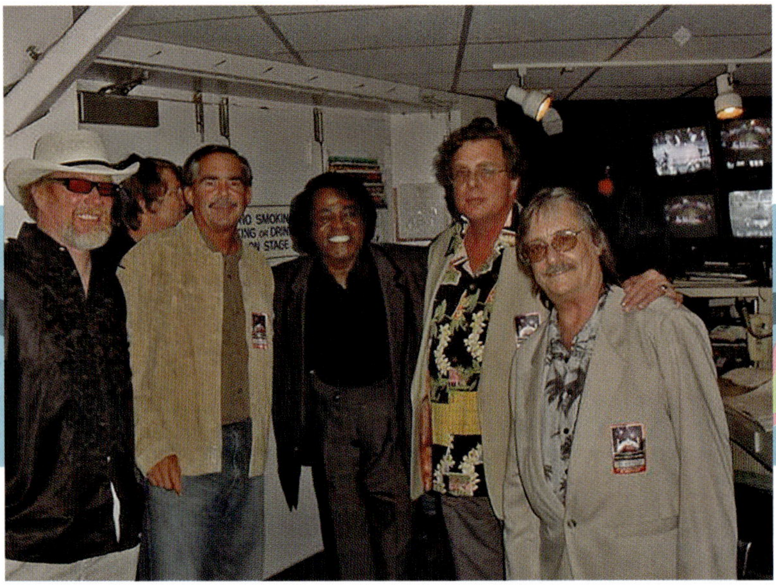

The Godfather of Soul meets the Godfather of Surf Guitar. Backstage at the Hollywood Bowl in the fall of 2004. From left: John Dordero, Ben Marcus, Randy Hunt, James Brown, Dennis Dooley and Surfari's guitarist Jim Fuller. Photo: Ben Marcus

CHAPTER 4.1 WIPE OUT

I WROTE A SIMPLE SONG

The Surfari's Guitarist Jim Fuller on the Birth and Long, Happy Life of ***Wipe Out!***

On the last Saturday in September 2004, a black limo rolled through LA traffic heading for the James Brown Revue at the Hollywood Bowl. On board were members of a San Marino Posse including John Dordero who runs the Orange Inn in Laguna and the cafeteria at Quiksilver. Randy Hunt was one of the founders of Quiksilver who now runs several Quiksilver Boardriders stores in Orange County. The ringleader was Dennis Dooley, a surfer, musician and record producer who has worked with everyone from Paul Revere and the Raiders to the Red Hot Chili Peppers. Sam McWhorter was in the limo as well, a record producer who has worked with Prince and ELO and Sonny and Cher and has at least one fine feather in his producer's cap: *Put a Little Love in Your Heart* by Jackie De Shannon. And then there was kind of a little guy in a suit who didn't say much but smiled quietly to himself. This was Jim Fuller, the original guitarist for The Surfaris and the guy who co-wrote *Wipe Out*. This crew sat backstage at the Bowl and watched James Brown and his 29-piece band rock a packed house. On the ride back, Jim Fuller opened up about the simple song he wrote, way back in 1962.

This interview originally appeared in the book *Surfing USA!*, published by Voyageur Press in 2005.

Happy birthday to you. Happy birthday to you. Happy Birthday to you and your hit song "Wipe Out"....
Thank you. Forty years. Eight million broadcasts.

Wow.
That is what I have been saying for 40 years.

It wasn't planned this way?
Not even close. It was a fluke. We needed a B side.

A B Side to what?
Surfer Joe. It was a song that came to Ron Wilson in his sleep. We recorded it and it came out pretty good. We were so young and naïve we didn't know we needed a B Side.

Who were "we" and how young were "you?"
We were The Surfaris. I was 15 and the others were around there: Ron Wilson, Bob Berryhill and Ron Connolly. We were all from the Glendale area and we were still in high school. Our parents were driving us to gigs.

What kind of gigs?
Skating rinks. Teen clubs. We were lucky if we'd earn $10 to $15 a night, each.

Fun.
It was fun. It was 1963. We were a surf band.

Did you guys surf?
Sure. We were all from Glendale but we spent as much time at the beach as possible.

Where did Wipe Out *come from?*
We had a manager named Ron Smallen and he thought if we recorded a song we could buy a van for the band and some new instruments.

And maybe some new surfboards.
And some new surfboards. We all went to a recording studio in Cucamonga in December of 1962 and recorded *Surfer Joe*. It came out okay and then someone noted that we needed a song for the *other* side of the 45.

Traditionally, yes. Where did it come from?
Well Ron Wilson was in the high school marching band and he had this drum cadence that he speeded up.

Where do the sound effects at the start come from?
That was our manager Ron Smallen. He broke a board covered with plaster and then cackled "Wipe out!" into the mic.

Where did your guitar riff come from?
It was just something I had in my head. Something I had been working on for a couple of weeks.

And it all gelled there in the recording studio.
It came together rather nicely

What was your axe?
I had a ¾ neck Fender DuoSonic with a lot of reverb that night. I really liked that guitar and I wish I had held onto it, but who was to know what was coming? When *Wipe Out* became a hit the Surfaris cut a deal with Fender. We did some ads in music magazines and they gave us a lot of equipment. I got a brand-new red Dakota Stratocaster. I've been playing Strats ever since, but I do wish I still had that DuoSonic.

So you got your new equipment?
That and a lot more.

Wipe Out *has to be the simplest song ever written.*
Simple, but effective. We rehearsed it in six takes and then we nailed it.

And that was that. When did you know you had a hit?
We knew it was a hit when we turned on the radio and they were playing it non-stop. But that didn't happen right away. After we recorded in December, Ron Smallen hit the pavement and went all around Hollywood shoving it under people's noses. We were still doing gigs and driving to the middle of nowhere to play it for disc jockeys. But it paid off. By the third or fourth month it was getting some play and by June of 1963 it went to Number Two.

Surprised?
I was surprised. The band was surprised. My mom was surprised. I was still living with my mom and she was mind-blown. I paid off her house.

Such a good son. What did you do for yourself?
I was 16. It was the early 60s. I bought a hot car. We all bought hot cars. I went from a 1951 Willy's panel truck to a brand new, fire engine red GTO. Bob Berryhill upgraded his rodded, '56 Ford F 100 for a '64 Ford Galaxy 500 with a 427 that he raced at the drags. Pat Connolly bought a ram-inducted Dodge and Ron Wilson bought a Ford Fairlane.

Surfing and hot rods. The 60s. You were completely styling.
We were.

And you could drive yourself to gigs at the Skating Rink and the Teen Center.
Well that got an upgrade too. We started doing TV shows. *Shin Dig. Shiveree. Shebang. Ninth Street West. Hullabaloo.*

Tonight Show? Ed Sullivan?
Rock bands weren't doing those TV shows yet, but that was changed soon after by the Beatles and the British Invasion. And we weren't just driving to gigs, we were flying to them.

Where?
Our first tour was Hawaii with Bobby Vinton and the Crystals, and the second big tour was through Australia and the South Pacific with the Beach Boys and Roy Orbison and Paul and Paula.

Damn.
Yeah. I will always remember that Australia tour. And then we played Japan in front of a hundred thousand people.

Crazy, man. How long did it last?
The Surfaris were touring through 1964 and 1965 and *Wipe Out* somehow went to #16 again in 1965. Then the British Invasion swept into America and started to knock a lot of California bands off the charts.

Did you get rich off Wipe Out?
Well, not rich. If you have a hit song like that these days you're living in the Malibu Colony. But *Wipe Out* has been a solid income over the last 40 years.

You kept all the rights?
Yes. The Surfaris retained all the publishing and copyright licenses.

Smart lads.
Yes. If you go to the BMI website and plug in *Wipe Out* you will see all the bands who have recorded it.

The Beach Boys, Camp California, The Challengers, Davie Allan and the Arrows, Fat Boys, Harlow Wilcox and the Oakies, Lively Ones, The Lucy Show, The Muppets, the Psychotic Frogs, The Tempos, Terry Gordon, Thunders Johnnny, Tony Lane and the Fabulous Spades and the Ventures.

I've heard the song used commercially for In and Out, Wendy's, some scrub cloths, Burger King. *Wipe Out* has been used in movie soundtracks for *Meet the Parents* and *Back to the Beach* and *Dirty Dancing*. We were on the *Dirty Dancing* soundtrack so I got a triple platinum plaque.

And you get a residual from all those uses?
Comes in quarterly.

That is just about the coolest thing I have ever heard. Are you still playing?
I play quite a bit with the Surfaris, mostly from spring through fall and in the winter we do corporate parties. And then Dennis Dooley and I play around our schedule with the Beatniks. We've got 8 pieces and that includes two backup singers who did some time with Boz Scaggs and J Lo.

You wrote a simple song.
We wrote and recorded a simple song and it is still going.

And now BMI is saying it has been played 8 million times on the radio.
Eight million times in 40 years. That is 200,000 times a year.

And that probably doesn't include high school marching bands.
Who would have thought?

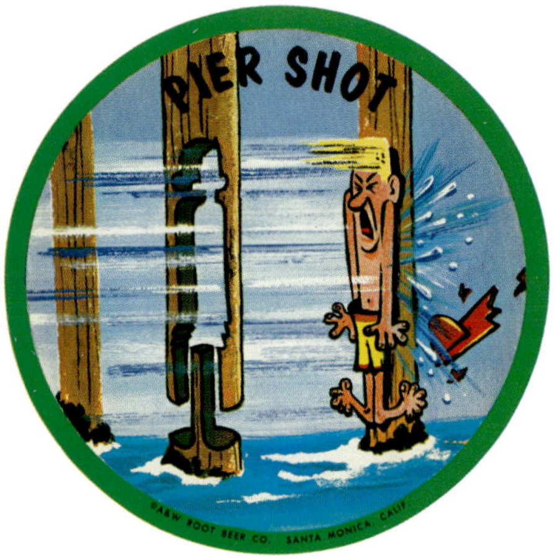
PIER SHOT
©A&W ROOT BEER CO. SANTA MONICA, CALIF.

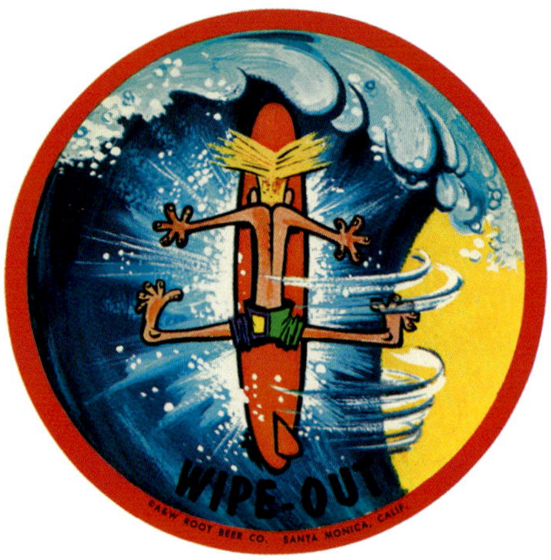
WIPE-OUT
©A&W ROOT BEER CO. SANTA MONICA, CALIF.

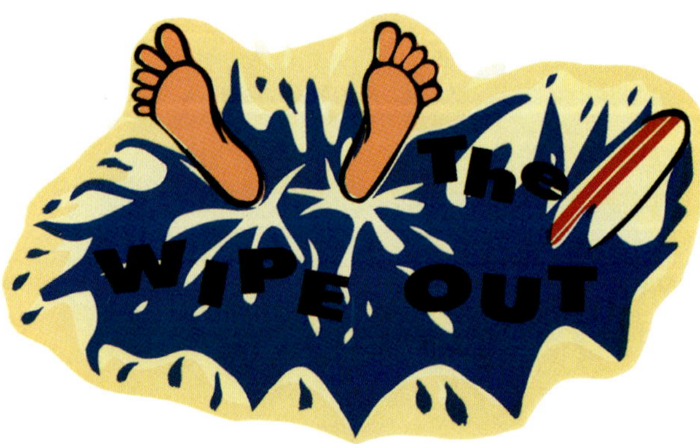
The
WIPE OUT

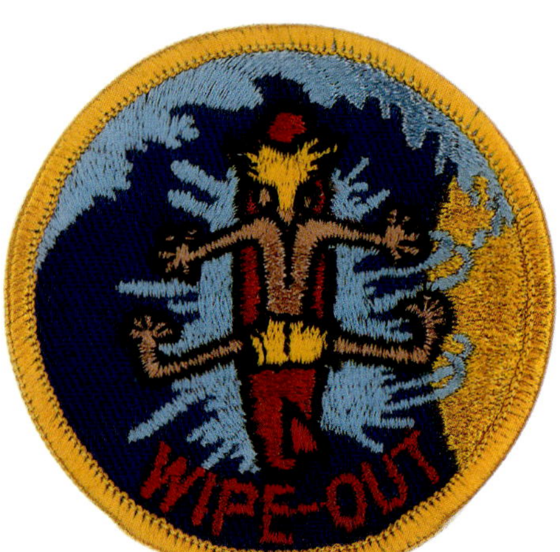
WIPE-OUT

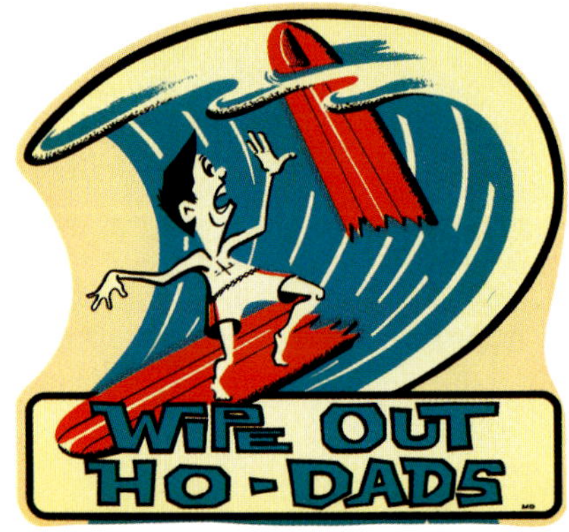
WIPE OUT
HO-DADS

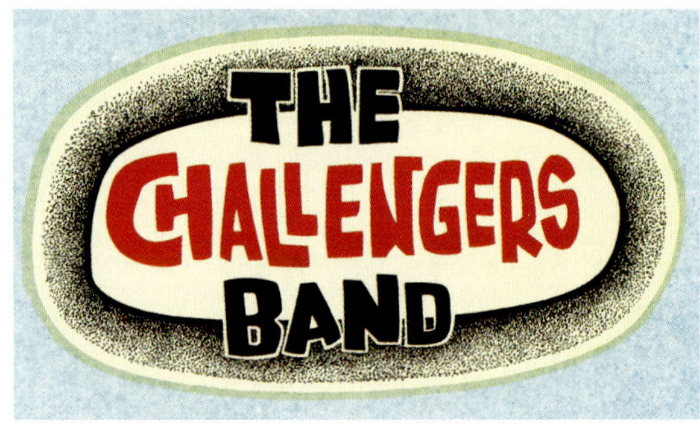
THE
CHALLENGERS
BAND

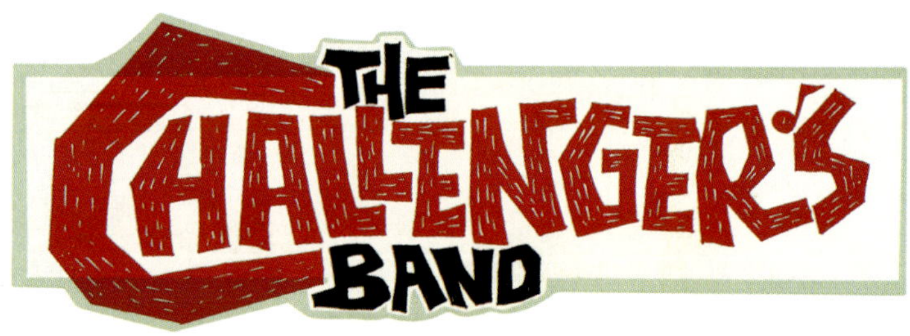
THE
CHALLENGER'S
BAND

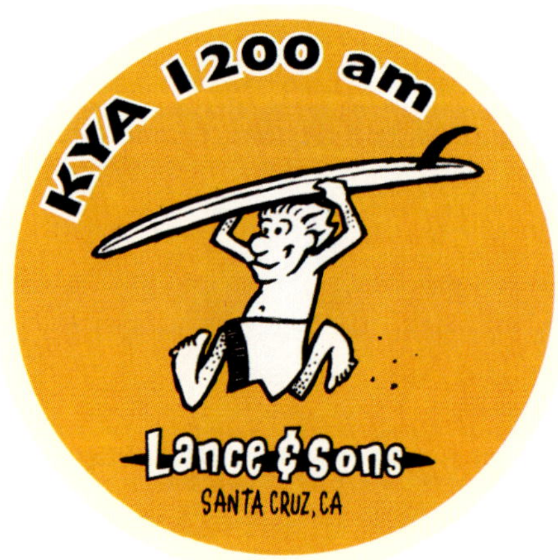
KYA 1200 am
Lance & Sons
SANTA CRUZ, CA

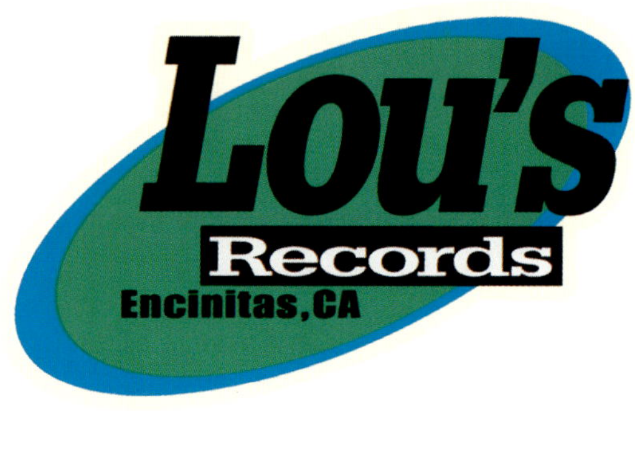
Lou's
Records
Encinitas, CA

CHAPTER 4.2
SURFER JOE

In 1962, The Surfaris sang: "Surfer Joe went to Huntington Beach one week for the annual surfing convention meet. He was hangin' five and walkin' the nose and when the meet was over, the trophy was Joe's."

In 1962, the big contest was the United States Amateur Surfing Championships in Huntington Beach. Surfers were required to wear plastic helmets in case they collided with the pier.

Since 1962, the number of surf contests around the world has mutated and now there are hundreds of contests around the world: local and international, amateur and professional.

These stickers represent some of those events, followed by stickers of the various organizations that run the events.

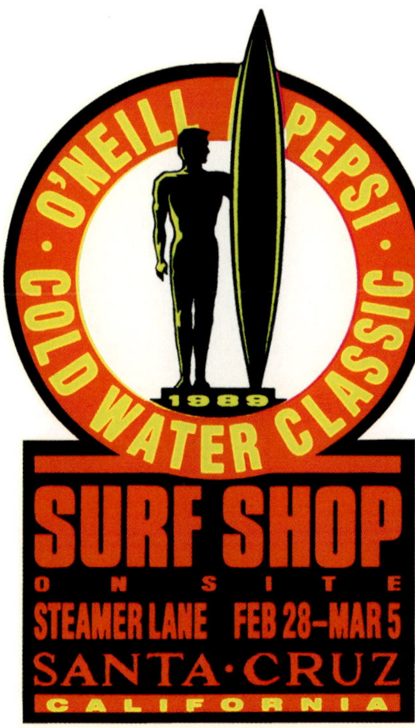

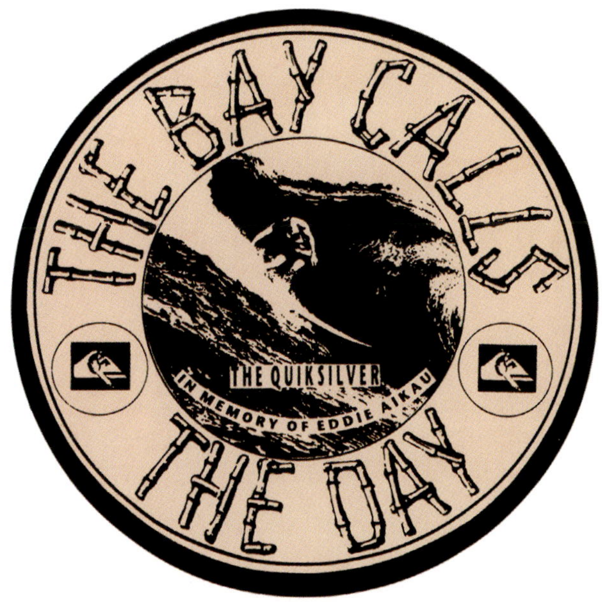

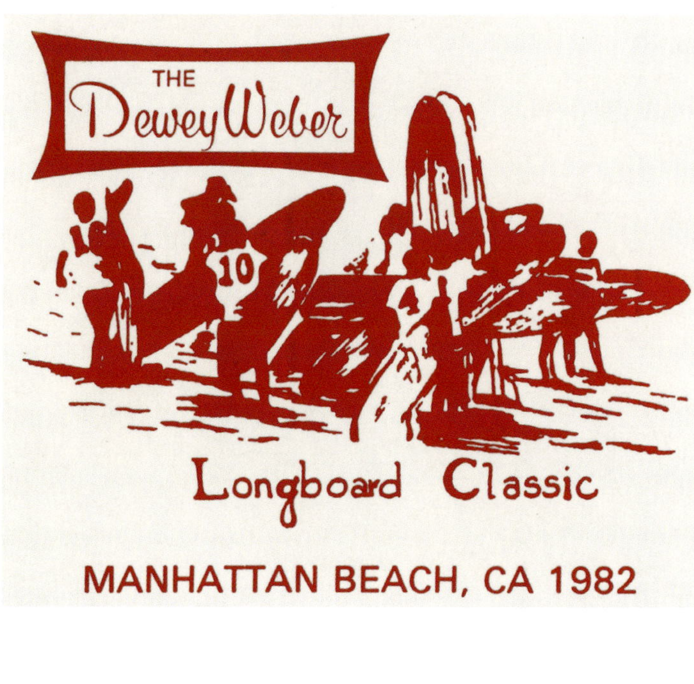

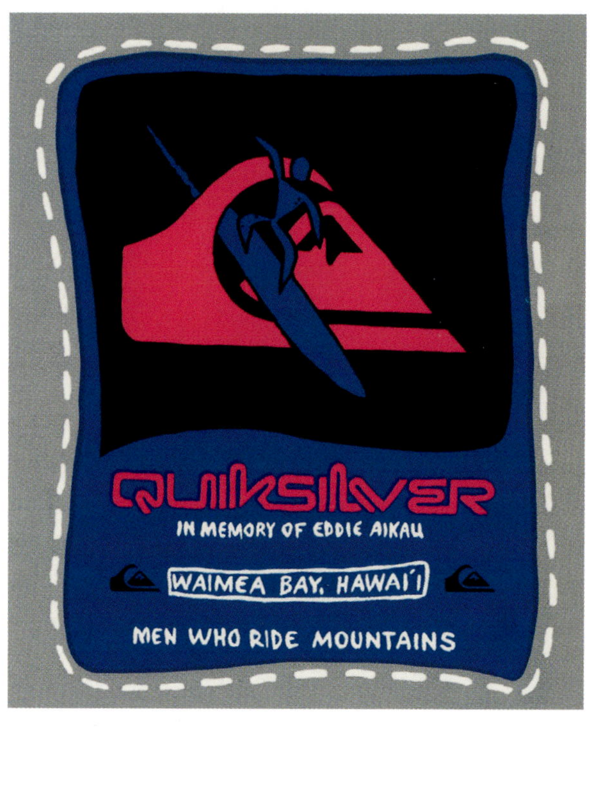

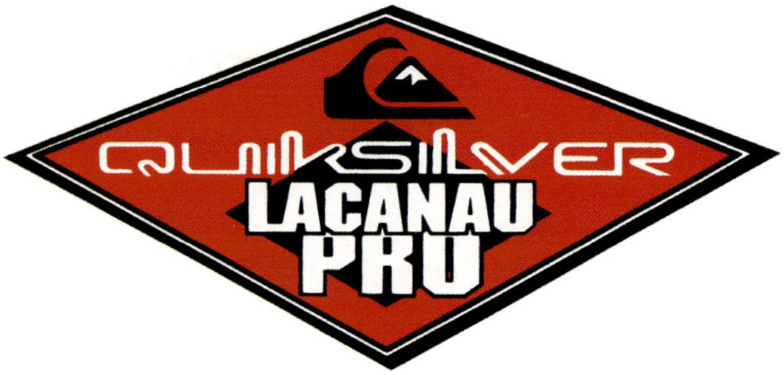
QUIKSILVER
LACANAU
PRO

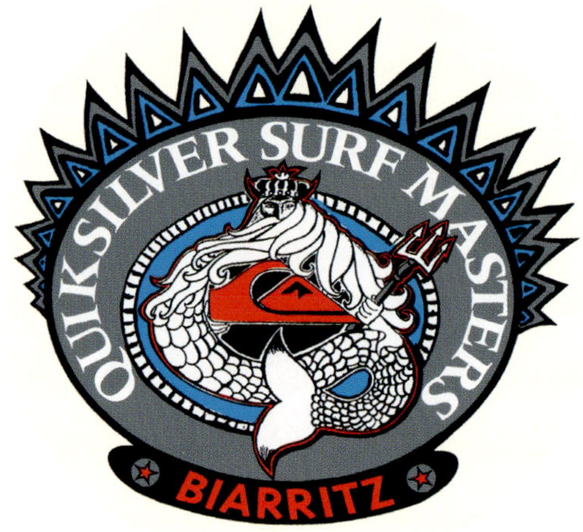
QUIKSILVER SURF MASTERS
BIARRITZ

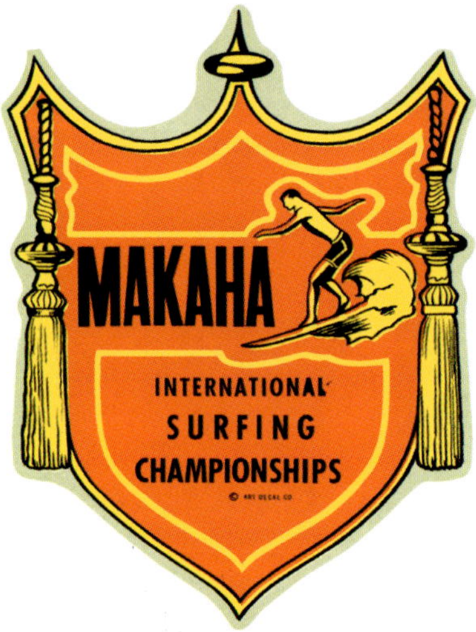
MAKAHA
INTERNATIONAL
SURFING
CHAMPIONSHIPS

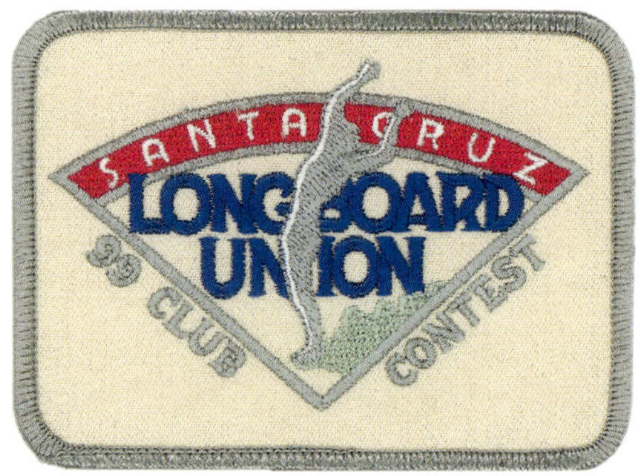
SANTA CRUZ
LONGBOARD
UNION
99 CLUB
CONTEST

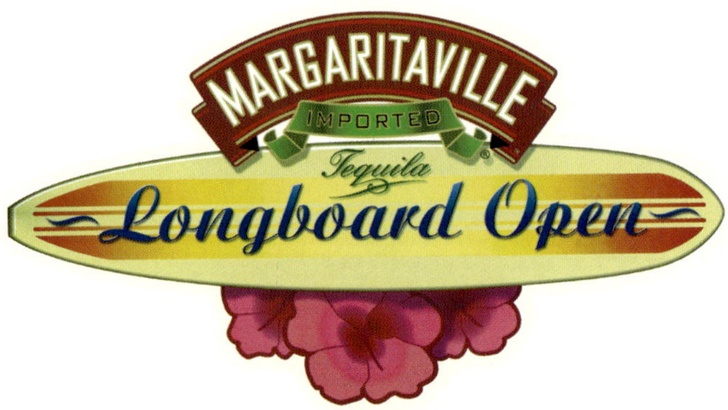
MARGARITAVILLE
IMPORTED
Tequila
Longboard Open

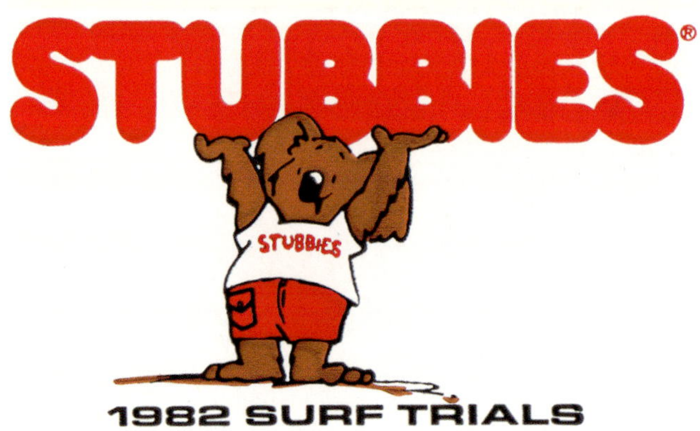
STUBBIES®
STUBBIES
1982 SURF TRIALS

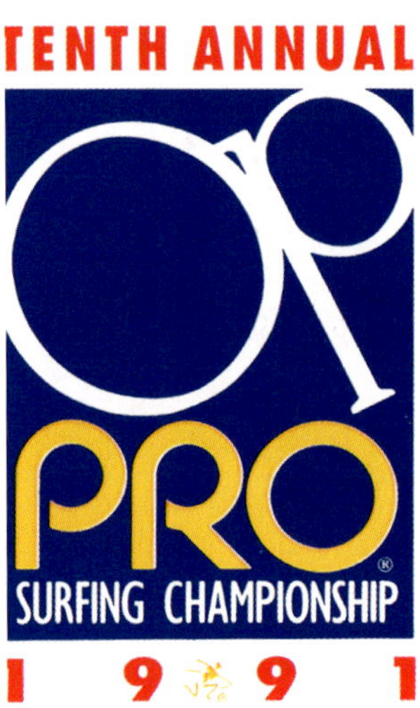
TENTH ANNUAL
OP
PRO®
SURFING CHAMPIONSHIP
1 9 9 1

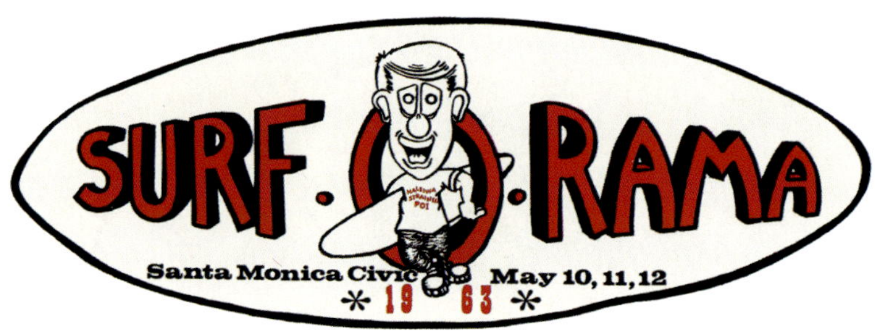
SURF-O-RAMA
Santa Monica Civic
May 10, 11, 12
19 63

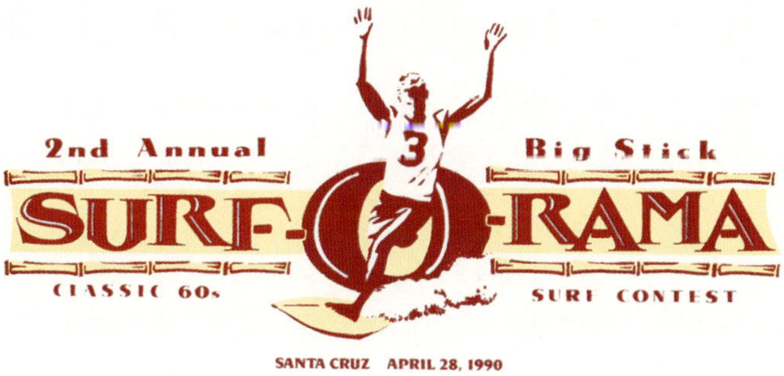
2nd Annual
Big Stick
SURF-O-RAMA
CLASSIC 60s
SURF CONTEST
SANTA CRUZ APRIL 28, 1990

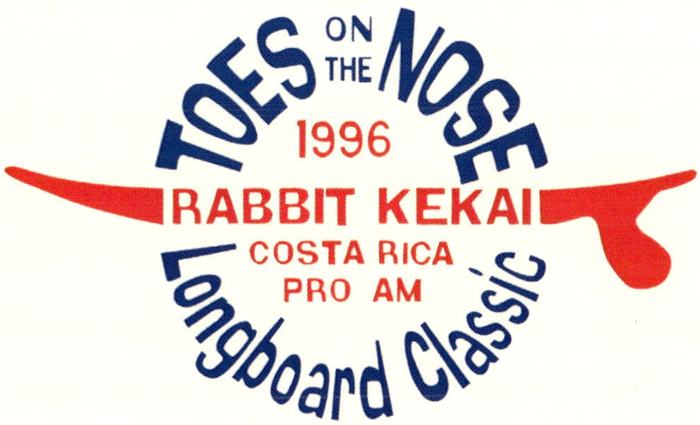
TOES ON THE NOSE
1996
RABBIT KEKAI
COSTA RICA
PRO AM
Longboard Classic

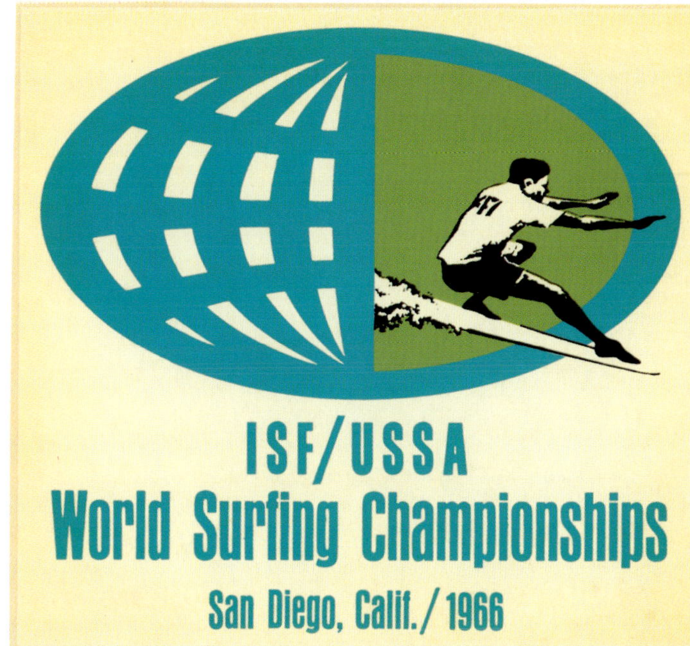
ISF/USSA
World Surfing Championships
San Diego, Calif./1966

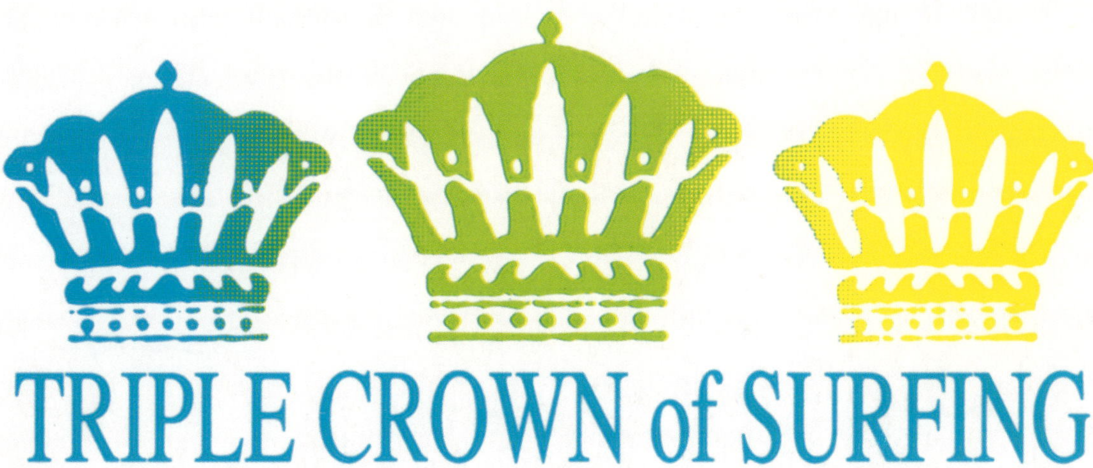
TRIPLE CROWN of SURFING

sunwear
WORLD CUP OF SURFING

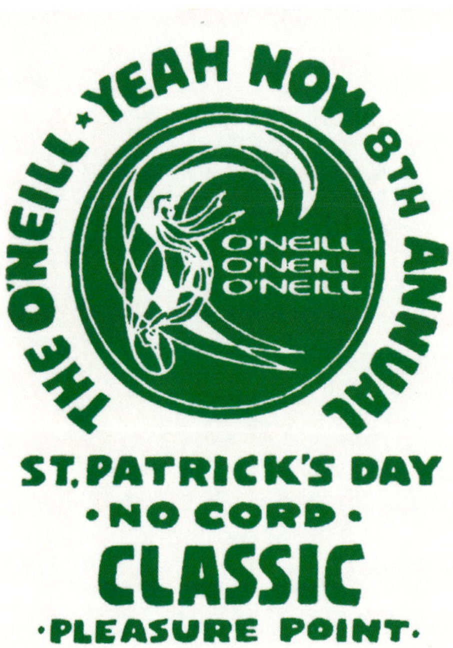
THE O'NEILL ★ YEAH NOW 8TH ANNUAL
O'NEILL
O'NEILL
O'NEILL
ST. PATRICK'S DAY
· NO CORD ·
CLASSIC
· PLEASURE POINT ·

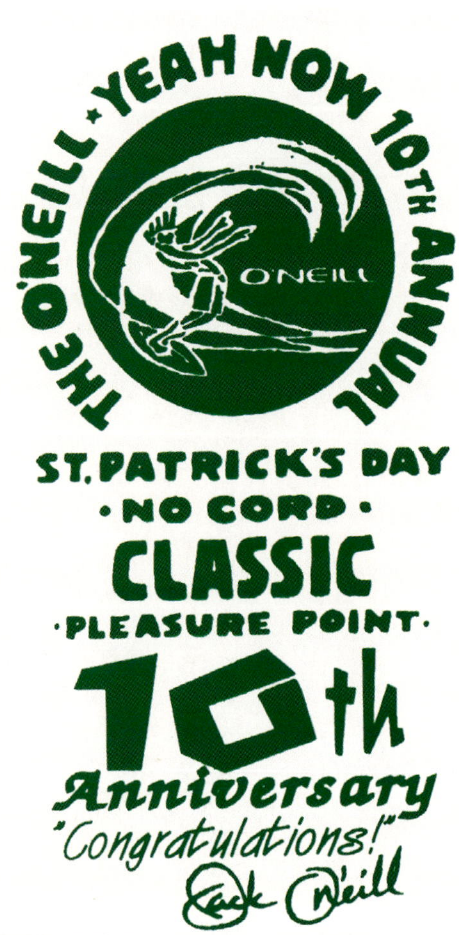
THE O'NEILL ★ YEAH NOW 10TH ANNUAL
O'NEILL
ST. PATRICK'S DAY
· NO CORD ·
CLASSIC
· PLEASURE POINT ·
10th
Anniversary
"Congratulations!"
Jack O'Neill

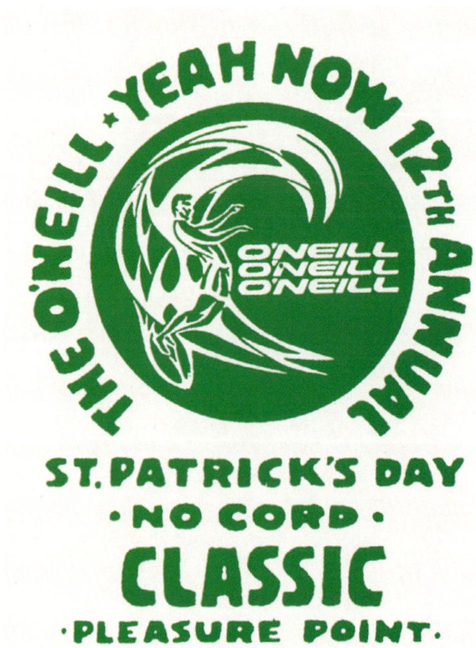
THE O'NEILL ★ YEAH NOW 12TH ANNUAL
O'NEILL
O'NEILL
O'NEILL
ST. PATRICK'S DAY
· NO CORD ·
CLASSIC
· PLEASURE POINT ·

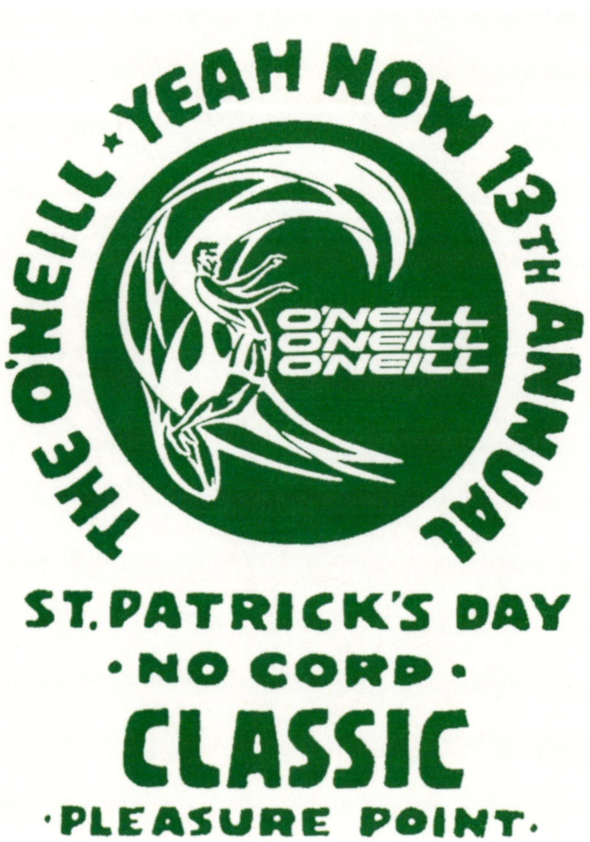
THE O'NEILL ★ YEAH NOW 13TH ANNUAL
O'NEILL
O'NEILL
O'NEILL
ST. PATRICK'S DAY
· NO CORD ·
CLASSIC
· PLEASURE POINT ·

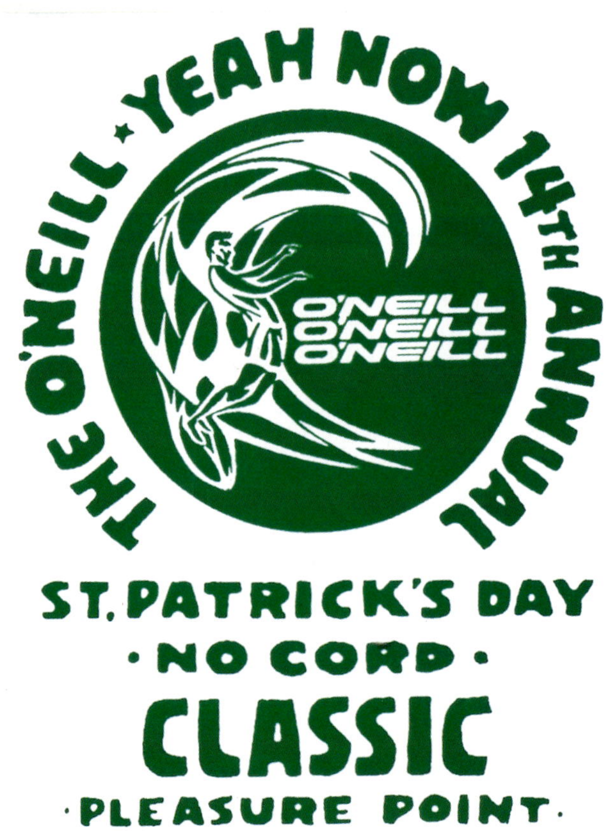
THE O'NEILL ★ YEAH NOW 14TH ANNUAL
O'NEILL
O'NEILL
O'NEILL
ST. PATRICK'S DAY
· NO CORD ·
CLASSIC
· PLEASURE POINT ·

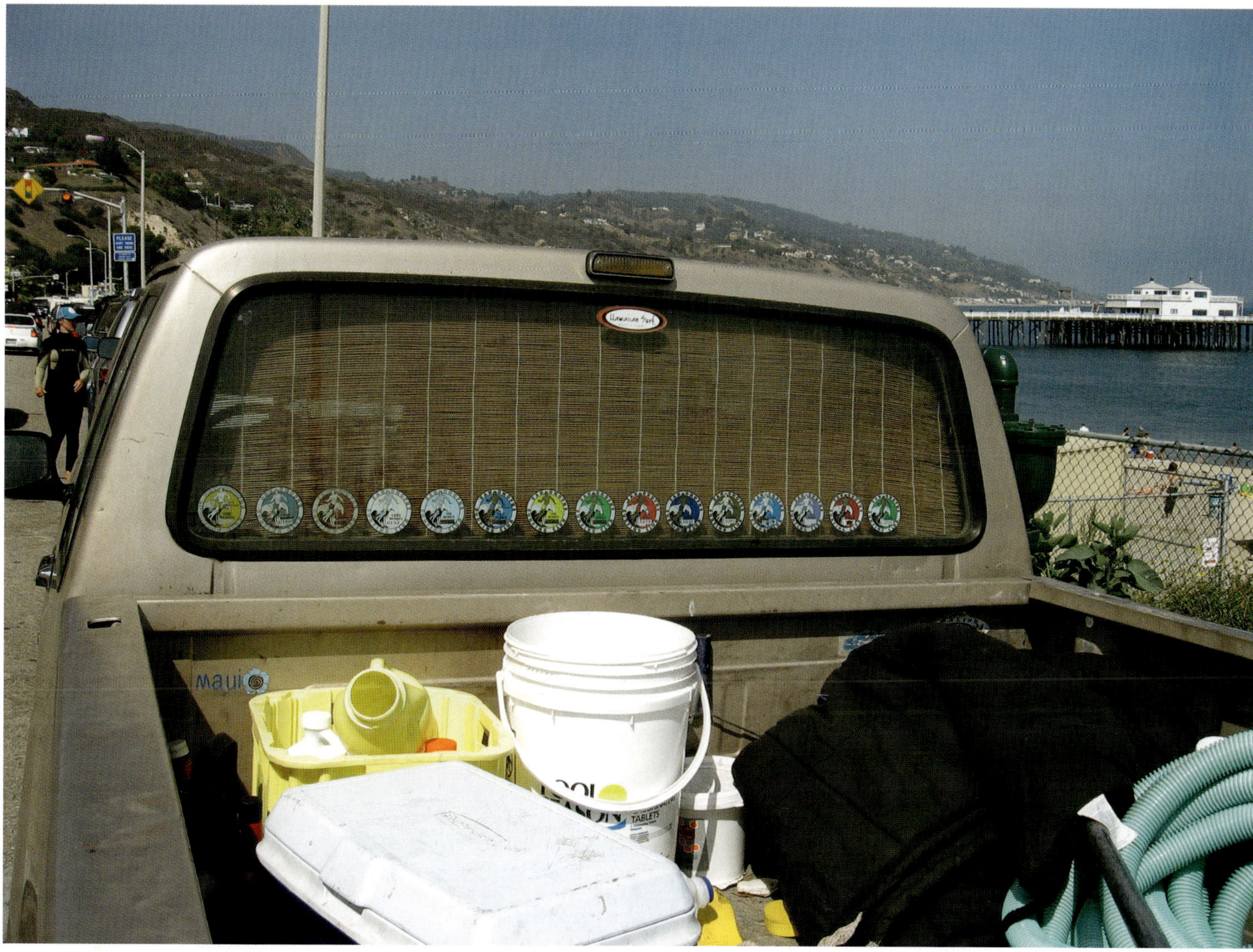

A pickup truck owned by Malibu Tom, showing 15 years of San Onofre Surf Club stickers. Photo: Ben Marcus.

4.3 CLUBS AND ORGANIZATIONS

The popularity of surf clubs has ebbed and flowed over the years. They were most popular in the 60s, when surfing beaches were worlds unto themselves and local surfers grouped into clubs to compete against other beaches up and down the coast.

Surf clubs died off a bit in the too-cool 70s, when surfing went underground. *Surfer Magazine* cancelled the Surfer Poll, and localism began to emerge up and down California, in Hawaii and around the world.

The longboard revival began in the late 70s and spread into the 80s and surf clubs began to appear again.

These are patches and stickers for surf clubs and competitive organizations around the world.

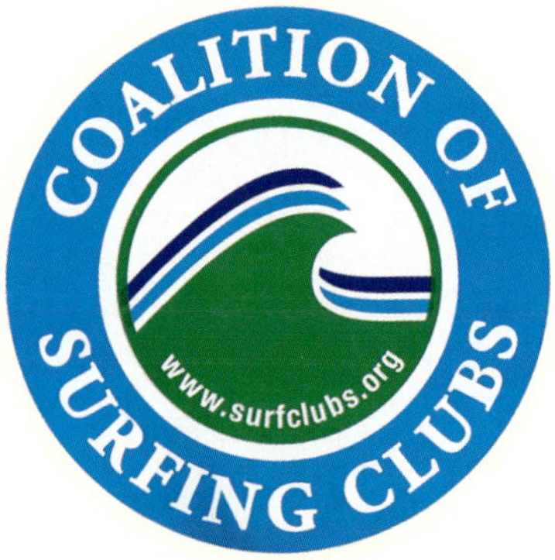
COALITION OF
SURFING CLUBS
www.surfclubs.org

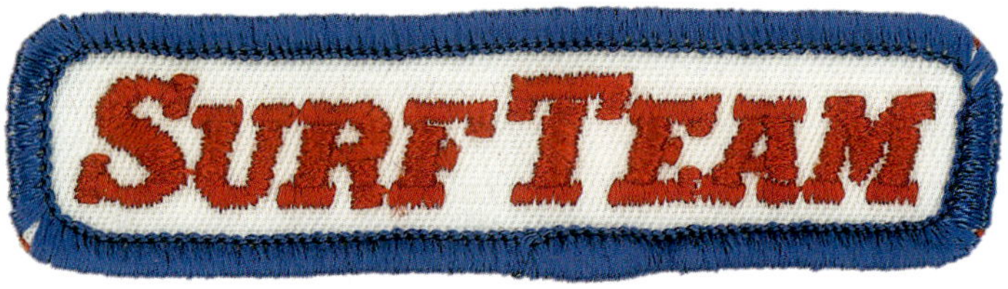
SURF TEAM

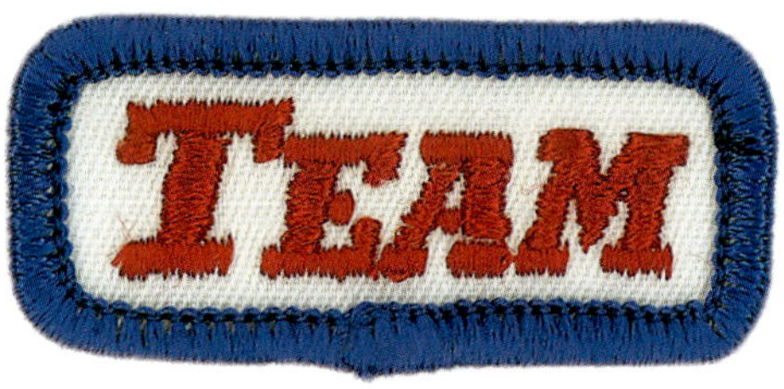
TEAM

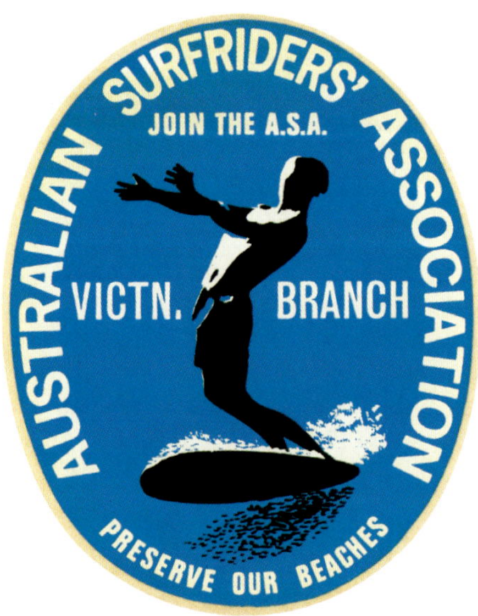
AUSTRALIAN SURFRIDERS' ASSOCIATION
JOIN THE A.S.A.
VICTN.
BRANCH
PRESERVE OUR BEACHES

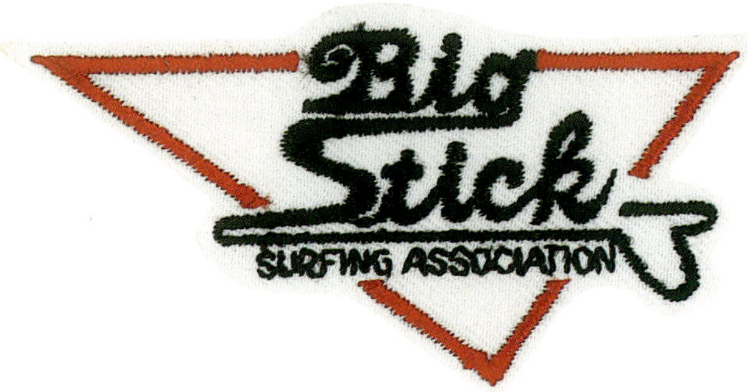
Big
Stick
SURFING ASSOCIATION

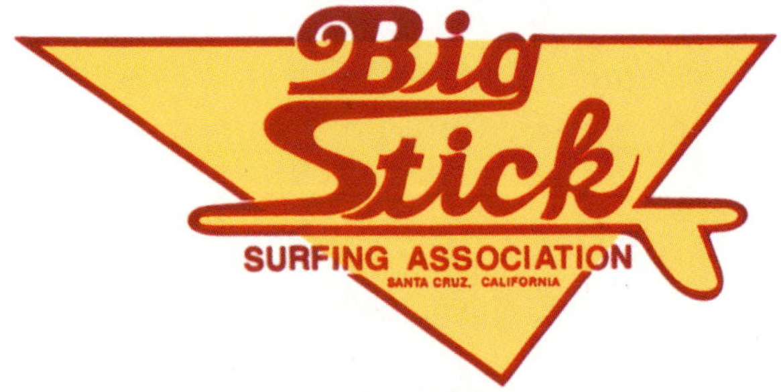
Big
Stick
SURFING ASSOCIATION
SANTA CRUZ, CALIFORNIA

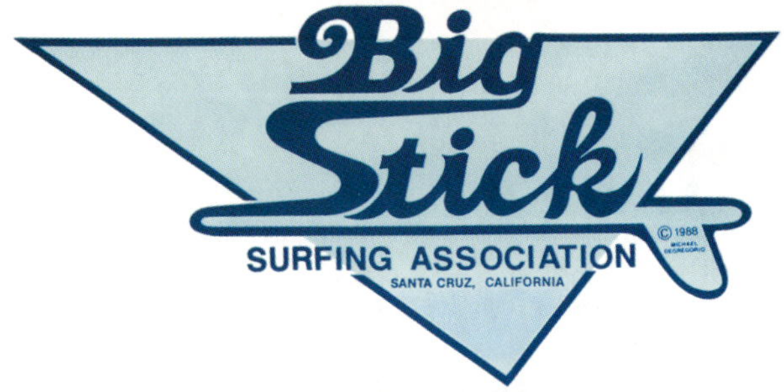
Big
Stick
SURFING ASSOCIATION
© 1988
SANTA CRUZ, CALIFORNIA

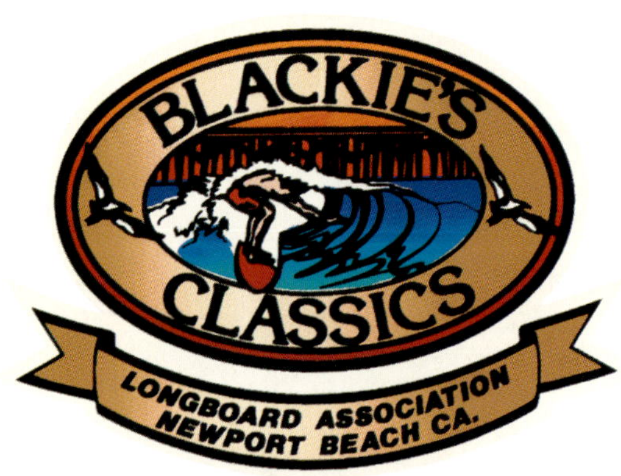
BLACKIE'S
CLASSICS
LONGBOARD ASSOCIATION
NEWPORT BEACH CA.

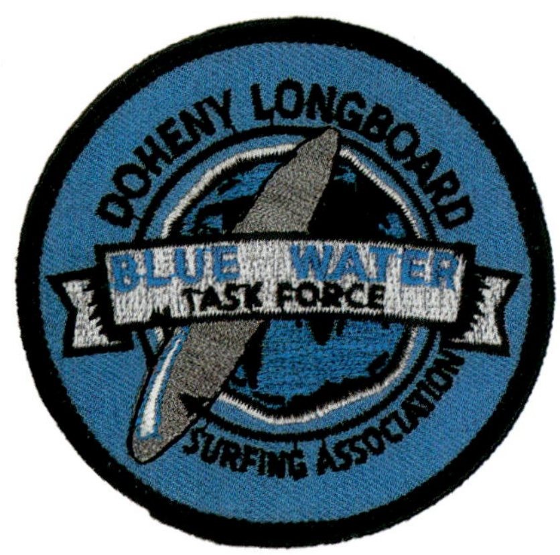
DOHENY LONGBOARD
BLUE WATER
TASK FORCE
SURFING ASSOCIATION

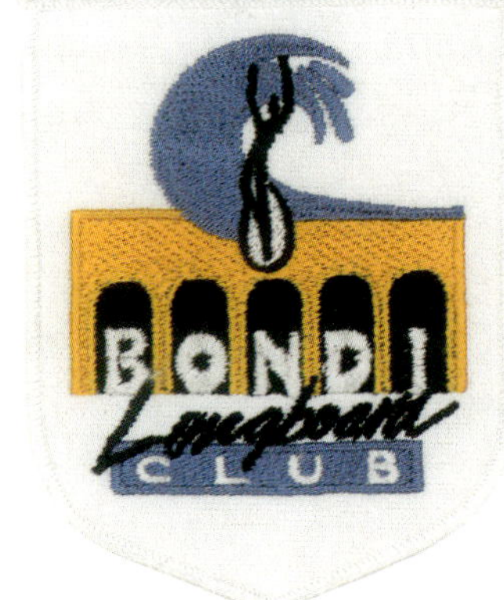
BONDI
Longboard
CLUB

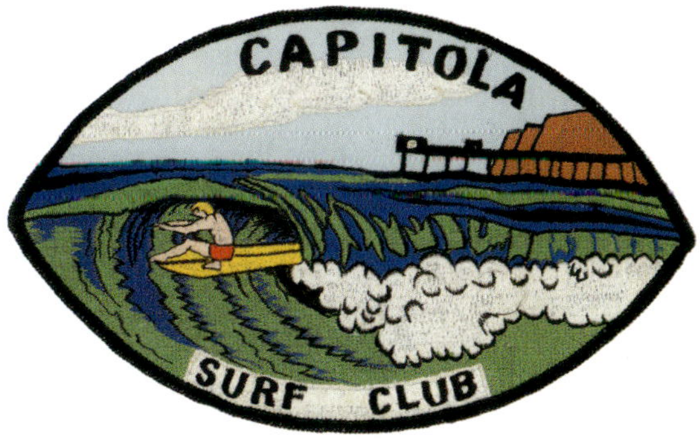
CAPITOLA
SURF CLUB

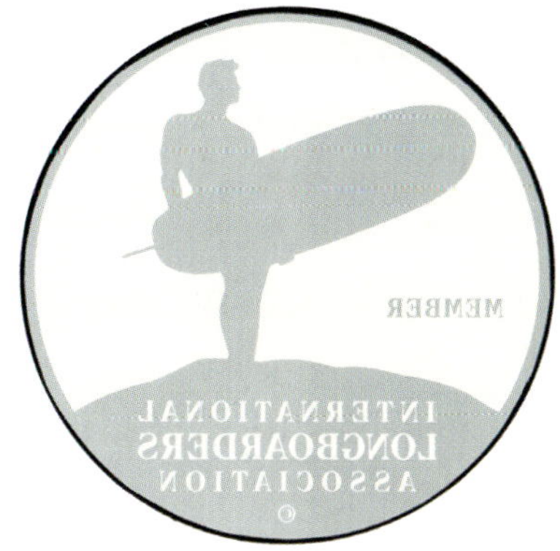
MEMBER
INTERNATIONAL
LONGBOARDERS
ASSOCIATION

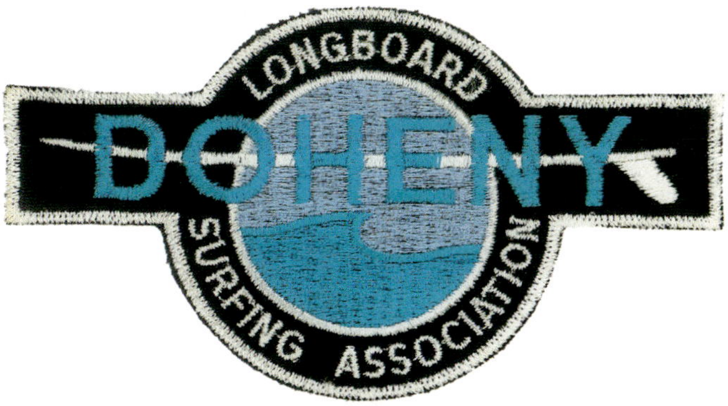
LONGBOARD
DOHENY
SURFING ASSOCIATION

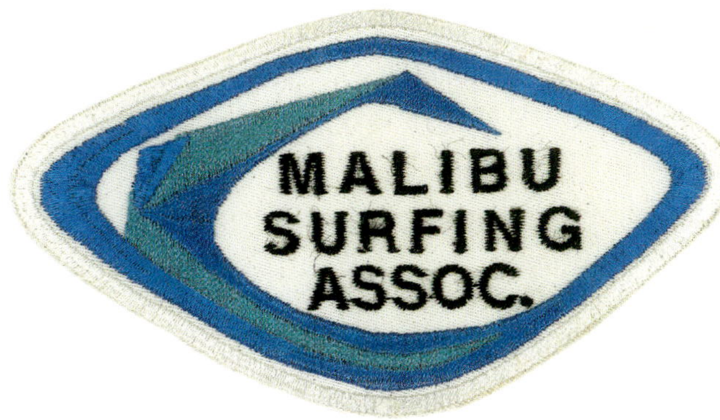
MALIBU
SURFING
ASSOC.

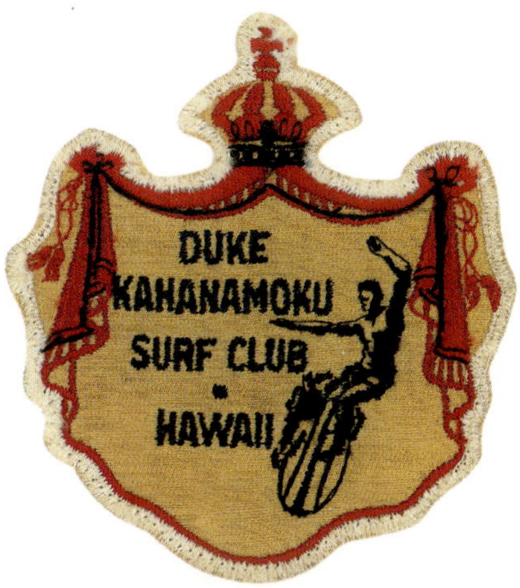
DUKE
KAHANAMOKU
SURF CLUB
HAWAII

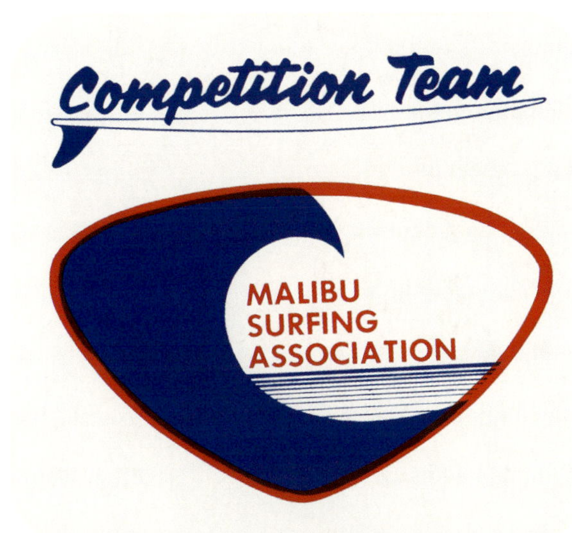
Competition Team
MALIBU
SURFING
ASSOCIATION

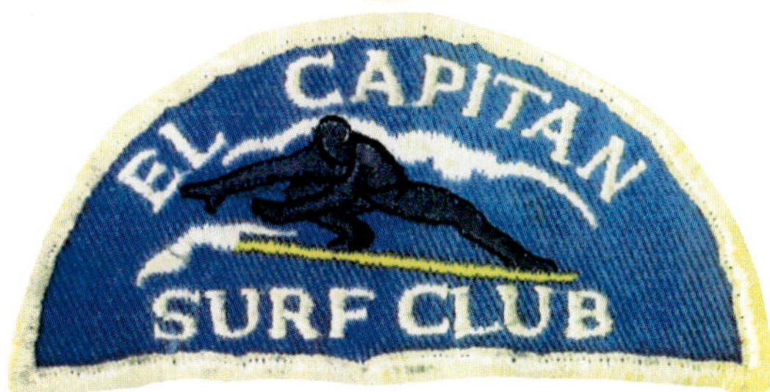
EL CAPITAN
SURF CLUB

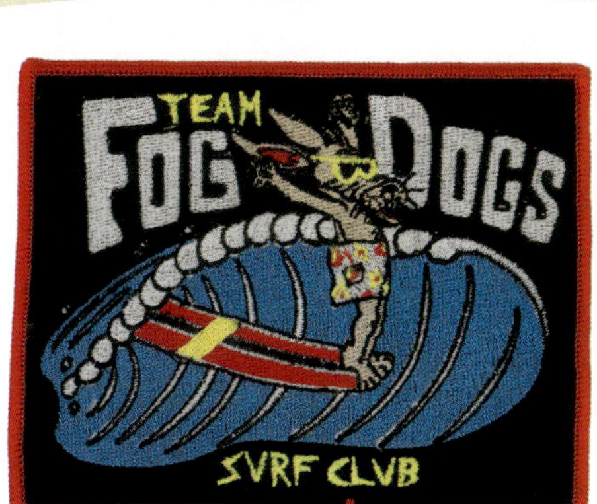
TEAM
FOG DOGS
SVRF CLVB

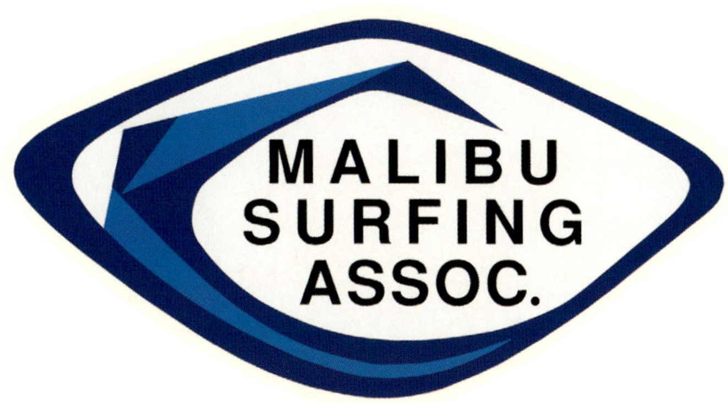
MALIBU
SURFING
ASSOC.

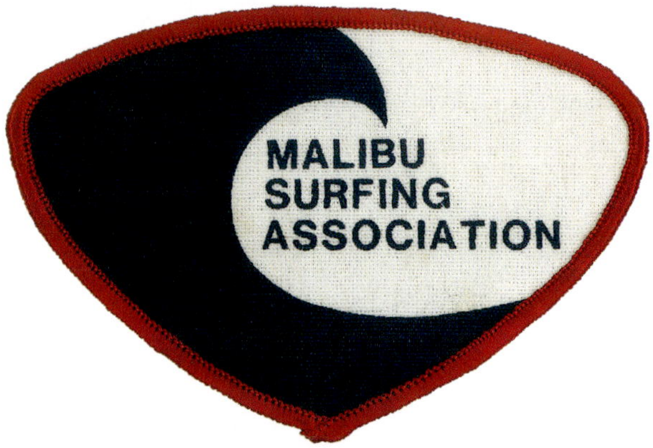
MALIBU
SURFING
ASSOCIATION

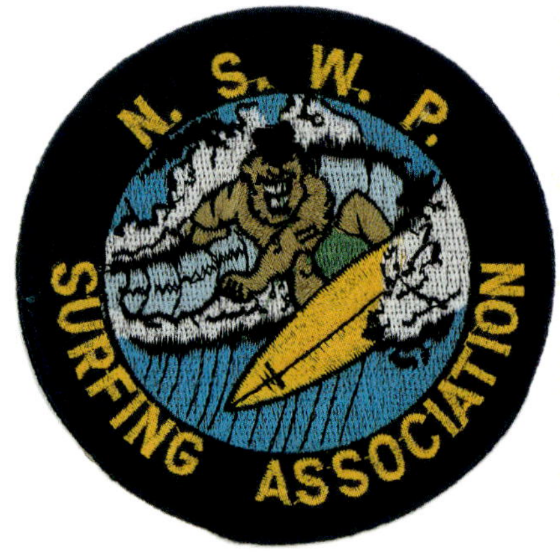
N. S. W. P.
SURFING ASSOCIATION

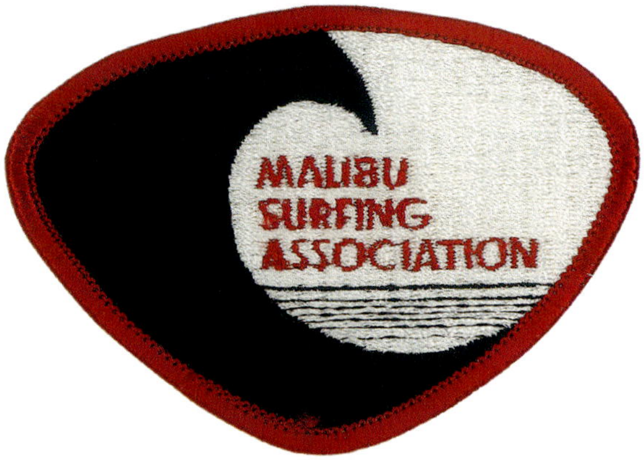
MALIBU
SURFING
ASSOCIATION

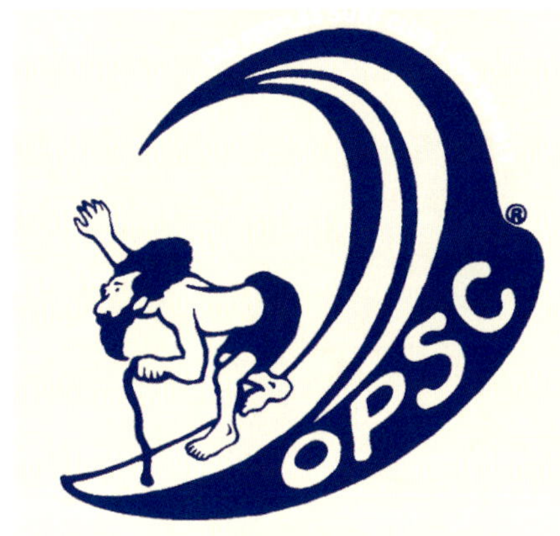
OPSC

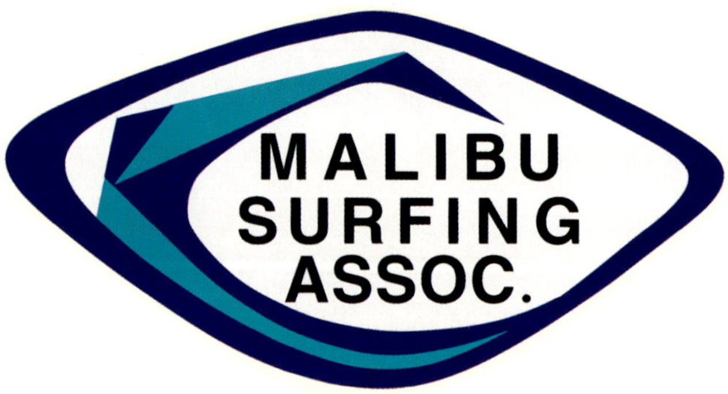
MALIBU
SURFING
ASSOC.

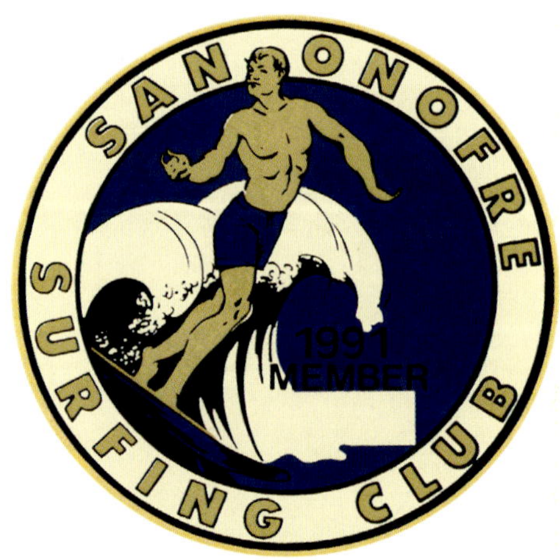
SAN ONOFRE
SURFING CLUB
1991
MEMBER

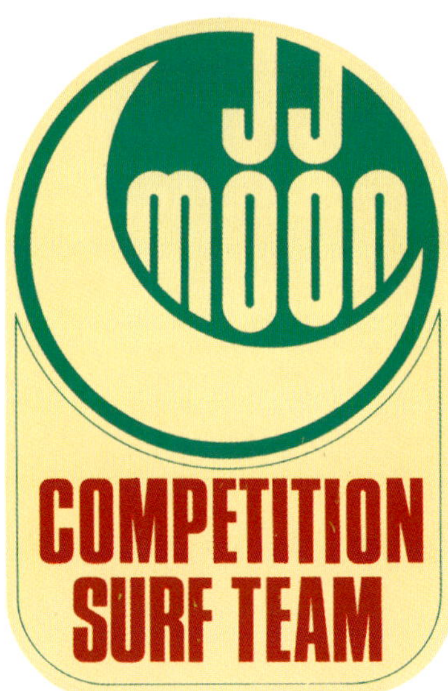
JJ
moon
COMPETITION
SURF TEAM

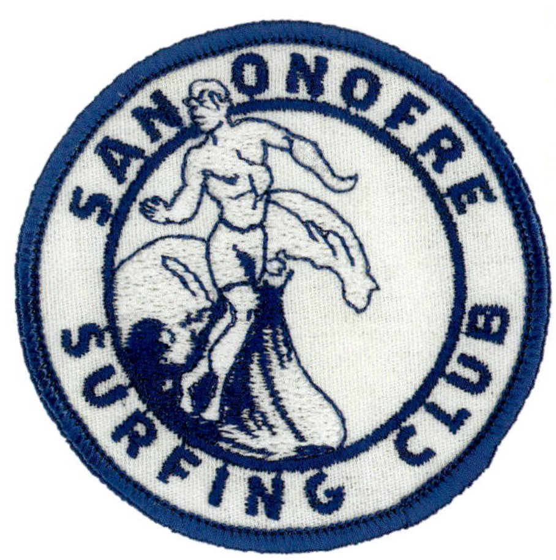
SAN ONOFRE
SURFING CLUB

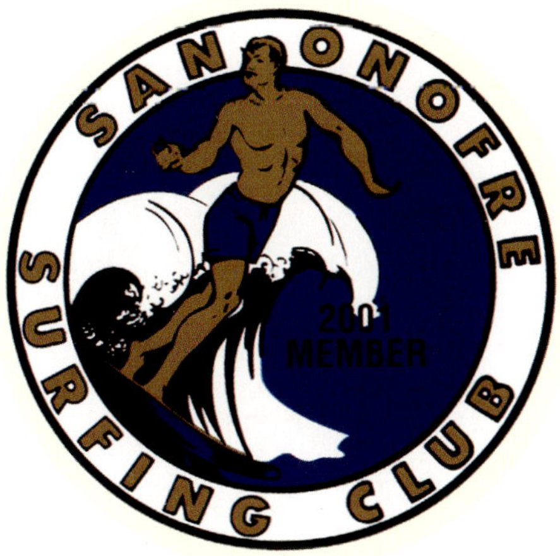
SAN ONOFRE
SURFING CLUB
2001
MEMBER

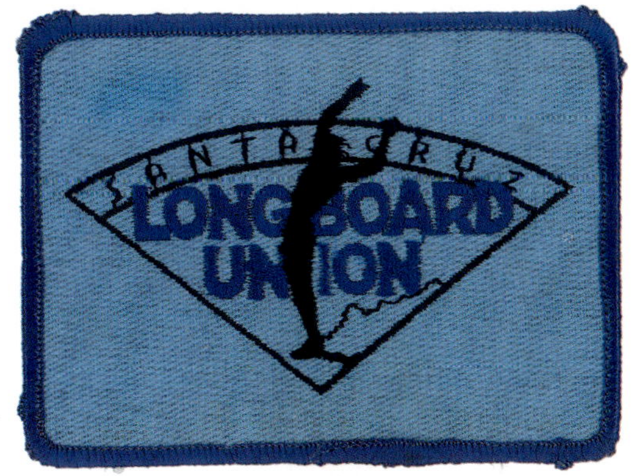
SANTA CRUZ
LONGBOARD
UNION

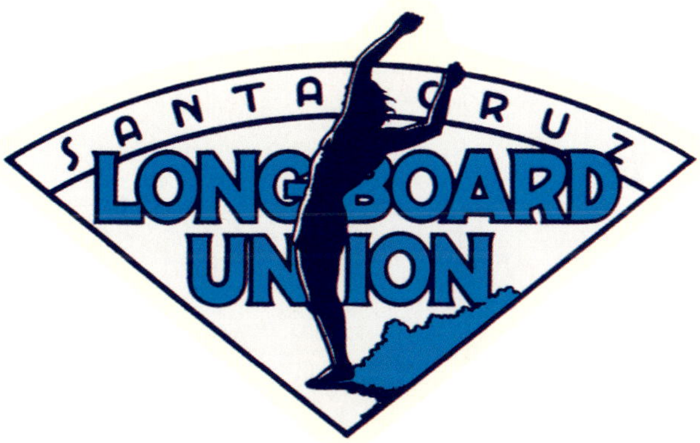
SANTA CRUZ
LONGBOARD
UNION

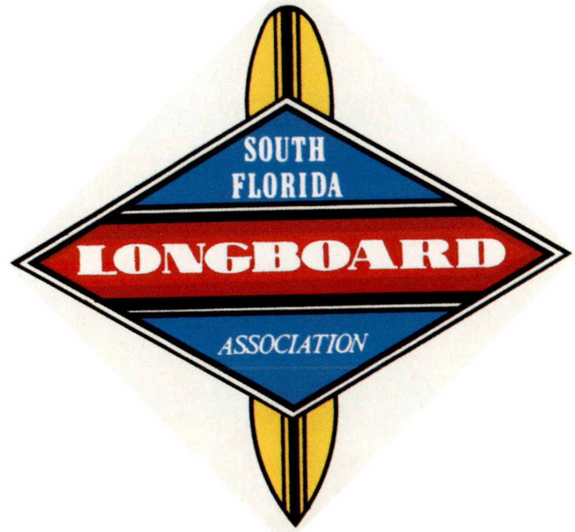
SOUTH
FLORIDA
LONGBOARD
ASSOCIATION

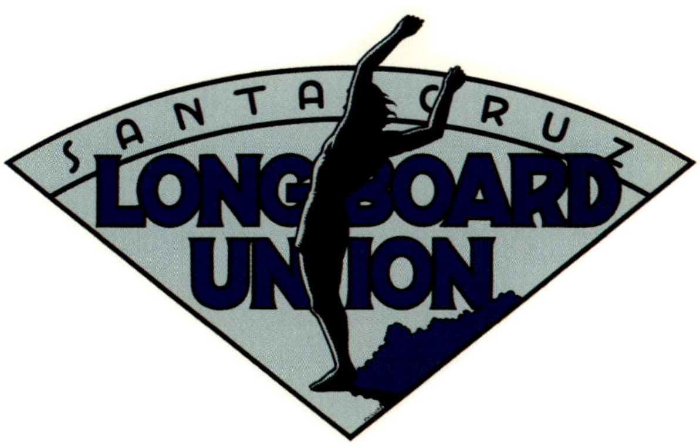
SANTA CRUZ
LONGBOARD
UNION

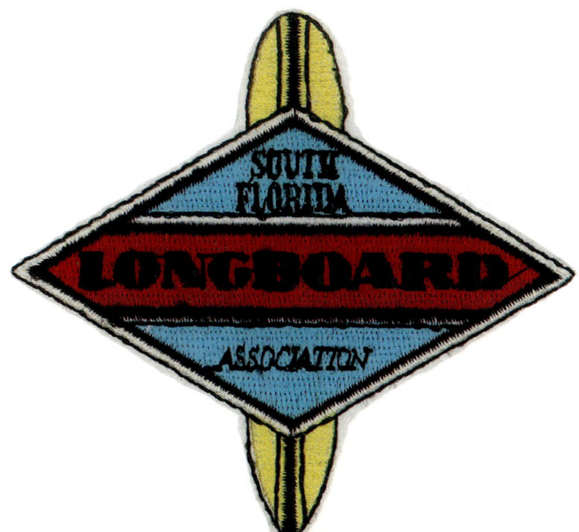
SOUTH
FLORIDA
LONGBOARD
ASSOCIATION

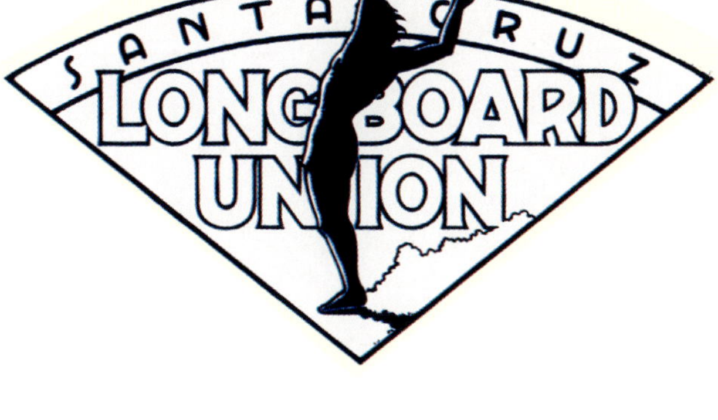
SANTA CRUZ
LONGBOARD
UNION

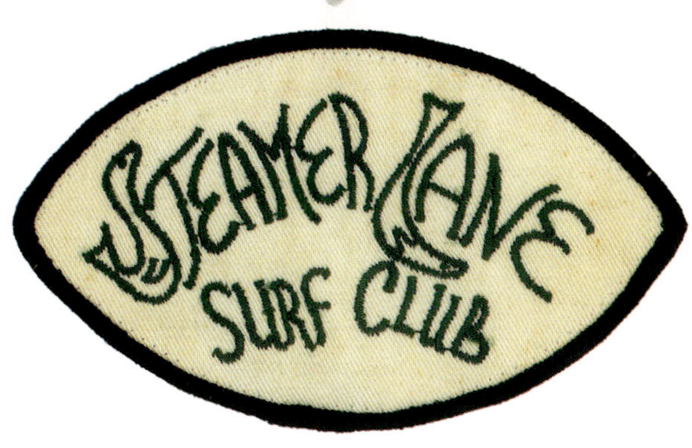
STEAMER LANE
SURF CLUB

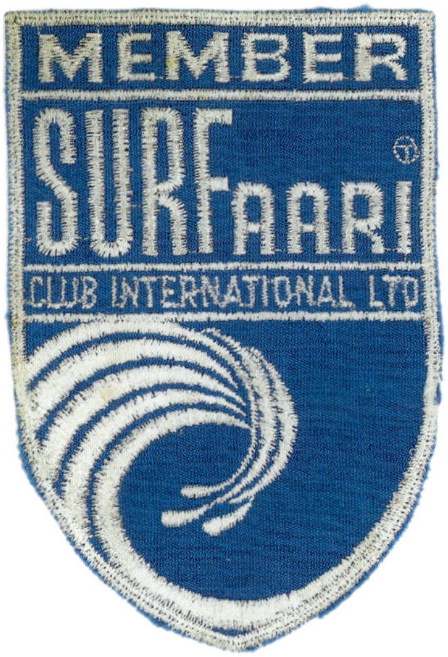
MEMBER
SURFAARI
CLUB INTERNATIONAL LTD

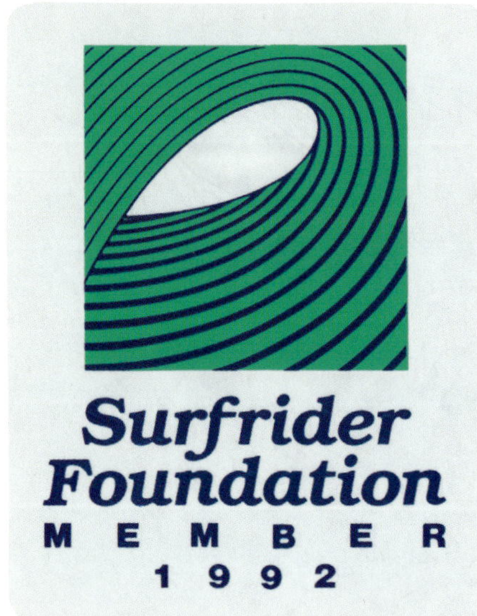
Surfrider
Foundation
MEMBER
1992

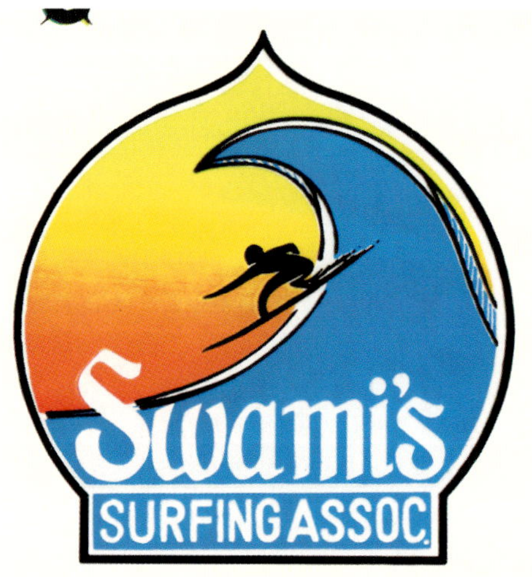
Swami's
SURFING ASSOC.

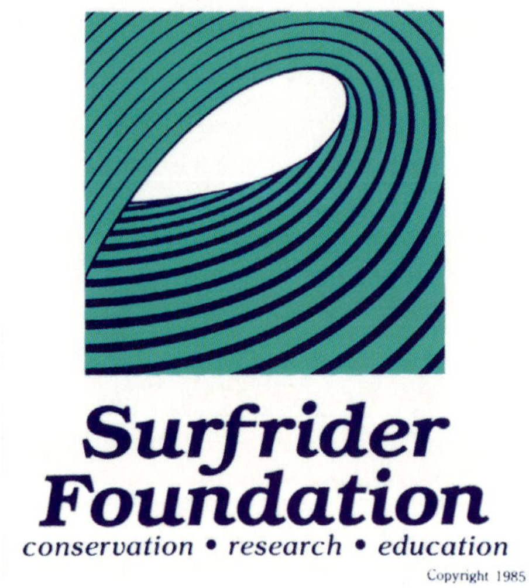
Surfrider
Foundation
conservation • research • education
Copyright 1985

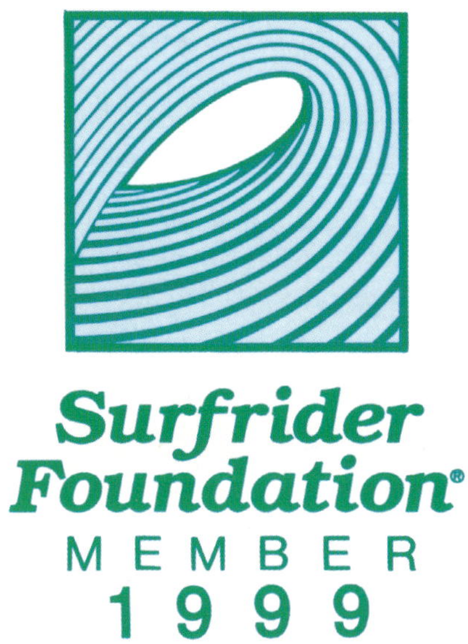
Surfrider
Foundation®
MEMBER
1999

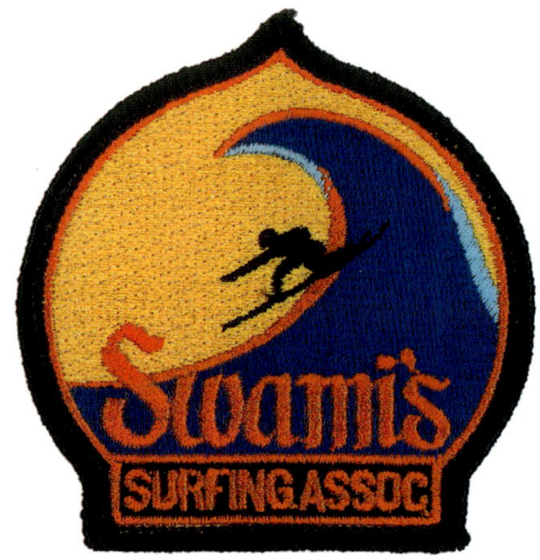
Swami's
SURFING ASSOC

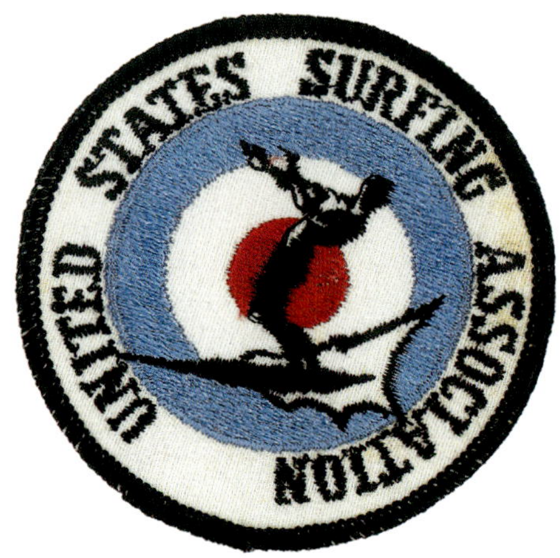
UNITED STATES SURFING ASSOCIATION

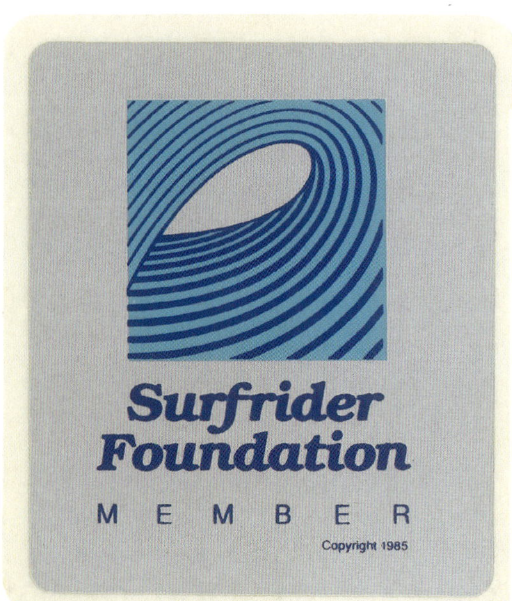
Surfrider
Foundation
MEMBER
Copyright 1985

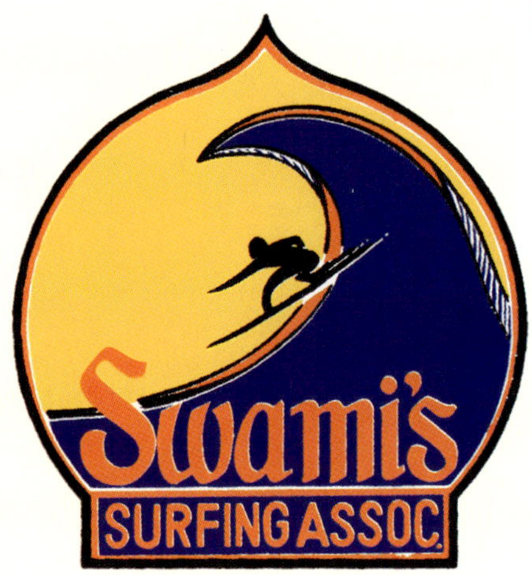
Swami's
SURFING ASSOC.

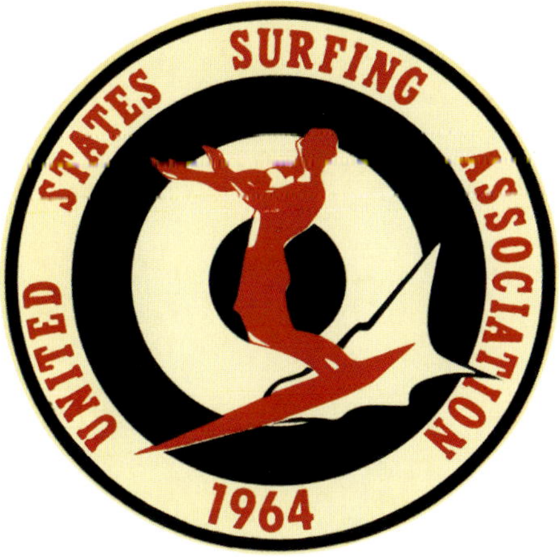
UNITED STATES SURFING ASSOCIATION
1964

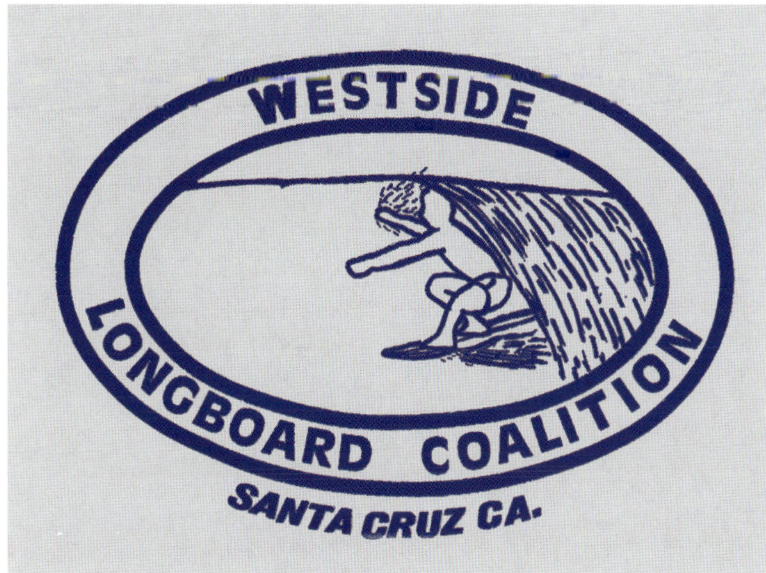
WESTSIDE
LONGBOARD COALITION
SANTA CRUZ CA.

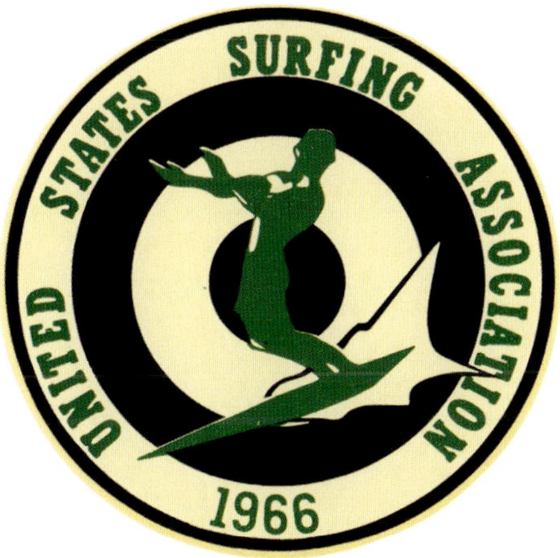
UNITED STATES SURFING ASSOCIATION
1966

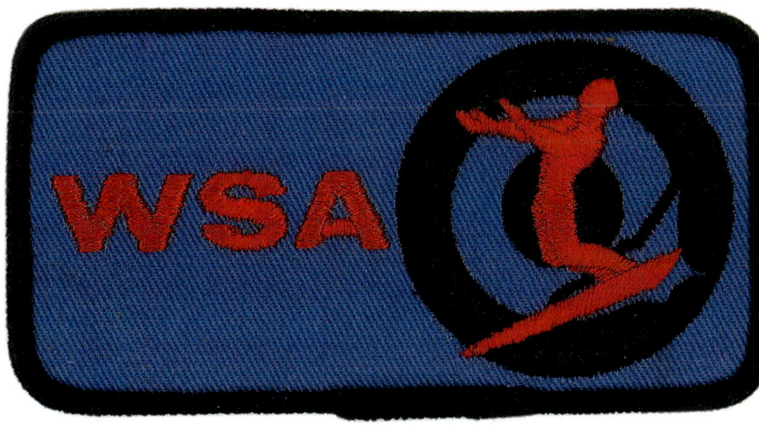
WSA

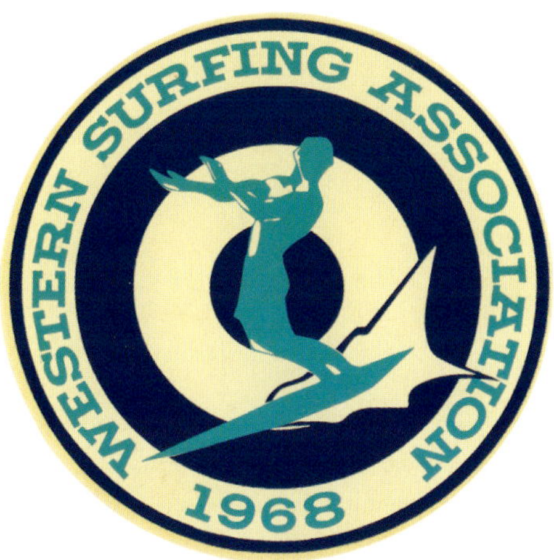
WESTERN SURFING ASSOCIATION
1968

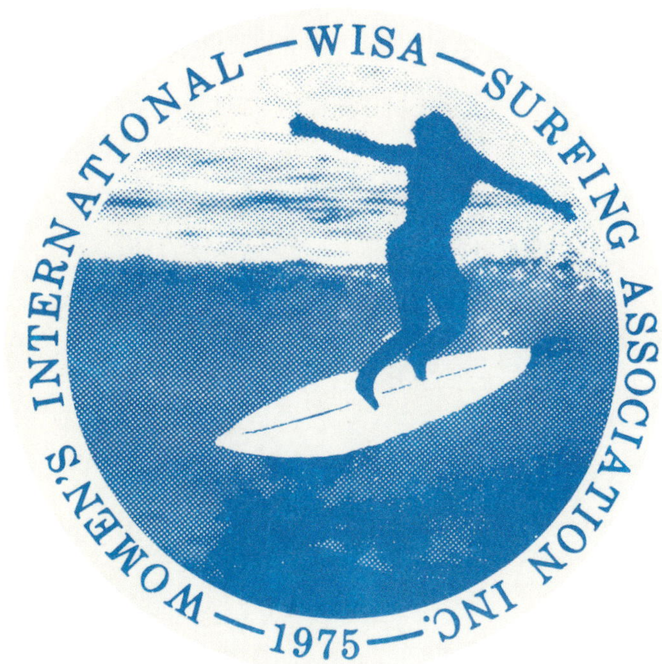
WOMEN'S INTERNATIONAL—WISA—SURFING ASSOCIATION INC.
—1975—

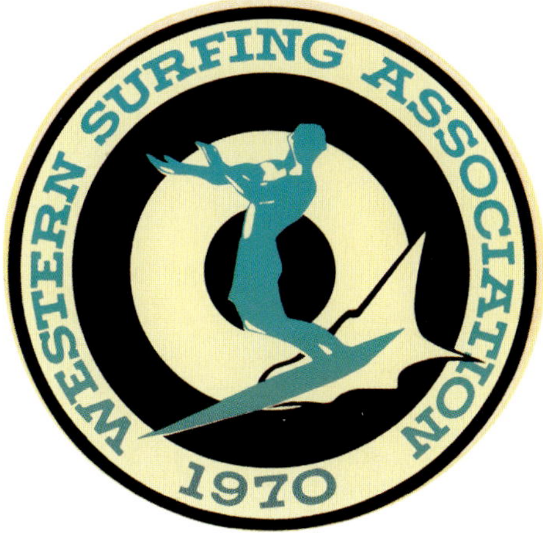
WESTERN SURFING ASSOCIATION
1970

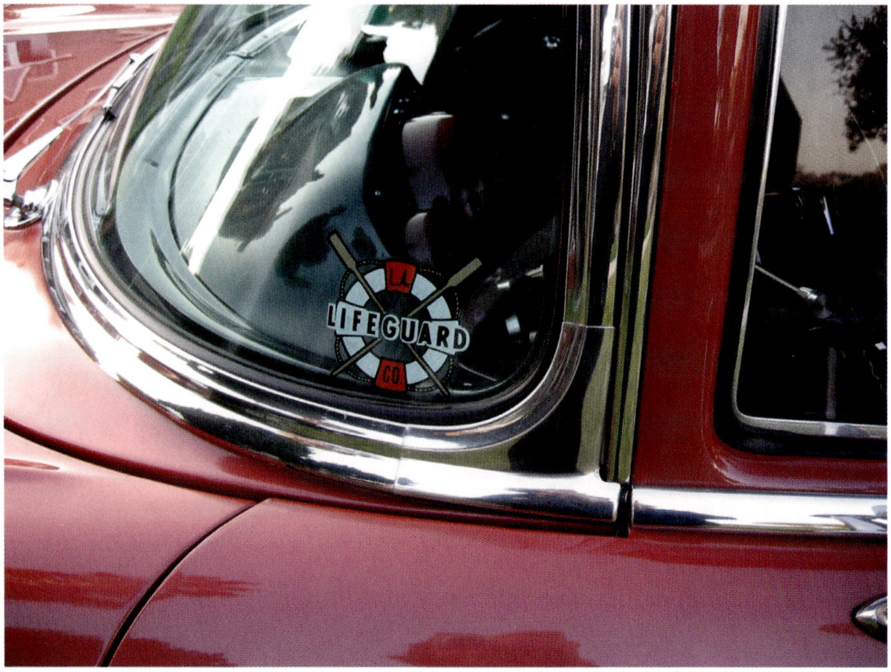

An LA County lifeguard sticker on the windshield of Tim McNulty's 1957 Chevy Bel Air wagon. Photo: Ben Marcus.

4.4 RESCUE ME

Lifeguard on duty and some of them are wearing cool patches.

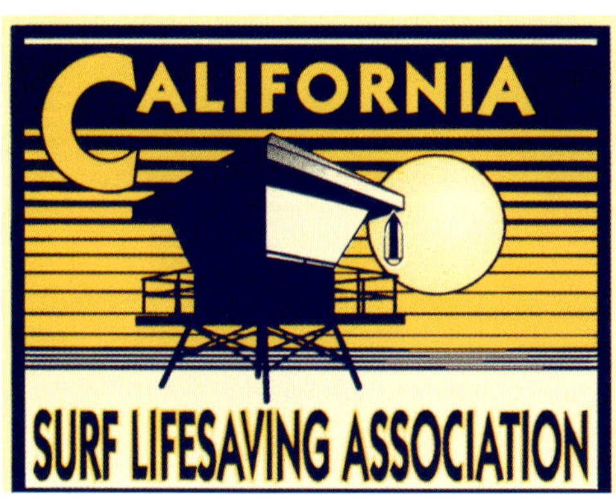

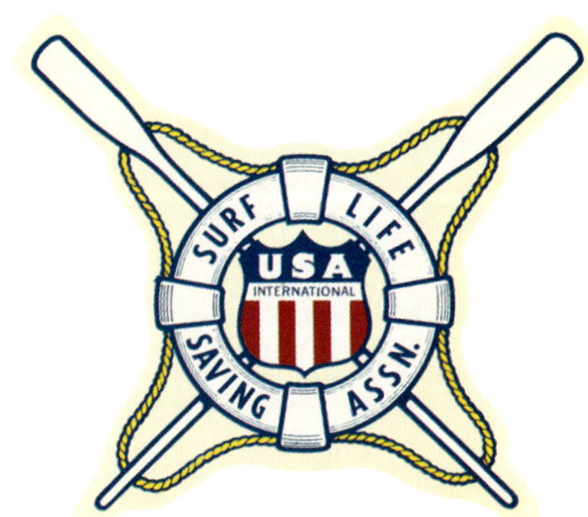

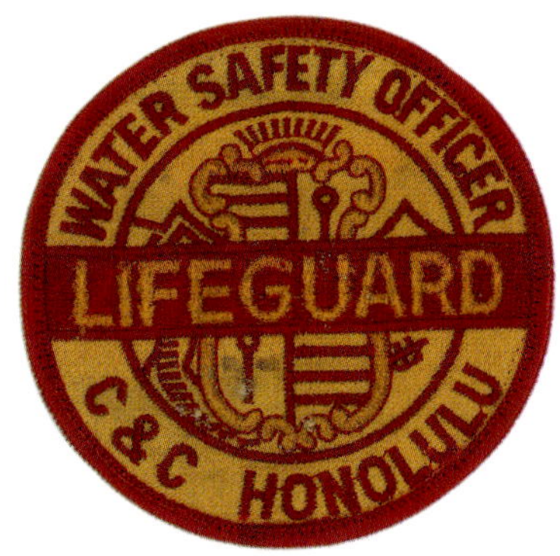

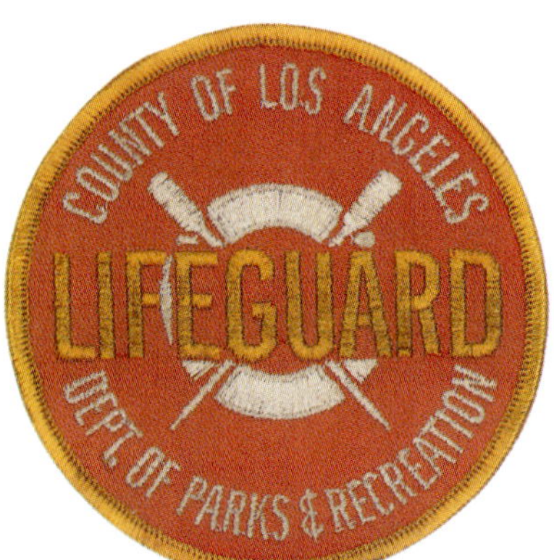

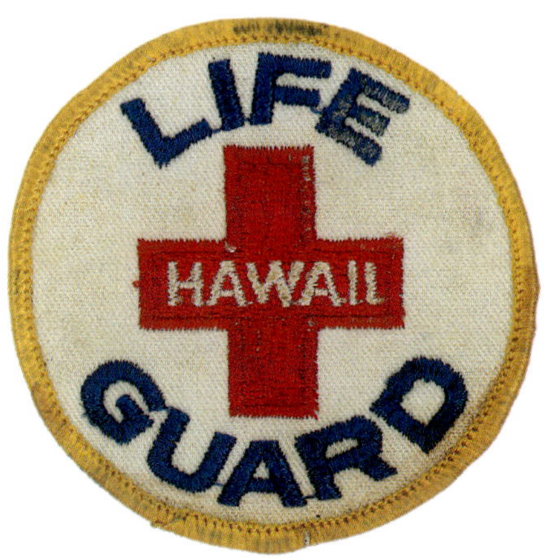

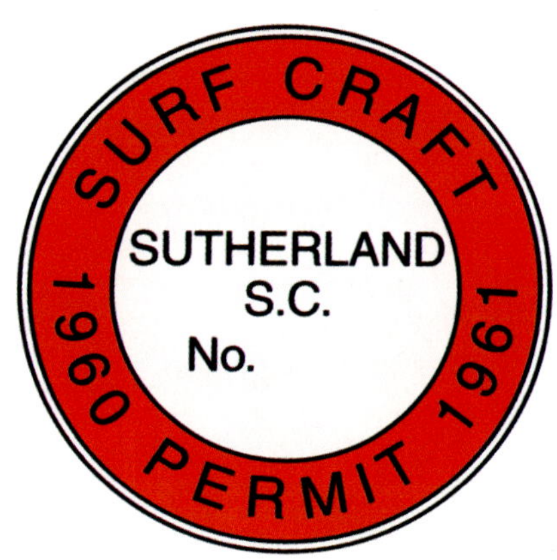

CHAPTER 4.5
YOU'LL CATCH 'EM SURFING AT....

In *Surfing USA*, the Beach Boys mentioned places like Trestles and Santa Cruz and Waimea Bay – locations in California, Hawaii and around the world. These stickers are from two of the three main surfing areas in the United States: California and Florida.

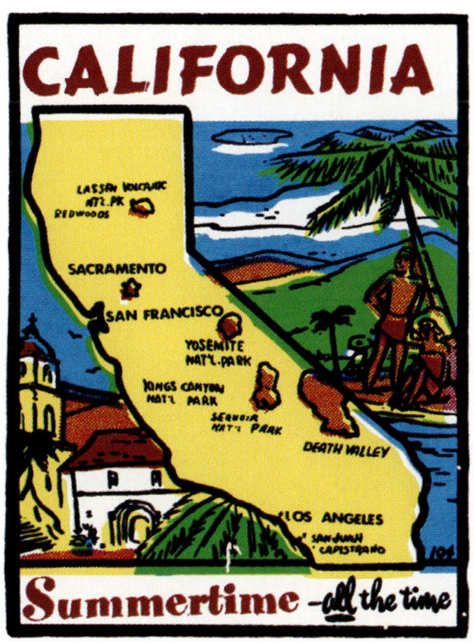

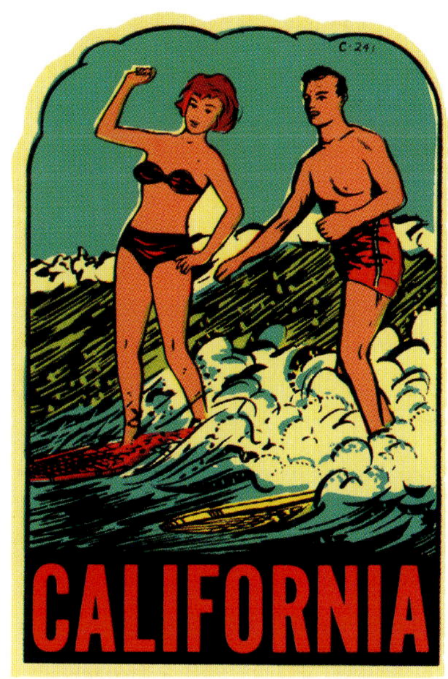

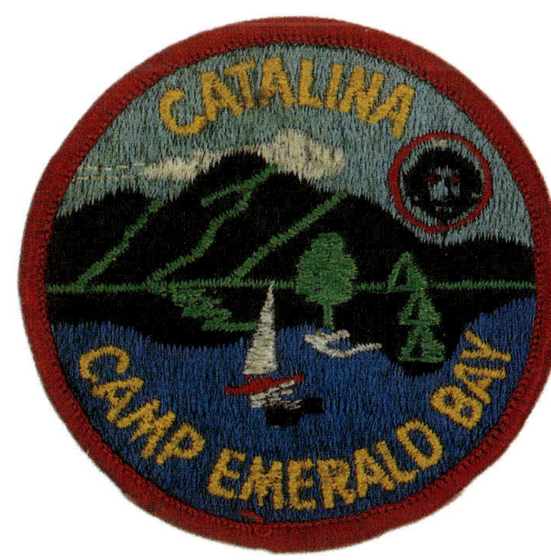

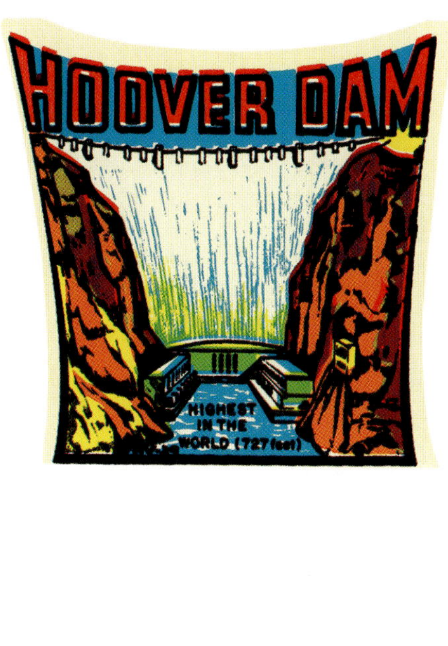

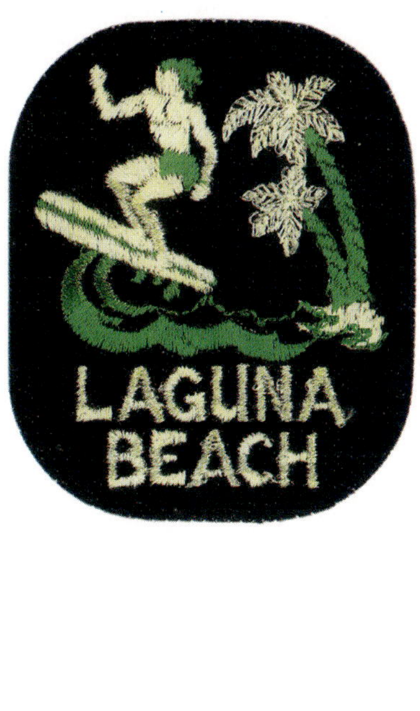

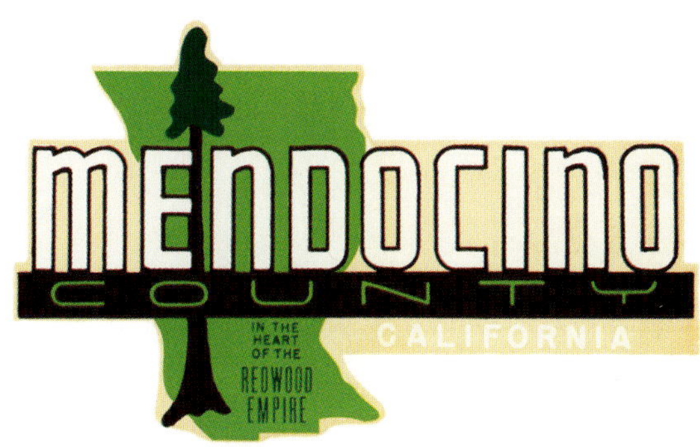

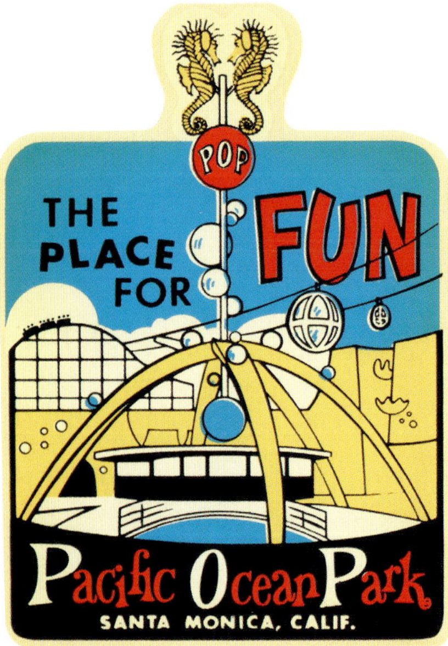
POP
THE PLACE FOR FUN
Pacific Ocean Park
SANTA MONICA, CALIF.

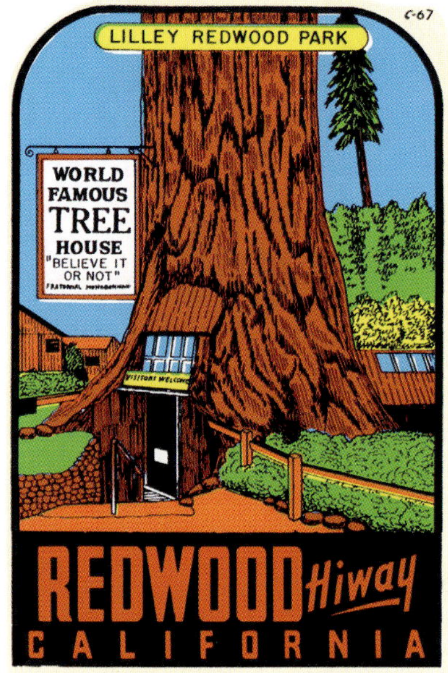
C-67
LILLEY REDWOOD PARK
WORLD FAMOUS TREE HOUSE
"BELIEVE IT OR NOT"
VISITORS WELCOME
REDWOOD Hiway
CALIFORNIA

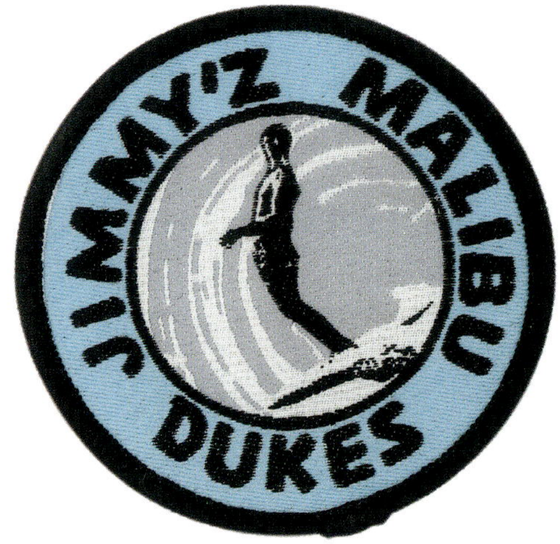
JIMMY'Z MALIBU
DUKES

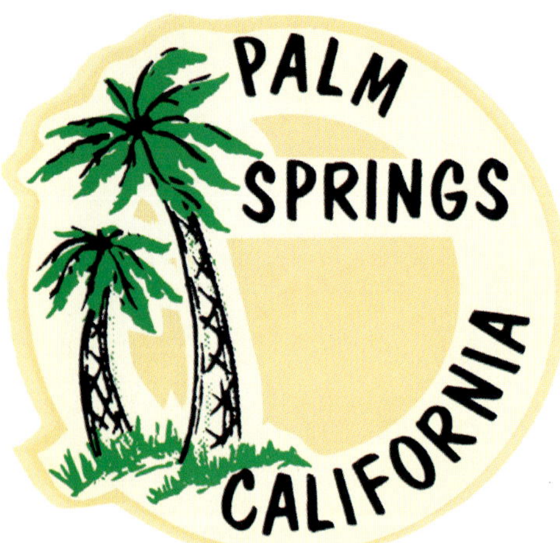
PALM
SPRINGS
CALIFORNIA

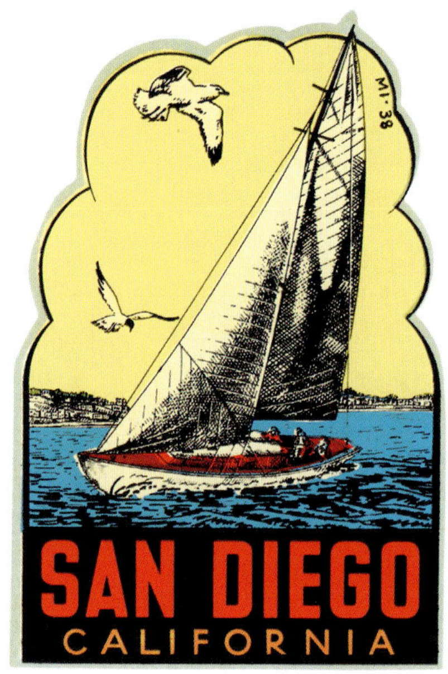
MI-38
SAN DIEGO
CALIFORNIA

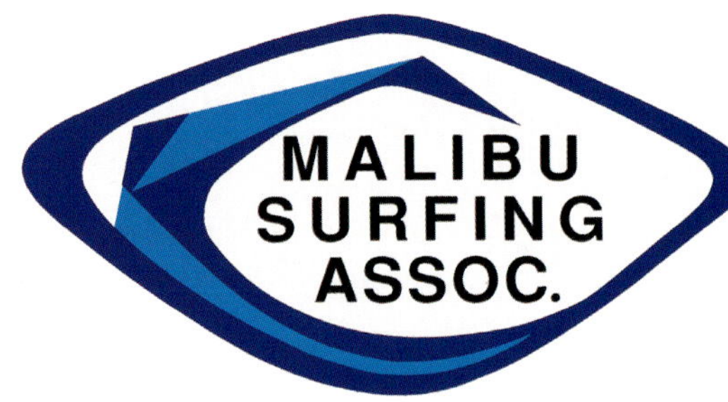
MALIBU
SURFING
ASSOC.

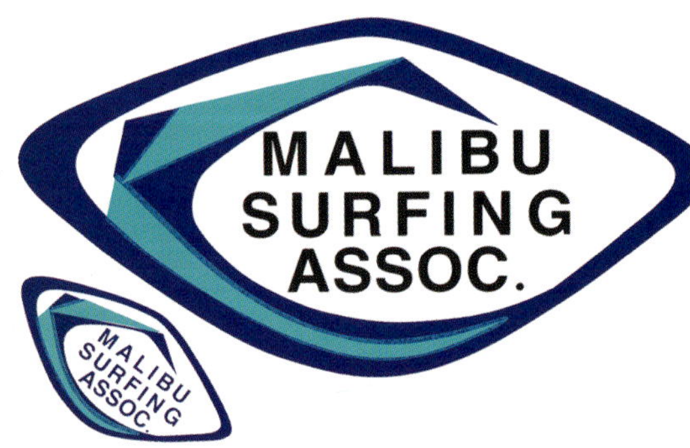
MALIBU
SURFING
ASSOC.
MALIBU
SURFING
ASSOC.

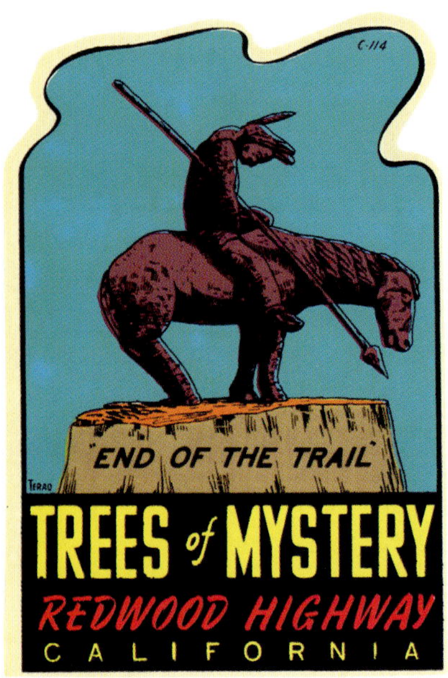
C-114
"END OF THE TRAIL"
TREES of MYSTERY
REDWOOD HIGHWAY
CALIFORNIA

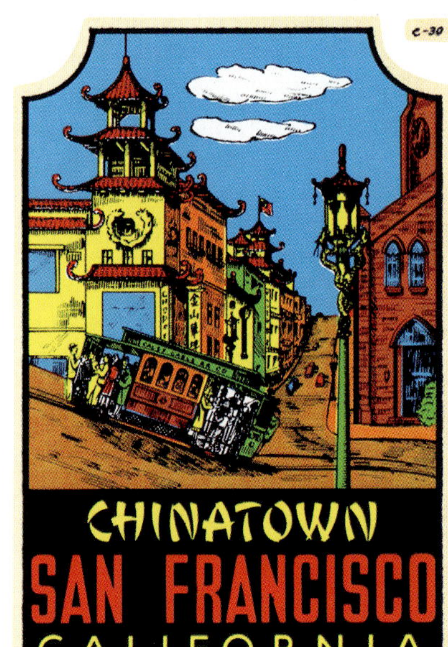
C-30
CHINATOWN
SAN FRANCISCO
CALIFORNIA

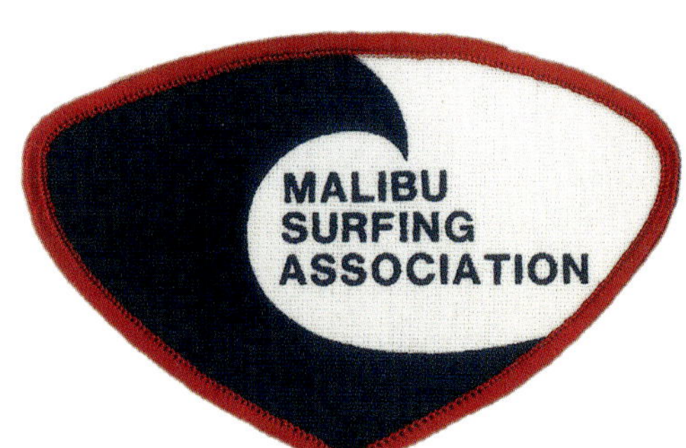
MALIBU
SURFING
ASSOCIATION

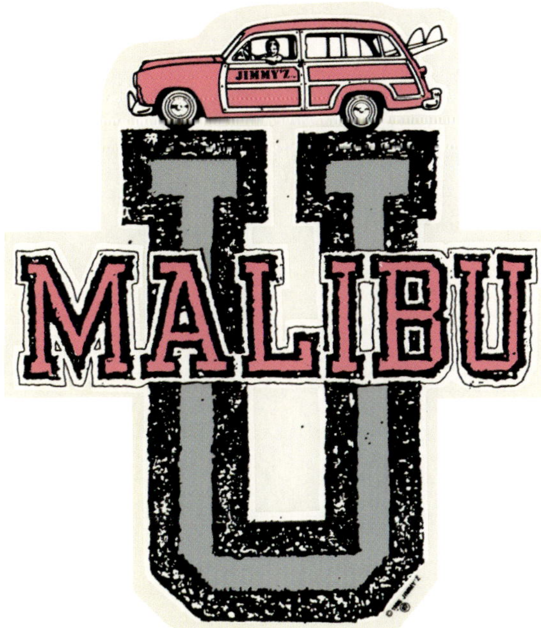
JIMMY'Z
MALIBU
U

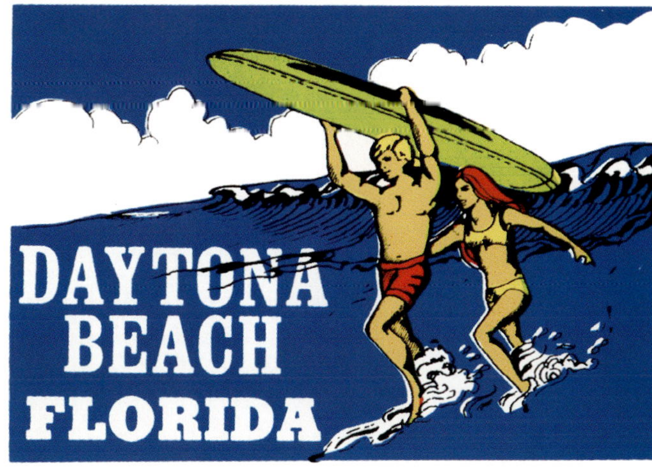
DAYTONA
BEACH
FLORIDA

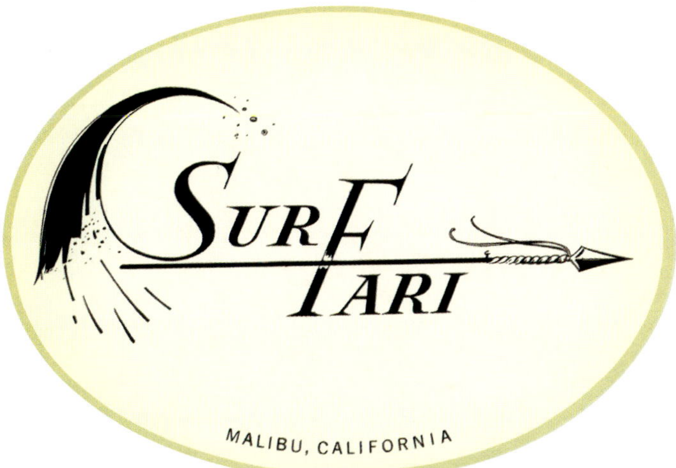
SURFARI
MALIBU, CALIFORNIA

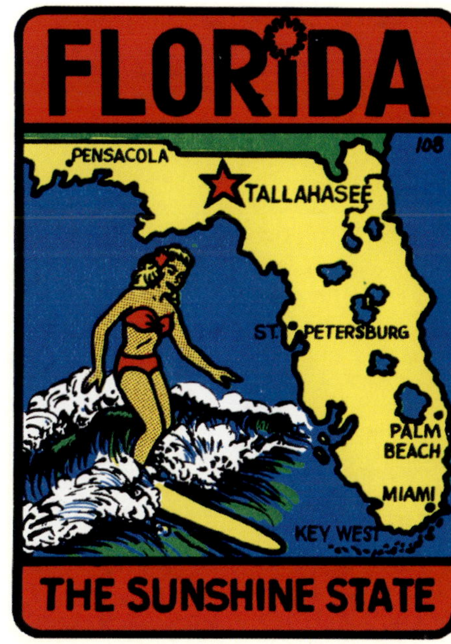
FLORIDA
108
PENSACOLA
TALLAHASEE
ST. PETERSBURG
PALM BEACH
MIAMI
KEY WEST
THE SUNSHINE STATE

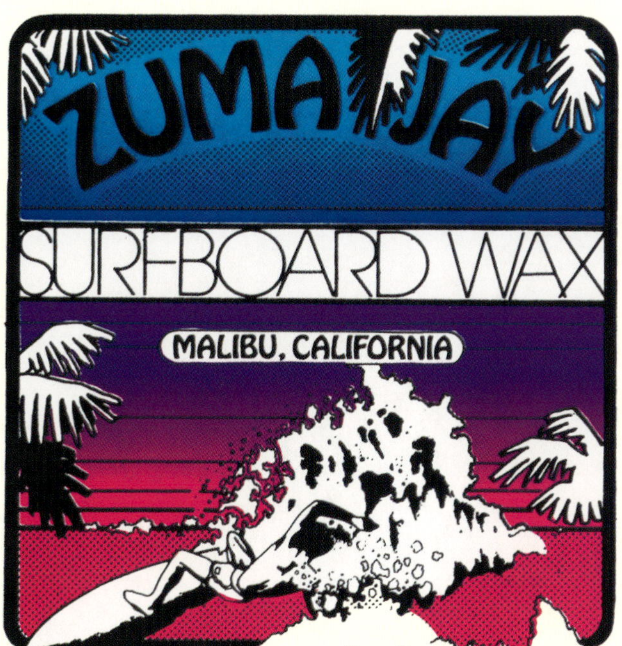
ZUMA JAY
SURFBOARD WAX
MALIBU, CALIFORNIA
60°-70° Temp.

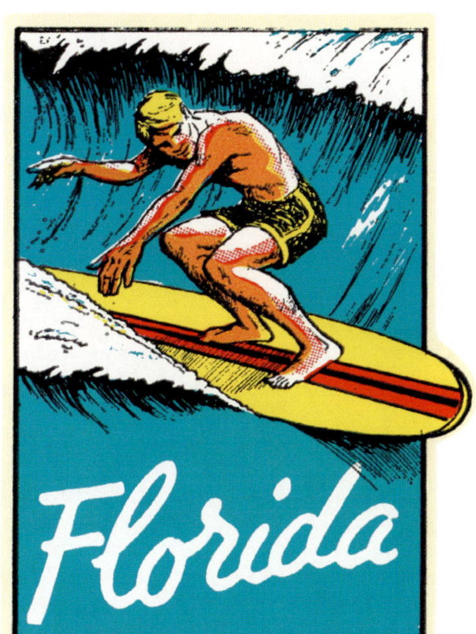
Florida

CHAPTER 4.6
TEQUILA!

Some say the 1958 song *Tequila!* is a surf instrumental, some say it's not a surf tune. Musical questions aside, Tequila is similar to *Wipeout!* in that it was thrown together in a studio as a B side and became a huge hit. The song was recorded in three takes by the Flores Trio in a Hollywood studio on December 23, 1957. It was the B Side for *Train to Nowhere*, but that song went nowhere and the country went ape for *Tequila*, an instrumental with honking saxophone and the word "Tequila!" shouted three times.

Tequila went to #1 on the Billboard Hot One Hundred chart. When everyone realized they had a fluky hit, they renamed the band The Champs and became a one-hit wonder. The song was popular because the drink was popular, and during the 50s and 60s, surf trips into Mexico were popular, for tequila and other things.

EAT ME
75 ¢

Just for the halibut
Rosarito Beach

Papas & Beer

Papas&Beer
ENSENADA ROSARITO

HUSSONG'S MR
ENSENADA, MEXICO

Rene's
SPORTS BAR-RESTAURANT
ROSARITO BEACH

HUSSONG'S MR
Centennial
ENSENADA, MEXICO

HUSSONG'S
Cantina
ENSENADA, MEXICO

Rock & Roll
TACO
Rosarito Beach
MEXICO

CHAPTER 4.7
SURF CITY

When Jan and Dean had a #1 hit with *Surf City* in 1963, they sang about loading up their woody and going to a place where the ratio of girls to boys was "two to one."

More than 30 years later, the city of Huntington Beach wanted to officially trademark their city as "Surf City." Up in northern California, the city of Santa Cruz took exception to that, claiming and going to court to argue that Santa Cruz deserved to be Surf City.

The argument raged back and forth with good arguments on both sides, but in the end, Huntington Beach won. Times may have changed, but in the 60s Huntington Beach was the surf city the song was about.

Here are some stickers representing both sides of the argument.

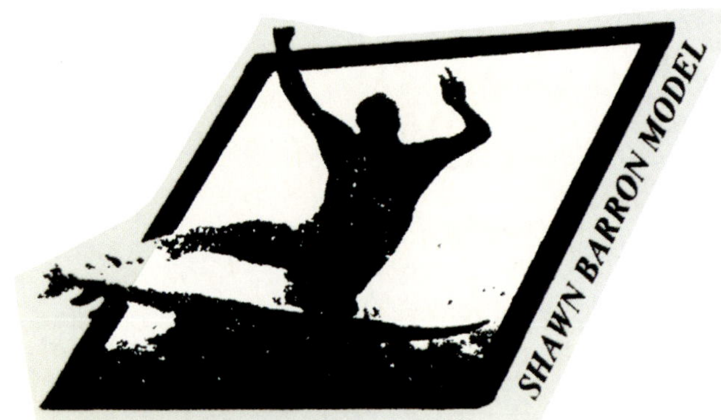

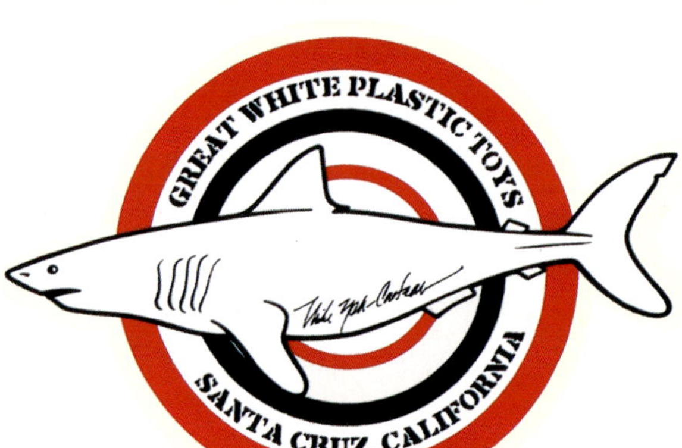

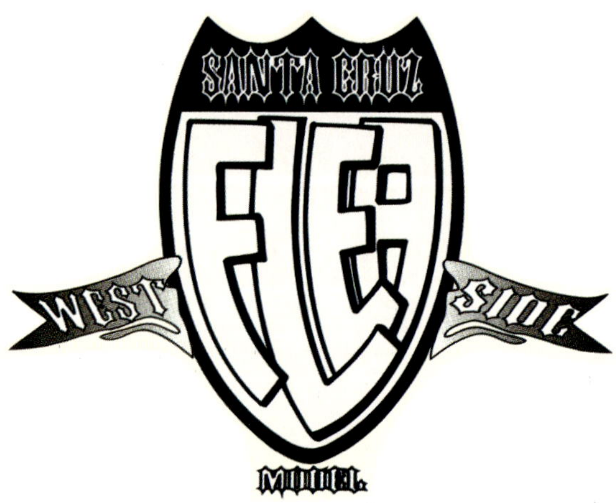

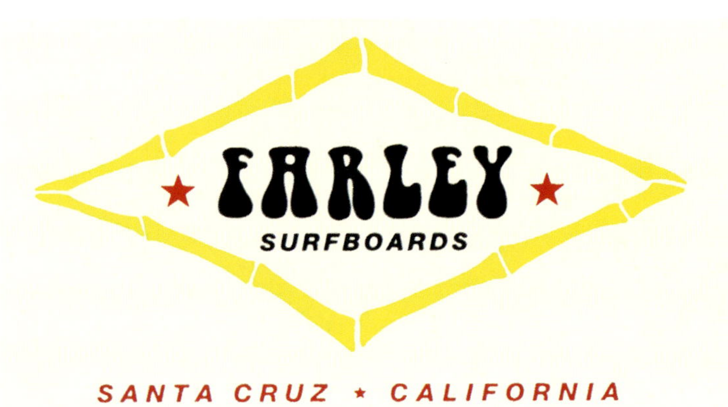

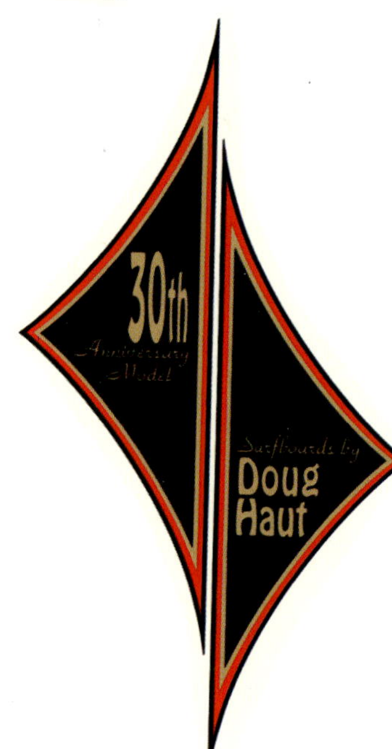

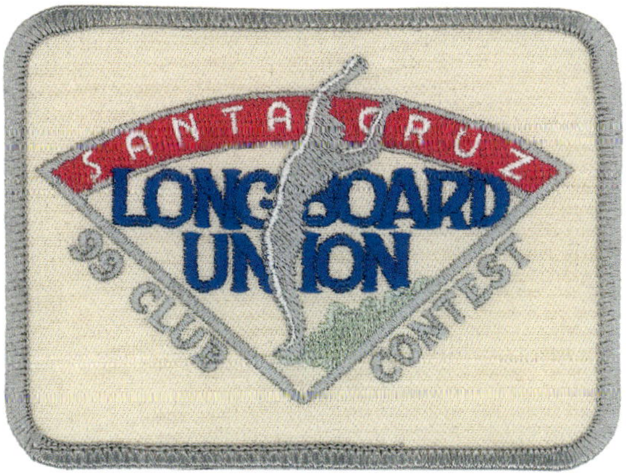
SANTA CRUZ
LONGBOARD UNION
99 CLUB CONTEST

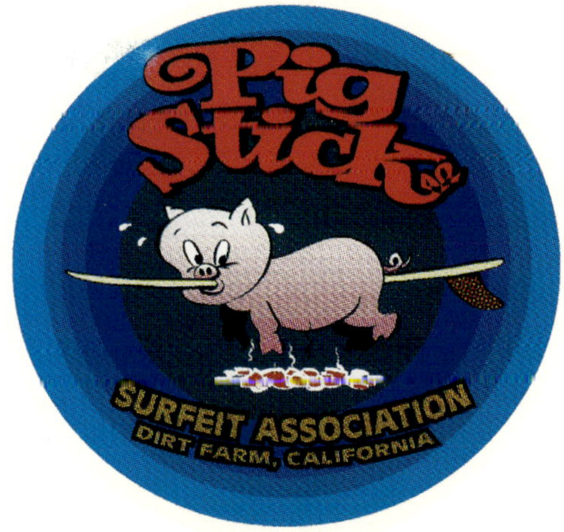
Pig Stick
SURFEIT ASSOCIATION
DIRT FARM, CALIFORNIA

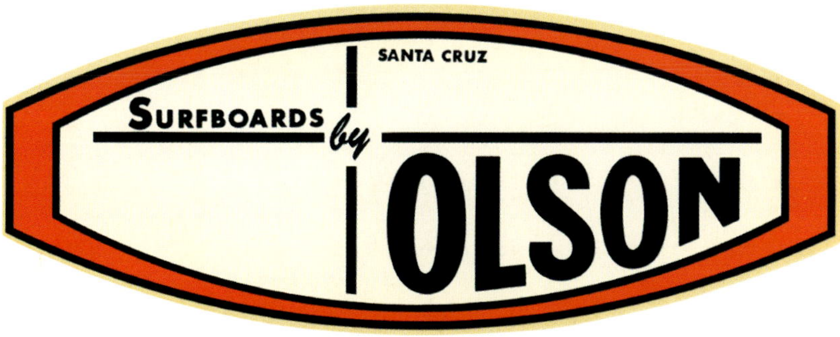
SANTA CRUZ
SURFBOARDS by
OLSON

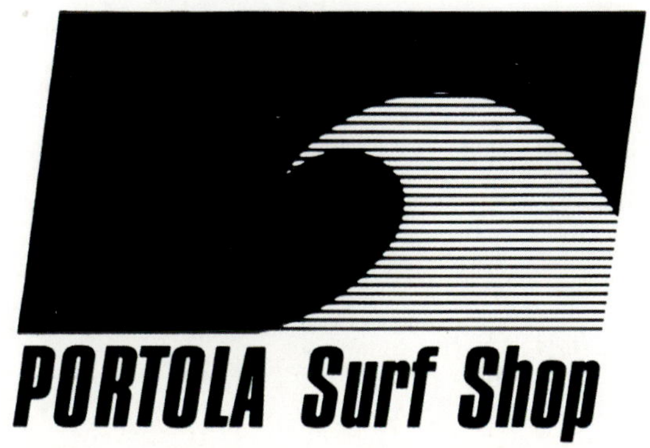
PORTOLA Surf Shop

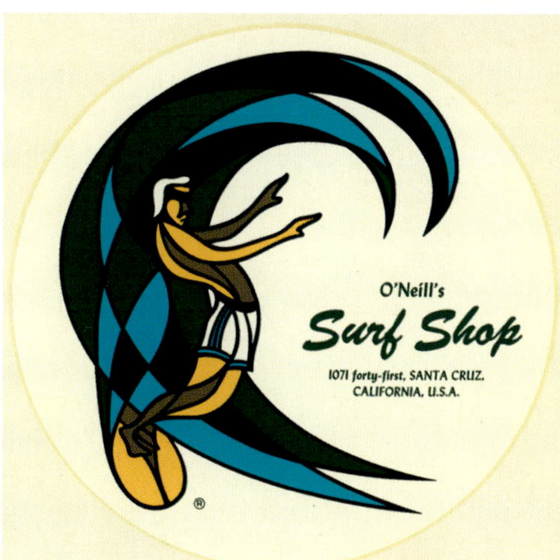
O'Neill's
Surf Shop
1071 forty-first, SANTA CRUZ, CALIFORNIA, U.S.A.

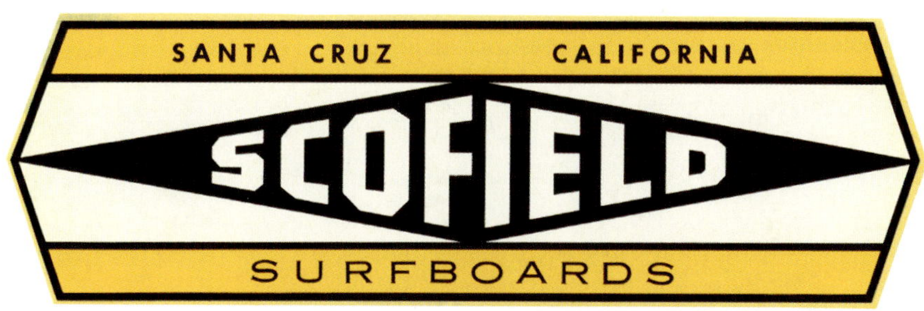
SANTA CRUZ CALIFORNIA
SCOFIELD
SURFBOARDS

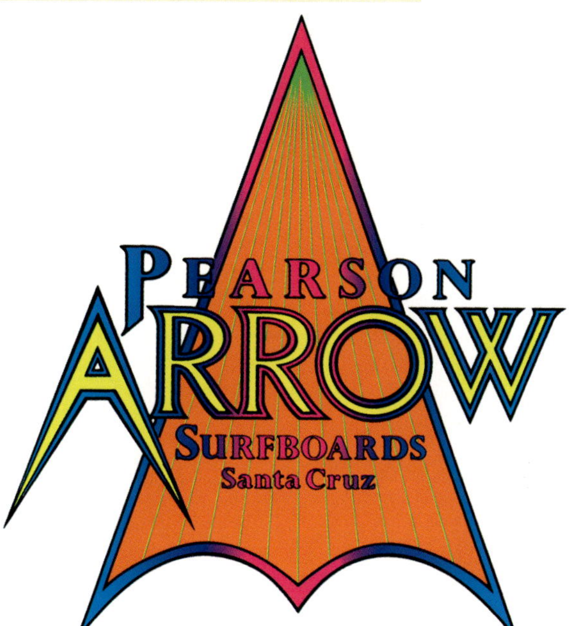
PEARSON
ARROW
SURFBOARDS
Santa Cruz

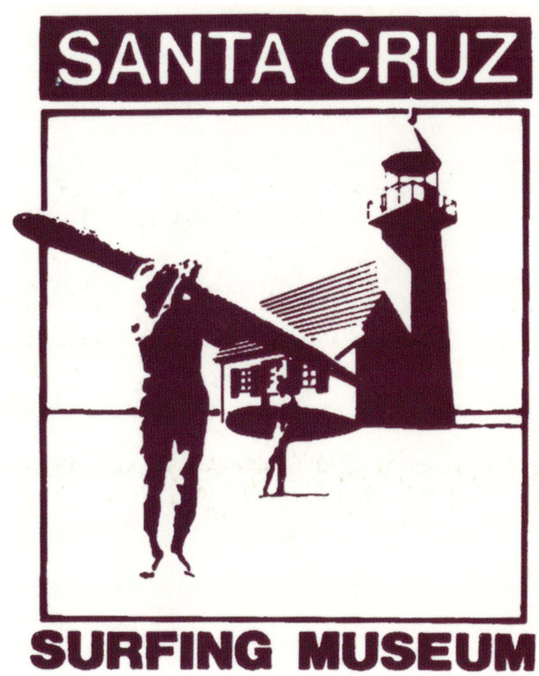
SANTA CRUZ
SURFING MUSEUM

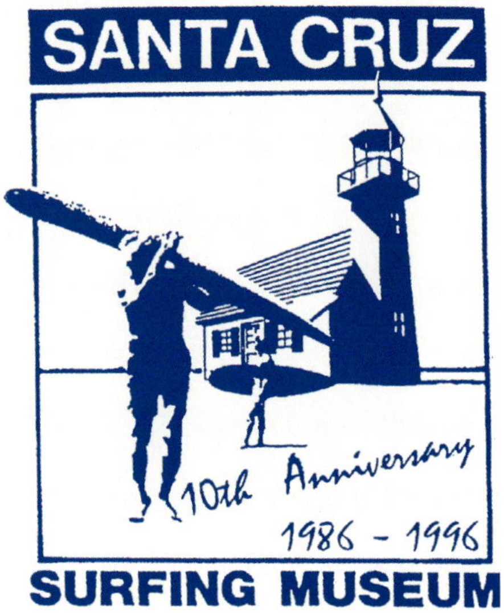
SANTA CRUZ
10th Anniversary
1986 - 1996
SURFING MUSEUM

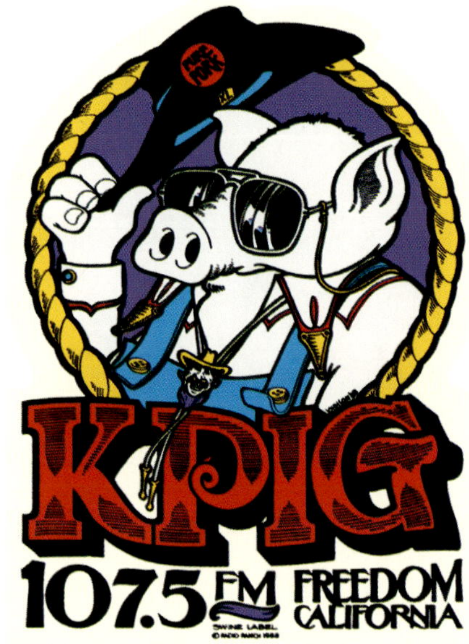
KPIG
107.5 FM
FREEDOM CALIFORNIA

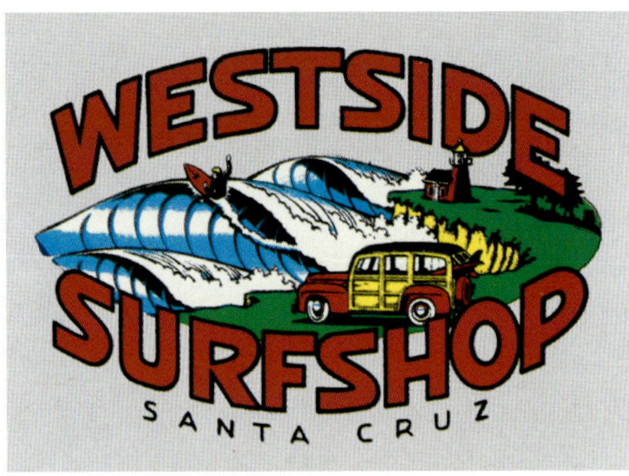
WESTSIDE
SURFSHOP
SANTA CRUZ

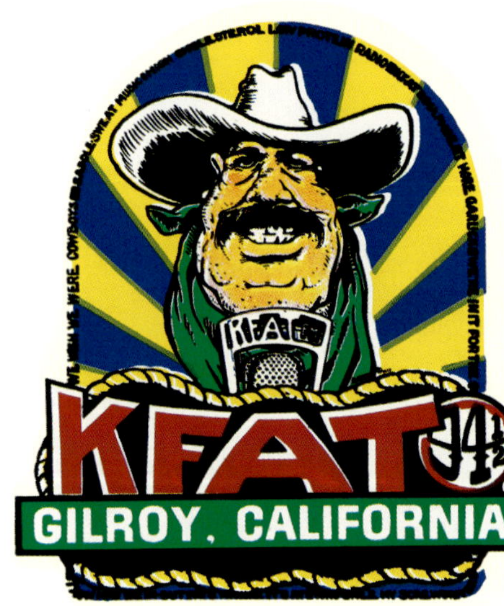
KFAT
94½
GILROY, CALIFORNIA

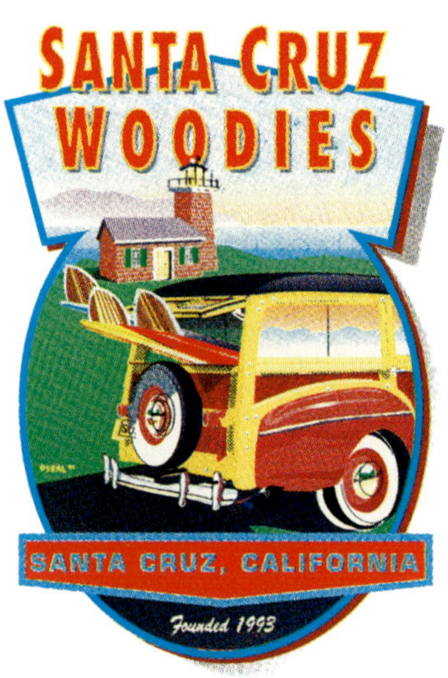
SANTA CRUZ
WOODIES
SANTA CRUZ, CALIFORNIA
Founded 1993

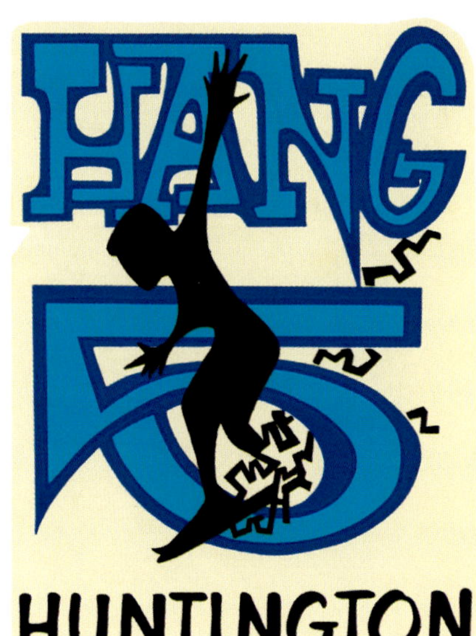
HANG
5
HUNTINGTON

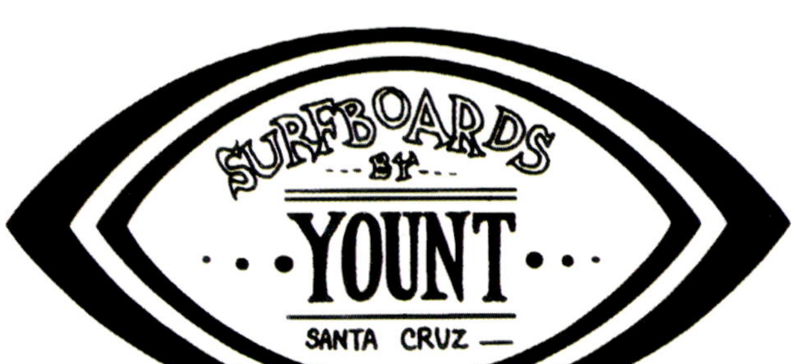
SURFBOARDS
BY
YOUNT
SANTA CRUZ

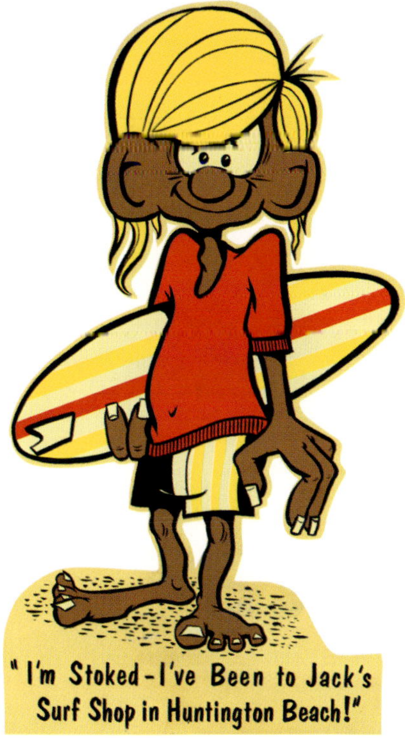
" I'm Stoked - I've Been to Jack's
Surf Shop in Huntington Beach!"

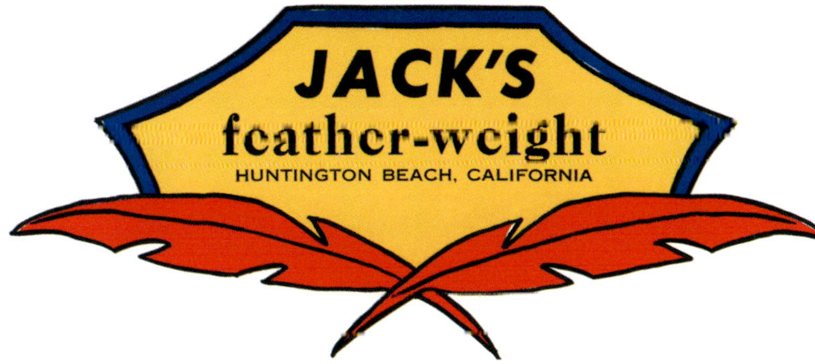
JACK'S
feather-weight
HUNTINGTON BEACH, CALIFORNIA

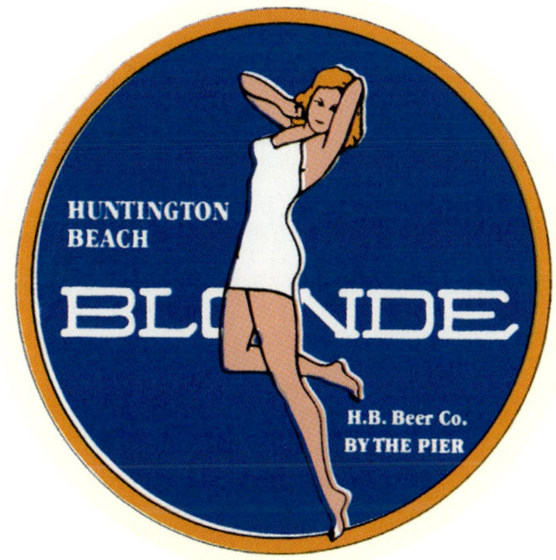
HUNTINGTON
BEACH
BLONDE
H.B. Beer Co.
BY THE PIER

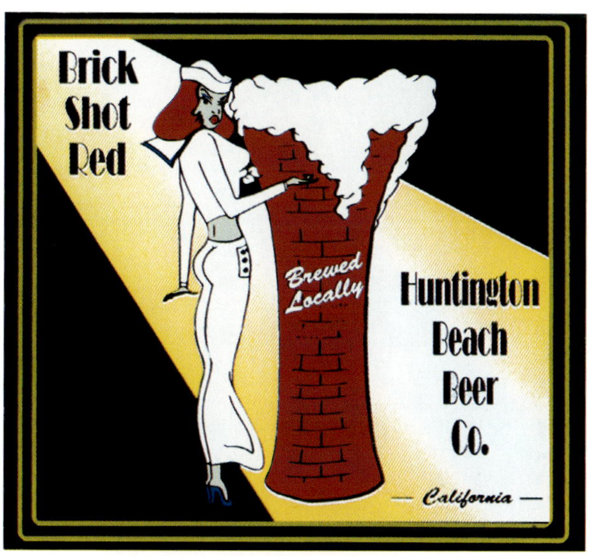
Brick
Shot
Red
Brewed
Locally
Huntington
Beach
Beer
Co.
— California —

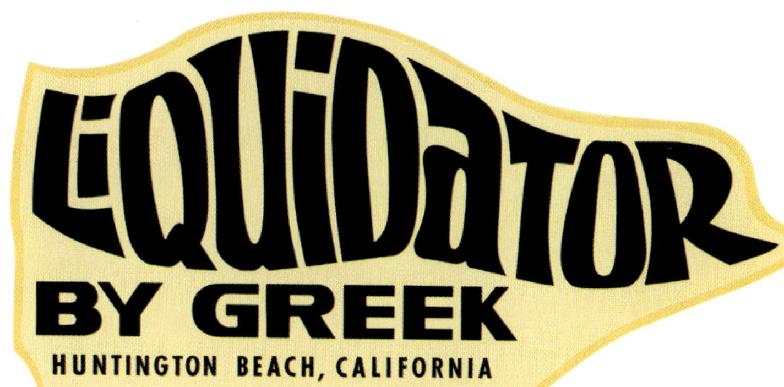
LiQUiDaTOR
BY GREEK
HUNTINGTON BEACH, CALIFORNIA

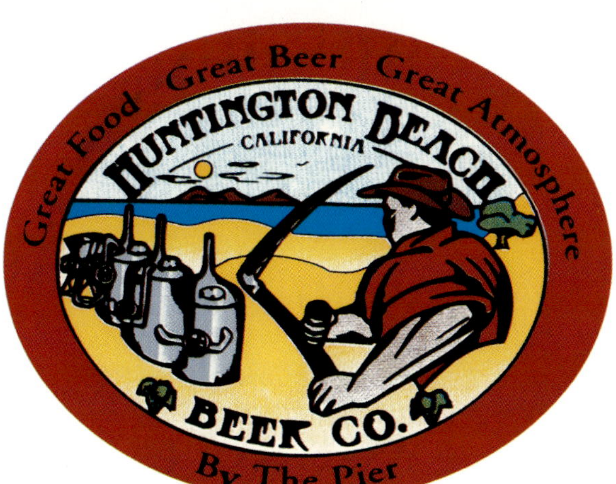
Great Food Great Beer Great Atmosphere
HUNTINGTON BEACH
CALIFORNIA
BEER CO.
By The Pier

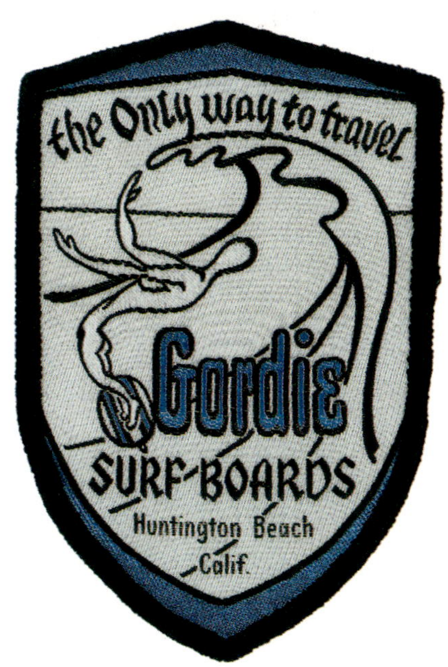
the Only way to travel
Gordie
SURF-BOARDS
Huntington Beach
Calif.

CHAPTER 4.8
I WISH THEY ALL COULD BE CALIFORNIA GIRLS.

The west coast has the sunshine and the girls all get so tan, and in 1965, Brian Wilson and Mike Love got a little greedy and wrote an ode that wished all girls north, south, east and west could be from the Golden State.

Rolling Stone Magazine rated *California Girls* as #71 on their 500 Greatest Songs of all Time, and David Lee Roth had a #3 hit with his cover of the song in 1985.

Most of these girlie stickers come from the collection of Cary Weiss: "I was at a woody show with my 48 Ford woody wagon and had some decals for sale. An older gentleman asked me if I would be interested in seeing some of his old travel decals he collected over the years and I ended up buying them. The Lady States were part of them. His wife would not let him put any on their wagon!!!"

That guy's loss was Cary Weiss' gain. These are some of the girls that the Beach Boys all wished could be west coast girls.

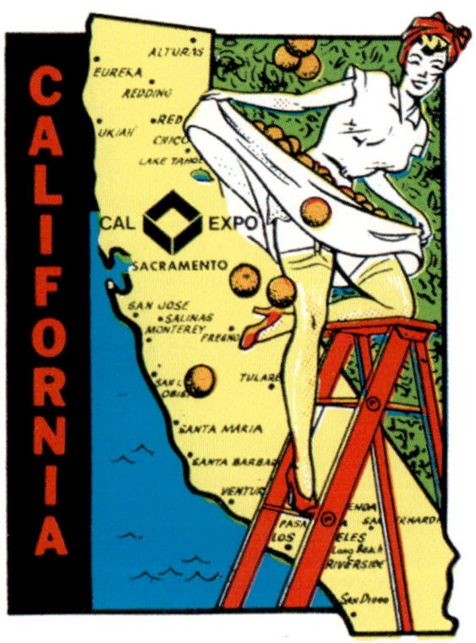

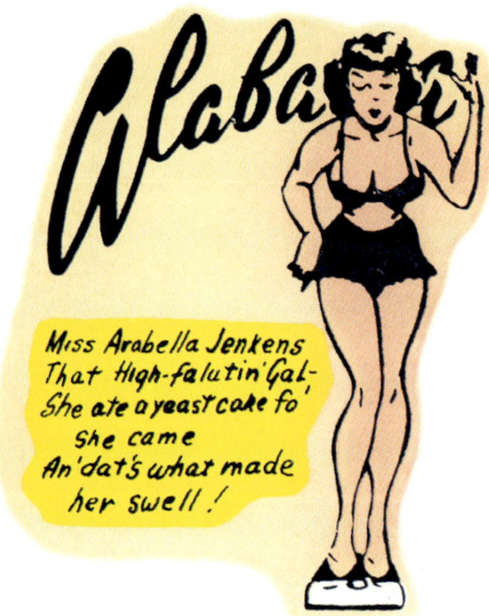

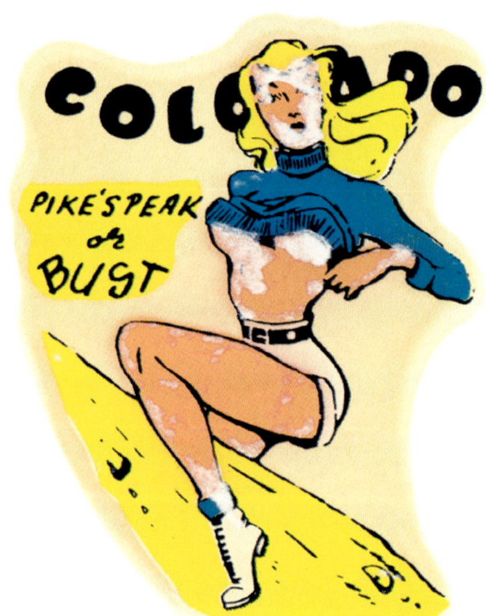

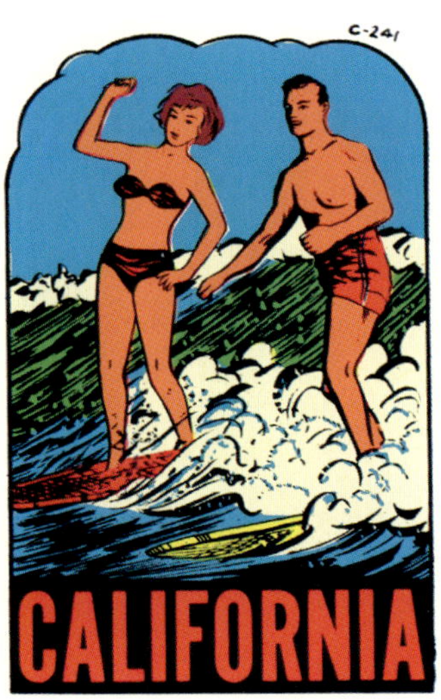

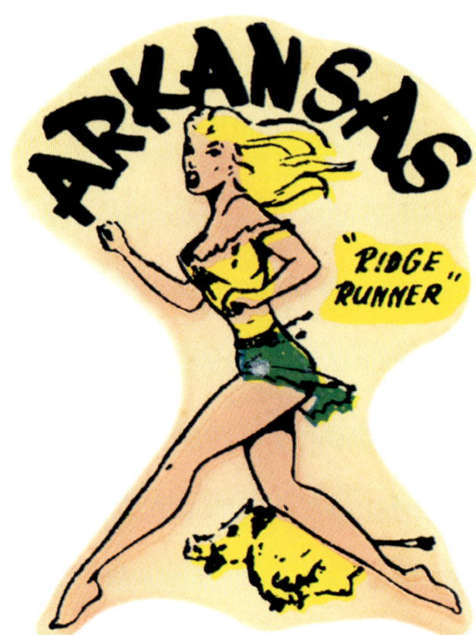

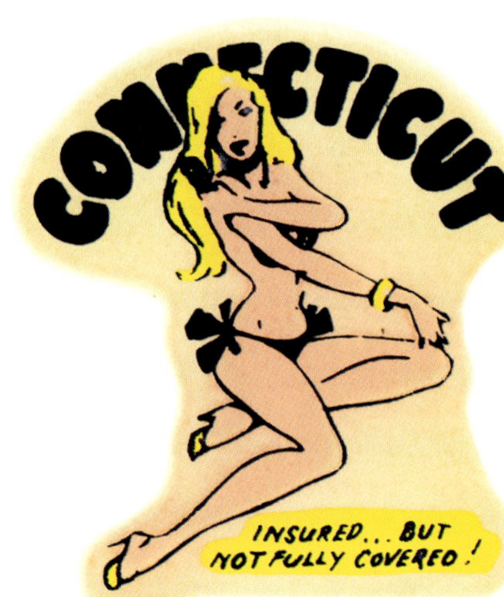

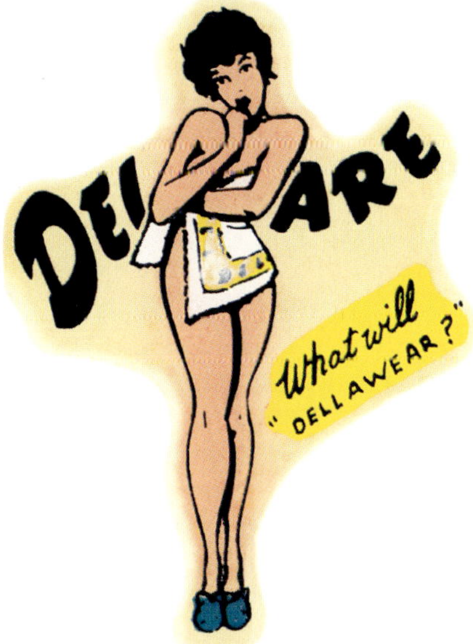
DEL
ARE
What will
"DELLAWEAR?"

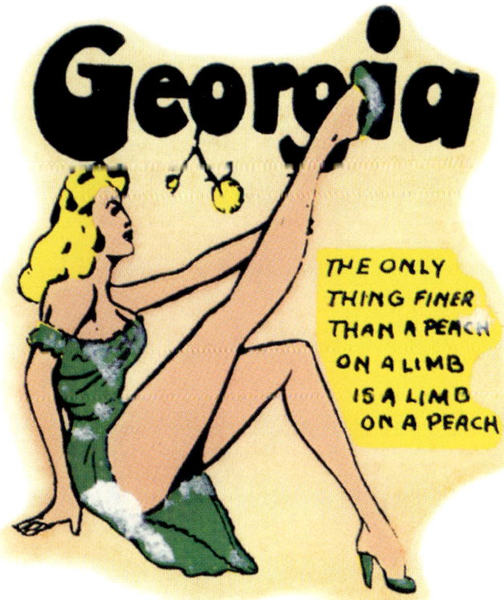
Georgia
THE ONLY THING FINER THAN A PEACH ON A LIMB IS A LIMB ON A PEACH

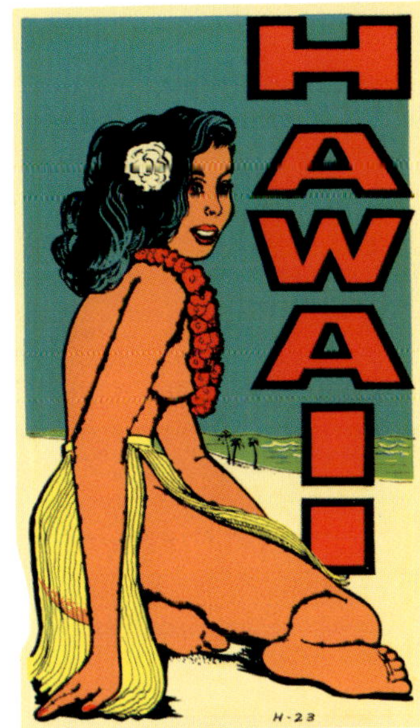
HAWAII
H-23

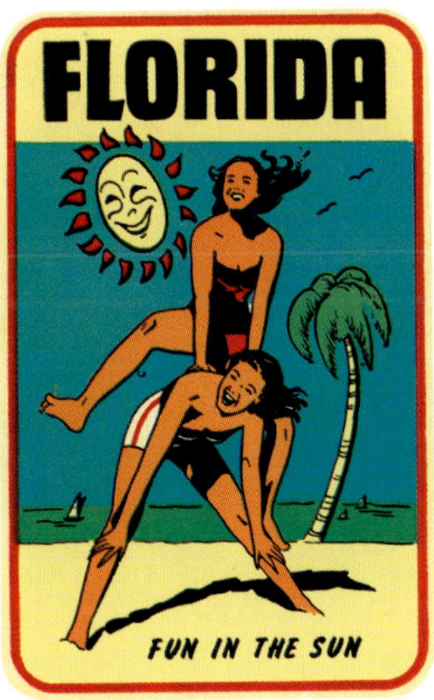
FLORIDA
FUN IN THE SUN

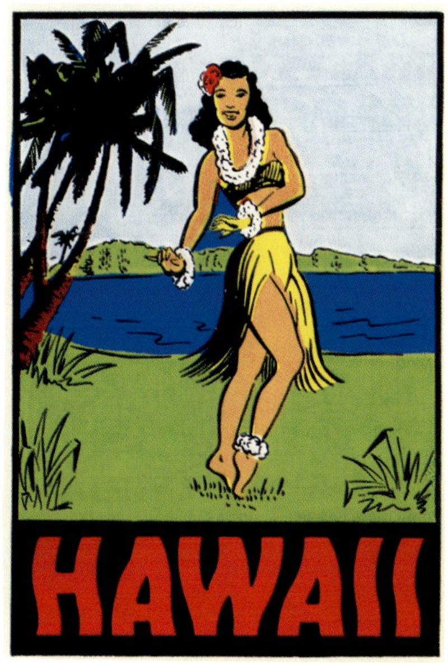
HAWAII

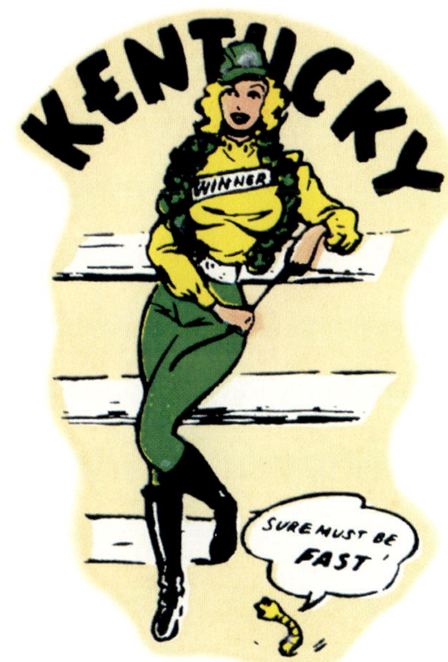
KENT
CKY
WINNER
SURE MUST BE FAST

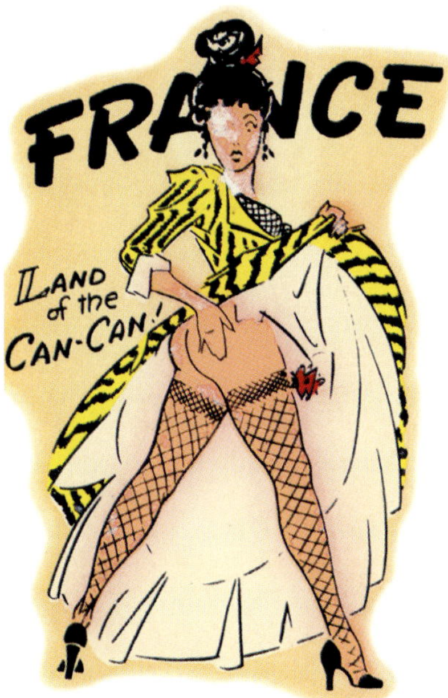
FRA
NCE
LAND of the CAN-CAN!

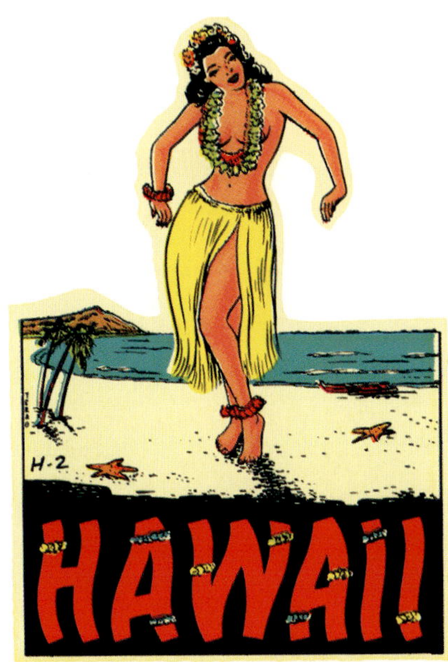
H-2
HAWAII

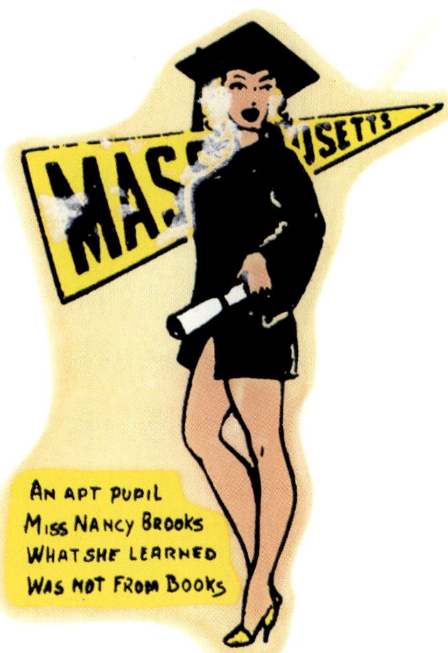
MAS
USETTS
AN APT PUPIL
MISS NANCY BROOKS
WHAT SHE LEARNED
WAS NOT FROM BOOKS

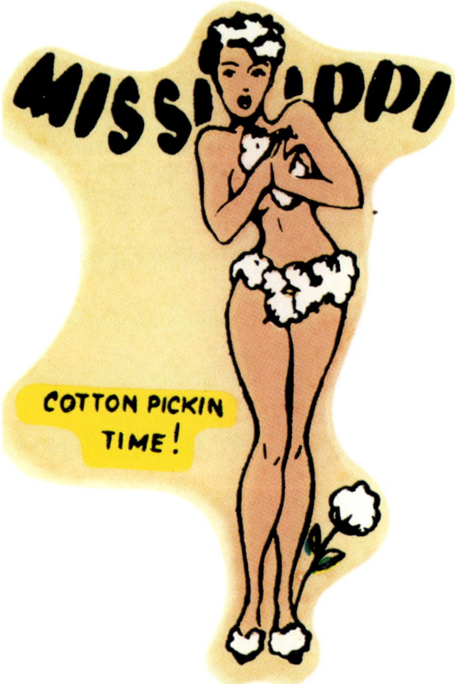
COTTON PICKIN TIME!

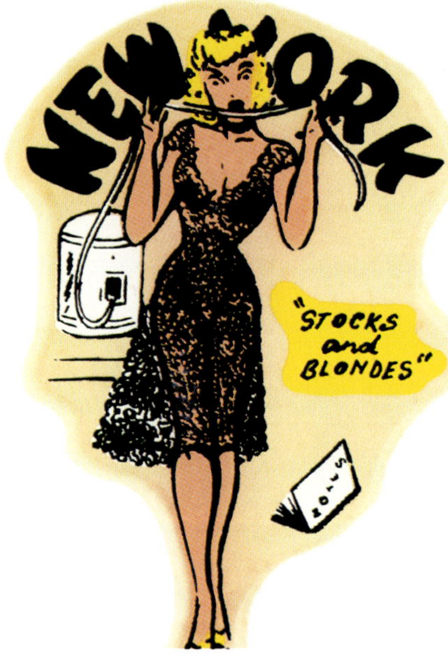
"STOCKS and BLONDES"

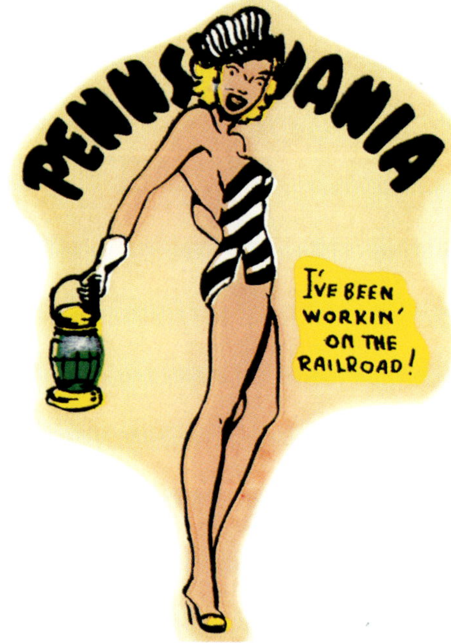
I'VE BEEN WORKIN' ON THE RAILROAD!

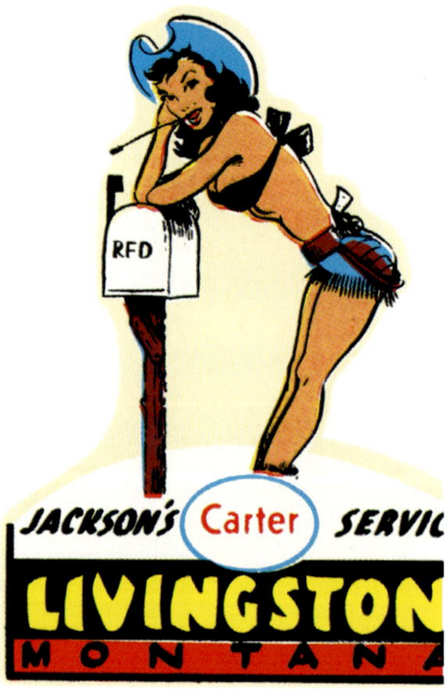
RFD
JACKSON'S Carter SERVIC
LIVINGSTON
MONTANA

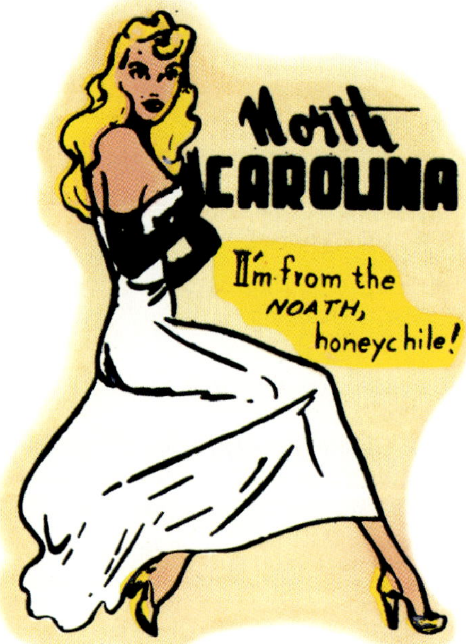
North CAROLINA
I'm from the NOATH, honeychile!

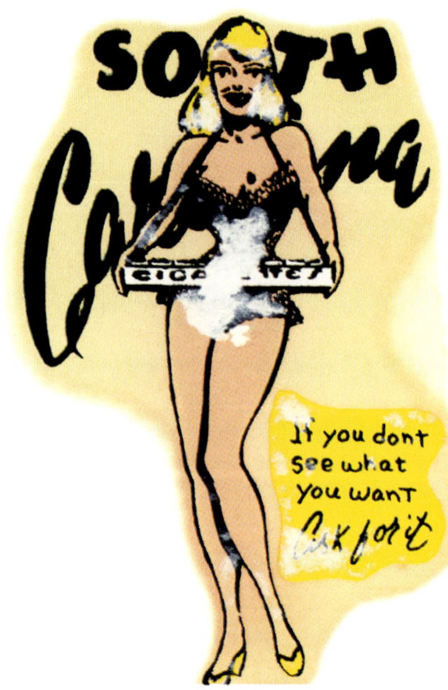
If you dont see what you want ask for it

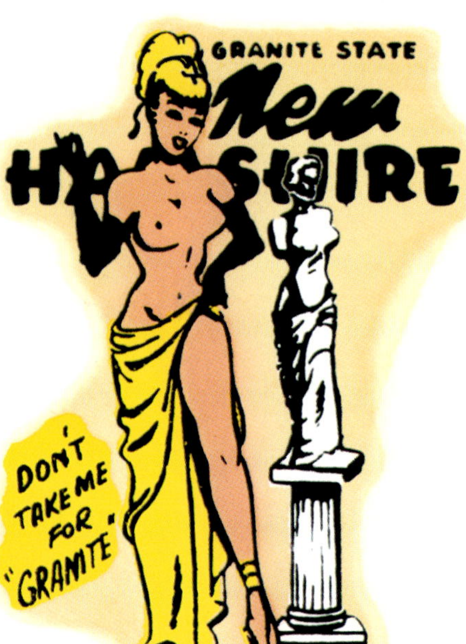
GRANITE STATE
DON'T TAKE ME FOR "GRANITE"

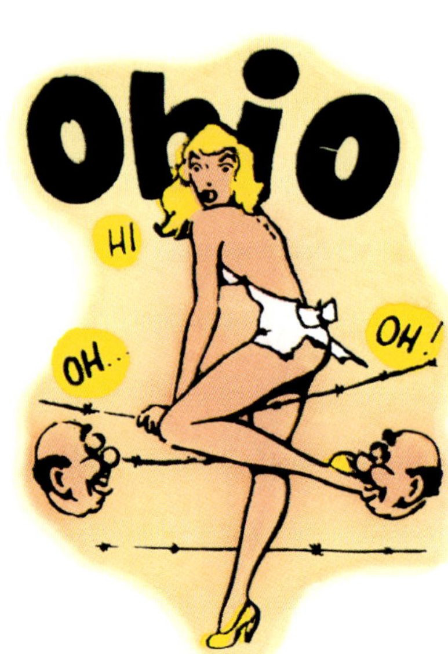
Ohio
HI
OH...
OH!

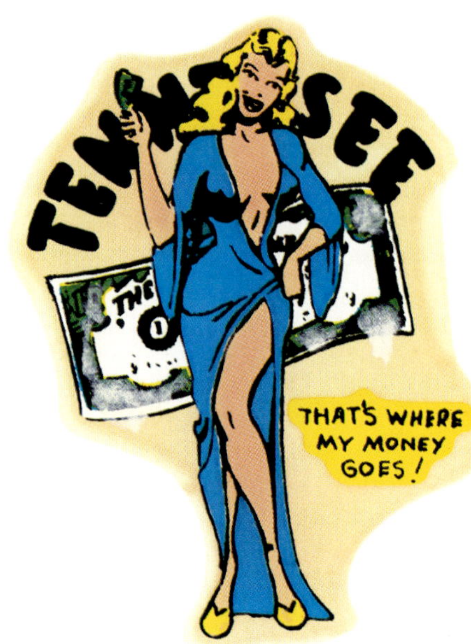
THAT'S WHERE MY MONEY GOES!

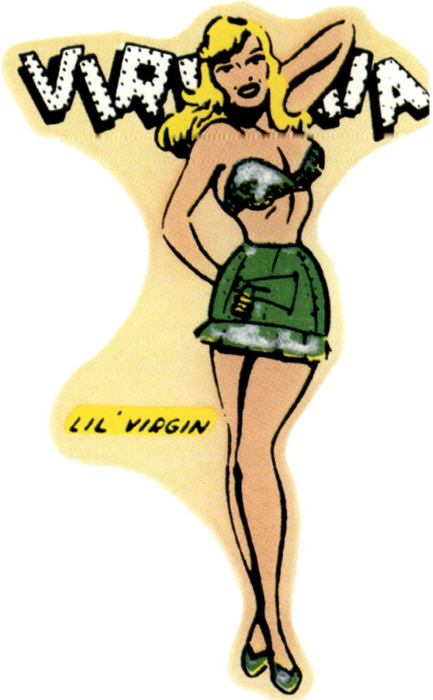
LIL' VIRGIN

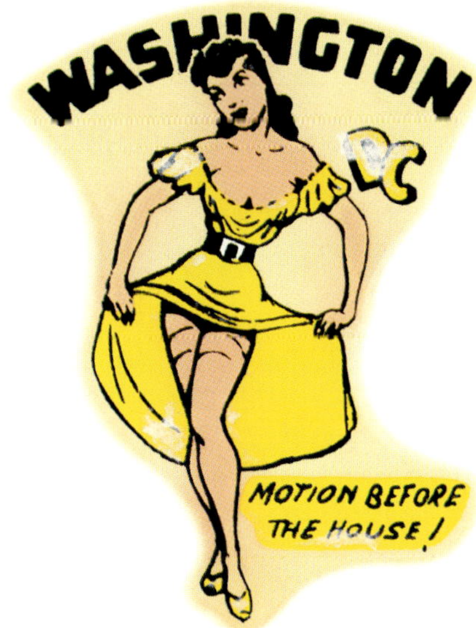
WASHINGTON
DC
MOTION BEFORE
THE HOUSE!

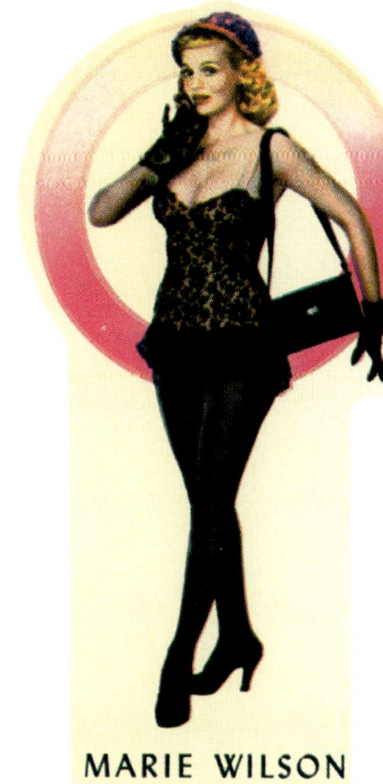
MARIE WILSON

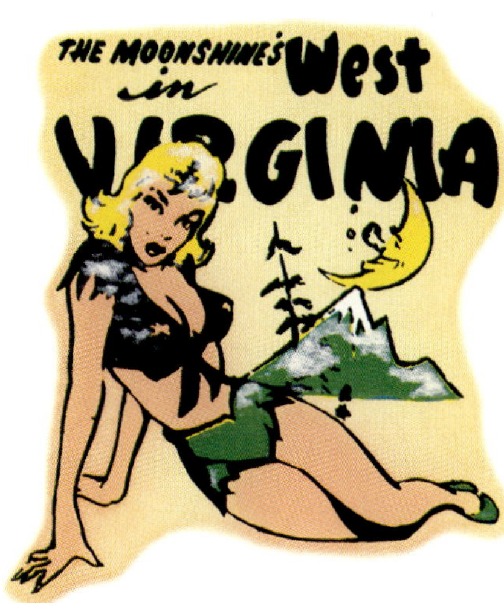
THE MOONSHINE'S West
in
VIRGINIA

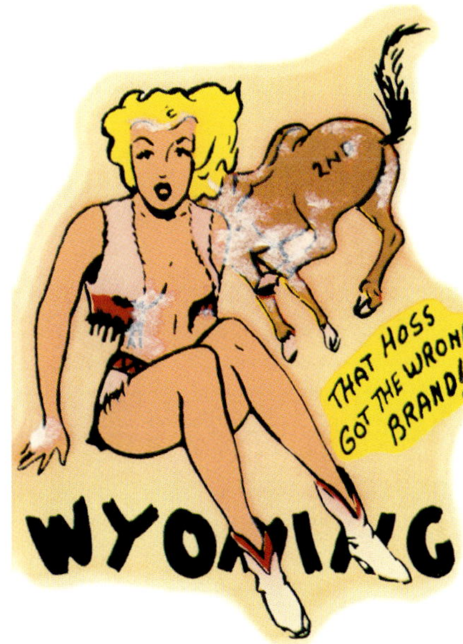
THAT HOSS
GOT THE WRONG
BRAND!
WYOMING

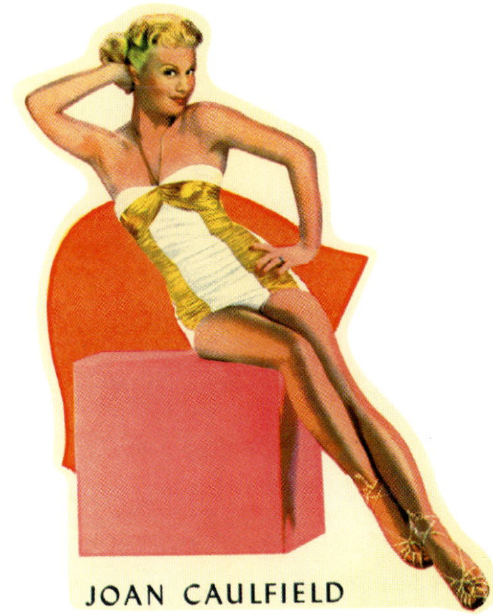
JOAN CAULFIELD

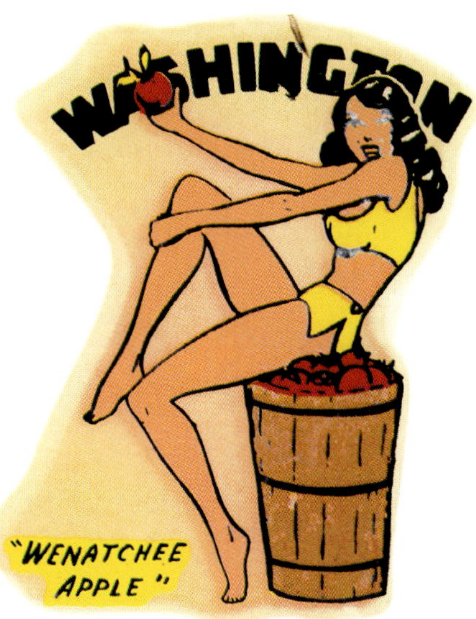
WASHINGTON
"WENATCHEE
APPLE"

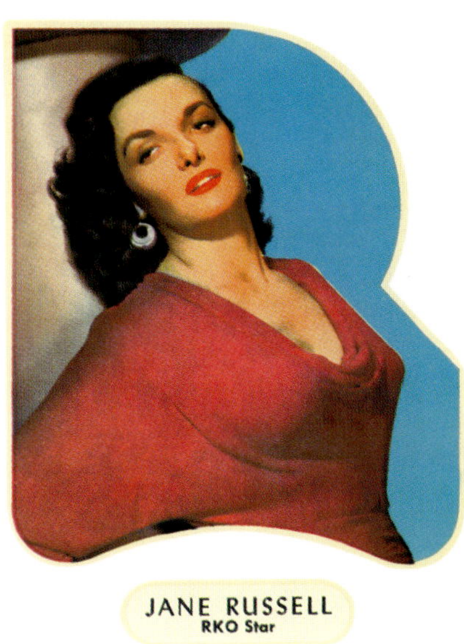
JANE RUSSELL
RKO Star

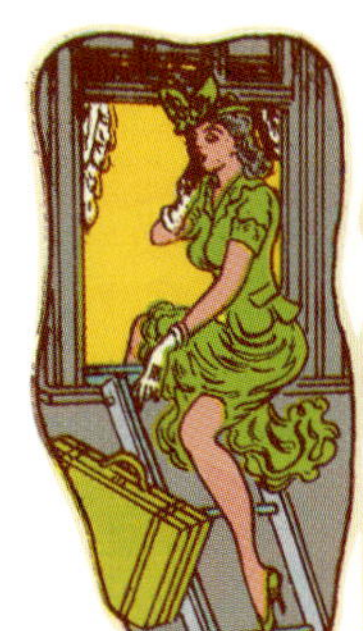

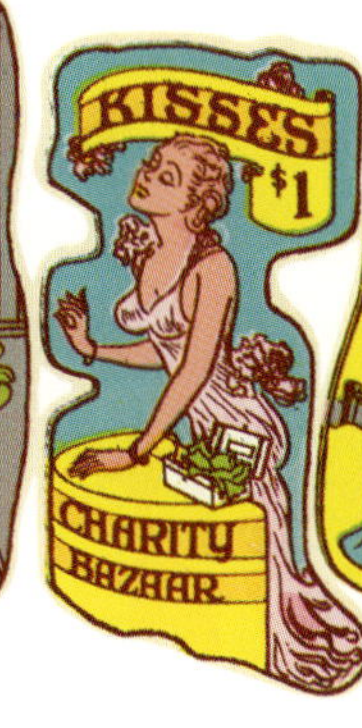
KISSES
$1
CHARITY
BAZAAR

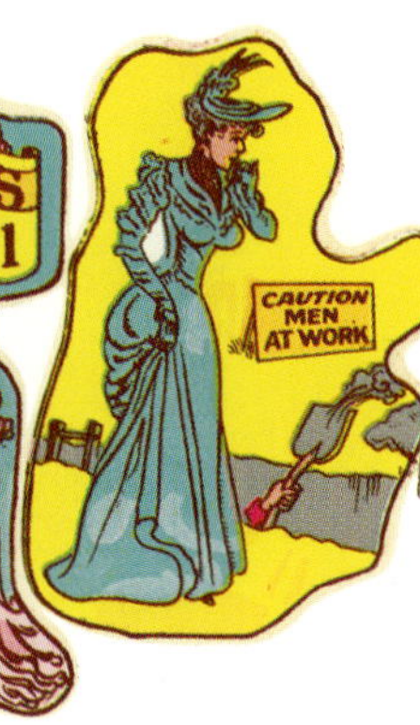
CAUTION
MEN
AT WORK

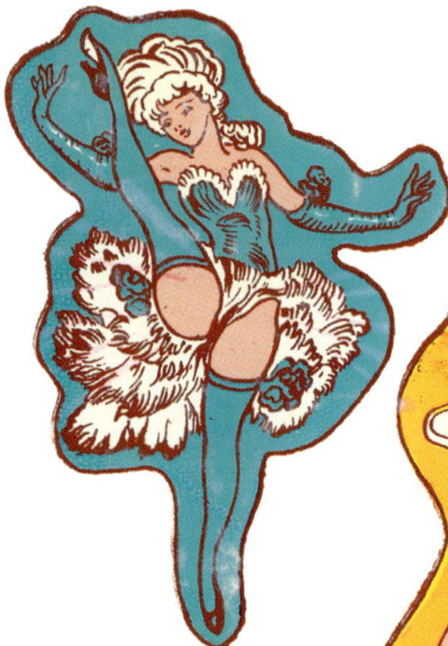

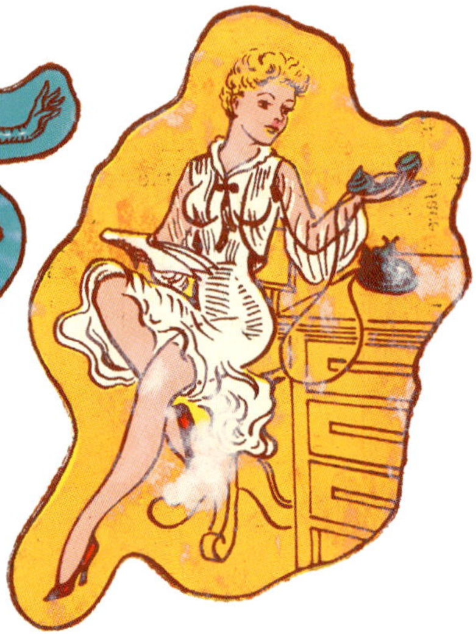

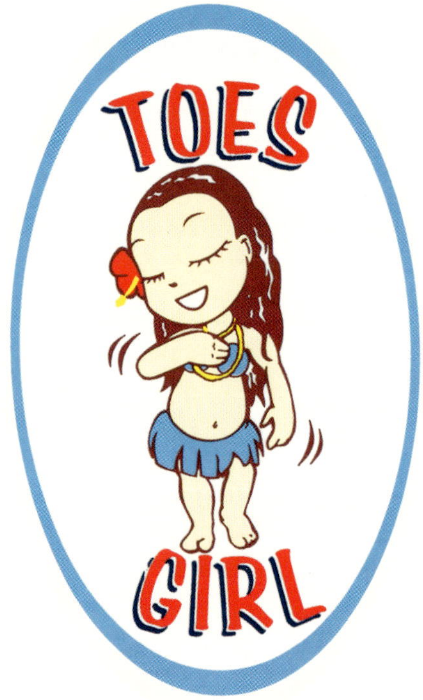
TOES
GIRL

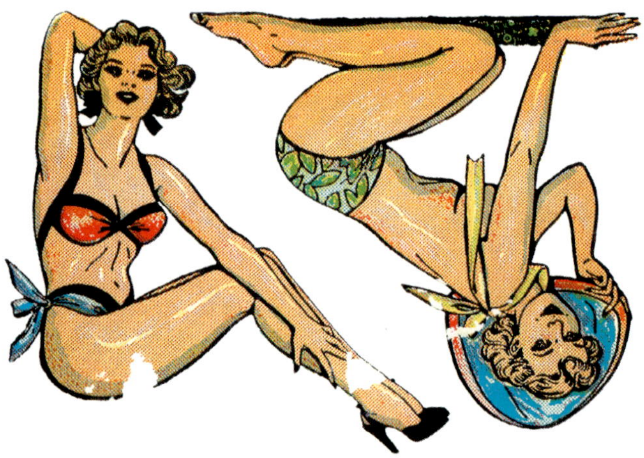

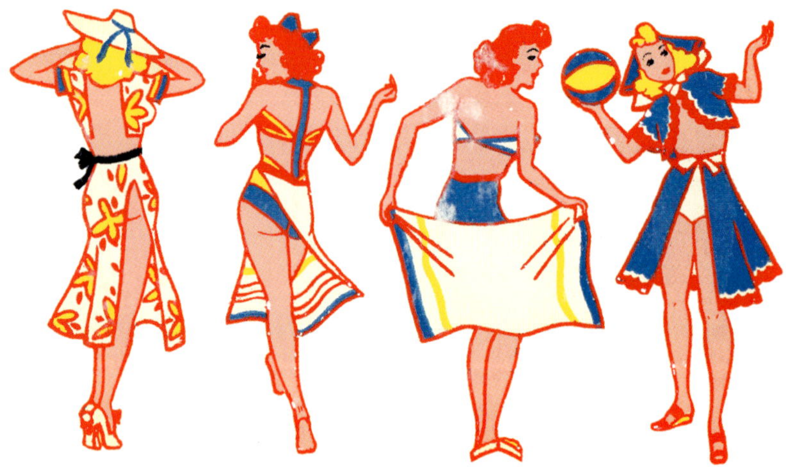

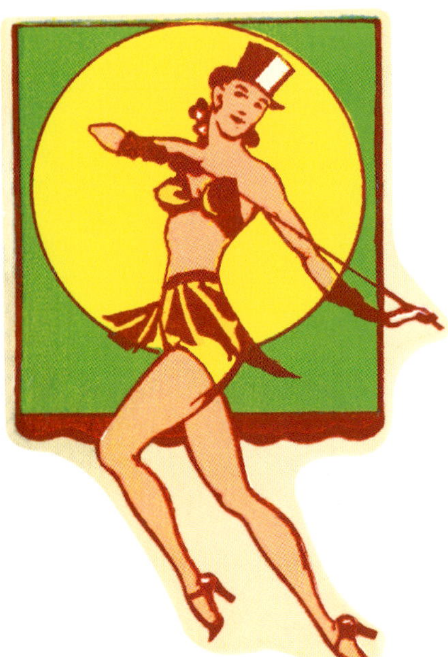

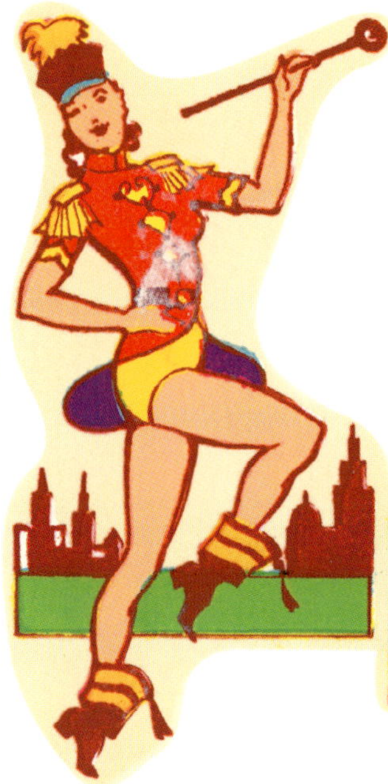

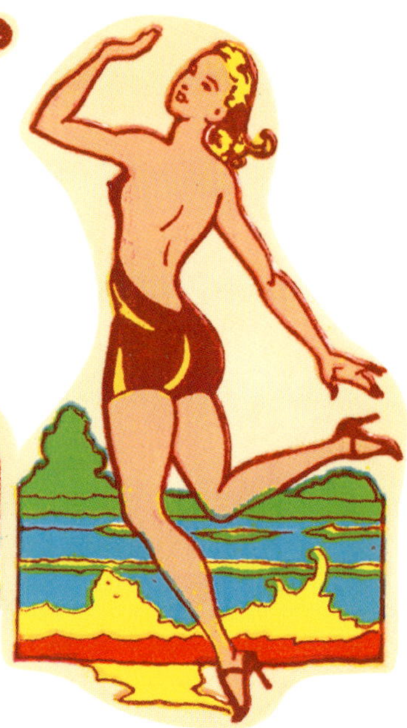

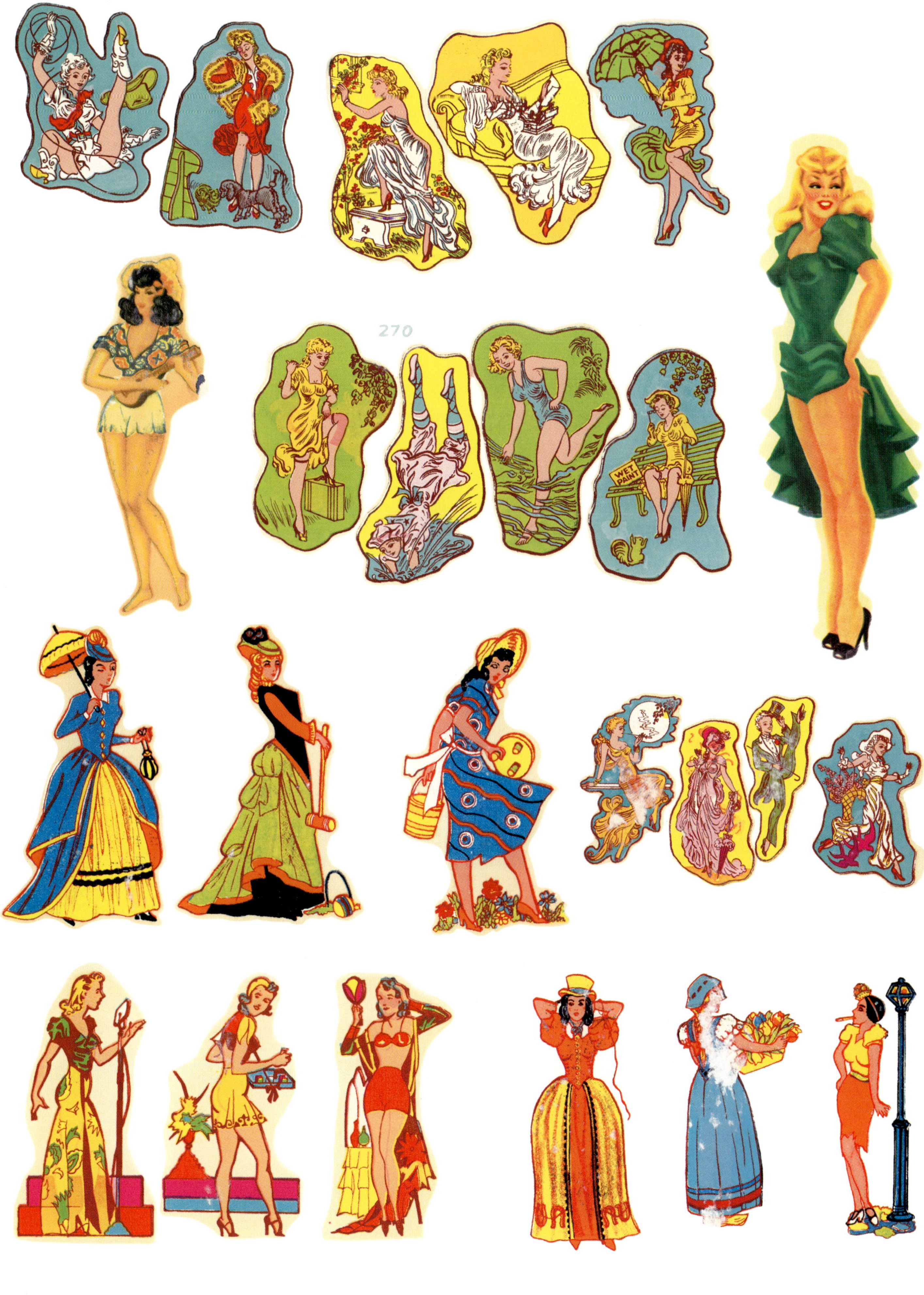
270
WET PAINT

CHAPTER 4.9
ROUND ROUND GET AROUND, I GET AROUND

Surfers have driven many different cars over the last 100 years, including panel vans, pickup trucks, Volkswagen buses, surfer vans, and SUVs. But in the 1960s, the Beach Boys sang about their "40 Ford wagon and I call it a Woody" in *Surf City*, and that image was fortified by other songs and a lot of movies, and the Woody has stuck in the minds of the world as the Surfer's Choice.

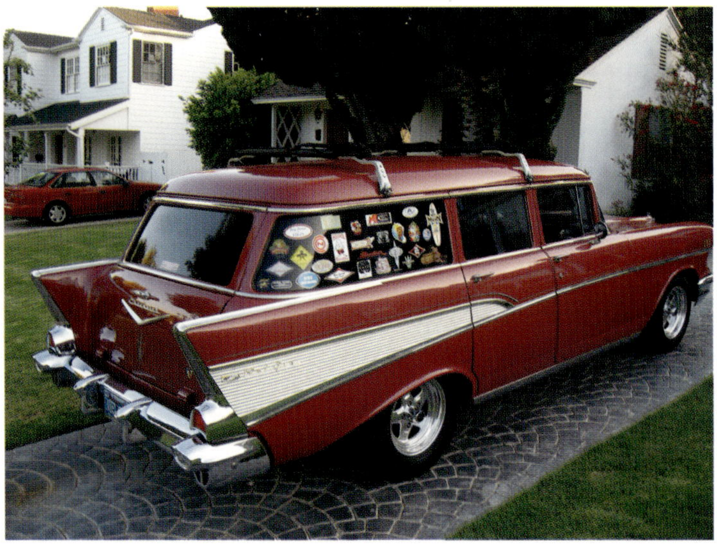

Tim McNulty's 1957 Chevy Bel Air wagon, tarted up with a couple decades of classic stickers. Photo: Ben Marcus.

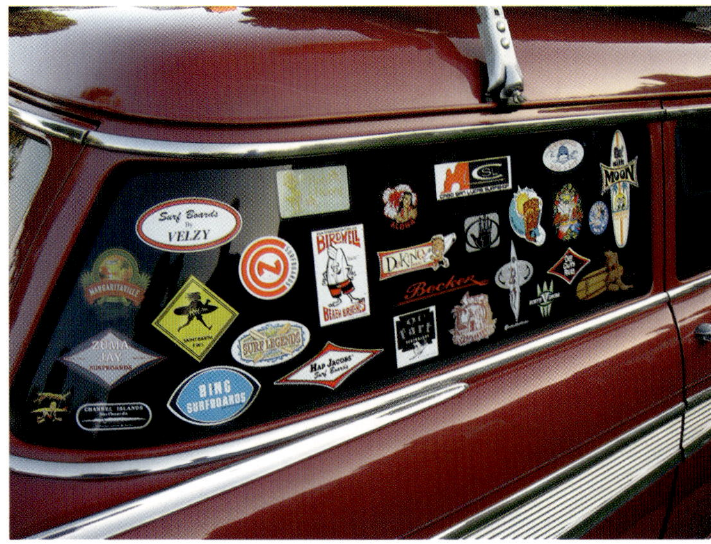

The right rear angle of Tim McNulty's '57 Bel Air wagon, featuring some of the most classic surf stickers from Birdwell to Becker. Photo: Ben Marcus.

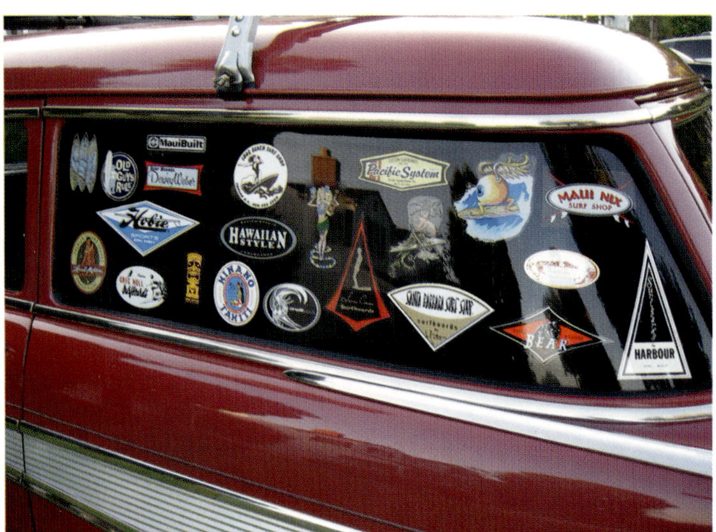

The left rear angle of Tim McNulty's '57 Chevy Bel Air wagon. Photo: Ben Marcus.

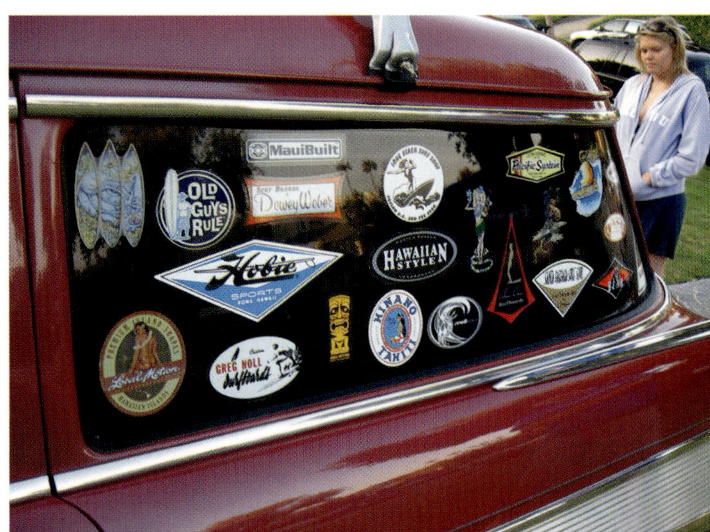

The left side of Tim McNulty's 1957 Bel Air wagon, with onlooker looking on. Photo: Ben Marcus.

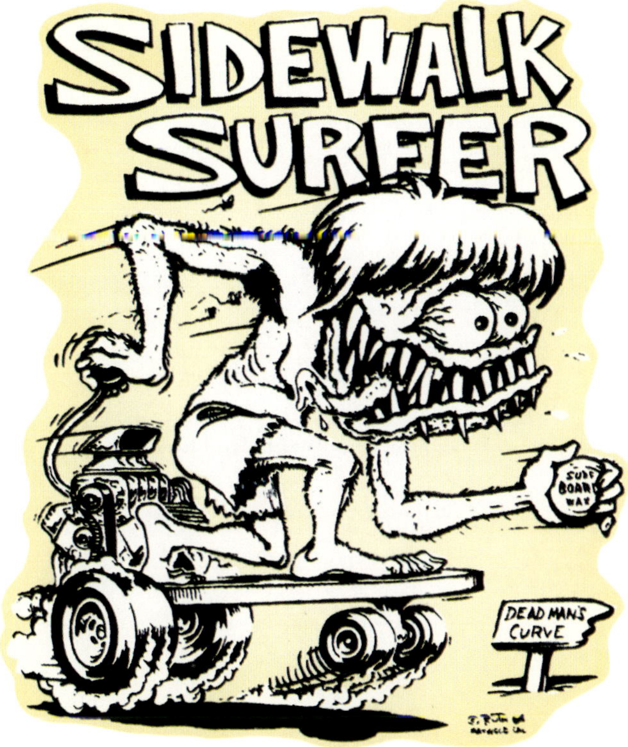
SIDEWALK
SURFER
DEAD MAN'S
CURVE

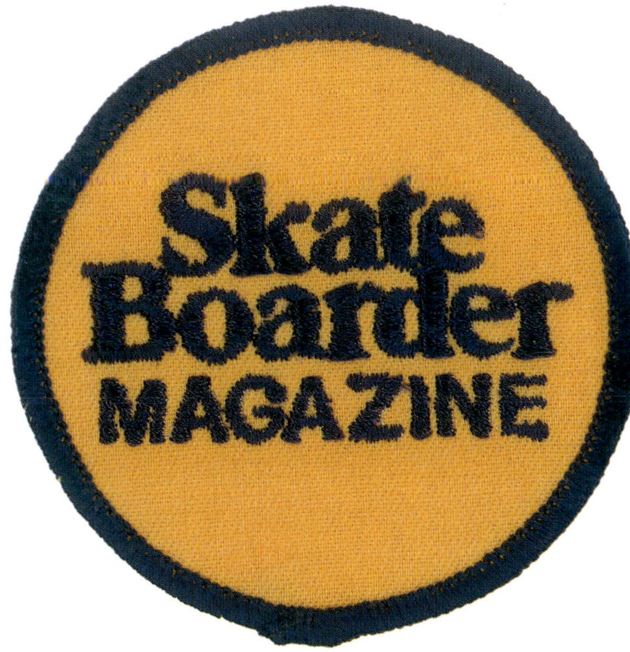
Skate
Boarder
MAGAZINE

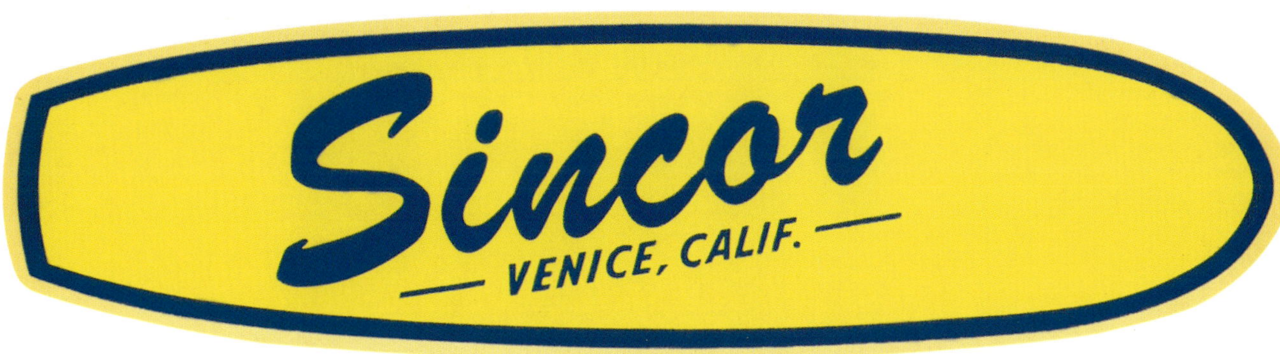
Sincor
VENICE, CALIF.

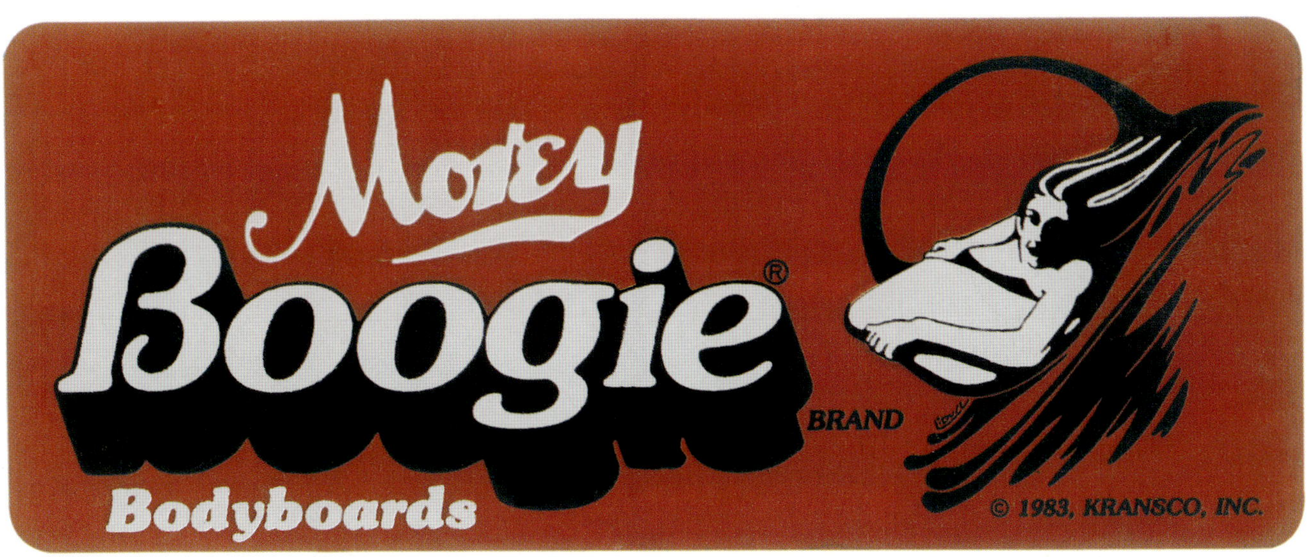
Morey
Boogie®
BRAND
Bodyboards
© 1983, KRANSCO, INC.

Blackies is a bar in Newport Beach, at the pier. It has no relationship to Blackie August, but it is a surf destination. The spot is named for the bar, not for the son of Robert August.

CHAPTER FIVE

SURF SHOPPING

Surf Shops and What to Buy There.

Surf shops are a business, sometimes a good business, sometimes a bad business, but like all businesses they need to advertise. The surf shop sticker was derived from the Surfboards By sticker, and they began to appear after Velzy and O'Neill opened their shops, and surf shops began to flower up and down the California coast, then around the country and around the world: "In the 70s, I would send Jack's Surf Shop, $10 or $20 and they would send 30 or 40 or 50 decals, and all of the examples of Jack's in my collection are a result of that," Pete Noble said. "Over the years I have given a ton away."

Noble gave tons away, but kept more than a few, and combined with the stickers of Keith Eshelman and Cary Weiss, here are a lot of surf shop stickers from A to Z.

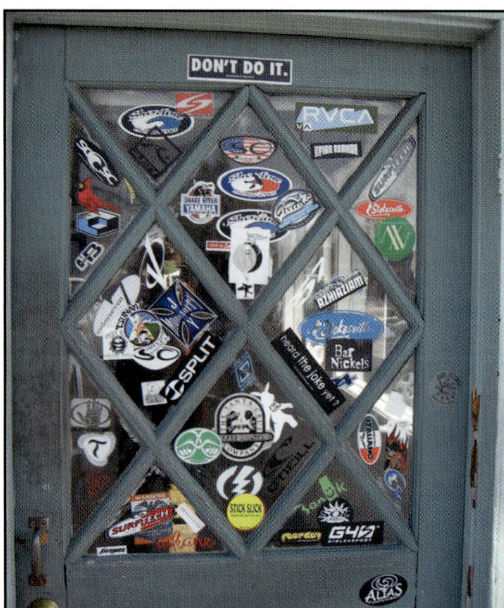

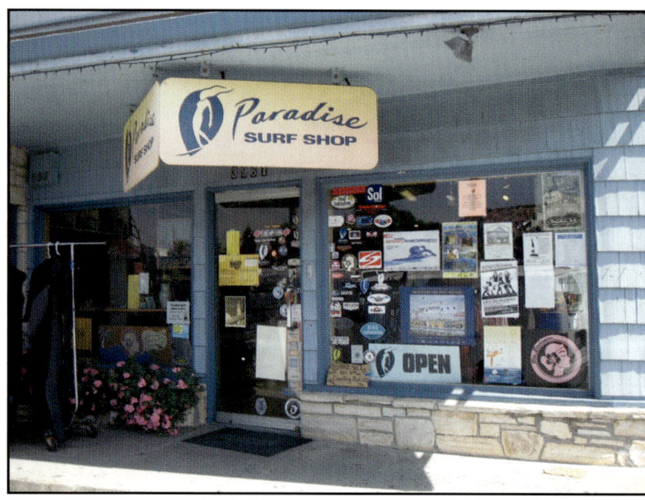

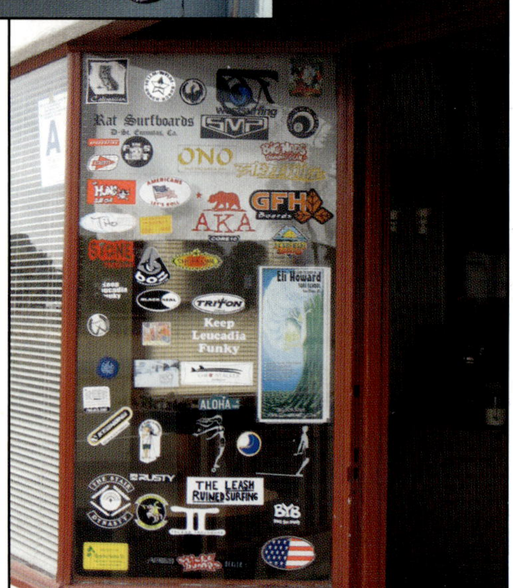

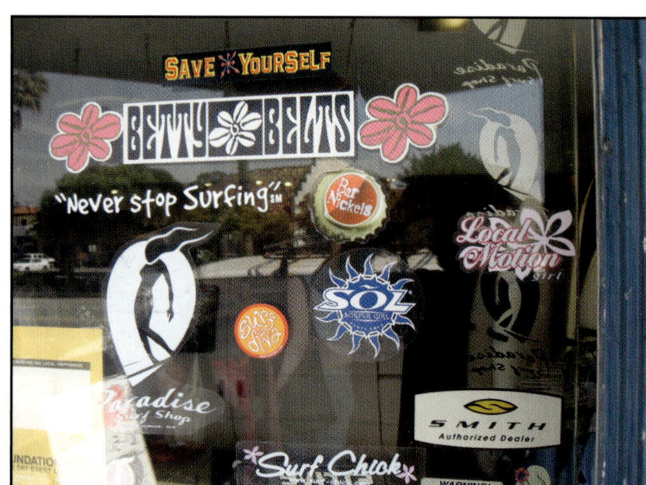

AUSTRALIAN
SURF SHOP

BREAKERS
SURF SHOP
MISSION BEACH • SAN DIEGO, CALIFORNIA

AUSTRALIAN
SURF SHOP

Since 1962
BRIGHTON BEACH
Surf Shop

Baja
BOARDHOUSE
ENSENADA BAJA MEXICO

CARBONELL
Surf Shop
LONG BEACH

Beach House
SANTA BARBARA

CASEY
625 PRINCES HWY. ROCKDALE SYD. AUSTRALIA
59 • 2472

Beach House
SANTA BARBARA

Cayucos
SURF COMPANY
CAYUCOS, CA.

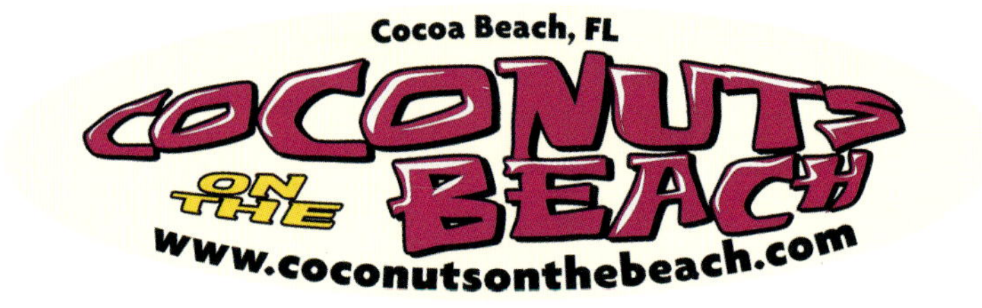

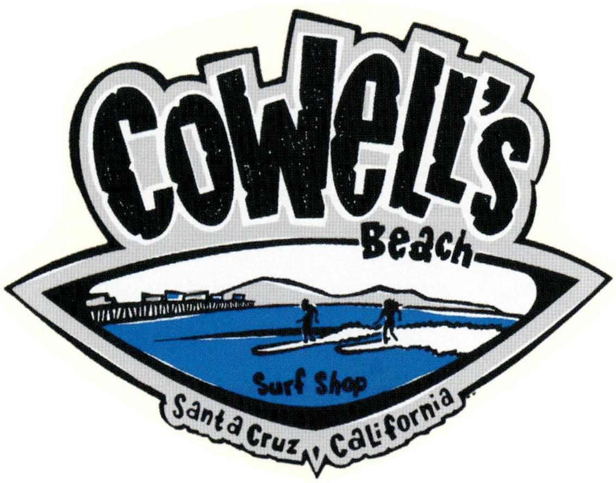

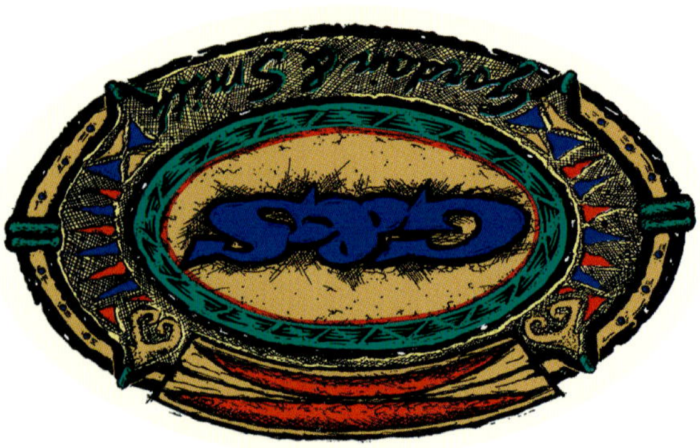

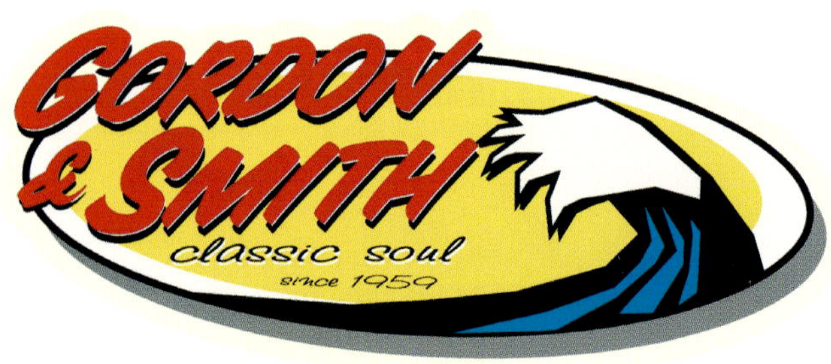

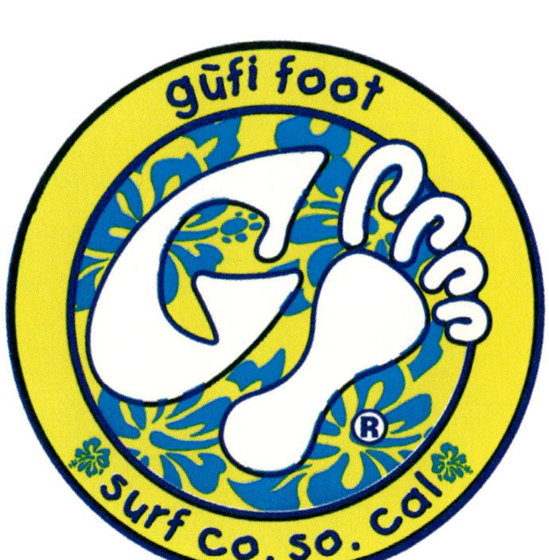

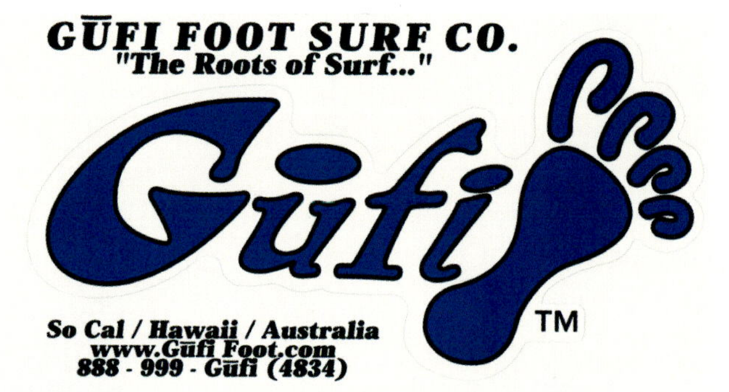

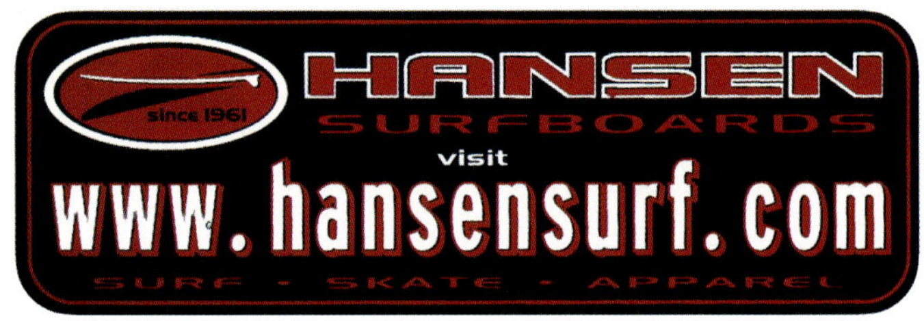

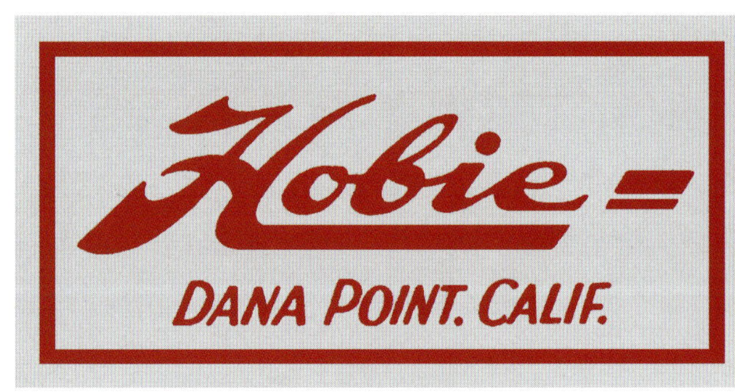

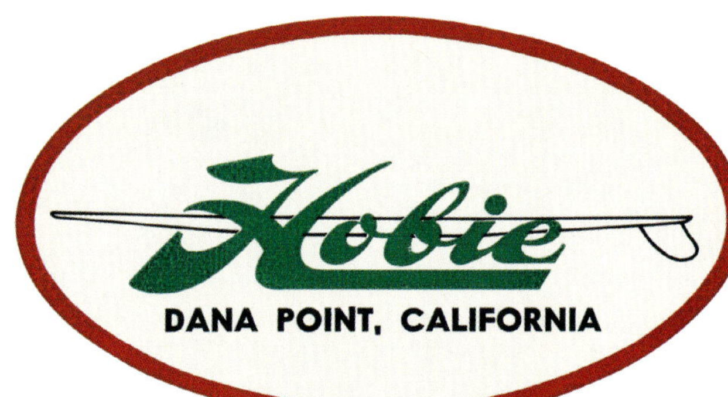

Those were Hobie laminates that Con Colbourn used for Hobie boards he bought from Hobie back in the 50s, because he couldn't glass them. Hobie would send up blanks with those laminates and they were glassed in Los Angeles. Con sold them in the surf house. – Pete Noble.

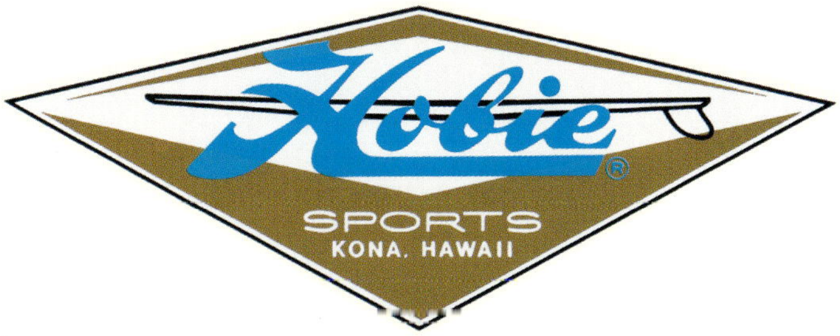
Hobie
SPORTS
KONA, HAWAII

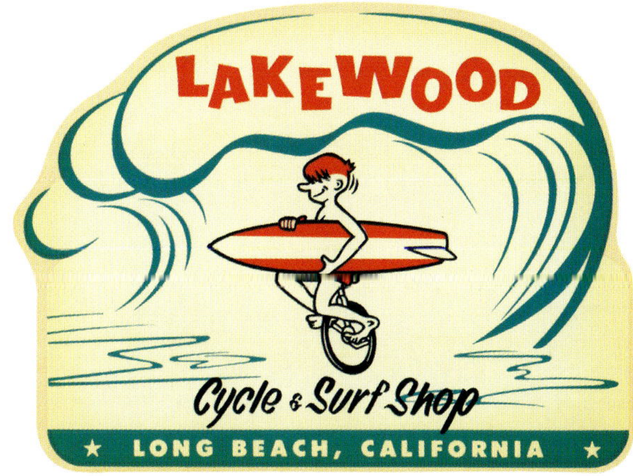
LAKEWOOD
Cycle & Surf Shop
LONG BEACH, CALIFORNIA

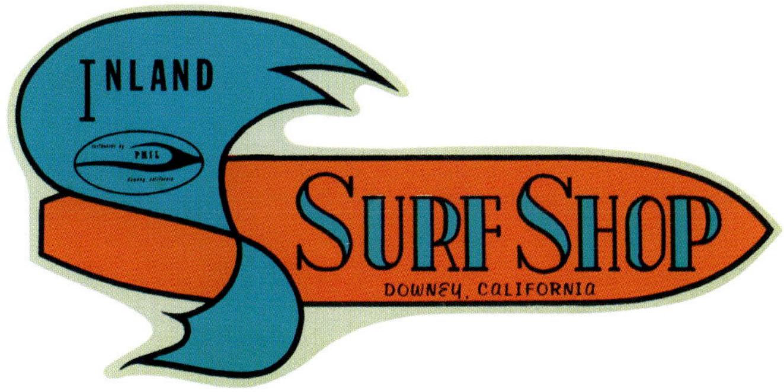
INLAND
SURF SHOP
DOWNEY, CALIFORNIA

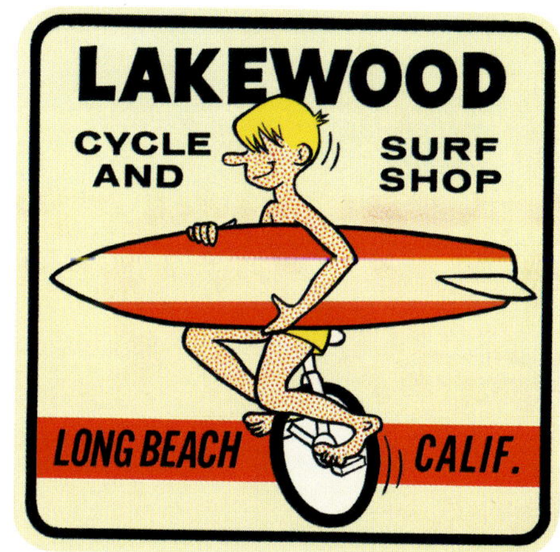
LAKEWOOD
CYCLE AND
SURF SHOP
LONG BEACH
CALIF.

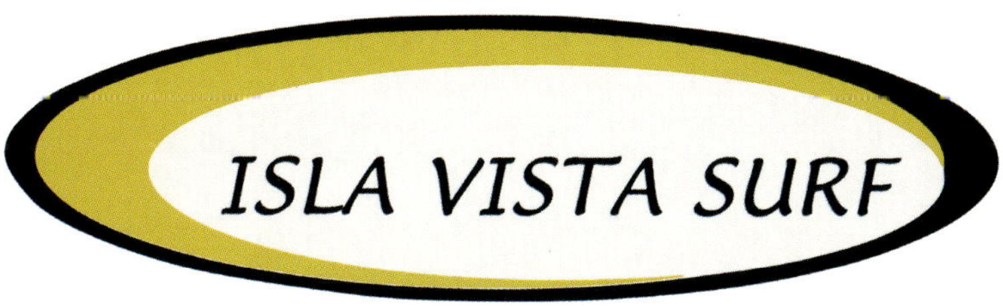
ISLA VISTA SURF

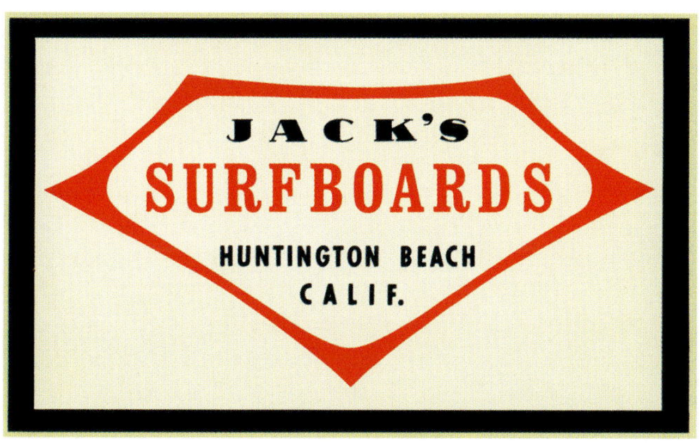
JACK'S
SURFBOARDS
HUNTINGTON BEACH
CALIF.

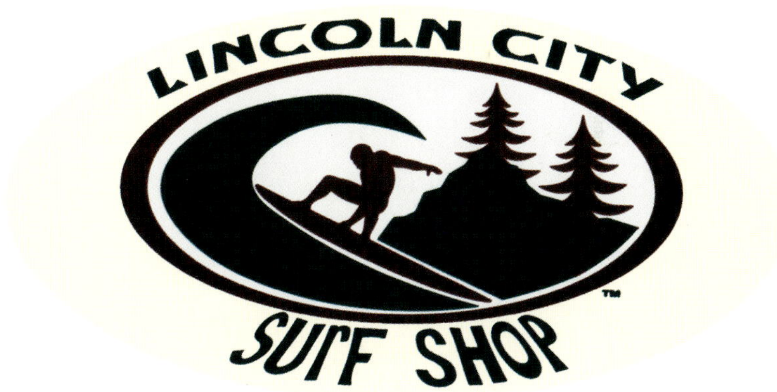
LINCOLN CITY
SURF SHOP

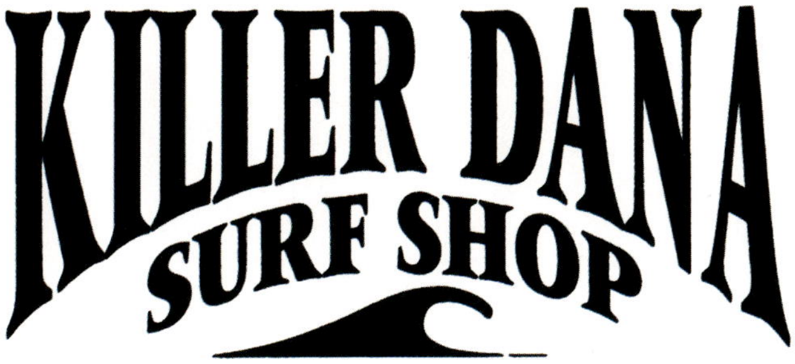
KILLER DANA
SURF SHOP

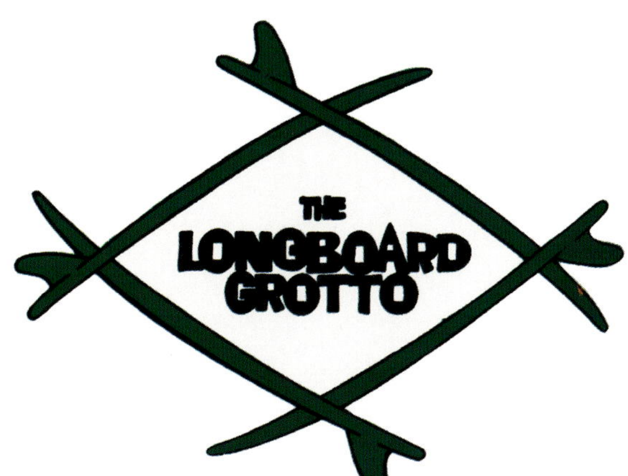
THE
LONGBOARD
GROTTO

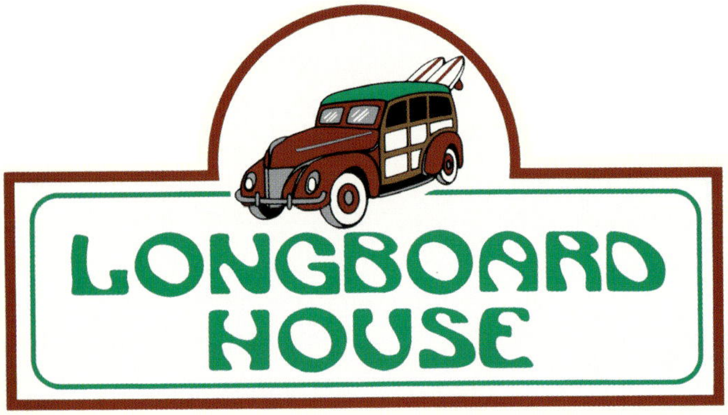

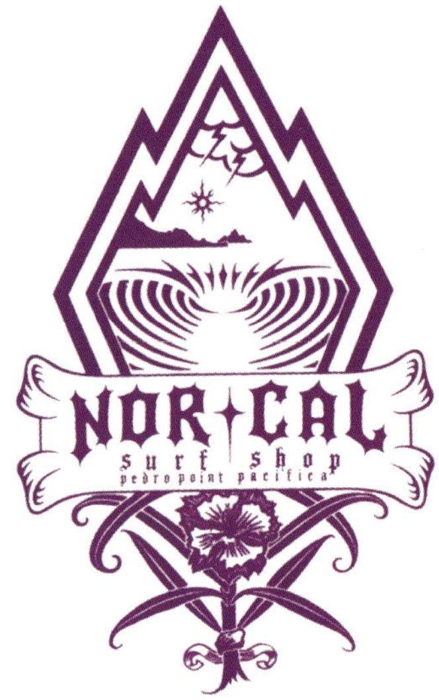

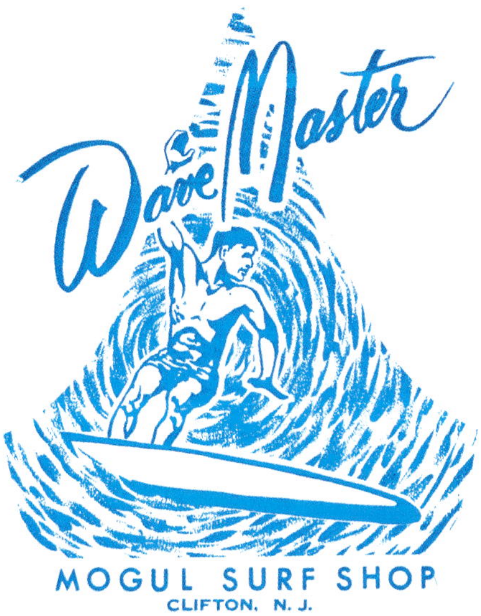

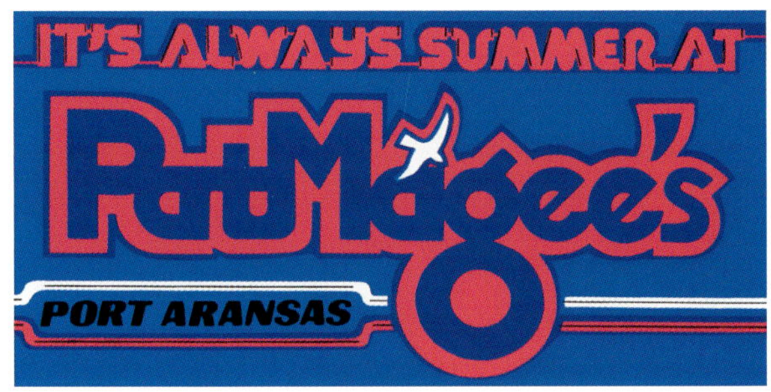

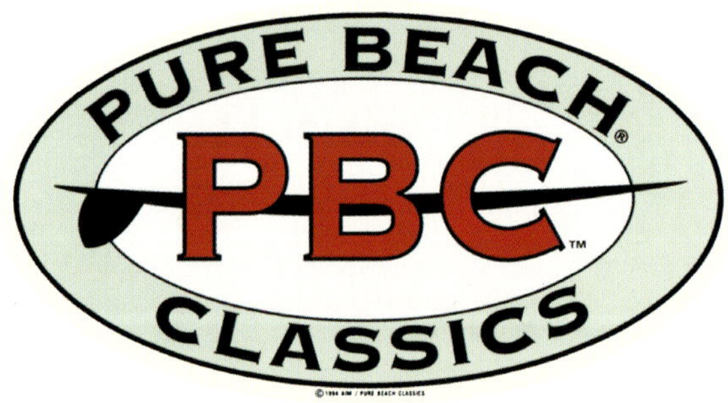

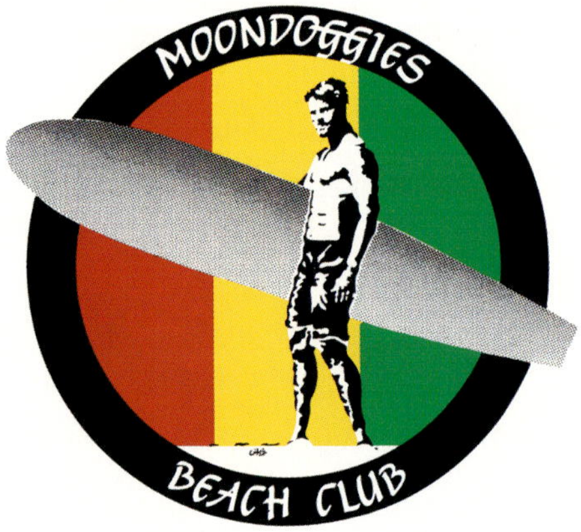

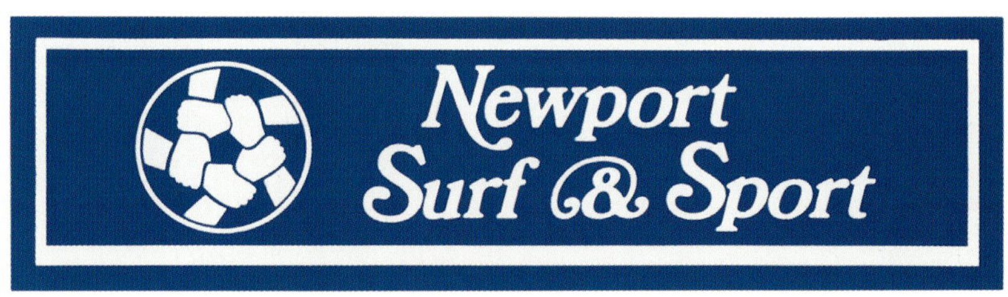

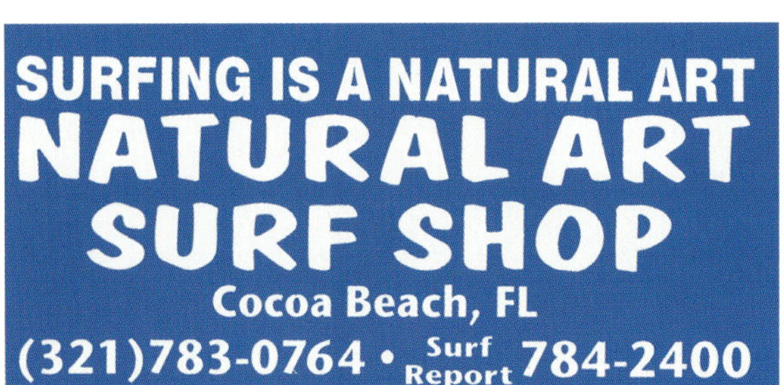

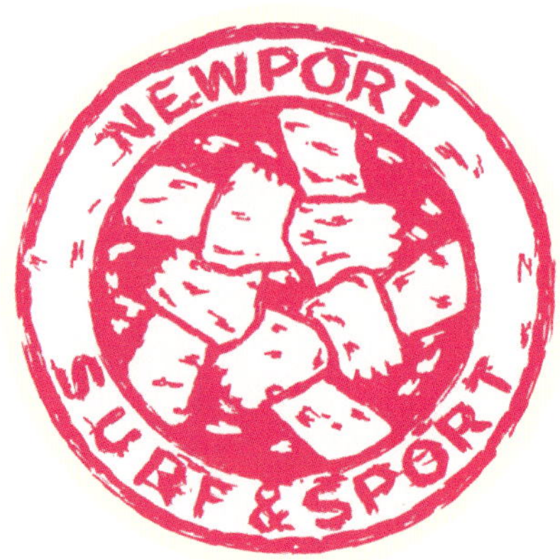

Tommy Noble was a partner in Newport Surf and Sport. The clenched hands are an international symbol of brotherhood. – Pete Noble

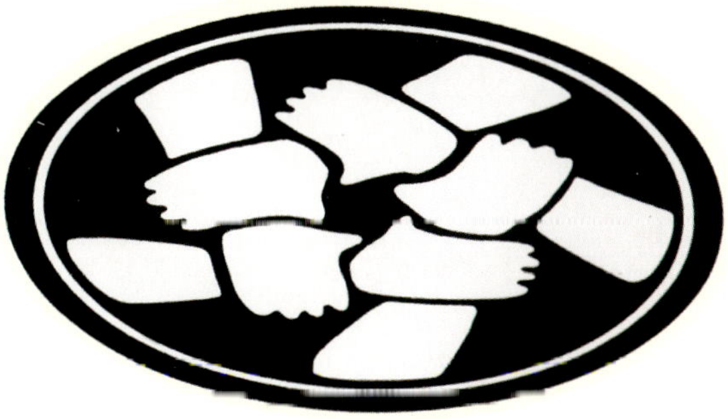

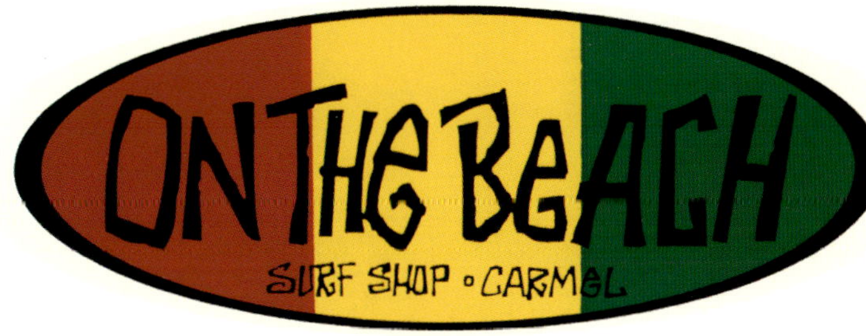
ON THE BEACH
SURF SHOP • CARMEL

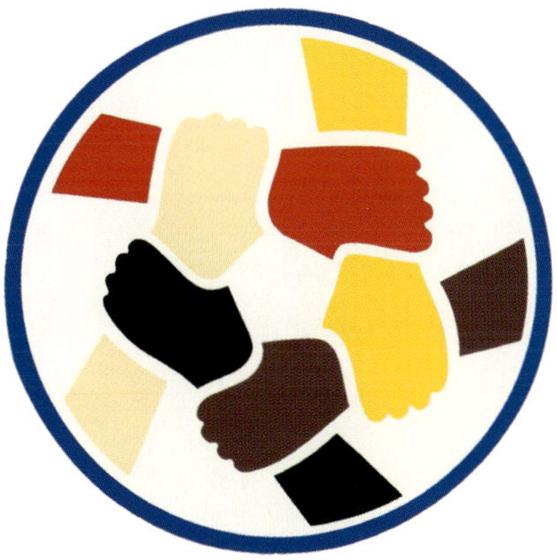

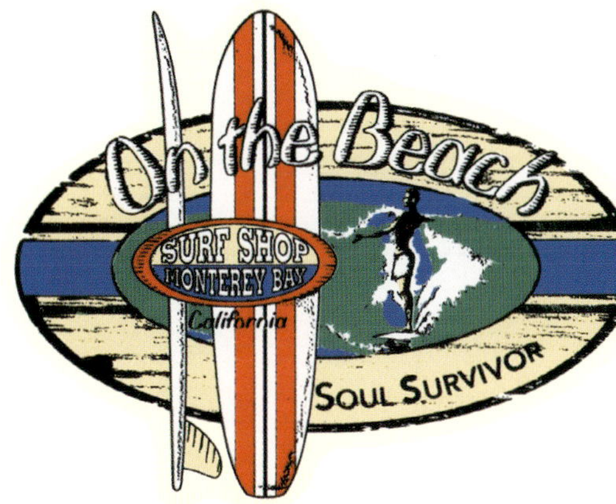
On the Beach
SURF SHOP
MONTEREY BAY
California
SOUL SURVIVOR

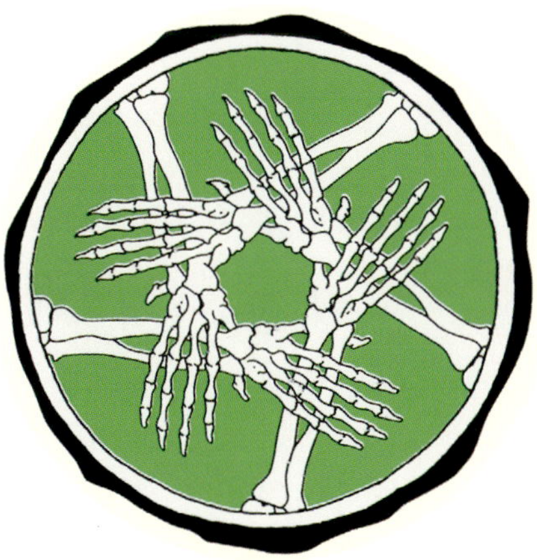

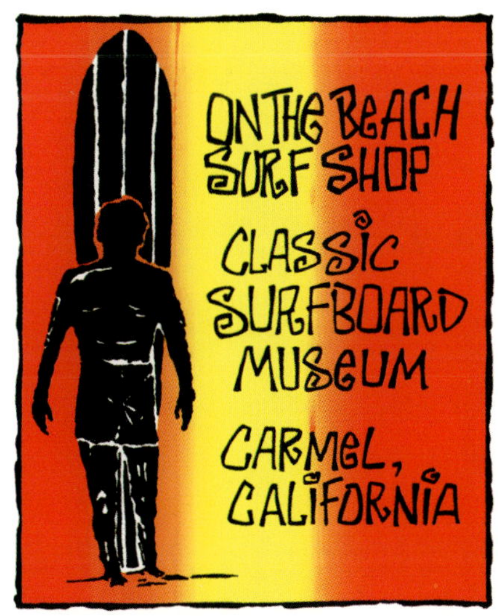
ON THE BEACH
SURF SHOP
CLASSIC
SURFBOARD
MUSEUM
CARMEL,
CALIFORNIA

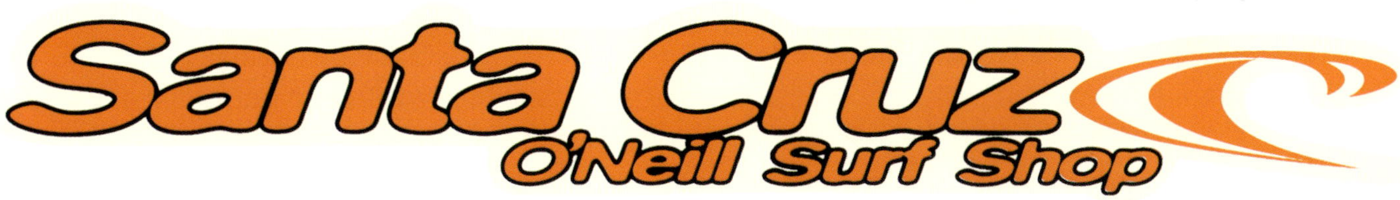
Santa Cruz
O'Neill Surf Shop

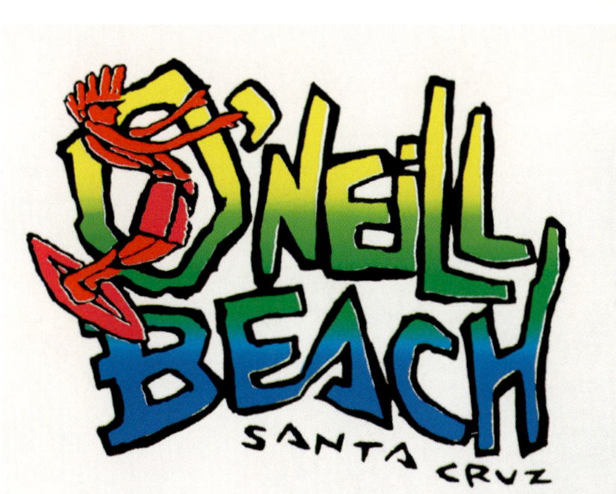
O'NEILL
BEACH
SANTA CRUZ

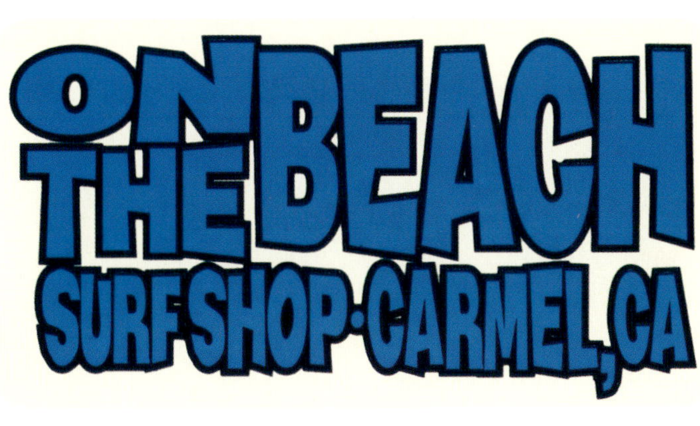
ON THE BEACH
SURF SHOP·CARMEL, CA

OTB
OnTheBeachSurfShop

OTB

ON THE BEACH
SURF SHOP • MONTEREY, CA

ON THE BEACH
SURF SHOP • MONTEREY, CA

on the
BEACH
SURF SHOP Carmel

On the Beach
SURF SHOP
MONTEREY BAY
California
SOUL SURVIVOR

OTB
1-800-455-WAVE

OTB

ON THE BEACH
SURFSHOP
Monterey Bay, CA
Est. 1986

OTB
1-800-455-WAVE

ON THE BEACH
SURFSHOP
Monterey Bay, CA
Est. 1986

ON THE BEACH
SURFSHOP
Monterey Bay, CA
Est. 1986

ON THE BEACH
SURF SHOP • MONTEREY, CA

OnTheBeach
surf shop - carmel, ca

ON THE BEACH
SURF SHOP·CARMEL, CA

OTB
OnTheBeachSurfShop

ON THE BEACH
SURFSHOP
Monterey Bay, CA
Est. 1986

PACIFIC BEACH
SURF CLUB
SAN DIEGO, CALIFORNIA

owl

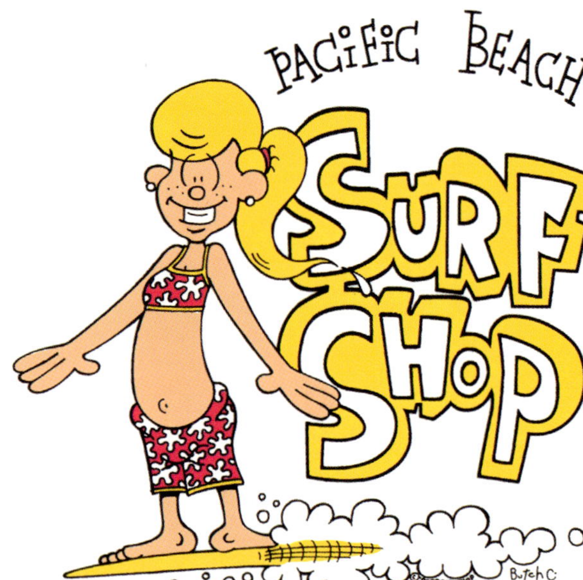

747 Pacific Beach Drive
San Diego, CA 92109

Jeff White is Owl Surfboards. He started in Santa Barbara and also had a shop in Santa Cruz, on Front Street, across from Ottos. He is still a partner in the Beach House in Santa Barbara. – Pete Noble

Portola
SURF SHOP
SANTA CRUZ

owl
SANTA BARBARA, CA

PORTOLA
Surf Shop

PORTOLA Surf Shop

ROBERTS SURF SHOP

RON JON SURF SHOP
"ONE OF A KIND"
Cocoa Beach, Fla.

ROBERTS SURF SHOP

RON JON SURF SHOP
LONG BEACH ISLAND - MANAHAWKIN, N.J.

ROBERTS SURF SHOP

SURF SAN ONOFRE SHOP

SURF SAN ONOFRE SHOP

ROBERTS SURF SHOP

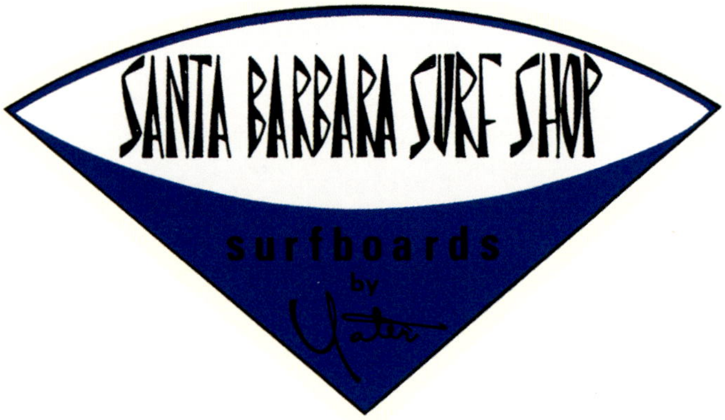
SANTA BARBARA SURF SHOP
surfboards
by

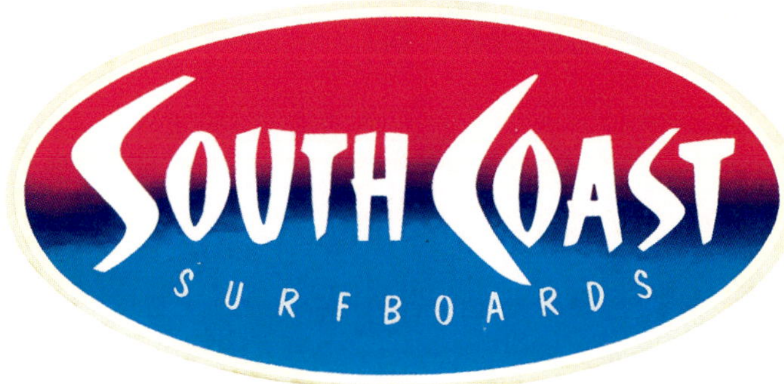
SOUTH COAST
SURFBOARDS

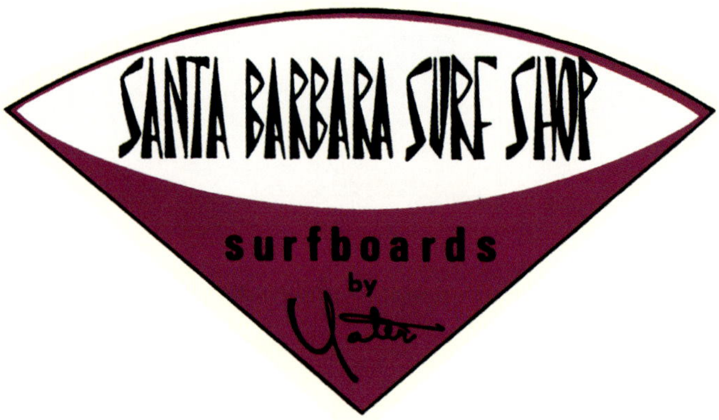
SANTA BARBARA SURF SHOP
surfboards
by

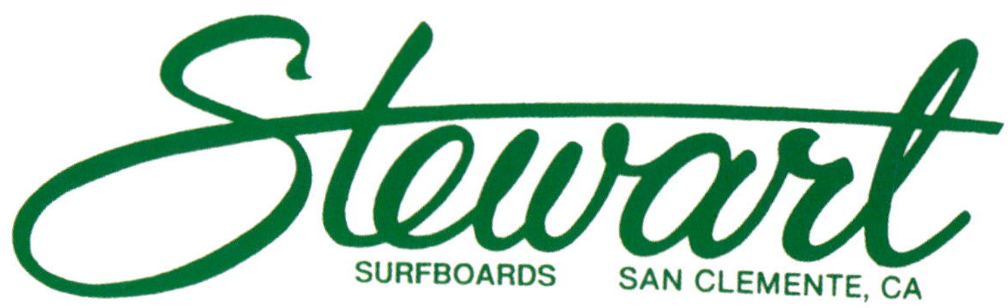
Stewart
SURFBOARDS
SAN CLEMENTE, CA

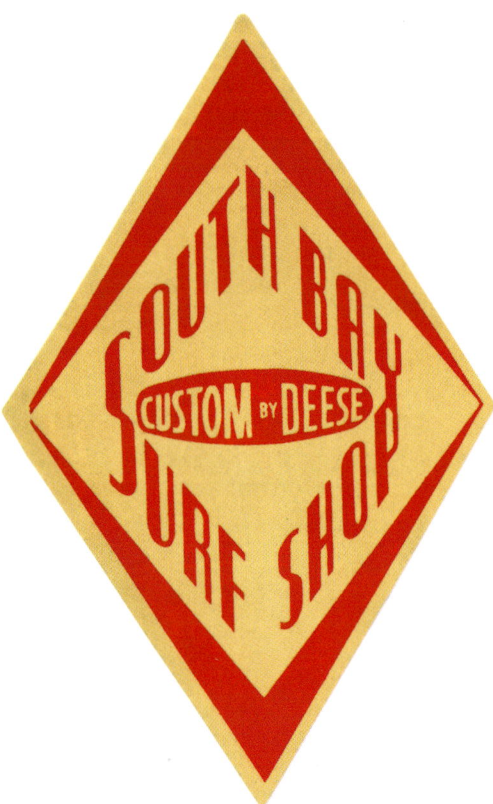
SOUTH BAY
CUSTOM BY DEESE
SURF SHOP

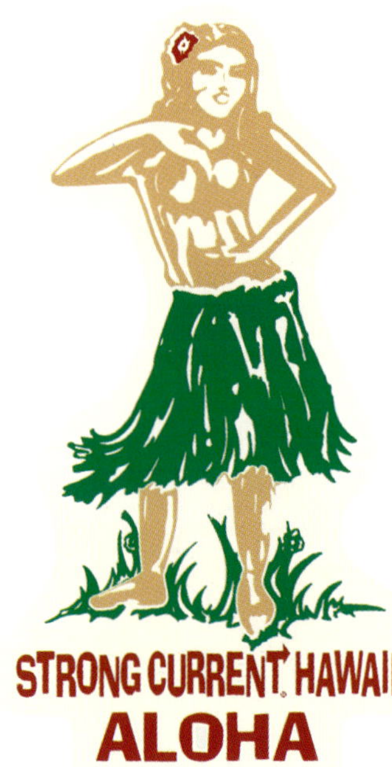
STRONG CURRENT® HAWAII
ALOHA

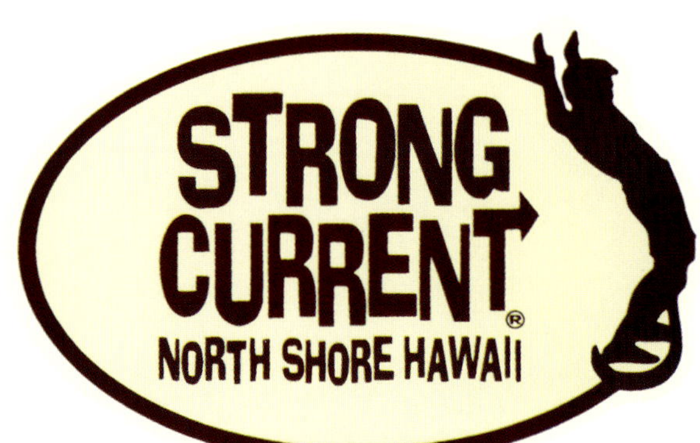
STRONG
CURRENT®
NORTH SHORE HAWAII

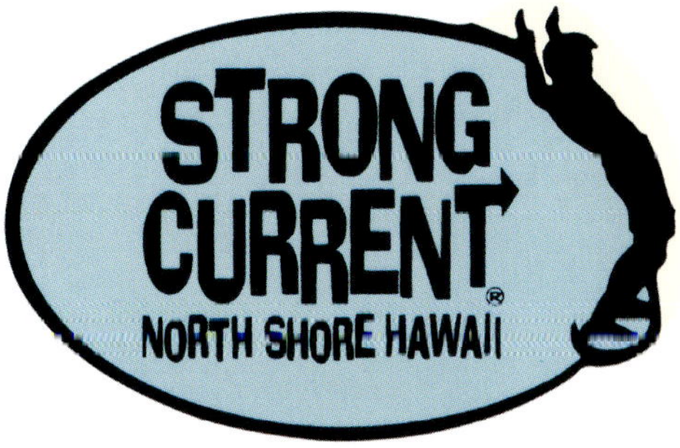
STRONG
CURRENT
NORTH SHORE HAWAII

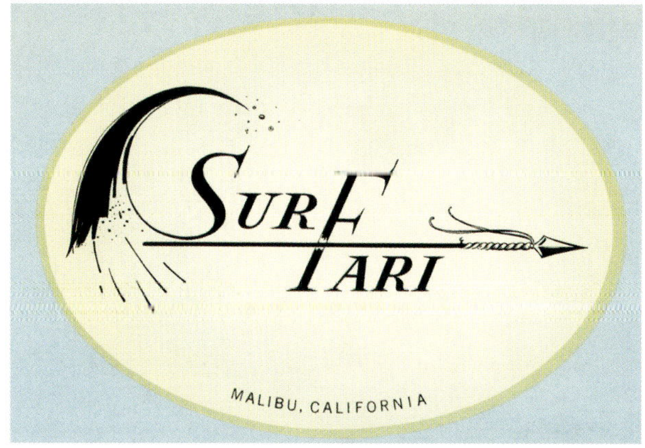
SURF
FARI
MALIBU, CALIFORNIA

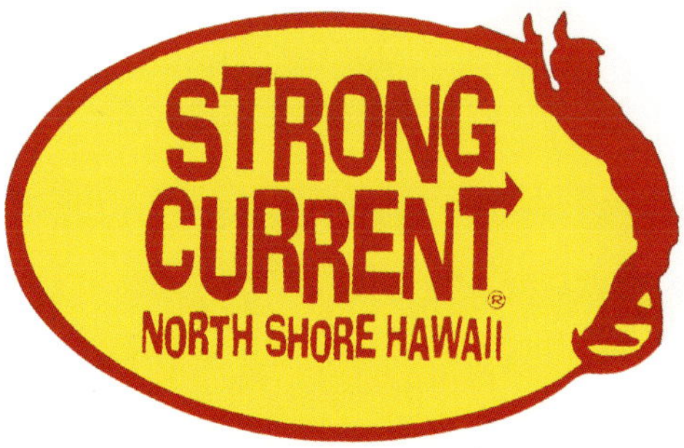
STRONG
CURRENT
NORTH SHORE HAWAII

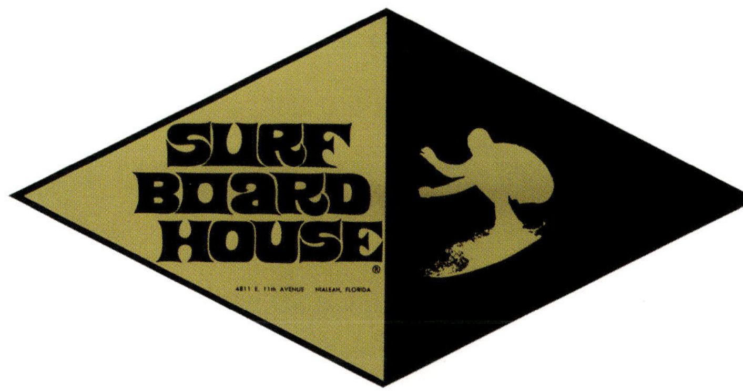
SURF
BOARD
HOUSE

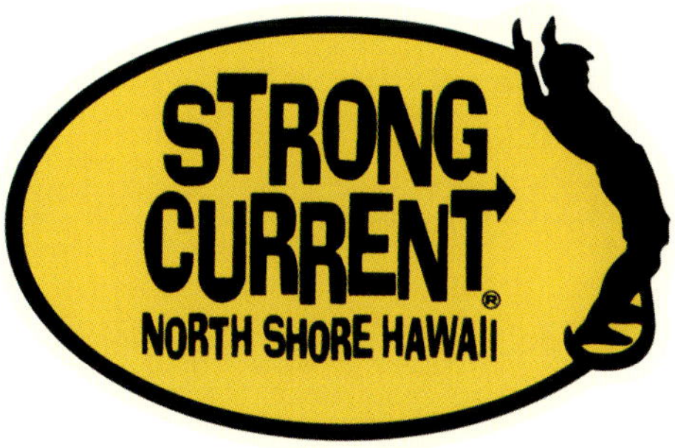
STRONG
CURRENT
NORTH SHORE HAWAII

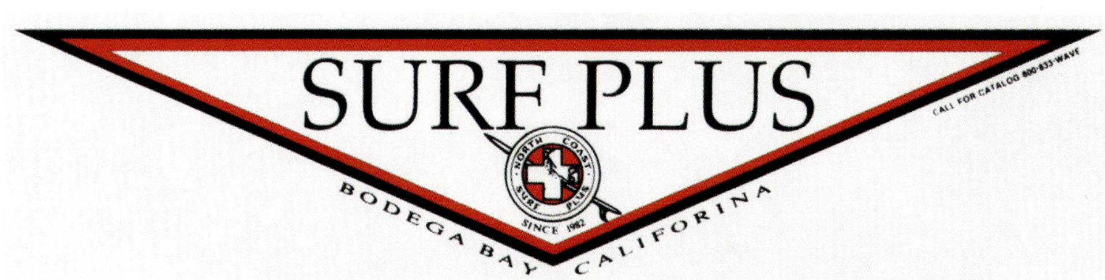
SURF PLUS
CALL FOR CATALOG 800-833-WAVE
NORTH COAST SURF PLUS
SINCE 1982
BODEGA BAY CALIFORINA

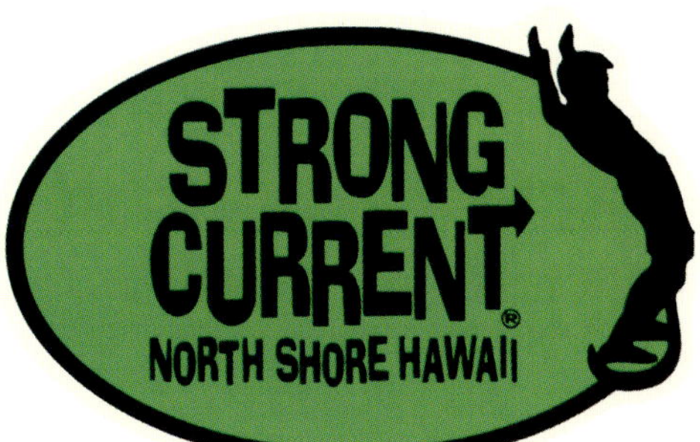
STRONG
CURRENT
NORTH SHORE HAWAII

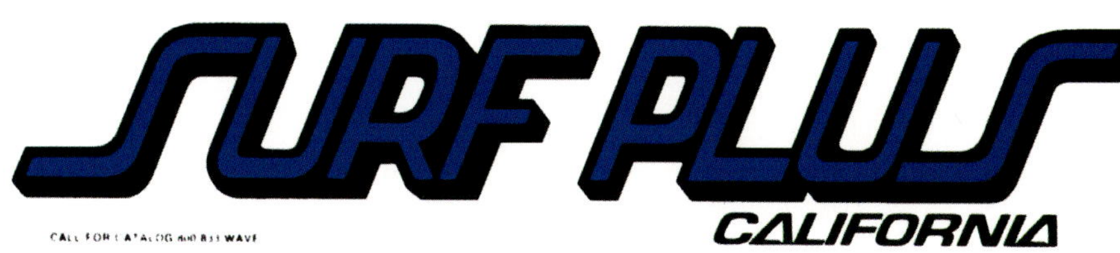
SURF PLUS
CALIFORNIA

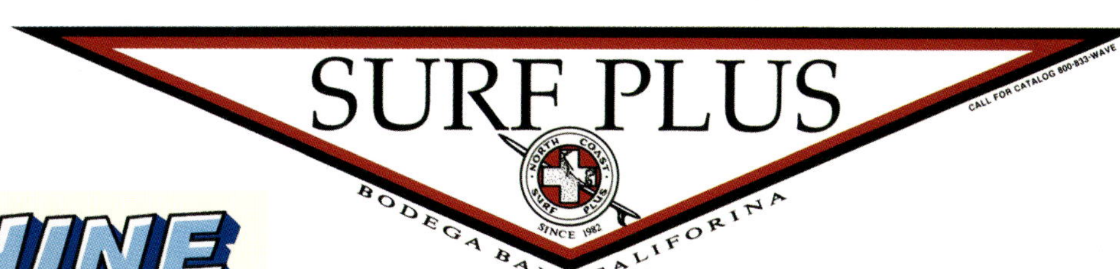
SURF PLUS
CALL FOR CATALOG 800-833-WAVE
NORTH COAST SURF PLUS
SINCE 1982
BODEGA BAY CALIFORINA

SUNSHINE
SURF
SHOP
14 Avenue Foch BIARRITZ

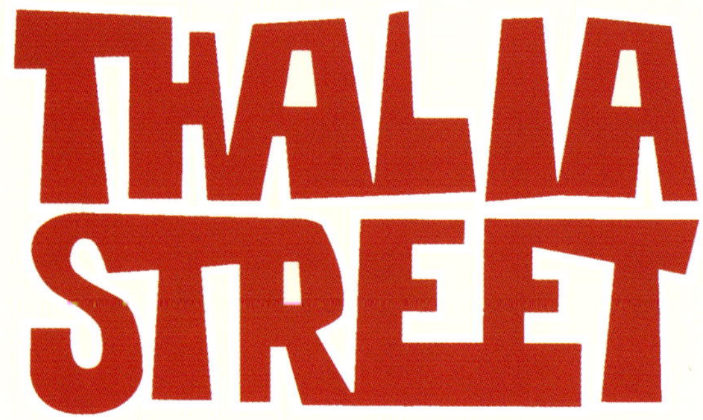
THALIA
STREET

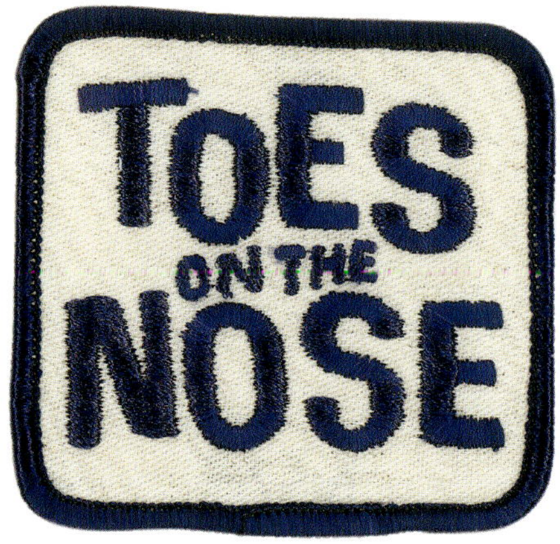
TOES
ON THE
NOSE

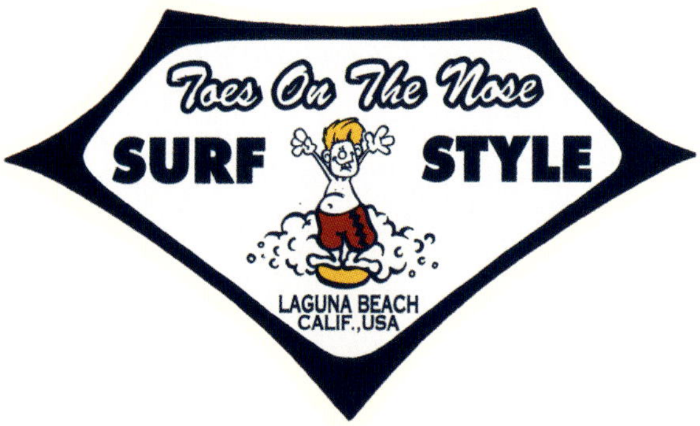
Toes On The Nose
SURF
STYLE
LAGUNA BEACH
CALIF., USA

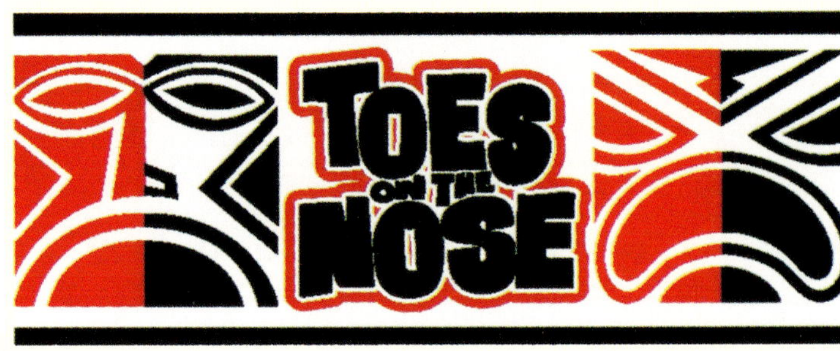
TOES
ON THE
NOSE

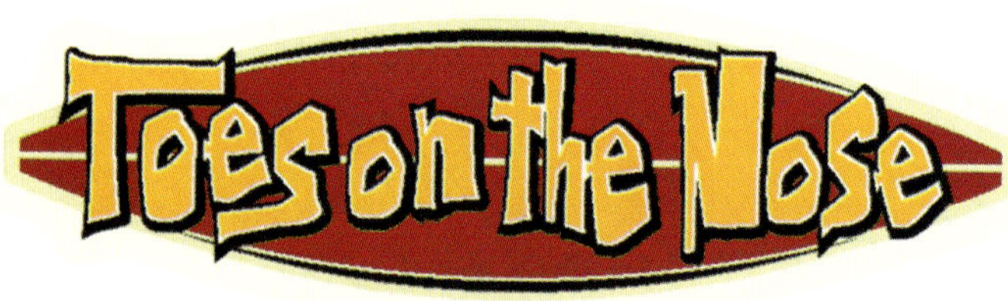
Toes on the Nose

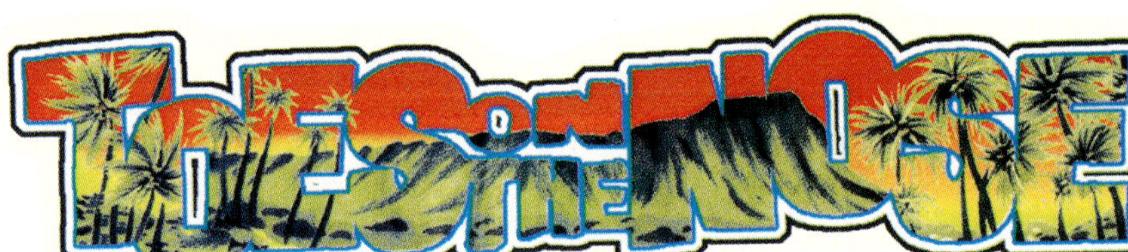
TOES ON THE NOSE

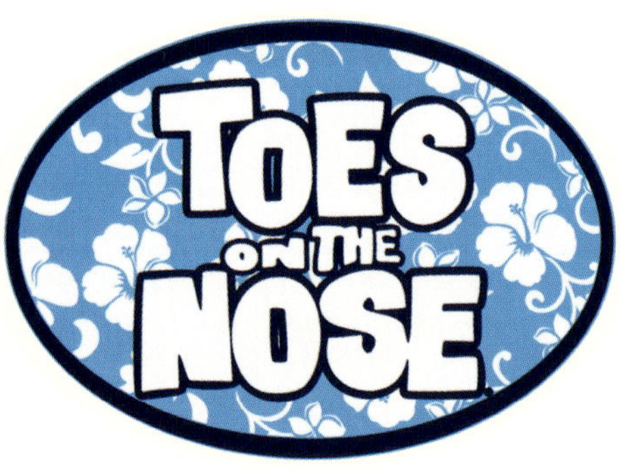
TOES
ON THE
NOSE

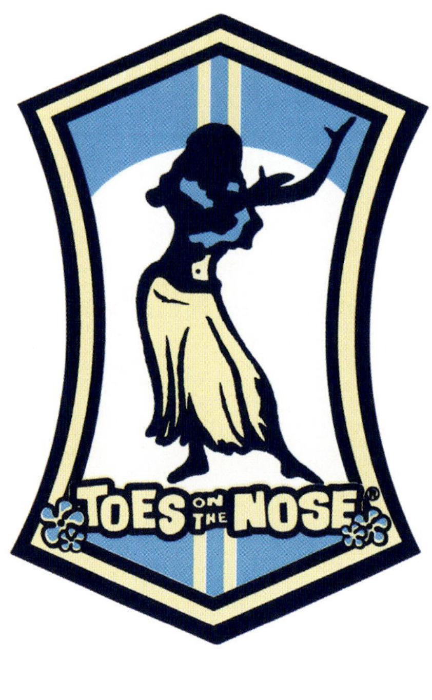
TOES ON THE NOSE

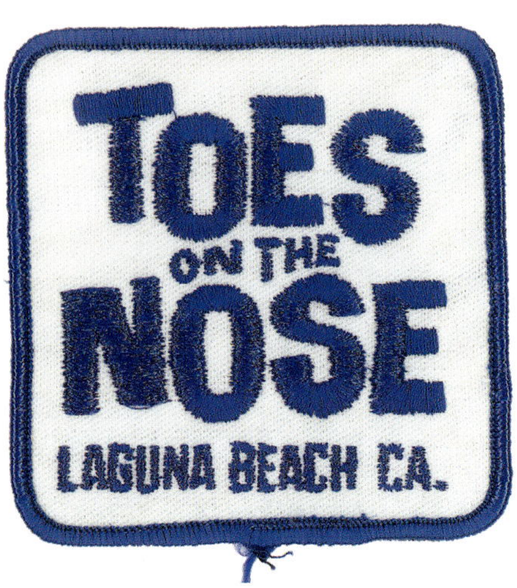
TOES
ON THE
NOSE
LAGUNA BEACH CA.

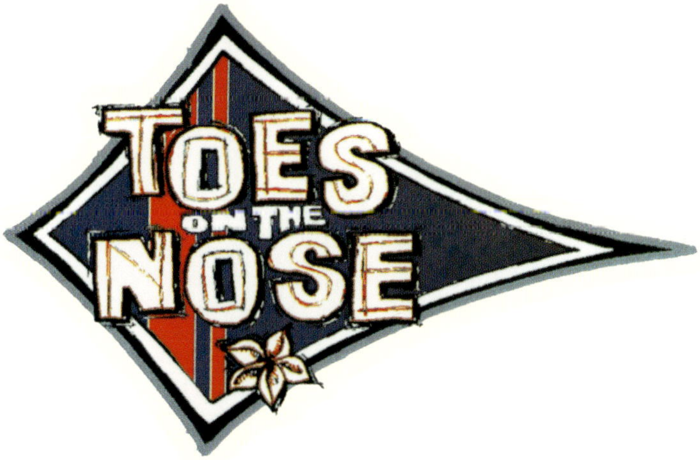
TOES
ON THE
NOSE

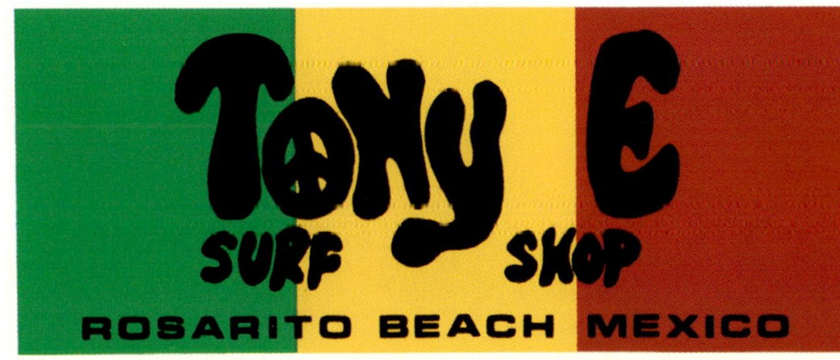
TONY E
SURF SHOP
ROSARITO BEACH MEXICO

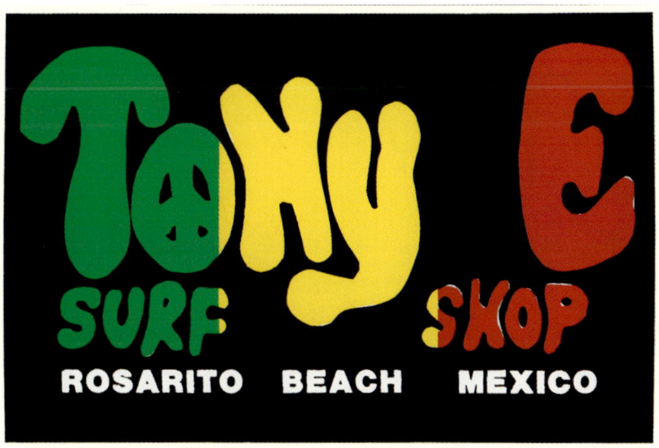
TONY E
SURF SHOP
ROSARITO BEACH MEXICO

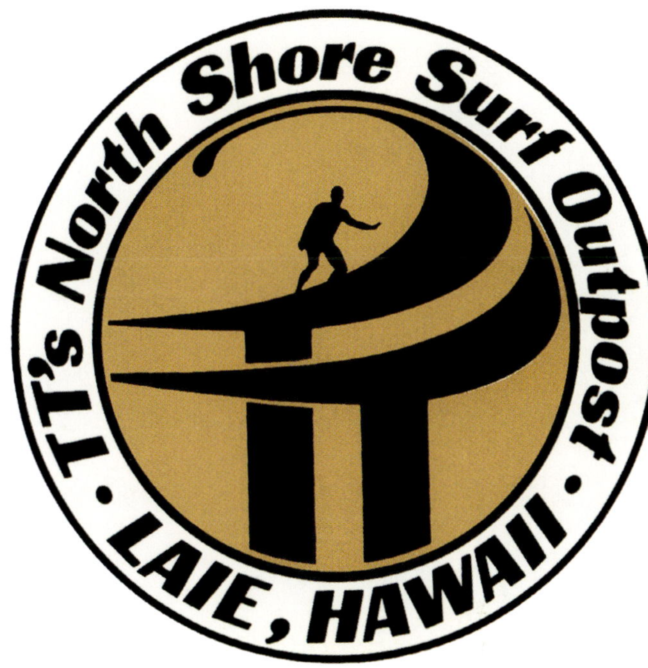
TT's North Shore Surf Outpost
LAIE, HAWAII

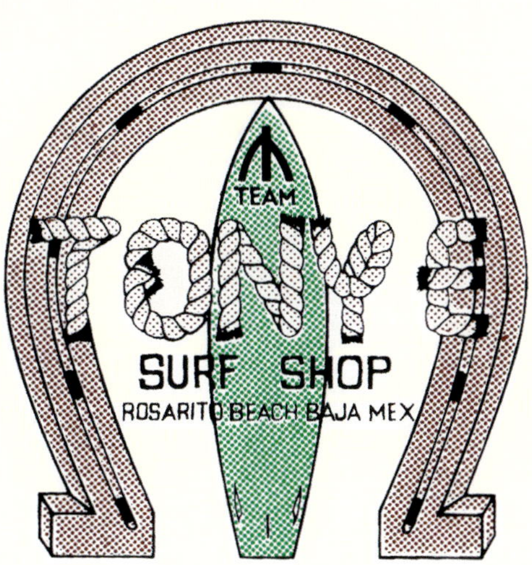
TEAM
TONY E
SURF SHOP
ROSARITO BEACH BAJA MEX

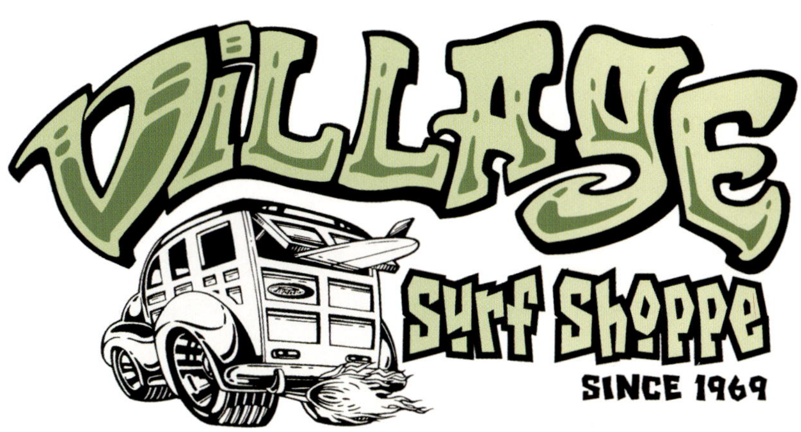
VILLAGE
Surf Shoppe
SINCE 1969

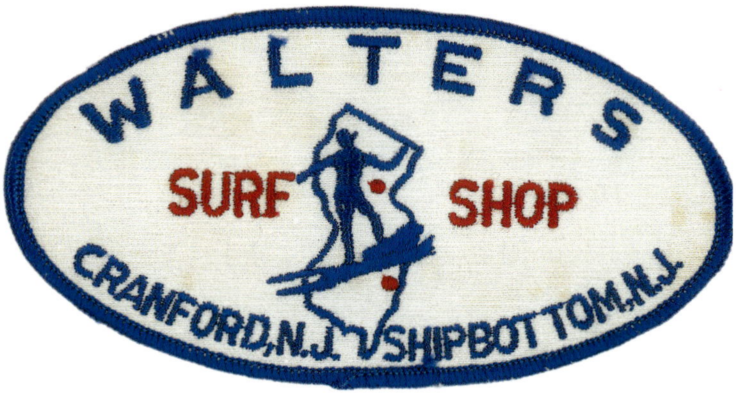
WALTERS
SURF SHOP
CRANFORD,N.J. SHIPBOTTOM,N.J.

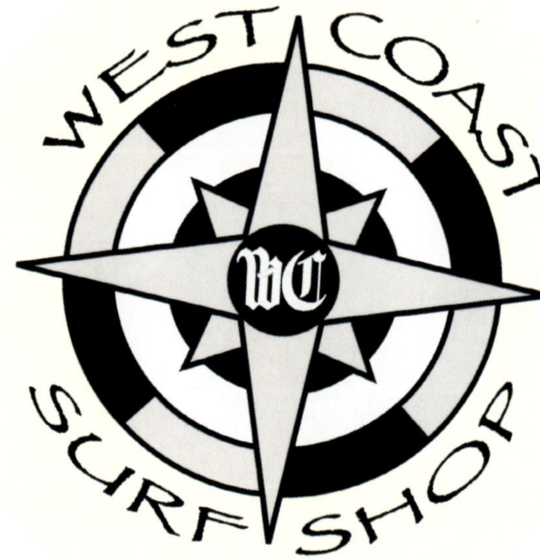
WEST COAST
WC
SURF SHOP

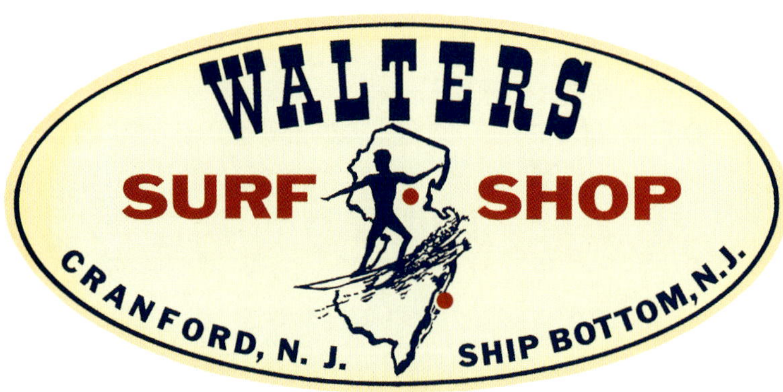
WALTERS
SURF SHOP
CRANFORD, N. J.
SHIP BOTTOM, N.J.

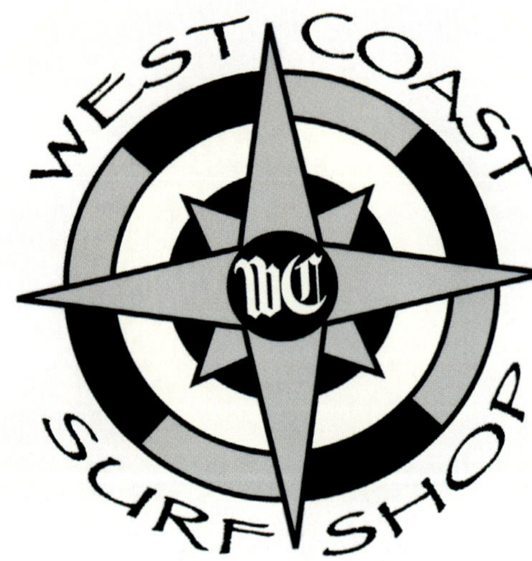
WEST COAST
WC
SURF SHOP

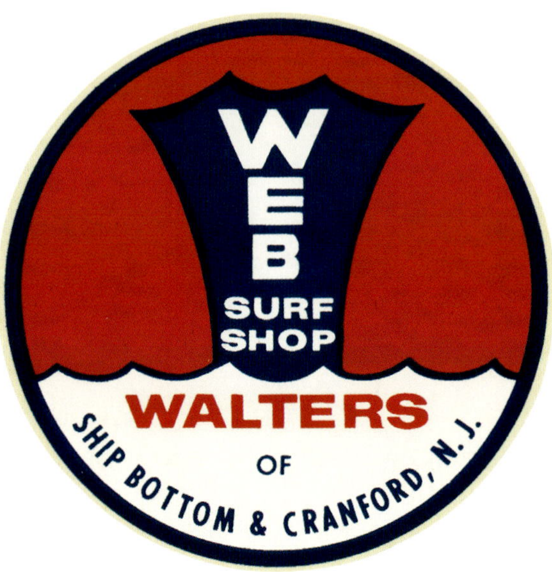
WEB
SURF
SHOP
WALTERS
OF
SHIP BOTTOM & CRANFORD, N.J.

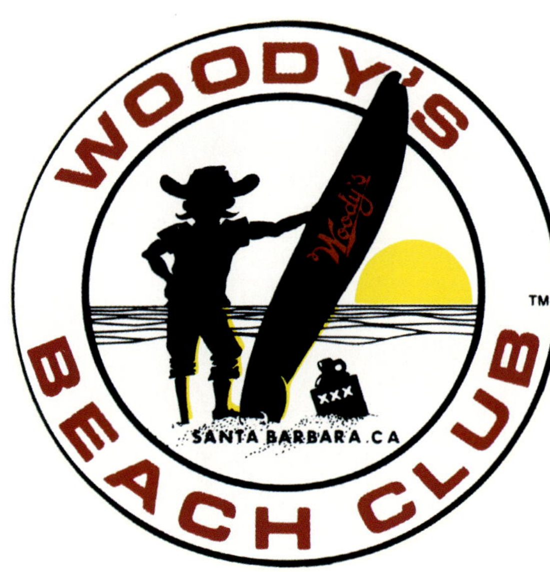
WOODY'S
Woody's
SANTA BARBARA.CA
TM
BEACH CLUB

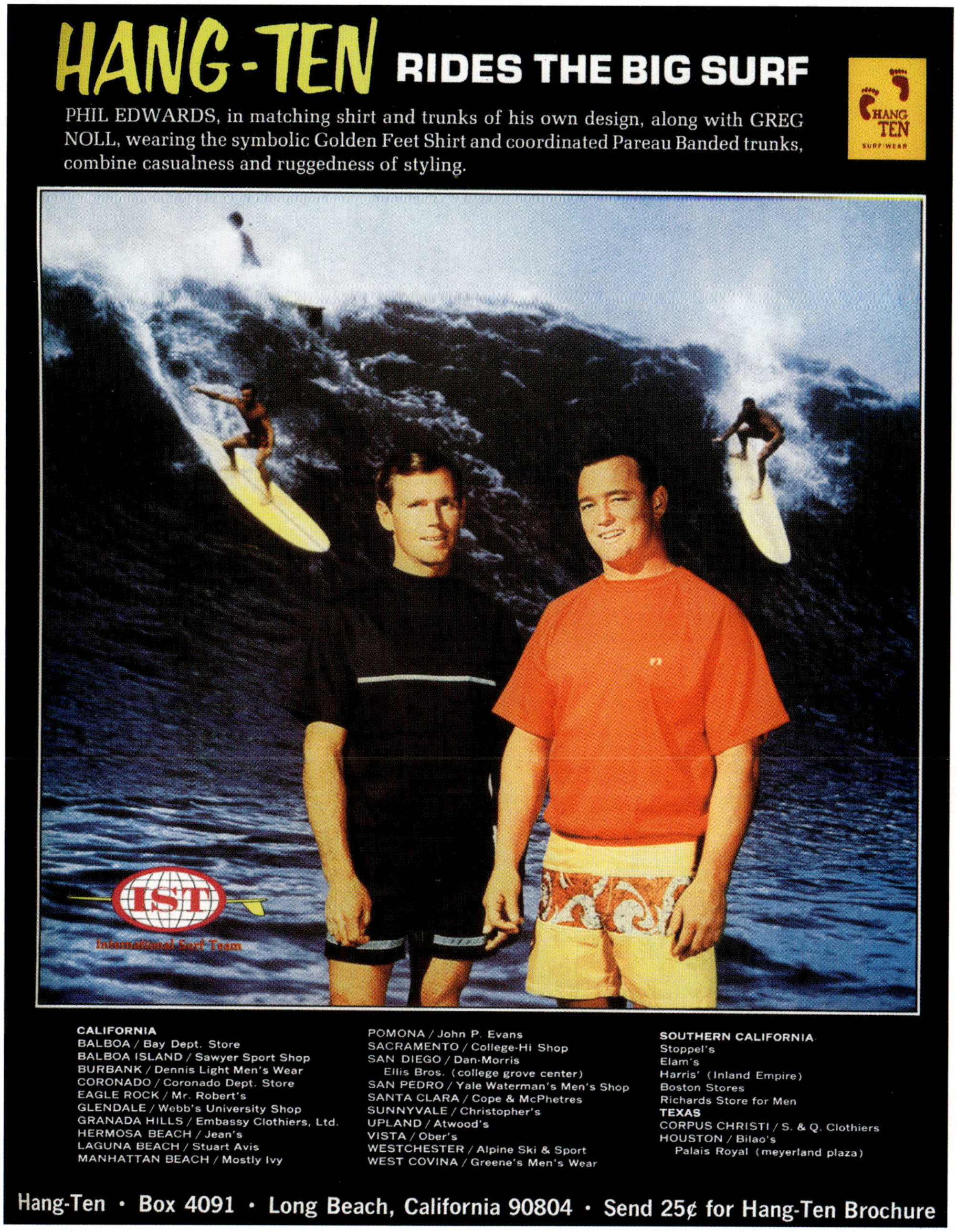

Phil Edwards and Greg Noll showing the colors in a 1966 ad for Hang Ten in *Surfer Magazine.*

5.1 LITTLE FEET

An Interview with Duke Boyd on The Genesis of Hang Ten

Hanging Ten is all about timing, positioning, skill, and finesse. The company was all about timing, and positioning, and the skill and the finesse came later. Hang Ten was the first surf company to go big – to cause a big sensation from the surfing world to the civilian world – and it was all about timing. The founder of the company, Duke Boyd, was a surfer noodling around for something to do in 1959, the year Gidget introduced the idea of the surfer as more than a bum to the world. Gidget lit the fuse that caused the surf culture explosion of the 60s. There was Gidget, then Frankie and Annette, and the Beach Boys, and within a couple of years, everybody wanted an ocean, across the USA. And Hang Ten was there to clothe the revolution, a company founded almost by accident, branded perfectly as an afterthought, and the first company started by a surfer that went off the richter and became an international sensation.

This interview with Duke Boyd was conducted for the *Trunk It* exhibit for the Surfing Heritage Foundation in 2005.

Duke is kind of an unusual name for a surfer. Where did you get that name?

Well my real first name is Francis.

Oh, okay.

I was born in Kansas City, Kansas in 1936, but at the age of two we moved to California and then at the age of 9 or 10 I moved to Hawaii. This was 1946. After the war there was a big need for Civil Servants so my step-father put in the paperwork and they approved him and we all jumped on a boat and sailed over there. I spent my youth barefooted and running around the islands and doing all the different kinds of things that you do in Hawaii when you're a young kid.

That sounds like fun.

I went surfing at Waikiki in 1946. I wasn't doing anything but laying down and holding on tight, but that's the beginning of all that.

Do you remember what you wore into the water as a kid growing up in Hawaii?

Actually I wore Hawaiian printed bathing suits that were very very flimsy and basically didn't stand up. They all tore and all the rest of it but that was the thing you would get from the Liberty House. The people that knew about surfing who were older than me, they would go out to Makaha to get their trunks custom made by a guy named M Nii. I'm not sure but I think he and his wife were Filipino, and they worked in a ratty old place with rats running around. But all the movie stars and the surfers who would go out there would get "Makaha surf trunks," which were a little high in the back and they came around the middle at the belly button level. They were shorter and that was a jump from the old tank suits that you see all the guys wearing, and the women were wearing too. I never did understand wool.

You lived in Hawaii for how long?

Just for a couple of years. We left there in 1949 and came back to California. I was 20 in 1954 and prime for the draft in the Korean War, so I got in the service when they were just passing out the last remnants of the GI Bill, which allowed me to go to college.

Where did you do your service?

Augusta, Georgia, then Paris.

How many years in the service?

About three and I think I got out early because they were getting rid of people. I was a private by the way, for the entire time. I finally came back to California in 1957 and that is when I started surfing again. You've got to remember I'm not a part of the... well let's just call them the Heritage Group which is Walter Hoffman, Mickey Munoz, and Woody Brown and all of those guys. I was a kid going to college who loved to surf. I got my first board from the Velzy shop. He basically rooked me on a junky board, took my money and laughed.

Manhattan Beach Velzy shop?

No it was San Clemente. Most of my surfing was as a lone wolf so to speak, or a lone surfer. I wasn't hanging around with any of those guys. When I first began venturing into that world the guys who ran the shops were the guys who shaped the boards. My first encounter with surfers was when I went into the

Ole Shop in Seal Beach and talked to Mickey Munoz, Steve Pezman, and Corky Carroll. These guys were deeply involved in the soul of surfing and had done all the pioneering and riding of big waves and all the rest of it. I've always been sort of like a waterboy in this thing. I was never one of the highly skilled surfers that I encountered and began to get involved with in business. I'm basically an average surfer for the most part who enjoyed it and loved it.

You got out of the service in 1957 and you were surfing around California. Where was the first glimmer of Hang Ten?

That was probably around 1959/1960. I was in college at Long Beach City College and eventually Long Beach State. My concept is that I was surfing and I was at school and that's where my head was at at the time, but I also needed money. I was an art minor so I thought I would design a jacket for surfing. After the surf was over you would put on the jacket and the jacket was nice. I lined it with silk and it had sleeves and big boxing pockets and a big hood on it. It was a pretty good thing for surfing.

So it was jackets at first?

After running around for quite a while I finally found somebody who would make them for me. I made an appointment to see a lady named Doris Moore who was in Long Beach. I brought in art work and showed it to her and she said, "What about the trunks that you'd design underneath it?"

And I said, "What about them?"

She said, "I won't make the jacket right now but I would like to make the trunks."

And I said, "Well okay, what does that mean?"

She said, "Well you go and have the samples made and then I will price them out and you will go off and sell them." And that's what happened. I went off and did that.

So you stumbled into the rag trade basically because you were in college and you needed some money.

Nothing more to it than that and it was a big stumble because I was destined to go become a teacher some place.

What do you think you were going to teach?

Probably History and Art and I hoped to eventually coach something.

Were you working on a teaching credential at Long Beach State?

I was working on my masters when I stumbled into it. I was designing a jacket to make some money and the lady wanted the trunks. Back then surfers would get their trunks from what I called little cotton shops up and down the coast. There were mothers who would make these trunks to fit the surfers. They would ask how long the leg should be and the other details, like wax pockets and stripes. Those little mom cotton shops were all established at that time so when I came in and worked on it I basically just took what everyone wanted and added a little of this and a little of that.

Jantzen and Catalina were making bunhuggers at that time and the only trunk that was being produced for surfers was by a company called Sandcomber and they were not a real surf trunk. They were too short and they were a little too tight. The trunks I designed had more of a rise in the back of the trunk which would give it a longer torso, and it would fold over in the back of the waist and wouldn't bind around the stomach. The young people in those days – I guess like young people these days – they wanted to wear their clothing low around the crack of their butt. In surfing that didn't work as well but by raising the back and lowering the front you still got that look.

At some point Doris Moore asked what label she wanted me to put on the trunks. And I didn't know you had to have a label. That's how naïve I was.

How many names did you go through before you decided on Hang Ten?

The first idea was Boyd Trunks but we didn't ever make a label for that. I didn't like it. And then one day we were talking and Doris asked: "Well what is the equivalent in surfing to a home run?"

I said, "Well, obviously it's hanging ten."

And she said, "Well, that's a good name."

By the way Doris Moore was a brilliant business woman. And if you want a little history on her, she was a lady who made dickies. Dickies were little things that go on top of sweaters. Mamie Eisenhower wore them, and everybody wore them in the 50s. But when the Kennedy people came in, Dickies were out and that was when I approached her about the jackets and she swayed me into trunks. It was just a lucky thing that she was not doing Dickies because she was the queen of the Dickie business.

Good timing is good.

I was fortunate. Very very fortunate. Hang Ten was all about something that was authentic in the sense that there was a connection between what the surfer wanted and what functioned for him. At the time trunks were made of canvas and heavy twills and those materials were stiff and would soak up water. They were better than wool, but hardly suitable for surfing. I began to change that by thinking in nylon and so forth which wasn't used before. Eventually we got to a point where we shifted from surf trunks to knit wear and then to yarn-died knits and t-shirts and that ended up being probably more volume in our knit line than we did in our trunk line because there were more people who could throw on a shirt than there were to go surfing.

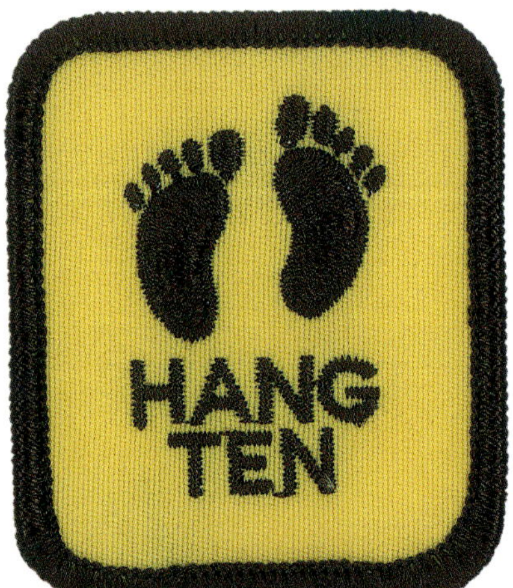

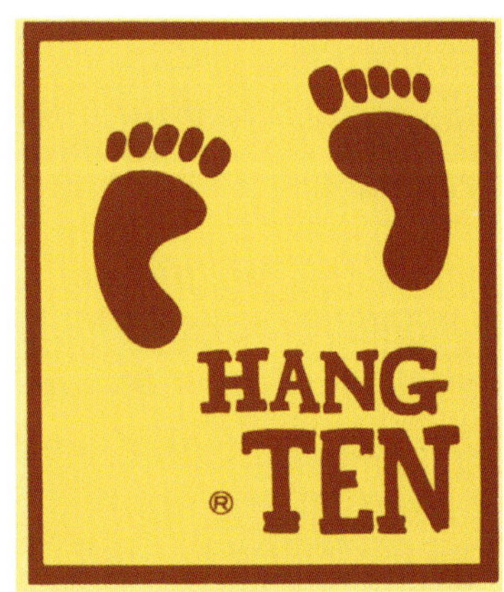

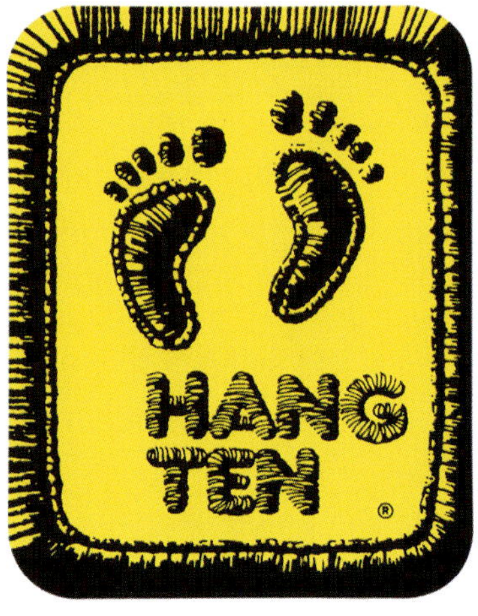

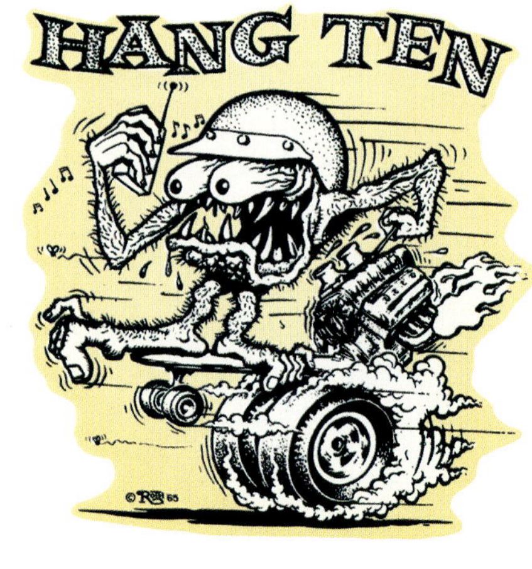

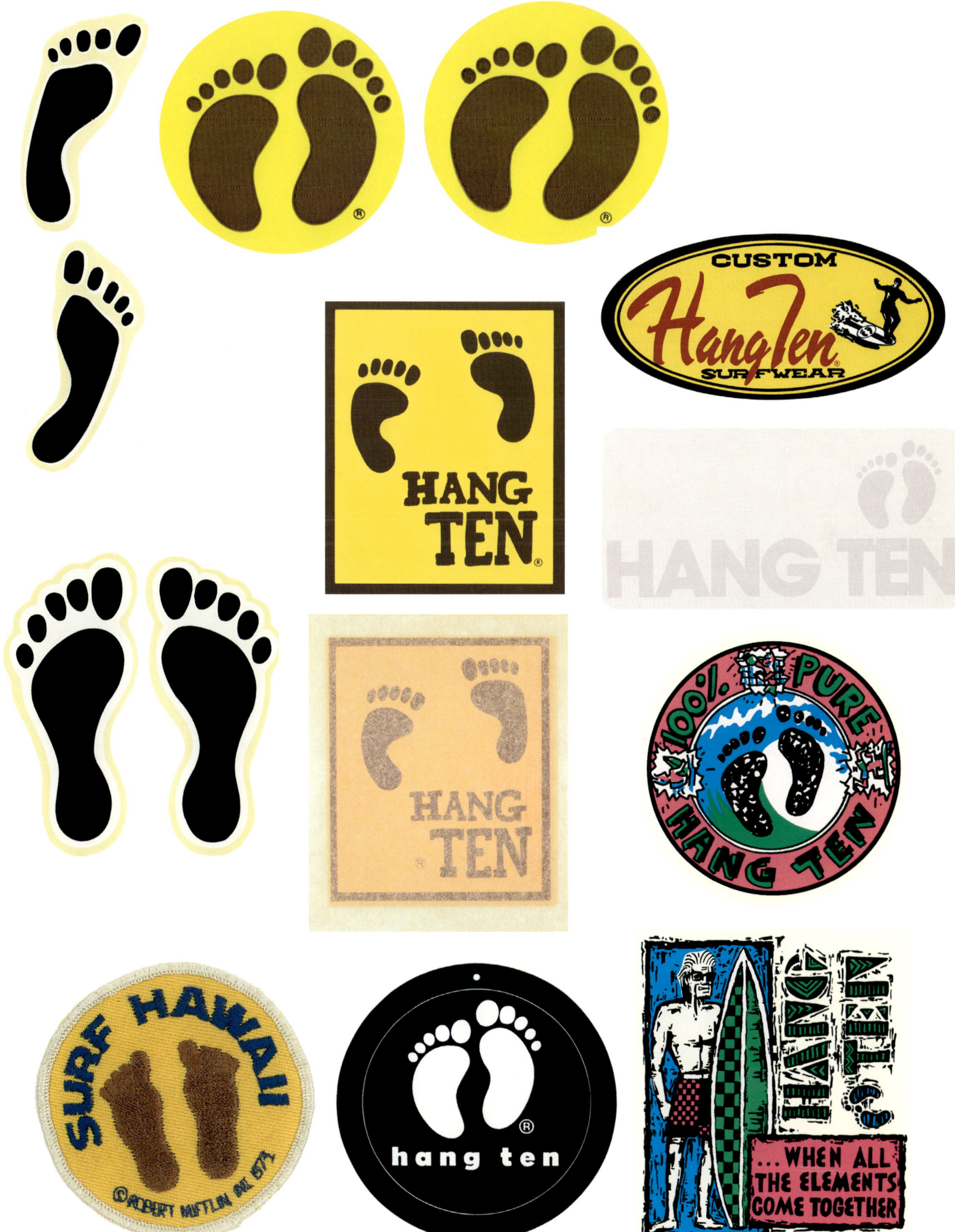
CUSTOM
HangTen
SURFWEAR
HANG TEN
HANG TEN
HANG TEN
100% PURE
HANG TEN
SURF HAWAII
©ROBERT MUFFLIN INC 1973
hang ten
...WHEN ALL THE ELEMENTS COME TOGETHER

5.2 RAG PATCHES

Clothing companies.

Hang Ten was the first clothing company to go big and become a national brand. Hang Ten did a great deal of business during the 60s and into the 70s. But around 1972, Hang Ten began to falter and a new crop of companies began to emerge, some from California, some from Hawaii and some from Australia and other foreign countries.

Now in the 21st Century, the surf clothing industry is worth many billions of dollars a year, as small companies try to get some of the market that the giant companies like Billabong, Quiksilver, and Roxy don't get.

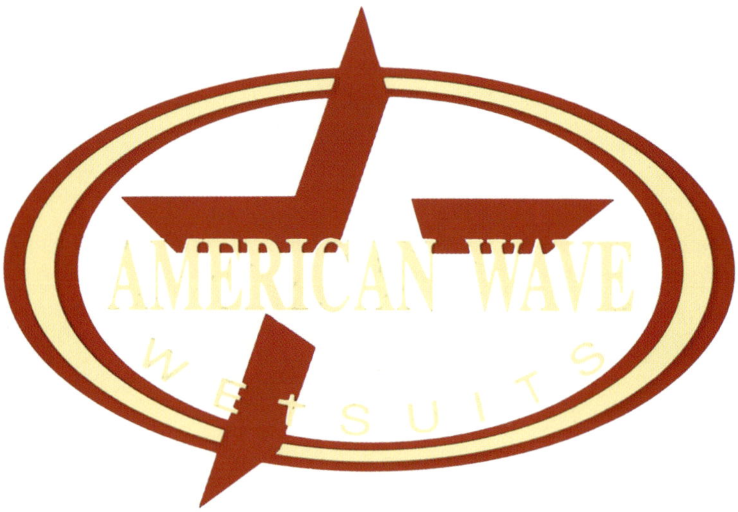

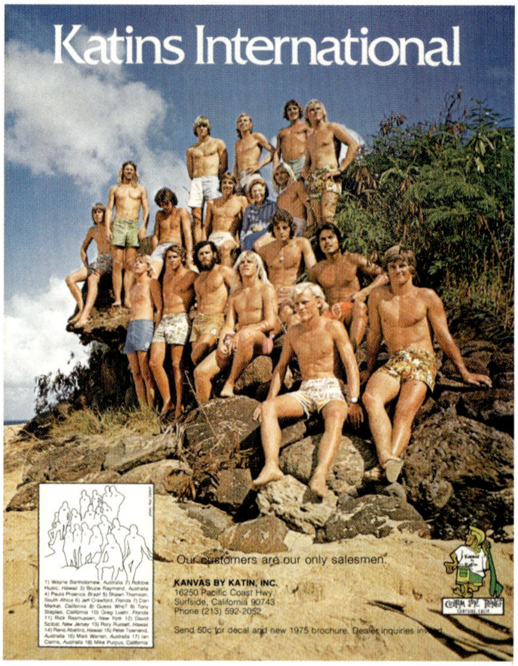

During the 70s, a group of two dozen of the best surfers posed on Hawaiian rocks for Kanvas by Katin.

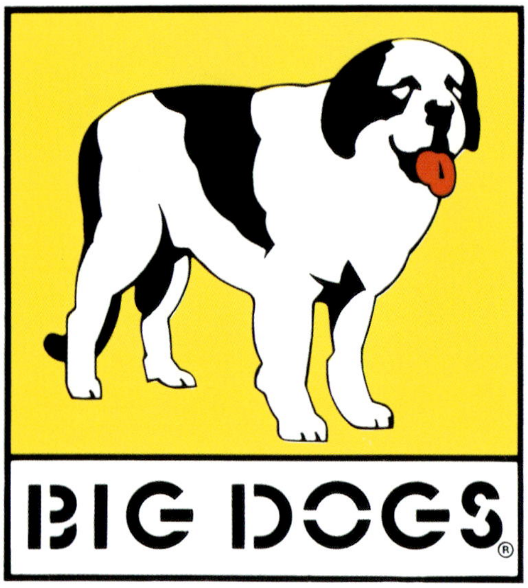

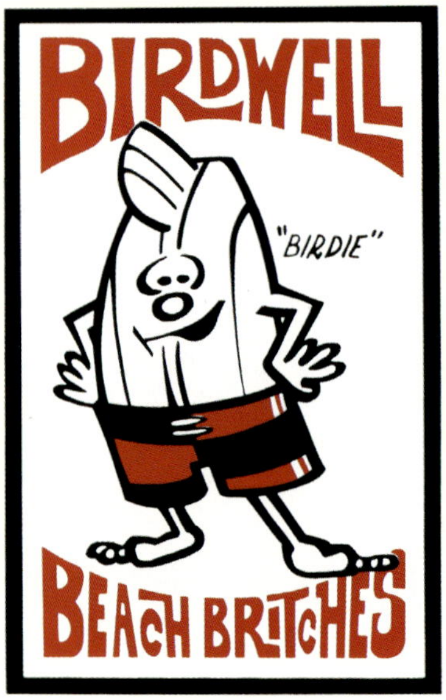

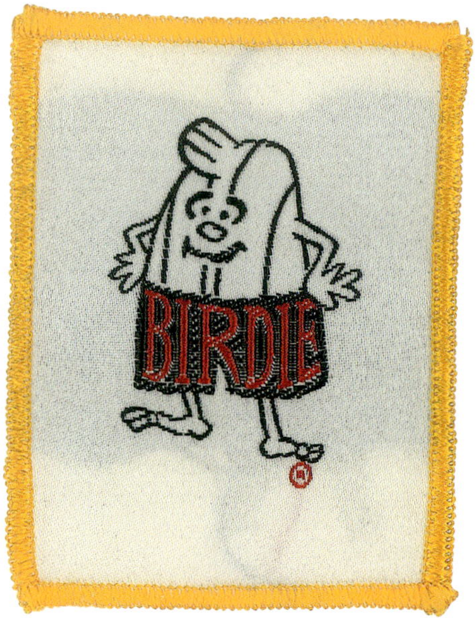

Black Flys
EYEWEAR
Est. 1992

Boards & Clothes
GORDON and SMITH
1 9 Since 5 9

CLASSIC
BEACH
U.S.A.

gotcha®

CLASSIC
BEACH
U.S.A.

GOTCHA®
ELECTRIC GYPSY
GOTCHA®

CLASSIC
BEACH
U.S.A.

CORAL REEF™

DA BULL

Graffiti Crimes
GOTCHA®

AFRICA • AUSTRALIA EUROPE • JAPAN • USA
ISLAND STYLE
SURF NECESSITIES
INTERNATIONAL

GOTCHA.®

© 1984
JIMMY'Z™

JIMMY'Z
© 1984
JIMMY'Z

INSTINCT
SURFWEAR

INSTINCT
SURFWEAR

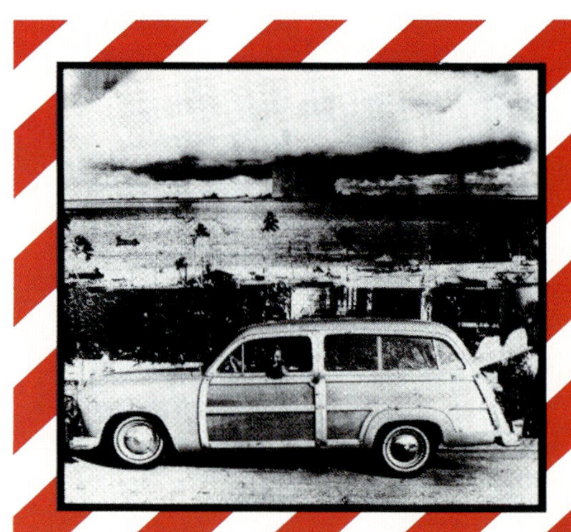

JIMMY'Z

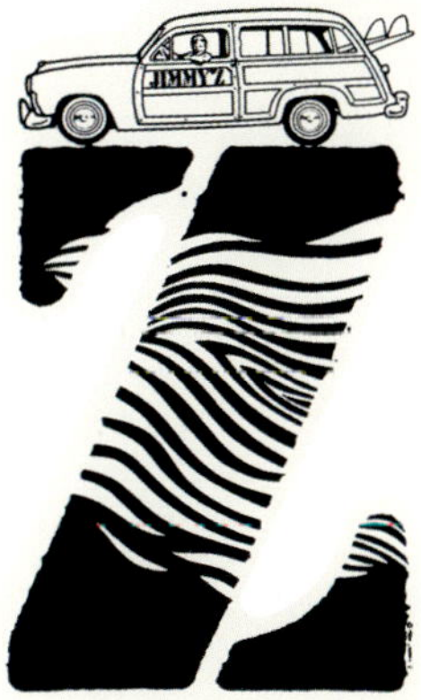
JIMMY'Z

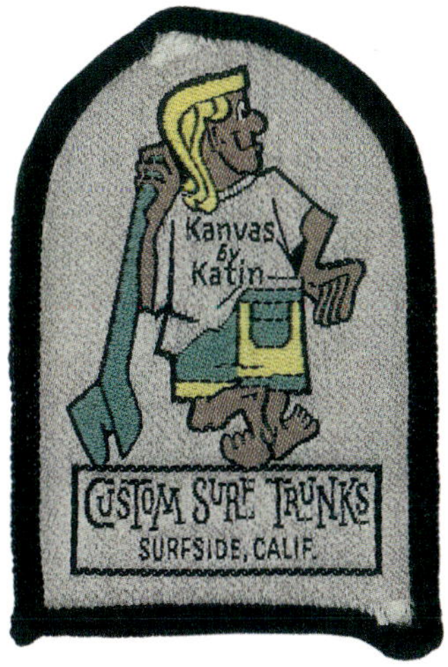
Kanvas
by
Katin
CUSTOM SURF TRUNKS
SURFSIDE, CALIF.

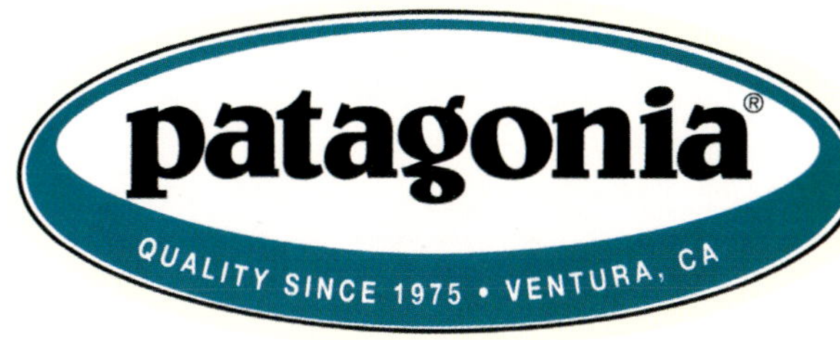
patagonia®
QUALITY SINCE 1975 • VENTURA, CA

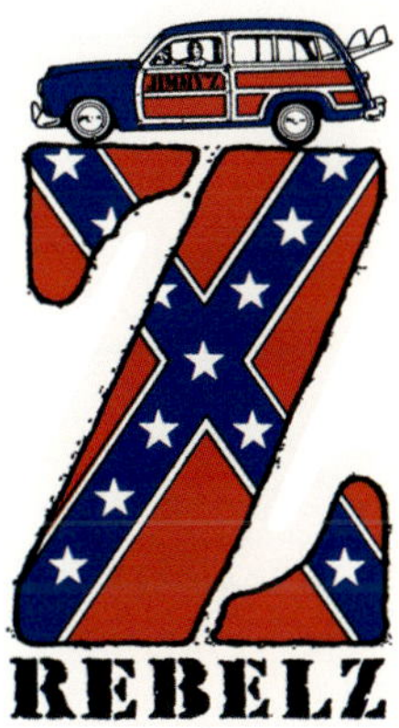
REBELZ

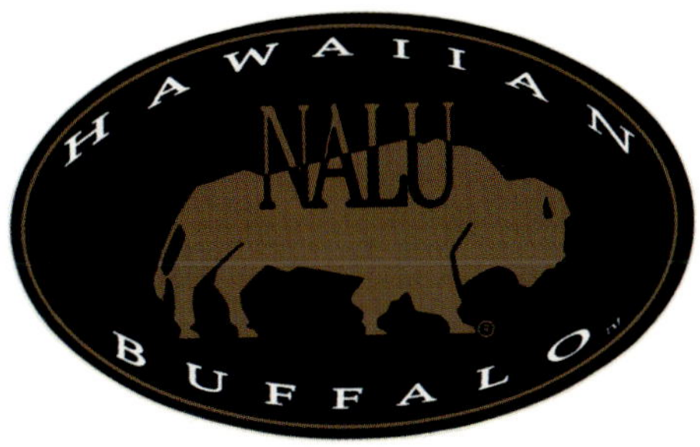
HAWAIIAN
NALU
BUFFALO

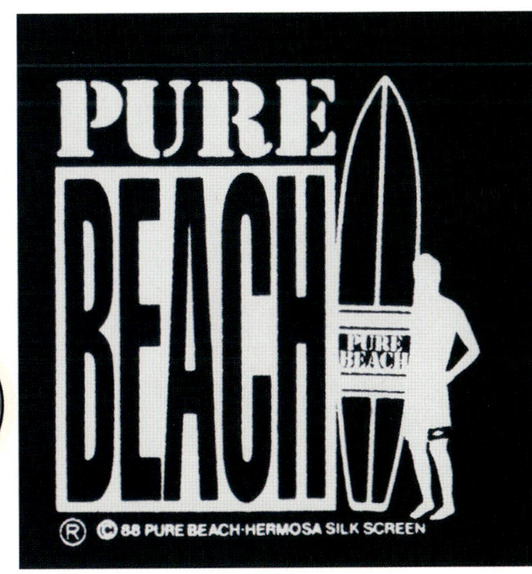
PURE
BEACH
PURE
BEACH
® © 88 PURE BEACH·HERMOSA SILK SCREEN

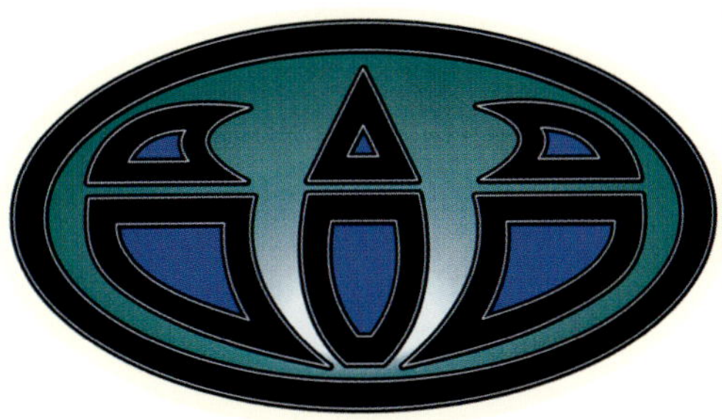

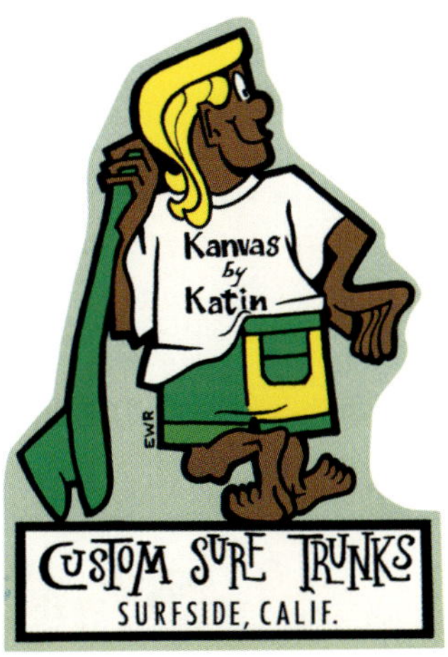
Kanvas
by
Katin
EWR
CUSTOM SURF TRUNKS
SURFSIDE, CALIF.

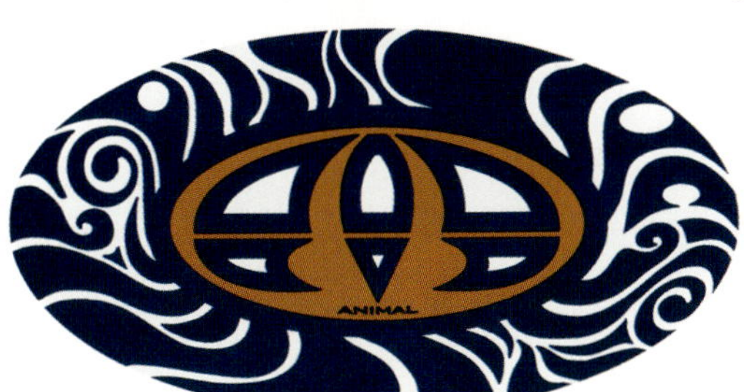
ANIMAL

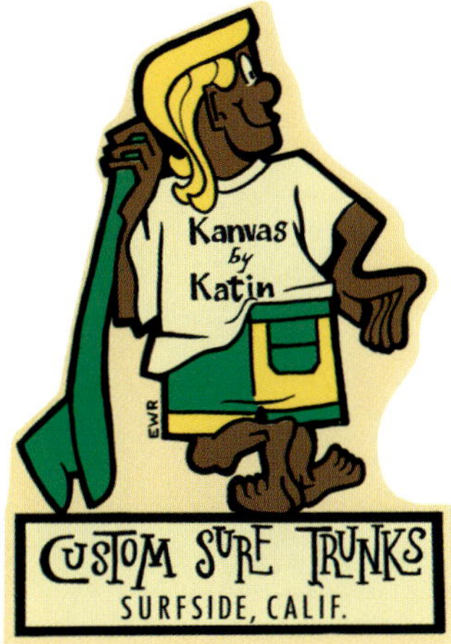
Kanvas
by
Katin
EWR
CUSTOM SURF TRUNKS
SURFSIDE, CALIF.

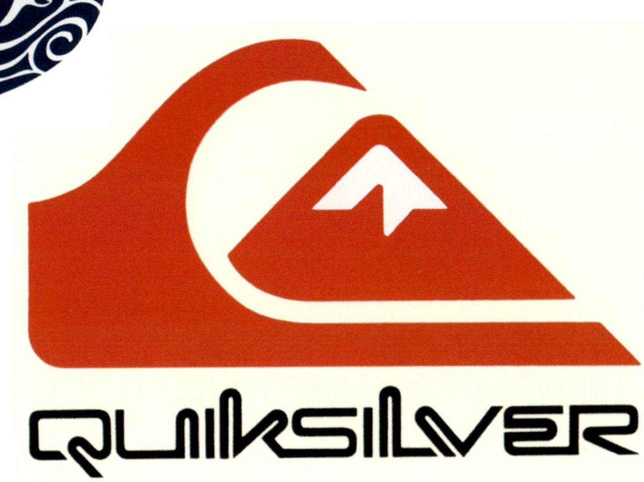
QUIKSILVER

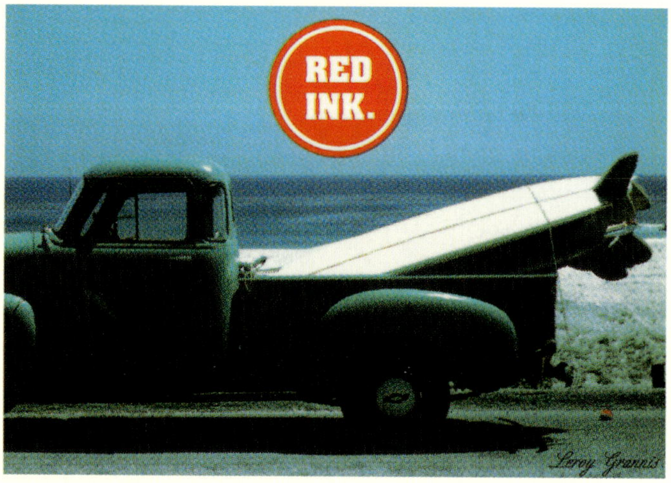

QUIKSILVER
WORLD TEAM

Redley®

QUIKSILVER

REDLEY
OCEAN SOUL™

The Rippers

REDLEY
TEAM

SINCE 1985
REDLEY®
SURF CO.

Redley®

Redley®

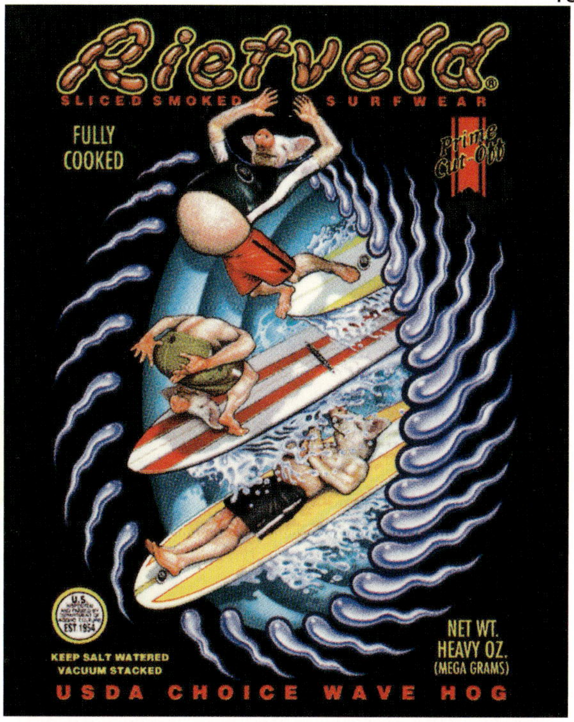

REEF
B·R·A·Z·I·L

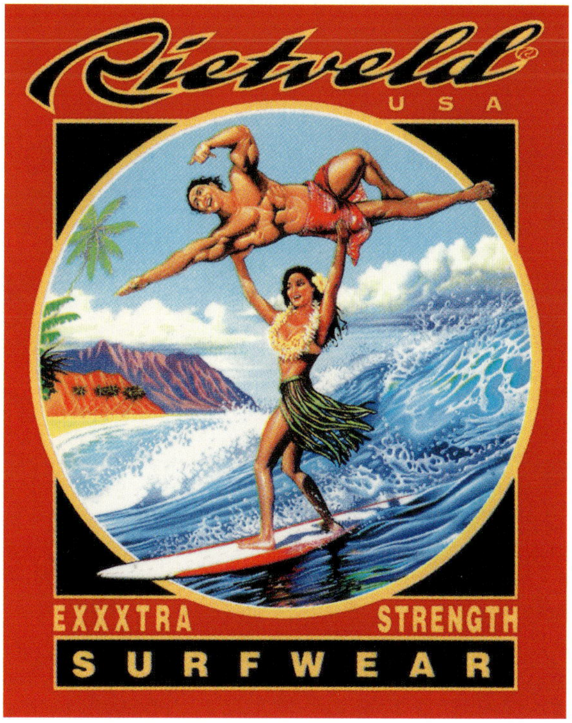

reyn spooner®
HAWAIIAN TRADITIONALS

RIFF RAFF
AMERICAN HARDCORE

ROXY

Sunset
Trading
Co.

ROXY

Stüssy

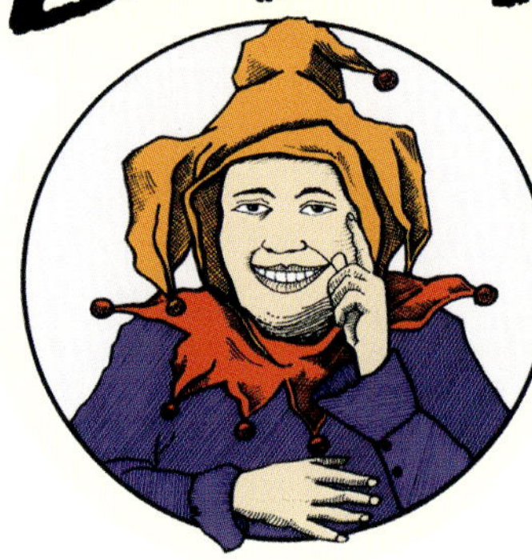

Roxy

ROXY

trading
Sunset
company

RYDIM · FOR JAH IRIE FEELING · STUSSY DESIGNS · ROOTS · REGGAE · SURF

URBANTAK
CLASSIC SURFSTYLE

Stüssy
POSITIVE VIBRATION INNA RUB A DUB STYLE!! AND I HAVE A GOOD VIBE...

5.3 SOFT CORE
Foam companies.

Since the middle 1950s, almost all of the surfboards made in America and around the world have been made of polyurethane cores – also called blanks. There were a number of companies involved in foam blanks through the 1960s – Clark Walker, Rogers and Dave Sweet – but by the 1970s, Clark Foam had claimed a near-monopoly on the foam market, which grew over the years into a business worth $20,000,000 to $30,000,000 a year.

In December of 2005, Gordon "Grubby" Clark, abruptly closed the doors of Clark Foam, creating a huge vacuum for that mountain of business, which dozens of companies have since rushed in to fill.

These stickers represent most of the old school foam companies.

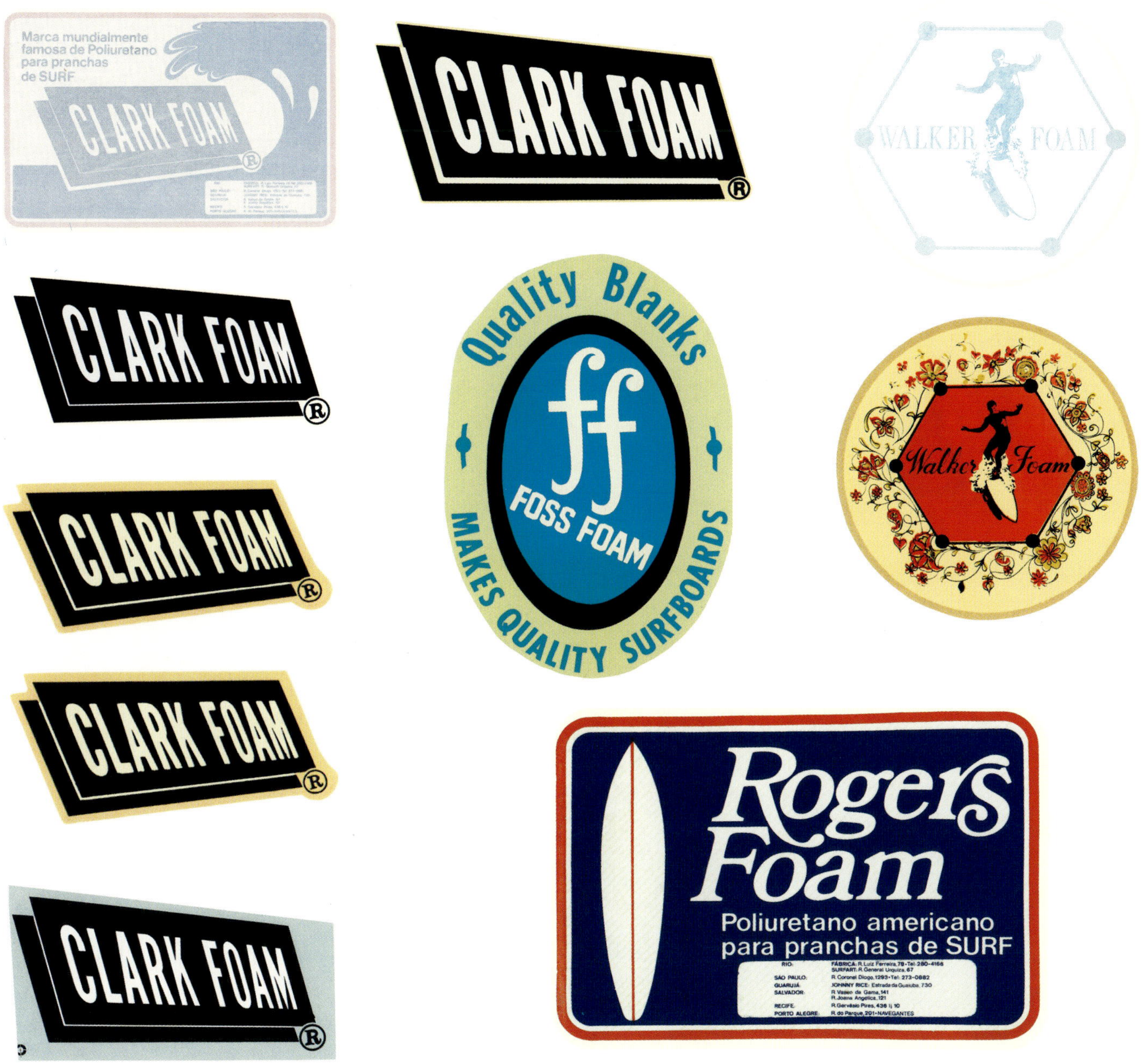

5.4 ACCESSORIZE

Wax and etc.

Surf shops are where you go to buy surfboards, wetsuits, and trunks, but also accessories, like surf wax, sun protection, and leashes. For a complete list of hundreds of surf wax labels, check out Schiffer Book's *Surfboard Wax: A History*.

Here are a few stickers from the accessories department of surf shops around the world.

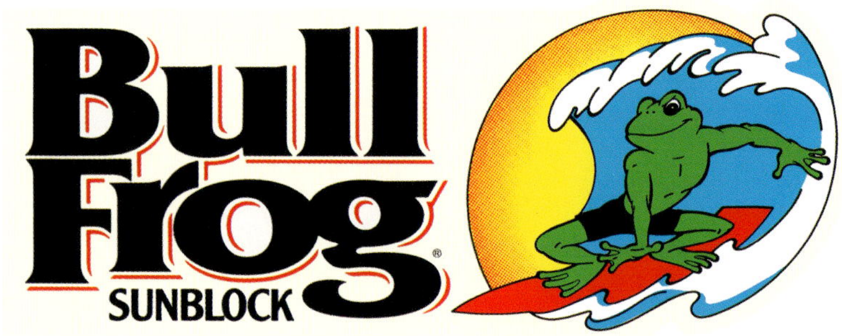

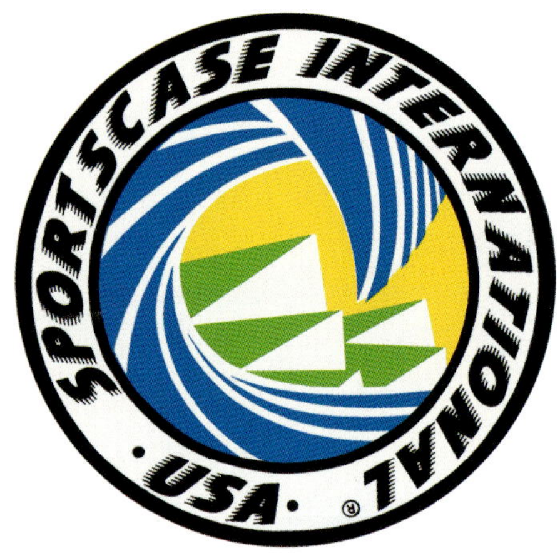

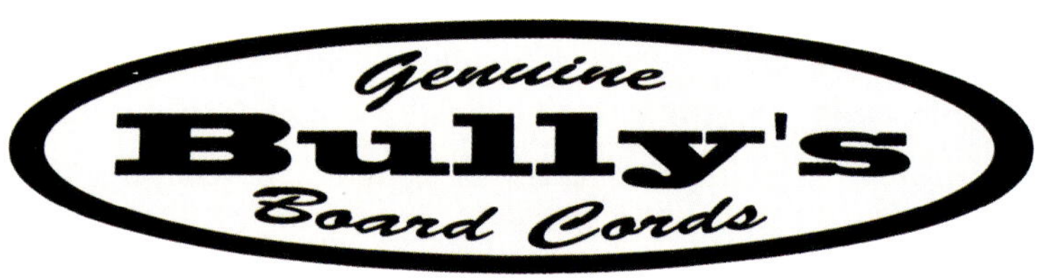

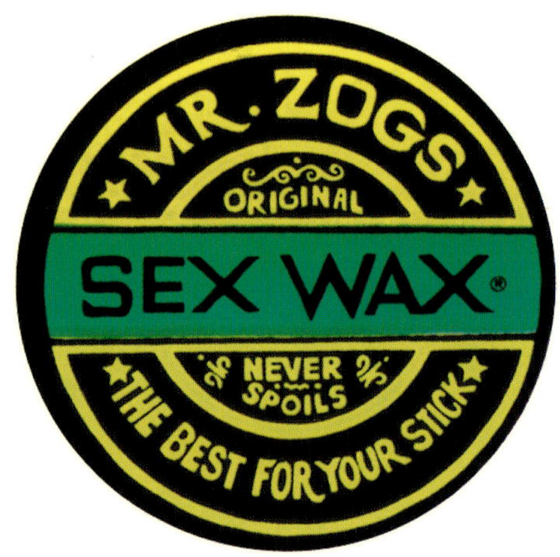

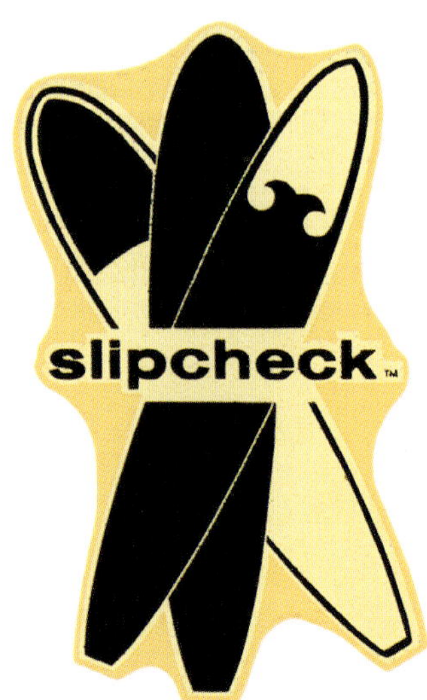

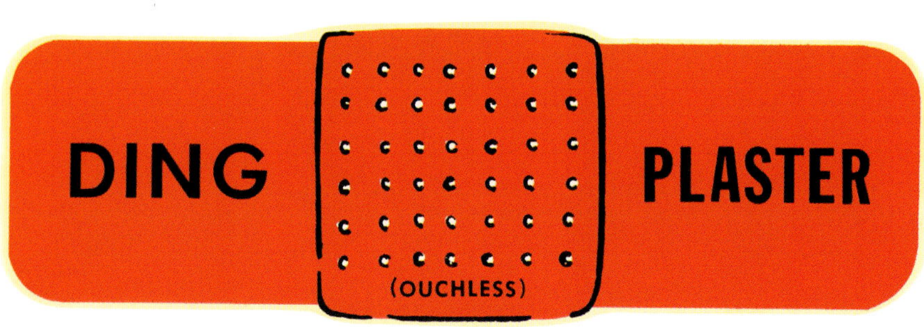

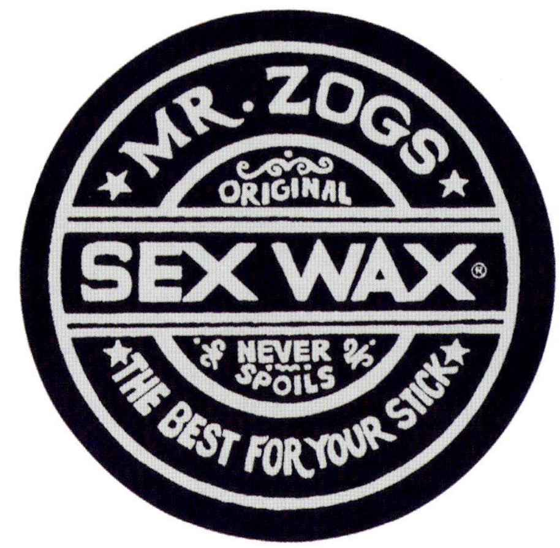

5.5 RUBBER SOUL

Wetsuit companies

In the late 1950s, Jack O'Neill was raising a family in San Francisco. He had a variety of jobs, including selling parking meters, but during his lunchtimes and off hours, he would sneak down to Ocean Beach and go bodysurfing in the big, cold waves along the Western front of San Francisco. At first O'Neill only had swim trunks for protection from the cold. Then he began experimenting with neoprene shorts and that lead to short john wetsuits and that lead to O'Neill opening a surf shop at Ocean Beach in 1959: "Everyone thought I was crazy," O'Neill has said many times over the last 50 years. "They said I would sell to the 13 guys on the beach, and that would be it."

O'Neill was perfectly positioned for the surf craze that bubbled and burst in the 1960s. He moved his family and his business to Santa Cruz in 1960, and was experimenting with better wetsuits when the world decided to go surfing. Almost 50 years later, O'Neill is now a multinational company selling wetsuits and clothing in America and around the world: "I didn't know this was going to happen," O'Neill has also said, many times over the years. " I was just trying to support my family."

Body Glove was originally founded as Dive and Surf by the Meistrell Brothers and Bev Morgan in the 50s, and those two companies were the foundation for the many surfing wetsuits companies that have come since.

This collection favors the O'Neill brand, because the bulk of the stickers are from Pete Noble, and Pete Noble is from northern California, and northern Californians tend to be loyal to the local wetsuit clan: "In the old days, the first O'Neill wetsuit vest I had cost $3.95," Pete Noble said. "We would take a razor blade to scrape the O'Neill logo off the left bottom, because we thought Jack O'Neill was ripping us off. We were still cold, but we were cool. The original O'Neill decal I got from Con Colbourn. Con got it in 1959 with one of his fictitious letters to the manufacturer to find out prices and so forth: 'Here is a quarter, send me a decal and a price list.' Con wanted his money back. He wanted $2 or $3 for these decals. I bought about 50 from him in the mid-80s."

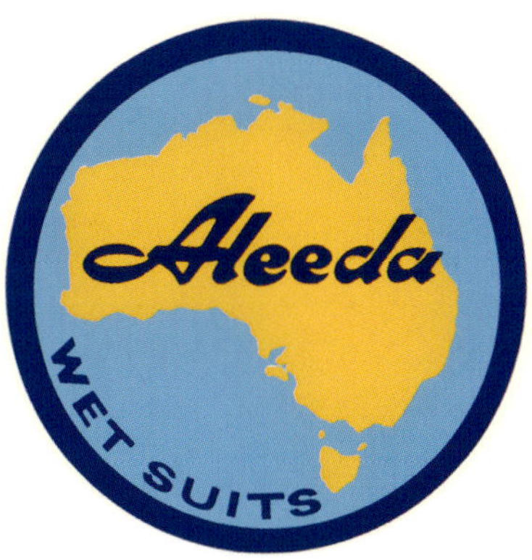

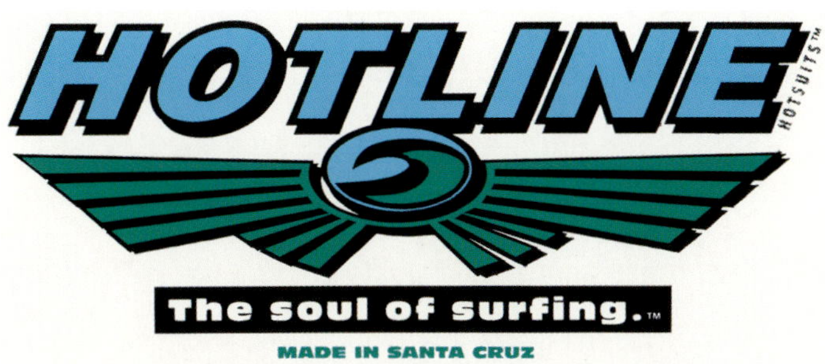

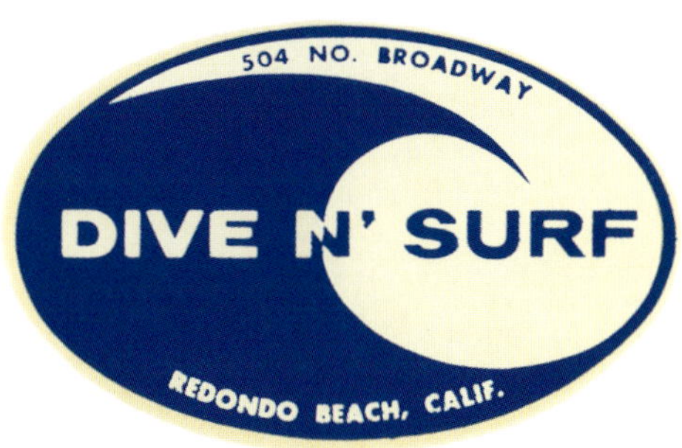

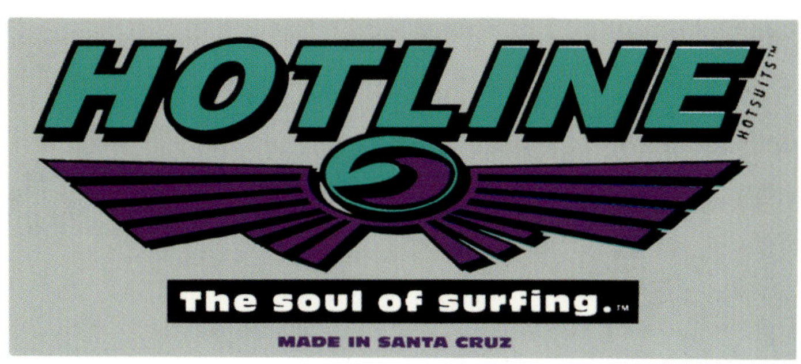

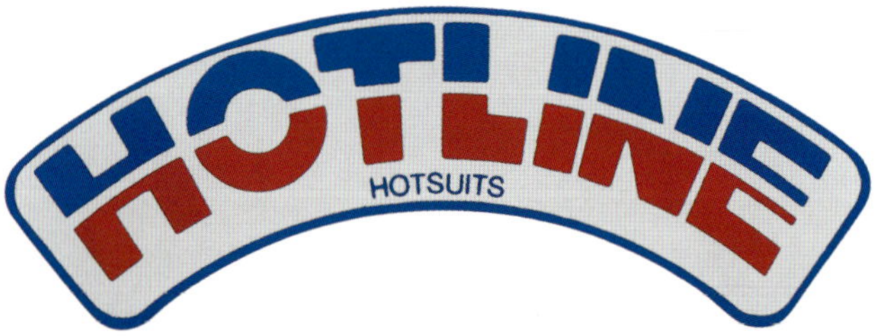

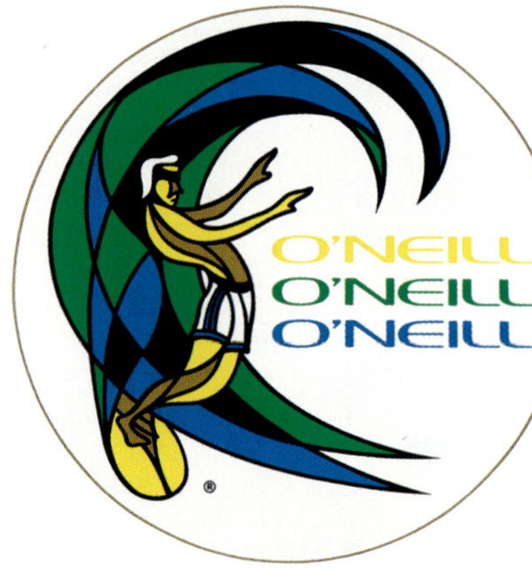

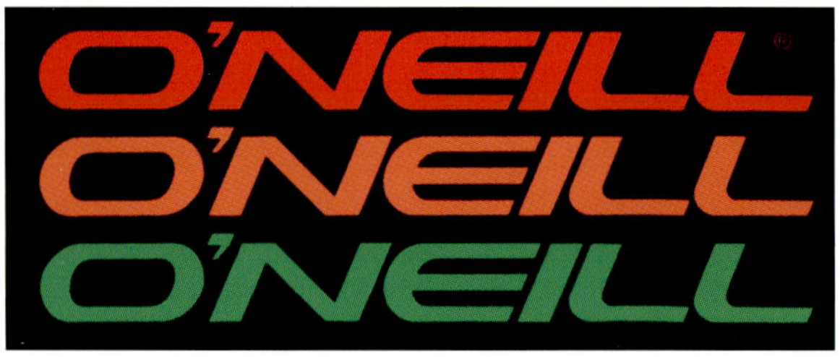

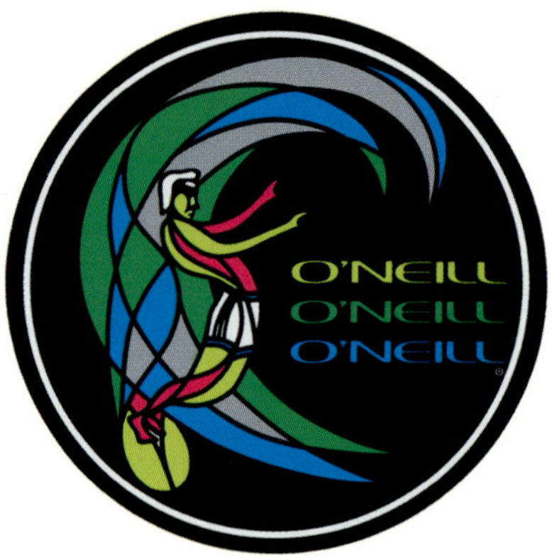

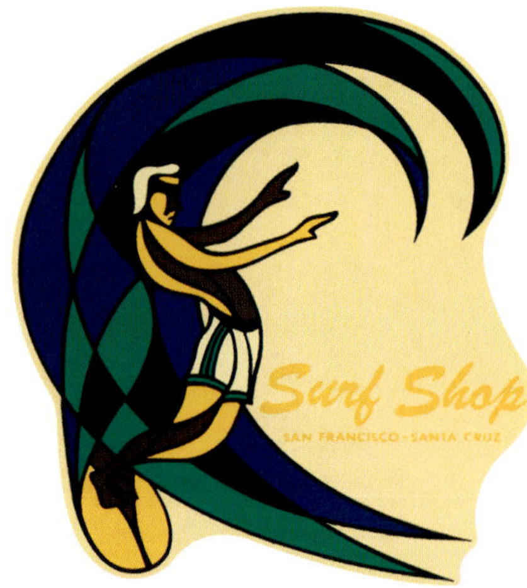

This was the first O'Neill water slide decal. It says Santa Cruz, San Francisco. – Pete Noble

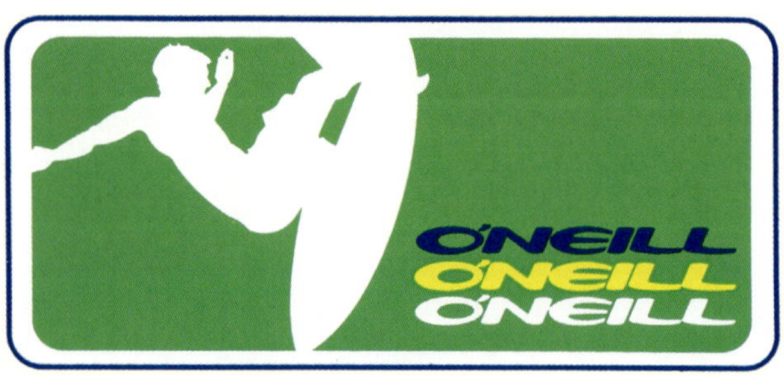

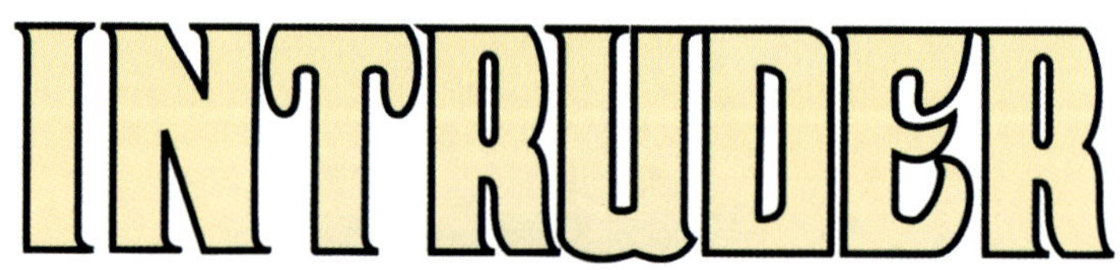

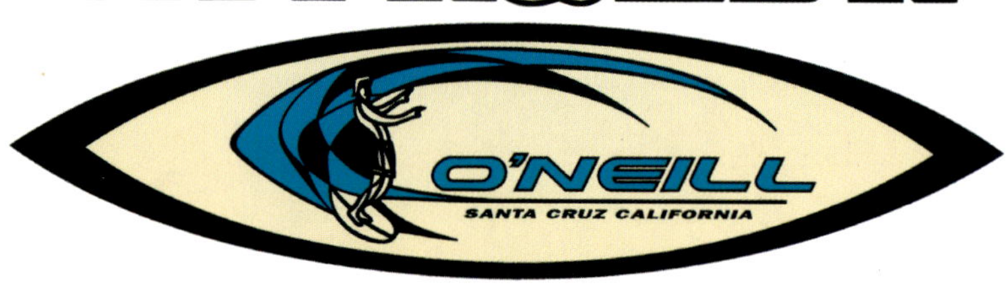

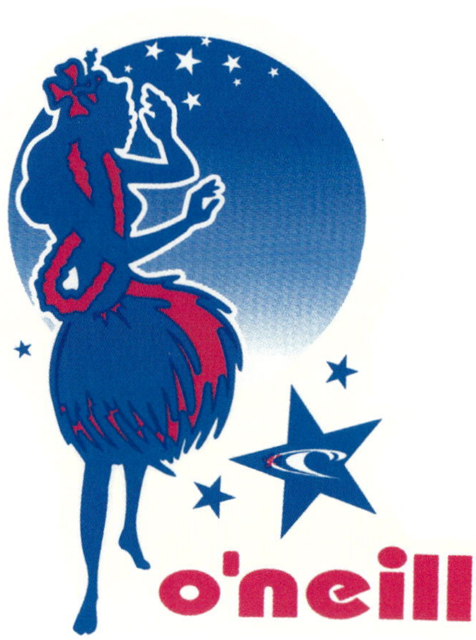

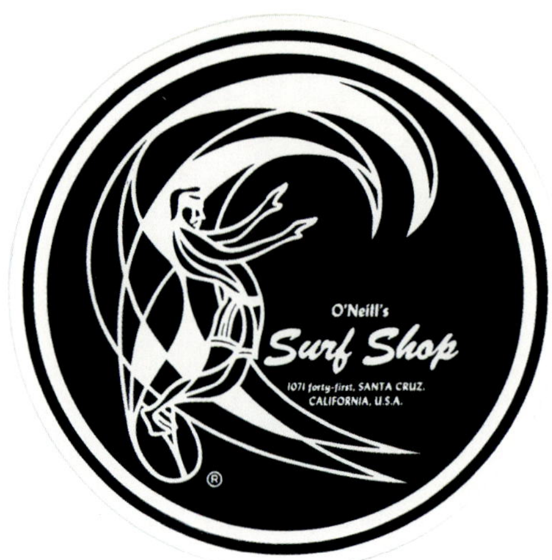

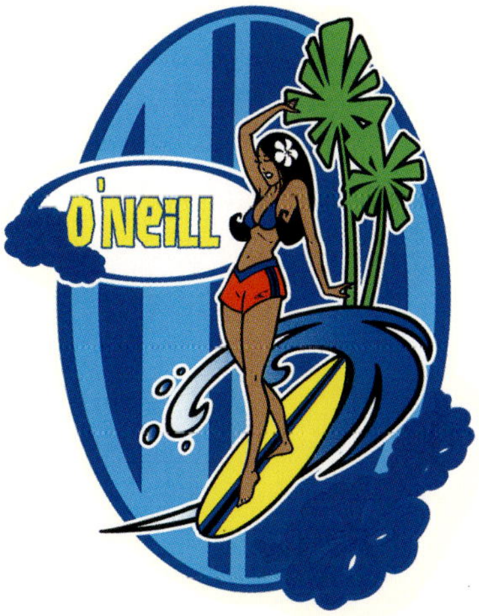
O'NEILL

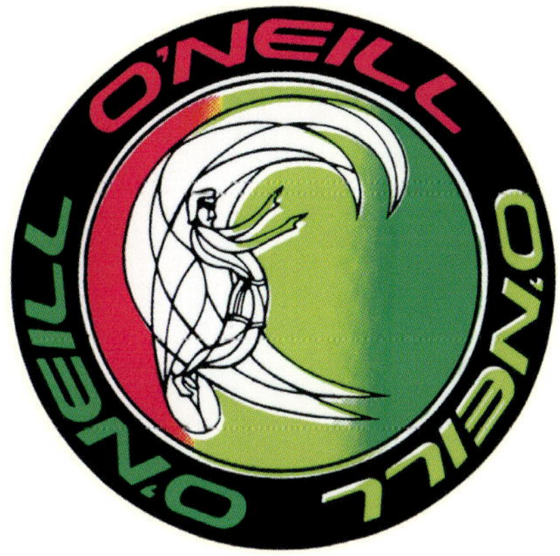
O'NEILL
O'NEILL
O'NEILL

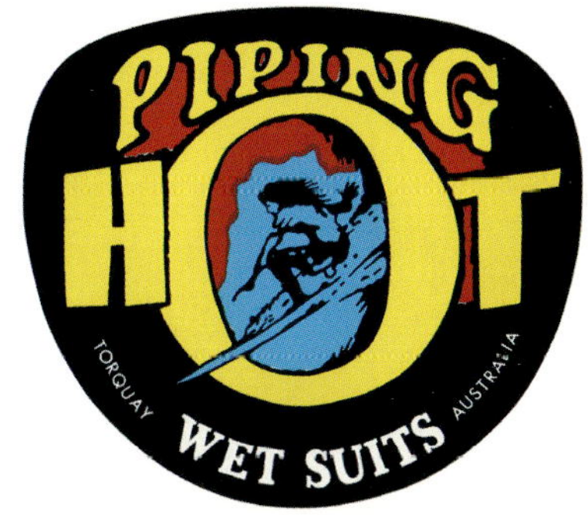
PIPING
HOT
TORQUAY
AUSTRALIA
WET SUITS

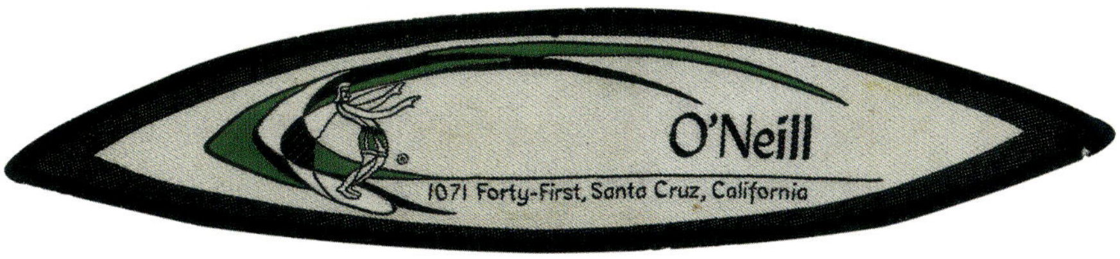
O'Neill
1071 Forty-First, Santa Cruz, California

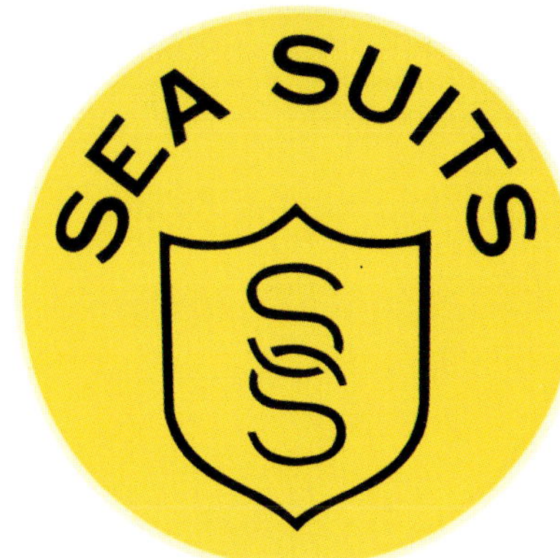
SEA SUITS

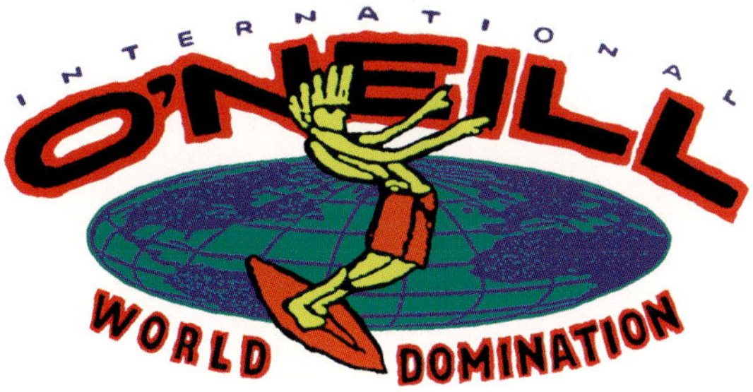
INTERNATIONAL
O'NEILL
WORLD DOMINATION

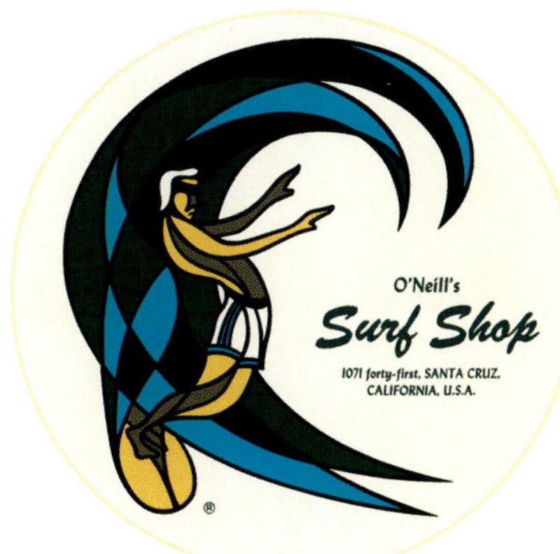
O'Neill's
Surf Shop
1071 forty-first, SANTA CRUZ,
CALIFORNIA, U.S.A.

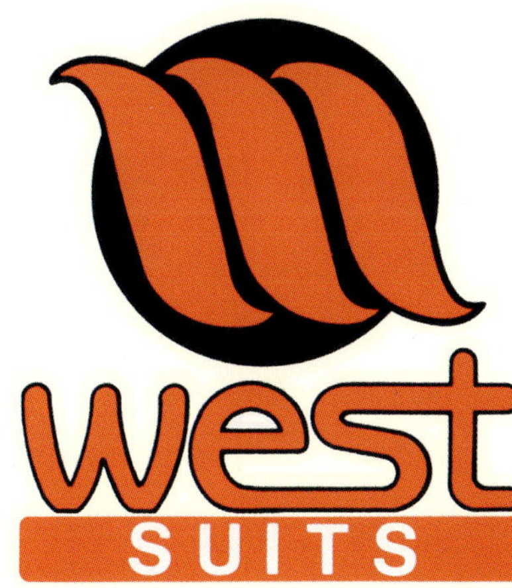
west
SUITS

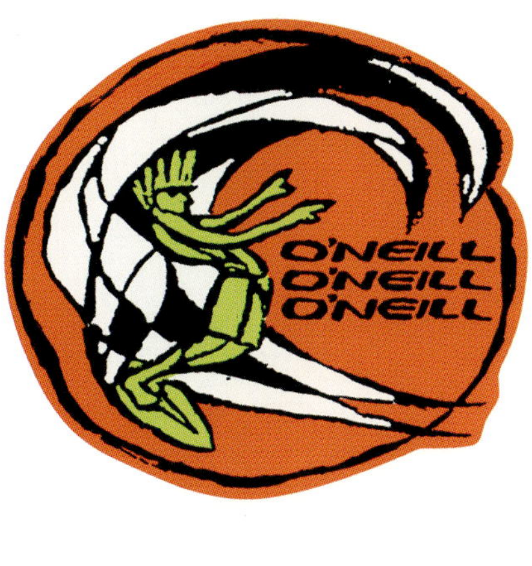
O'NEILL
O'NEILL
O'NEILL

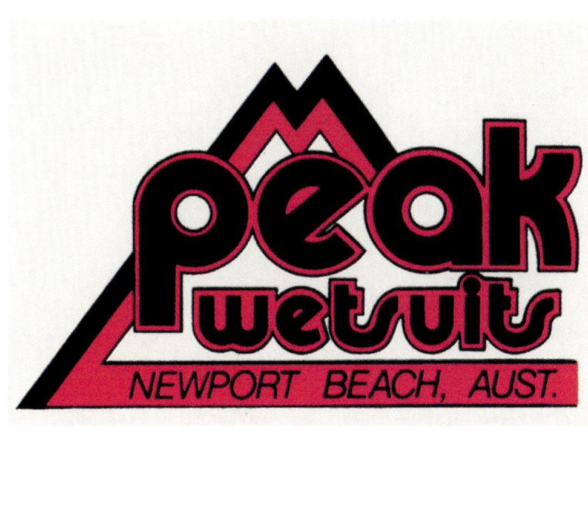
peak
wetsuits
NEWPORT BEACH, AUST.

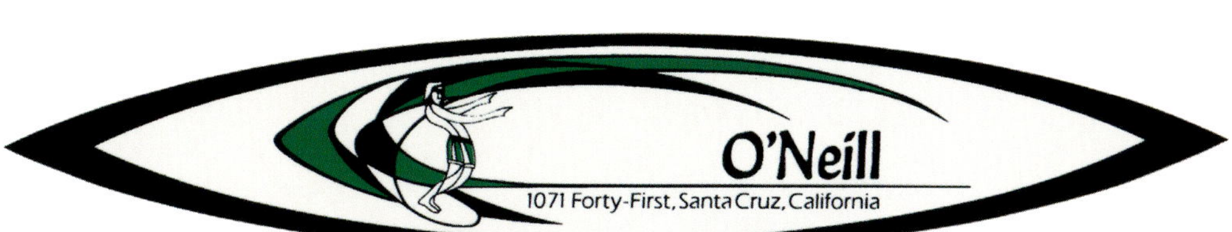
O'Neill
1071 Forty-First, Santa Cruz, California

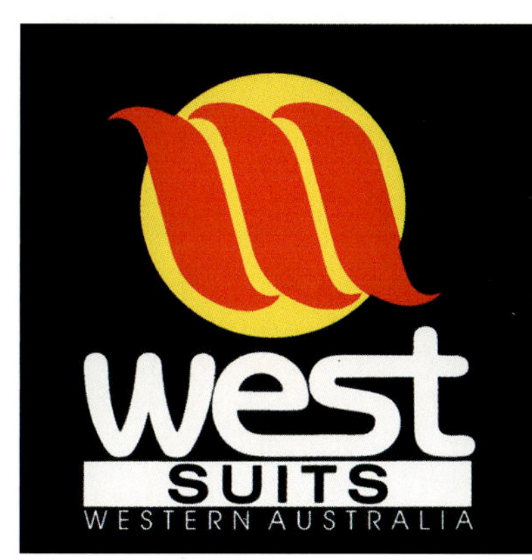
west
SUITS
WESTERN AUSTRALIA

5.6 MAG PATCHES

Surf magazines.

John Severson founded the first surf magazine in 1960, and called it *The Surfer*. Severson was an artist and surfer from Orange County, California, who made some great four-wall surf movies through the 1950s. As the surfing craze began to bubble, with the movie *Gidget* and the surf music of Dick Dale, Severson found that "people would buy any image of a surfer." The first issue of *The Surfer* was meant to be a brochure for one of his surf movies. But the magazine took off from there, and is still considered the Bible of the Sport.

In September of 1962, the third issue of the third volume of *The Surfer* had a cartoon of Murphy locked in, on the cover, and that cover is considered one of the all-time classics. Since *The Surfer*, dozens of surf magazines have come and gone. Some of them are represented here:

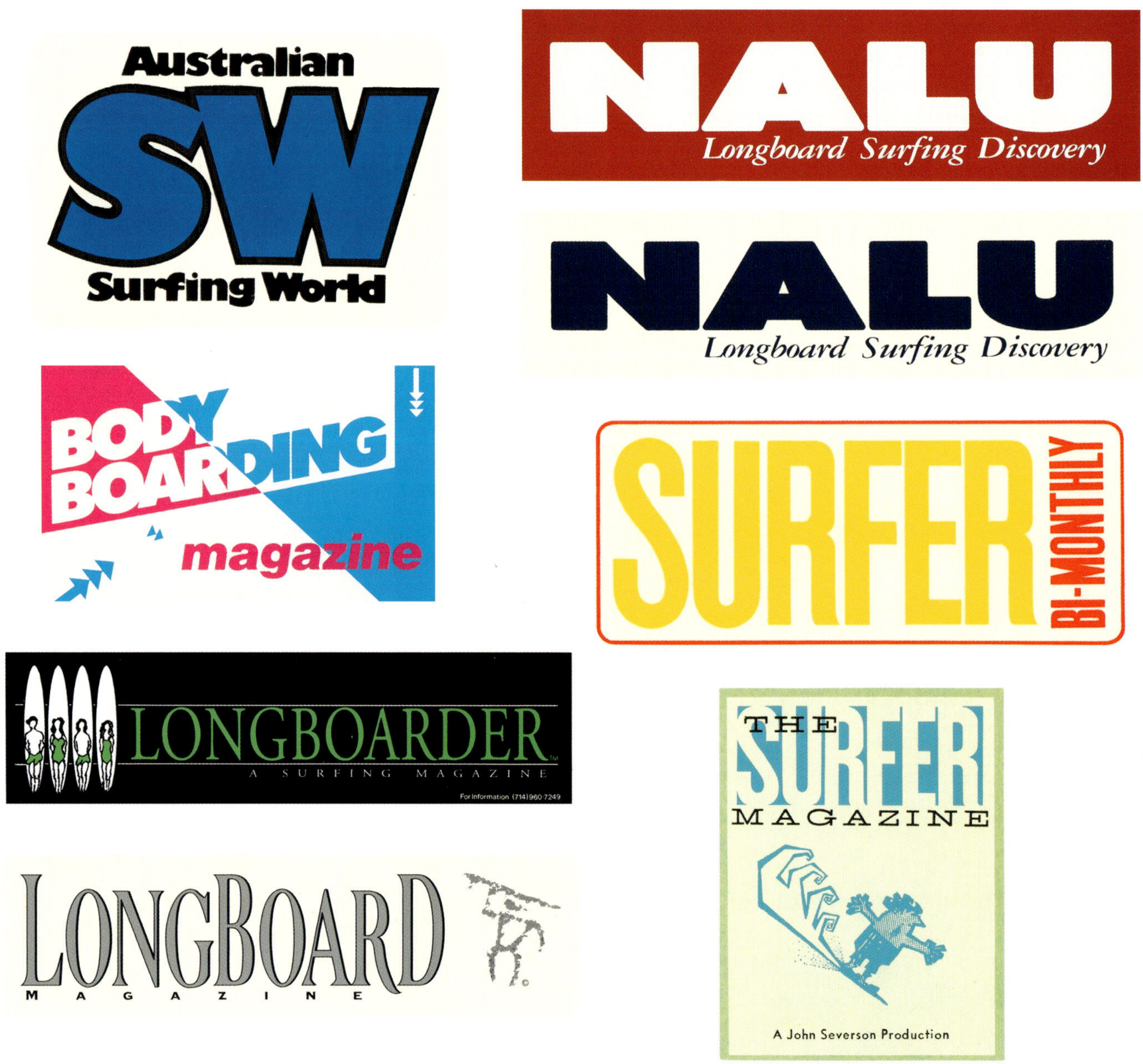

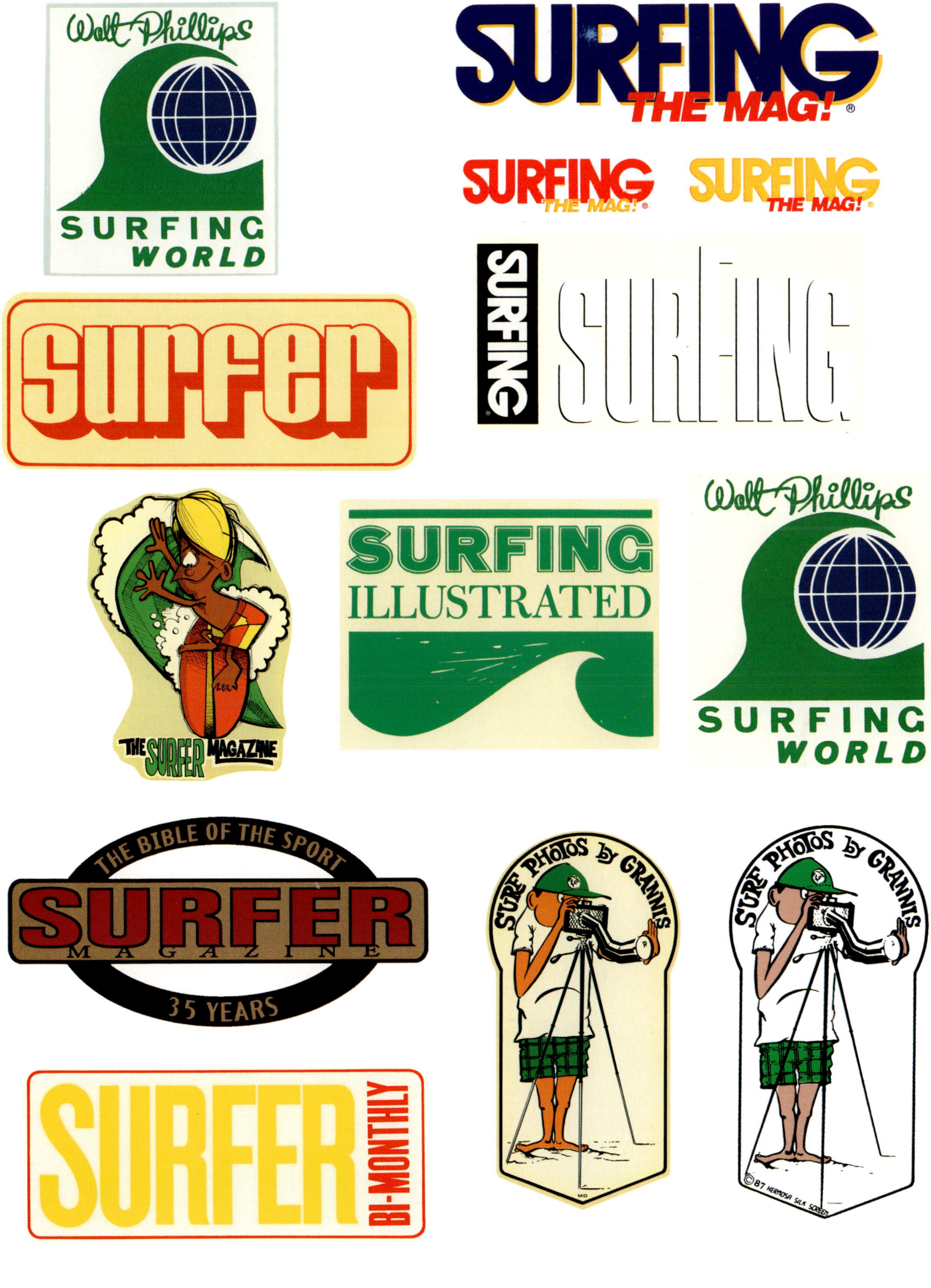
Walt Phillips
SURFING WORLD
SURFING THE MAG!
SURFING THE MAG!
SURFING THE MAG!
SURFING
SURFING
surfer
THE SURFER MAGAZINE
SURFING ILLUSTRATED
Walt Phillips
SURFING WORLD
THE BIBLE OF THE SPORT
SURFER
MAGAZINE
35 YEARS
SURF PHOTOS by GRANNIS
SURF PHOTOS by GRANNIS
©87 HERMOSA SILK SCREEN
SURFER
BI-MONTHLY

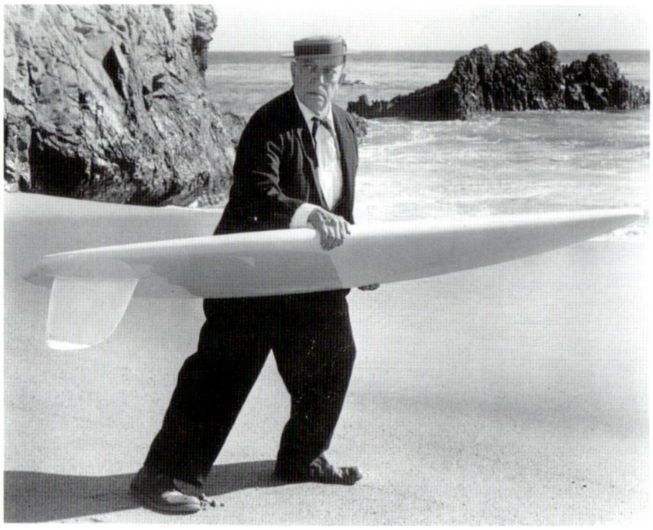

Buster Keaton, going surfing during the making of "Pajama Party," or "Beach Blanket Bingo" or "How to Stuff a Wild Bikini," at Zuma Beach in the middle 60s. Photo courtesy the Surfing Heritage Foundation.

5.7 NOW SHOWING
Surf movies.

INSERT MAGES AF07

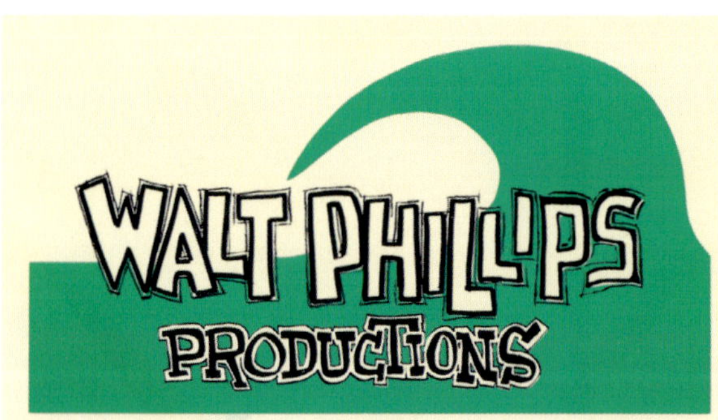

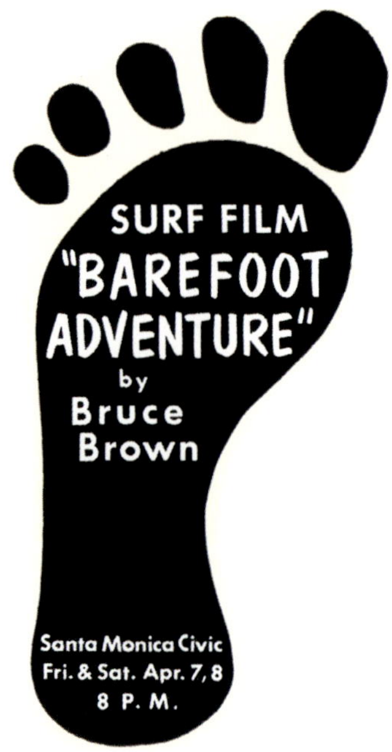

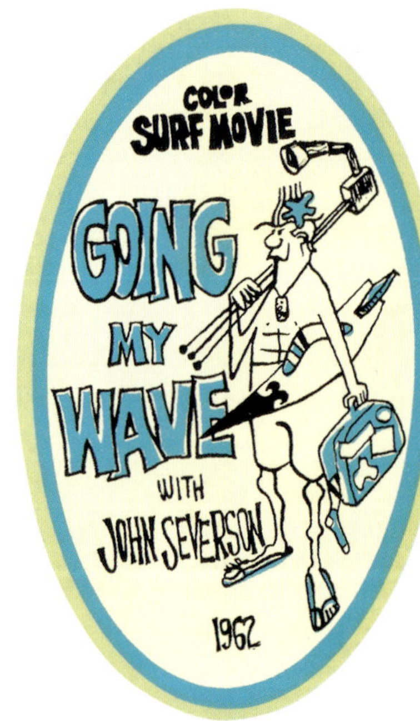

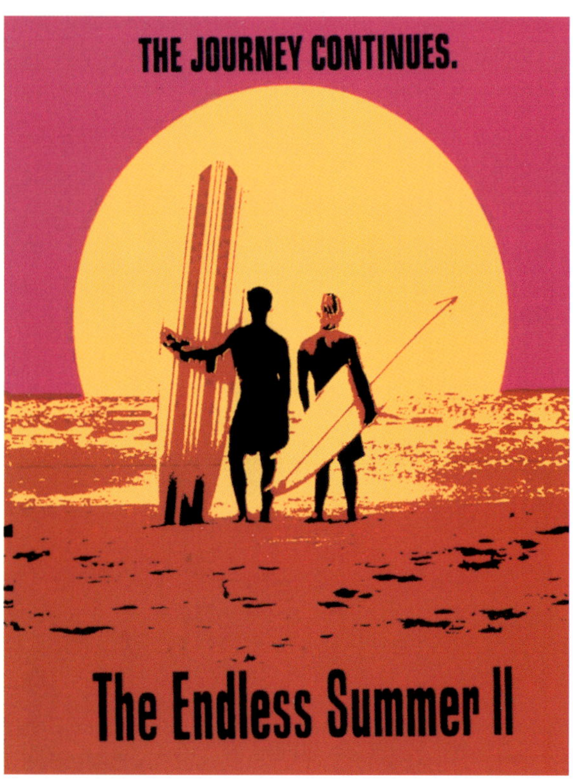

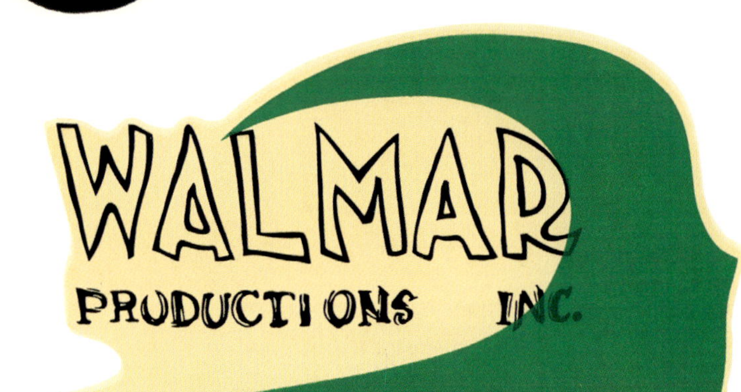

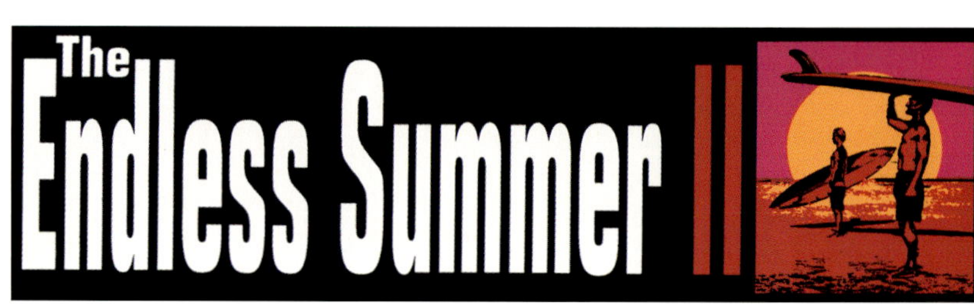

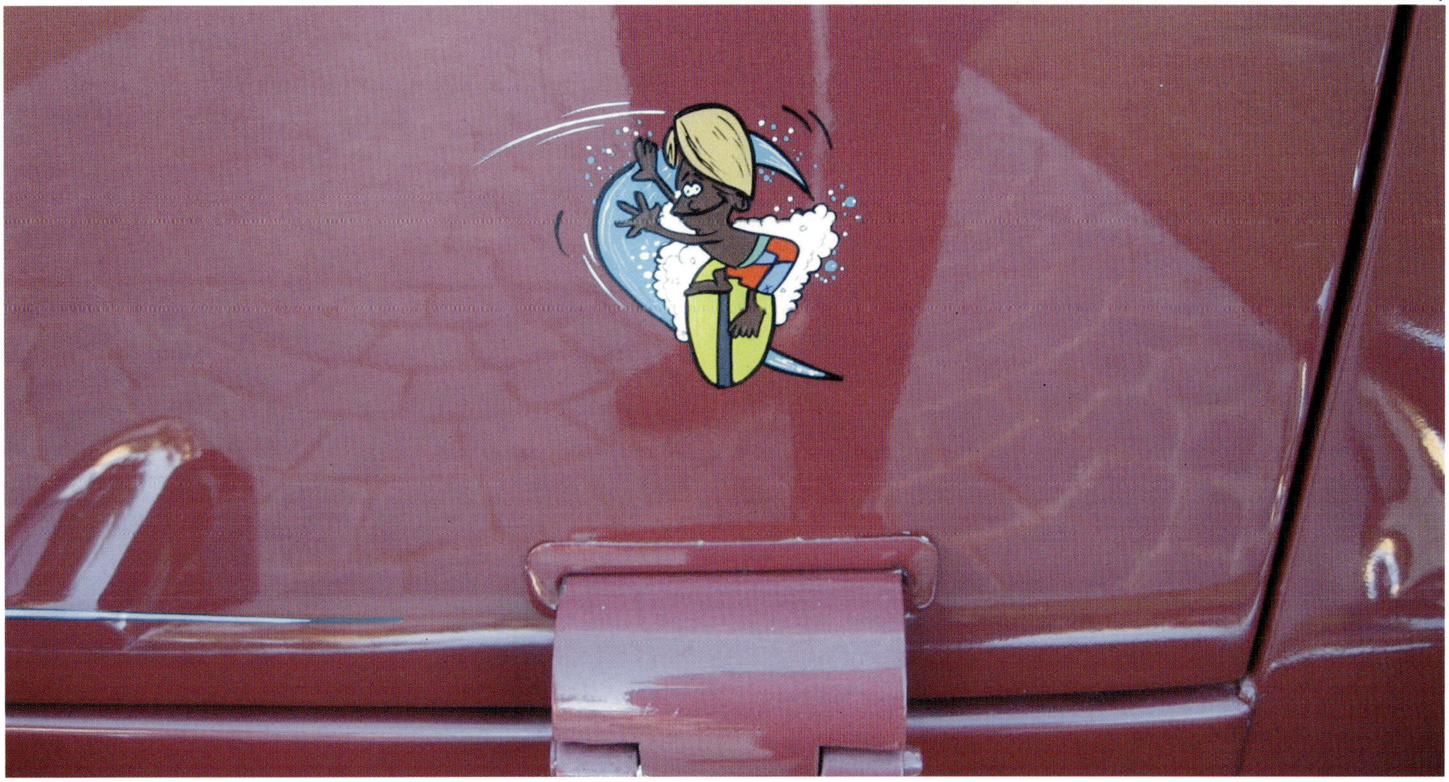

A custom Murphy illustration on the rear of a 1957 Chevy Bel Air belonging to Tim McNulty. Photo: Ben Marcus.

CHAPTER 6

MURPHY, GREMMIES AND OTHER CRITTERS

There are two truly great artists in the surfing world: John Severson, who was the founder of *Surfer Magazine*, and one of his first hires, Rick Griffin. In the early 60s, Griffin developed a character who was the "everygremmie," representing the perils and victories of a lot of young surfers getting into surfing.

Murphy was on the cover of *Surfer Magazine* and had a regular series of adventures that went well into the 60s. Murphy was very popular, and inspired a whole genre of yellow-haired, brown-skinned gremmies – an image that continues to this day.

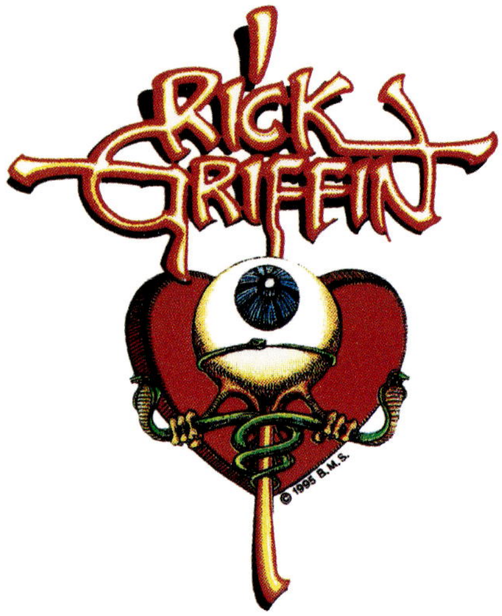
RICK GRIFFIN
© 1995 B.M.S.

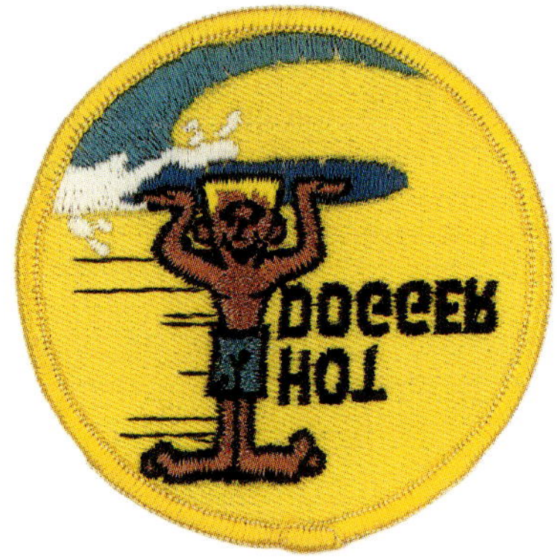

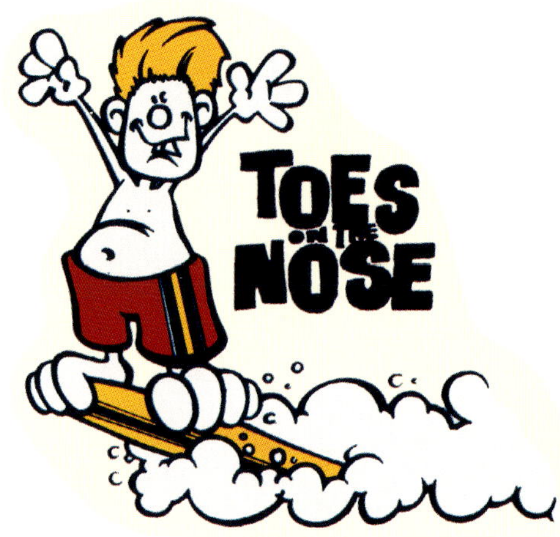
TOES ON THE NOSE

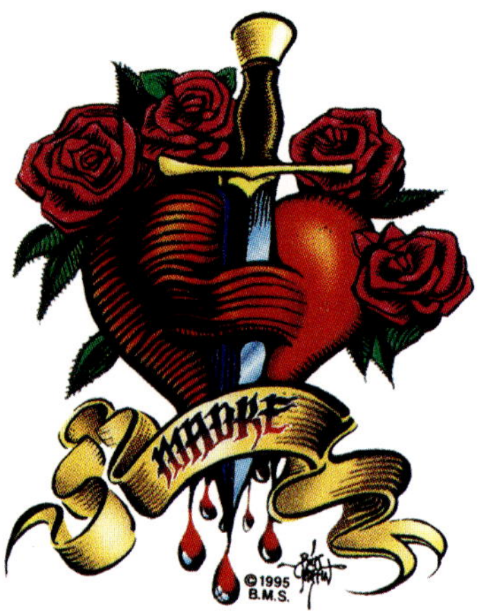

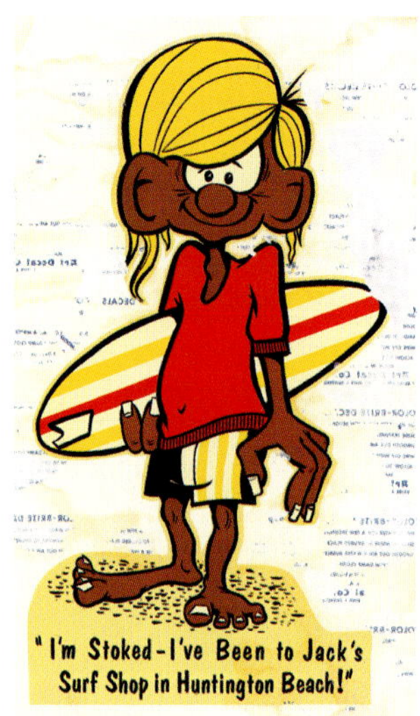
"I'm Stoked-I've Been to Jack's Surf Shop in Huntington Beach!"

ON THE BEACH
SURF SHOP
CARMEL & MONTEREY BAY
CALIFORNIA

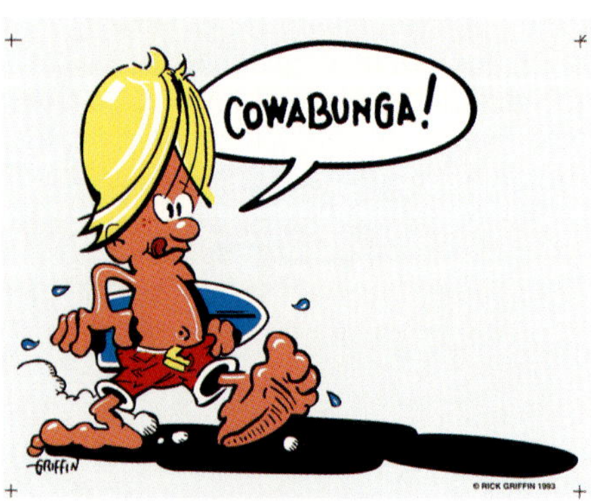
COWABUNGA!
GRIFFIN
© RICK GRIFFIN 1993

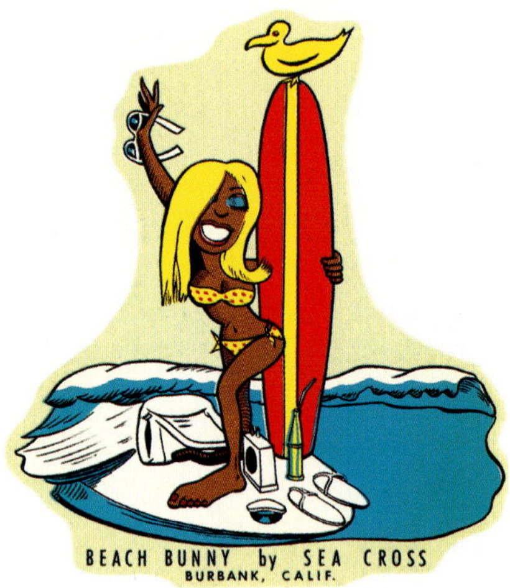
BEACH BUNNY by SEA CROSS
BURBANK, CALIF.

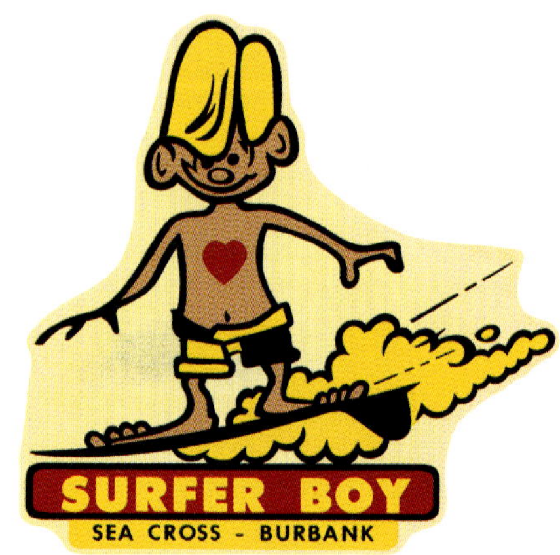
SURFER BOY
SEA CROSS - BURBANK

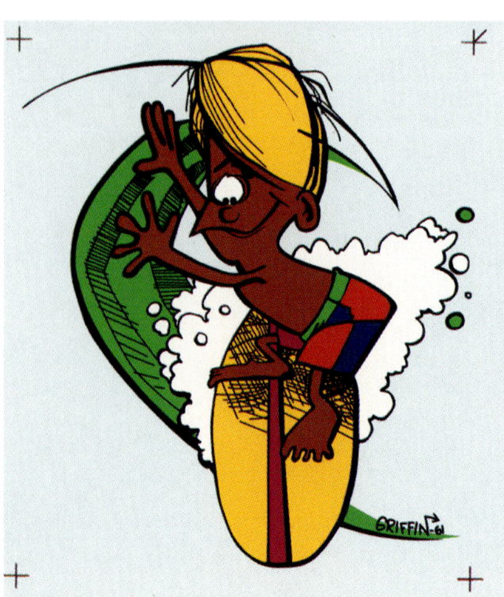
GRIFFIN

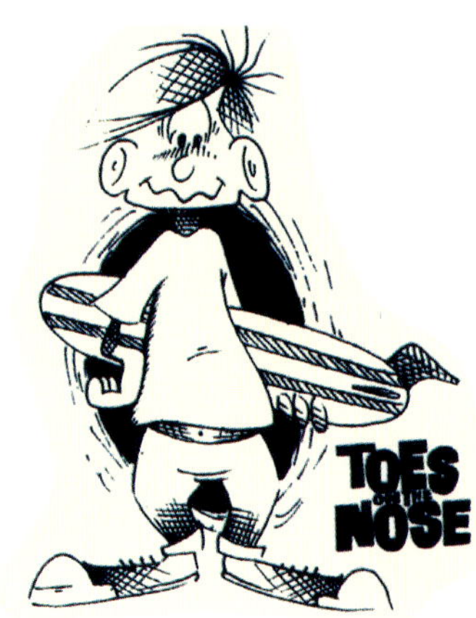
TOES ON THE NOSE

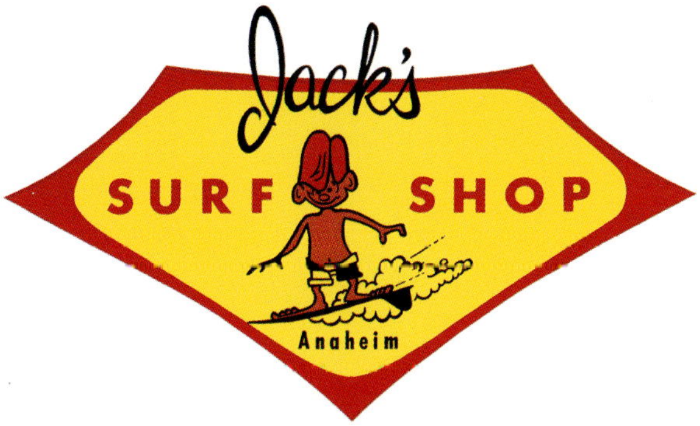
Jack's
SURF SHOP
Anaheim

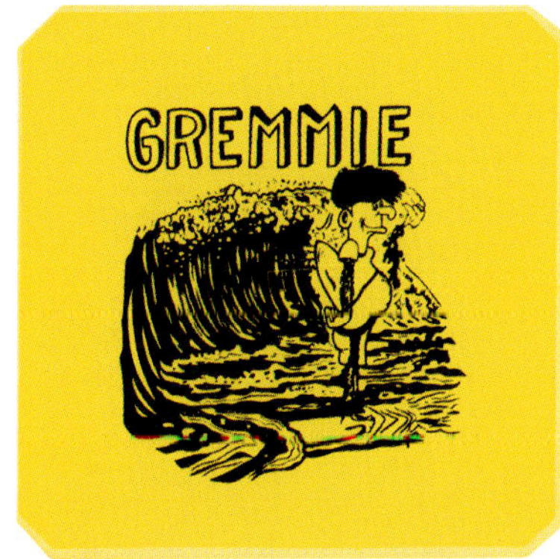
GREMMIE

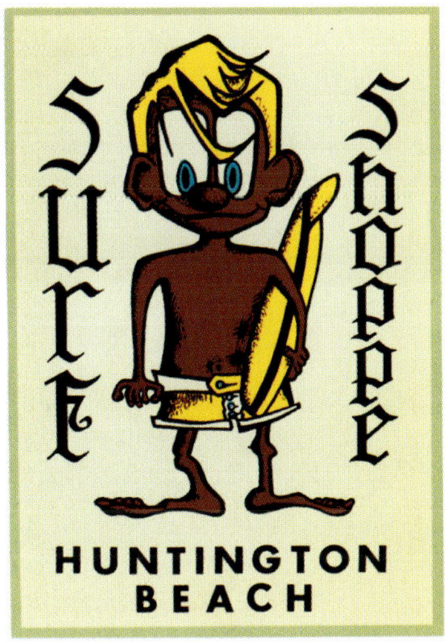
SURF
SHOPPE
HUNTINGTON
BEACH

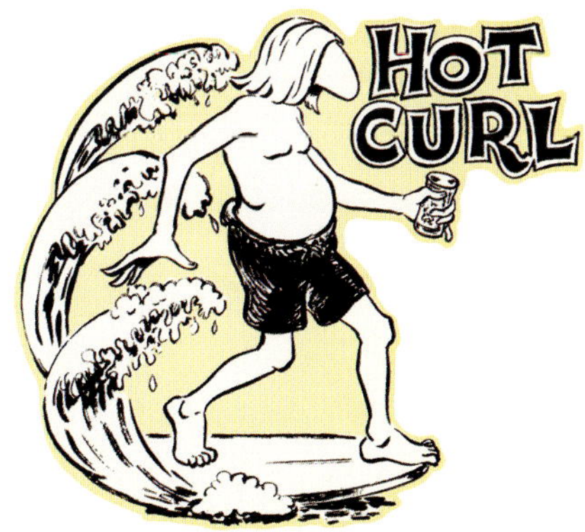
HOT
CURL

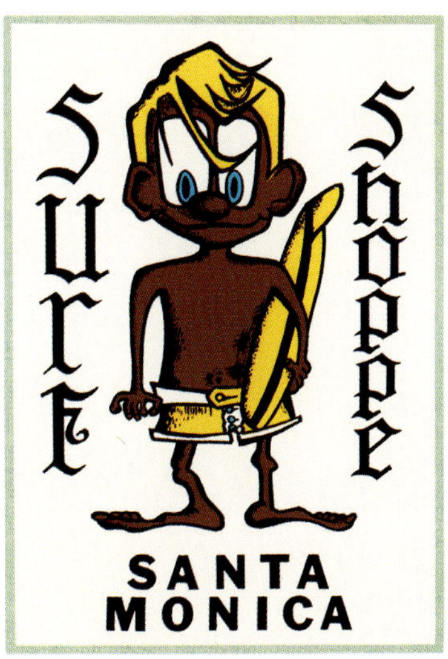
SURF
SHOPPE
SANTA
MONICA

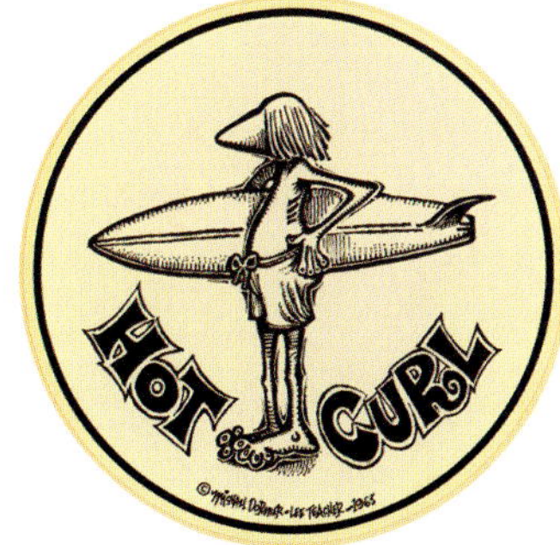
HOT
CURL

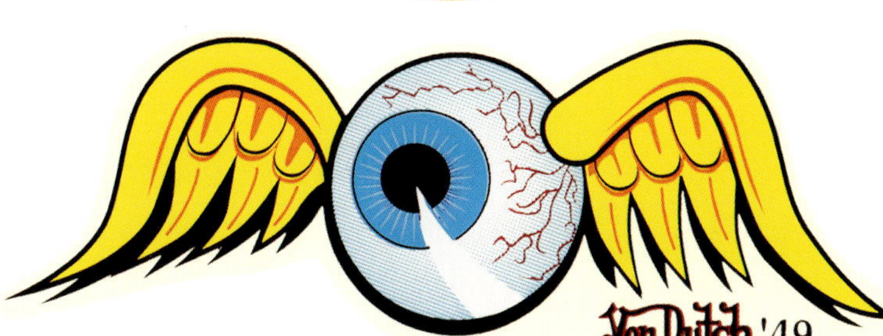
Von Dutch '49

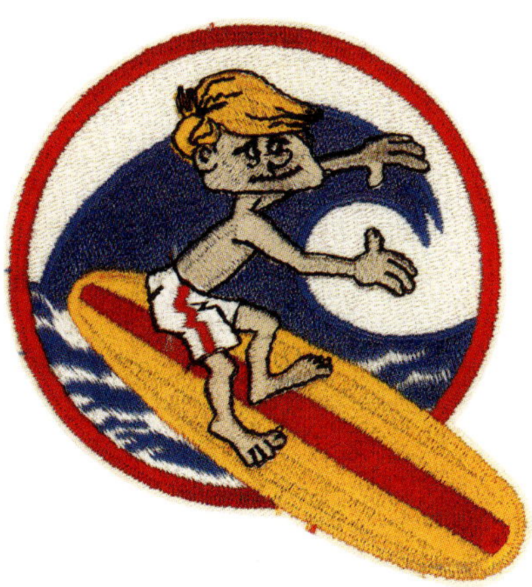

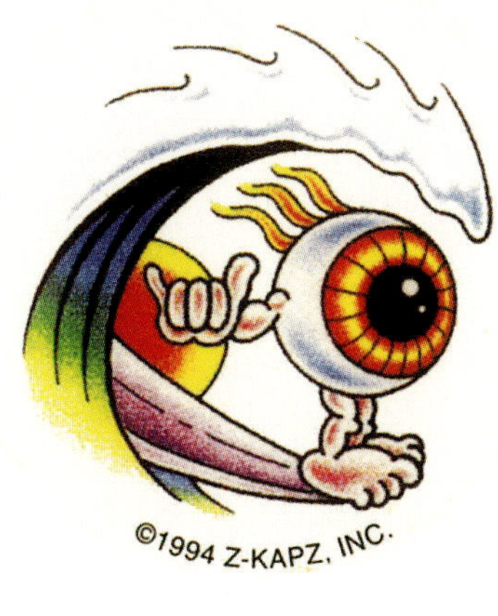
©1994 Z-KAPZ, INC.

6.1 CRITTERS

Lions, tigers and bears. Sharks, monsters and other creepy crawlies. Kids love critters and kids love stickers.

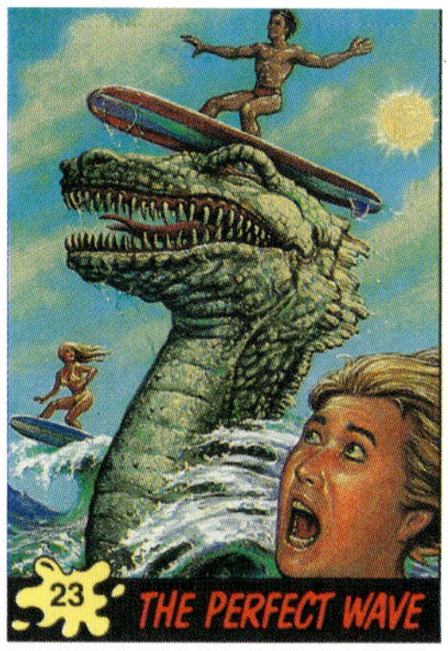

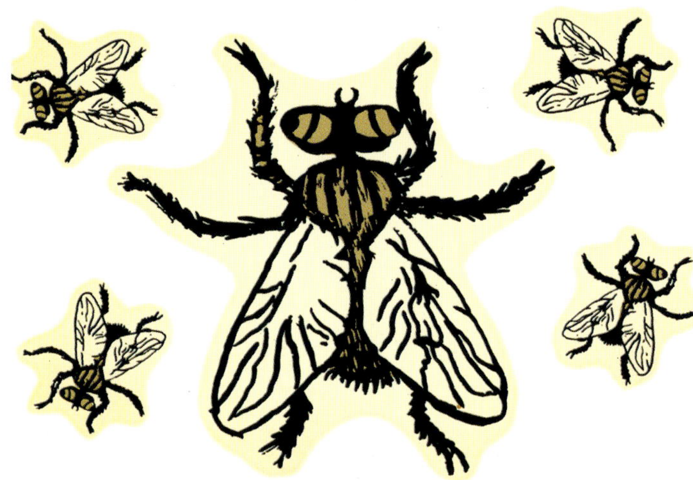

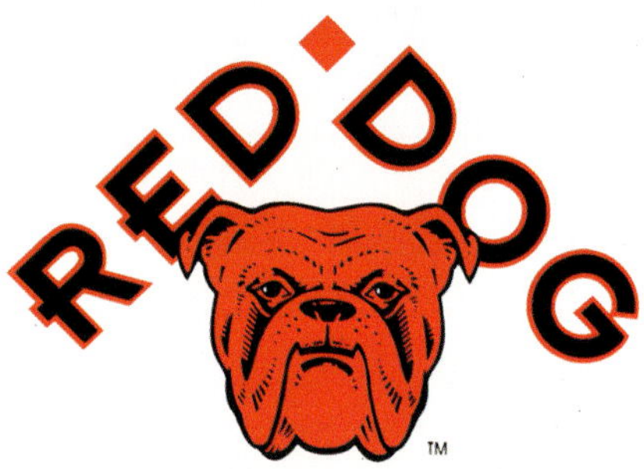

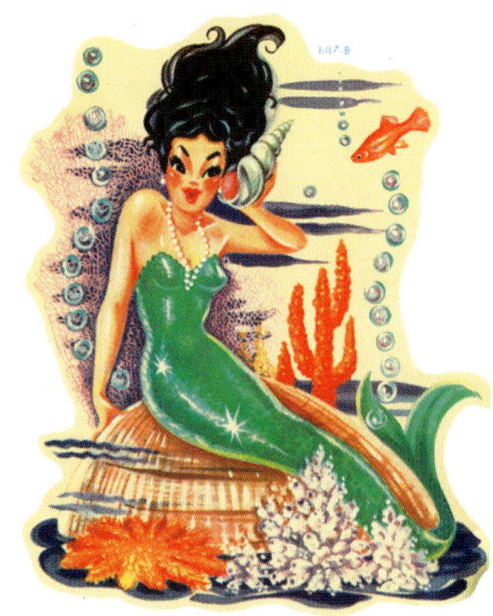

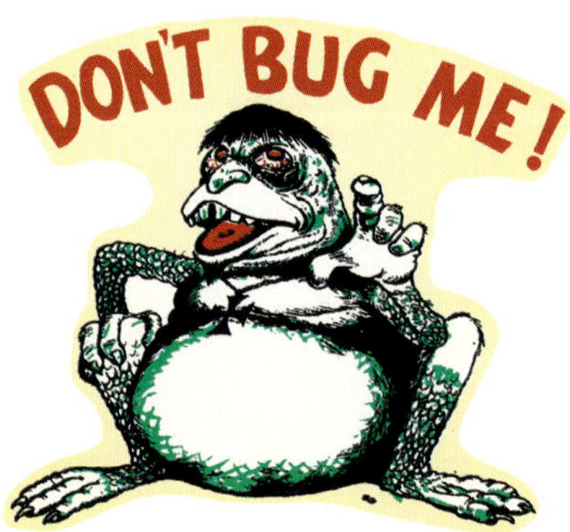

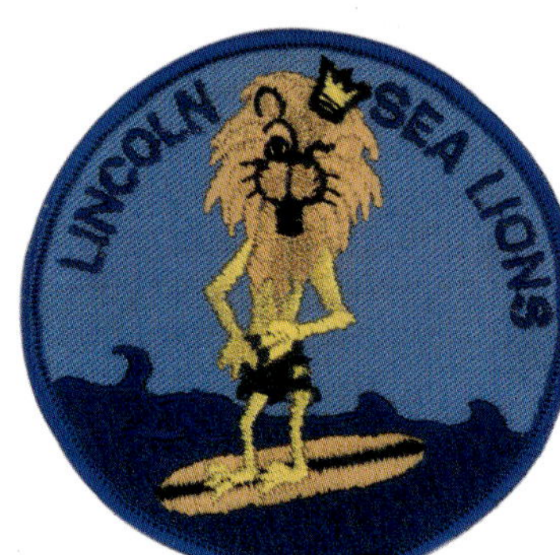

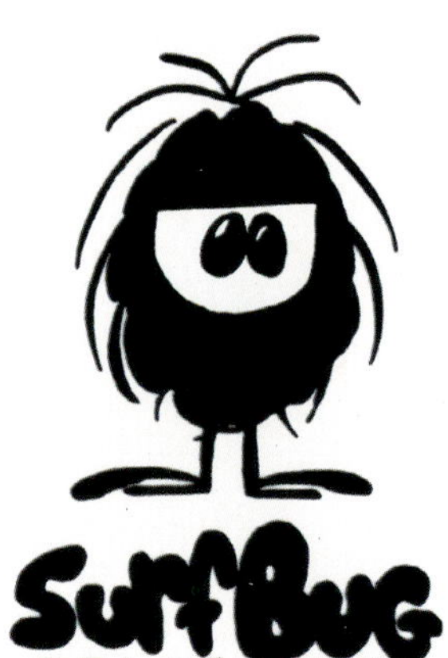

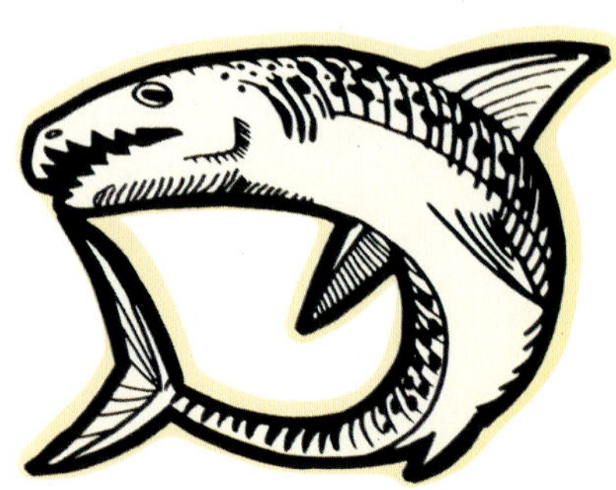

CHAPTER 7

DECLARE YOURSELF

Say it loud, you're a surfer and you're proud. Some surfers declare their pride loud and clear with bumper or other stickers.

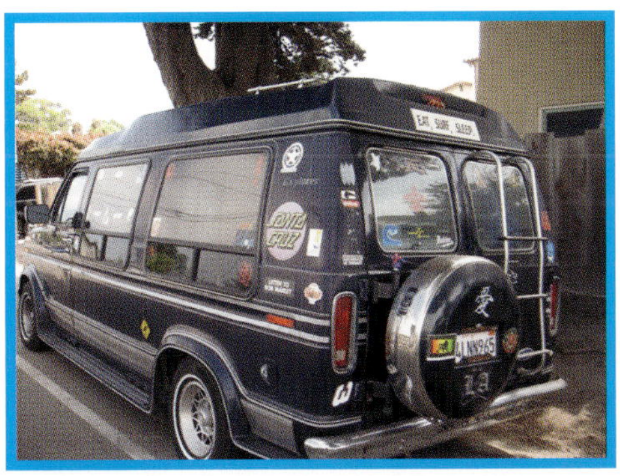

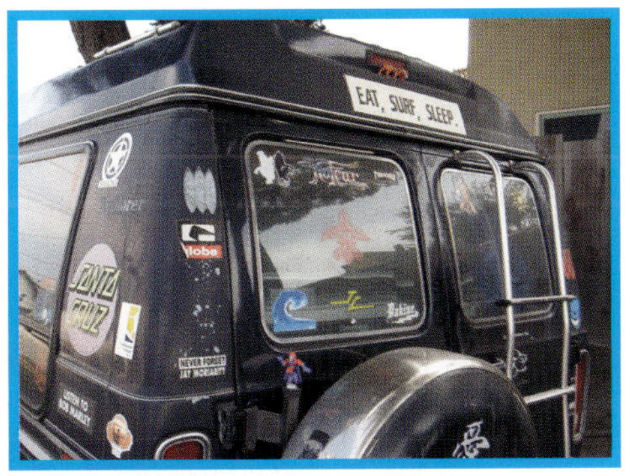

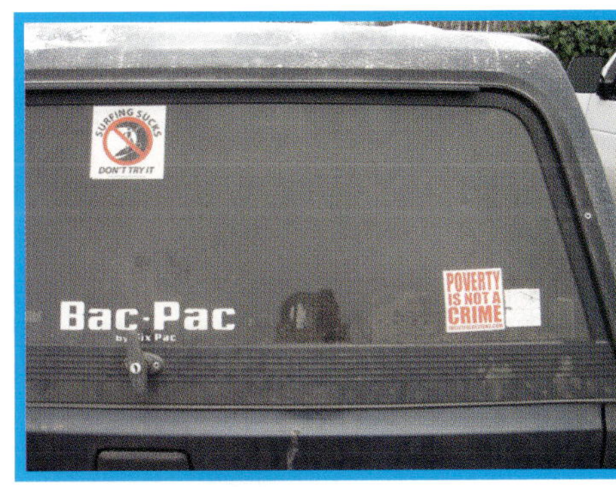

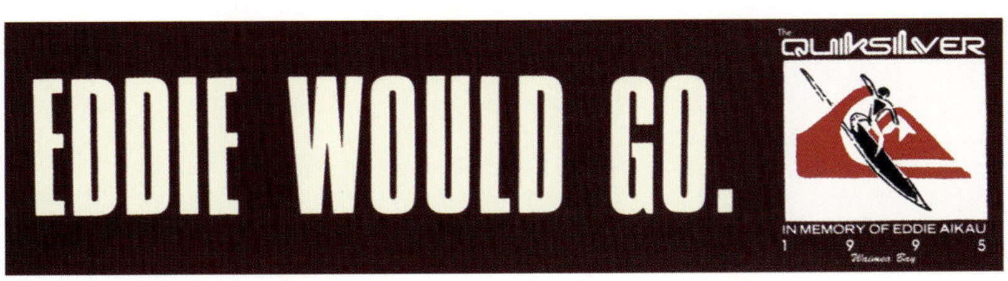

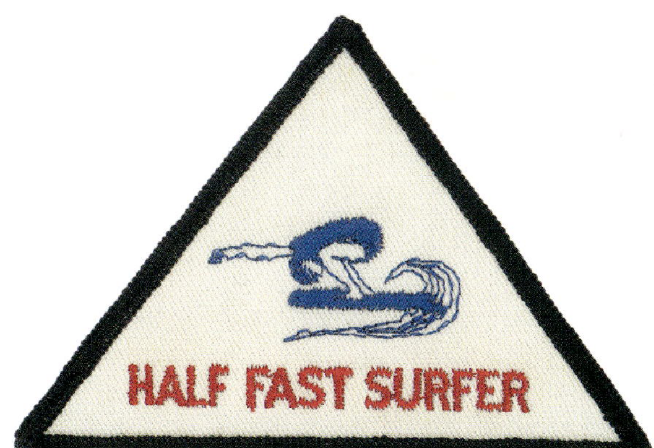

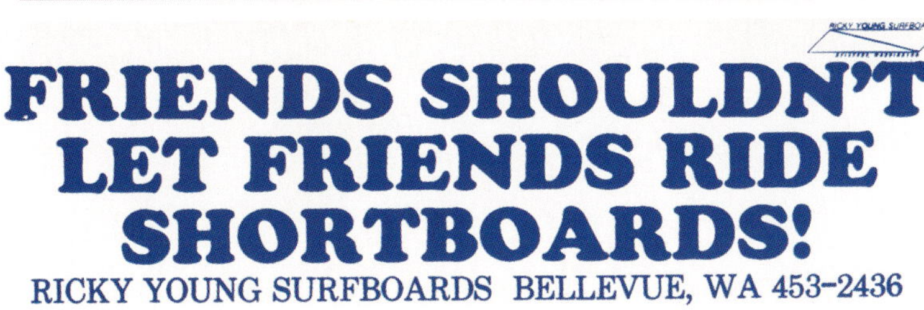

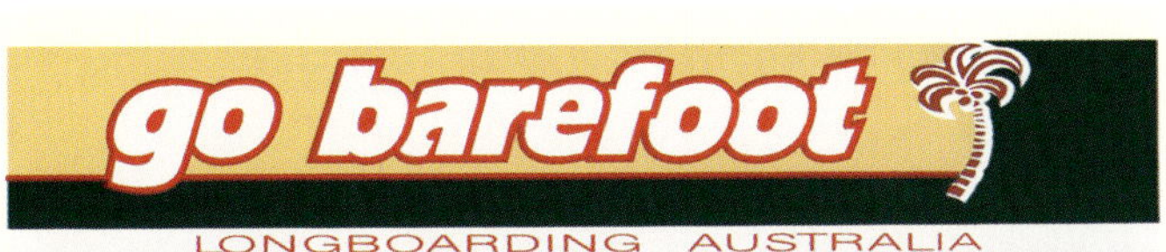

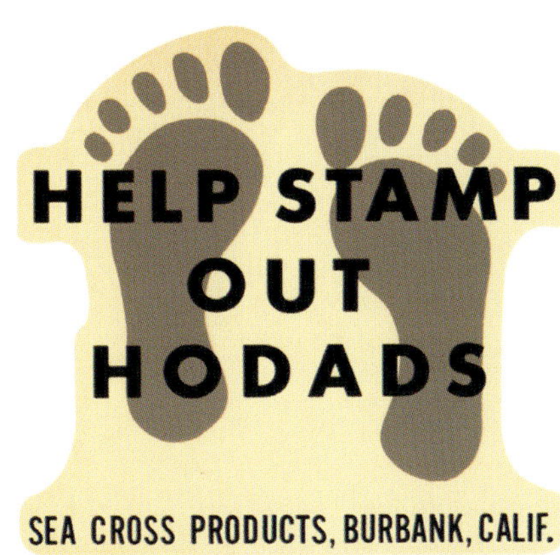

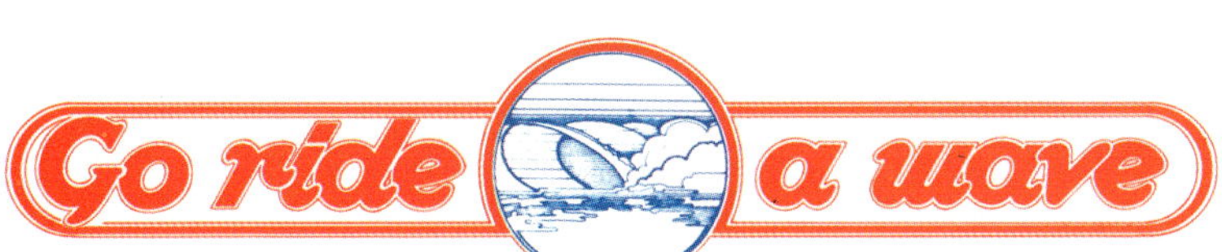

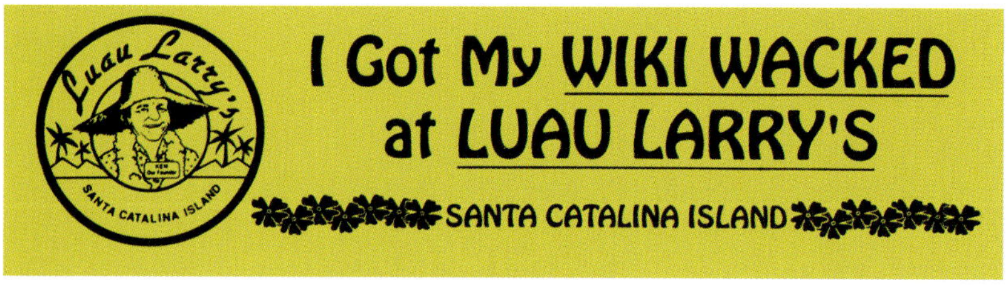
Luau Larry's
SANTA CATALINA ISLAND
I Got My WIKI WACKED
at LUAU LARRY'S
SANTA CATALINA ISLAND

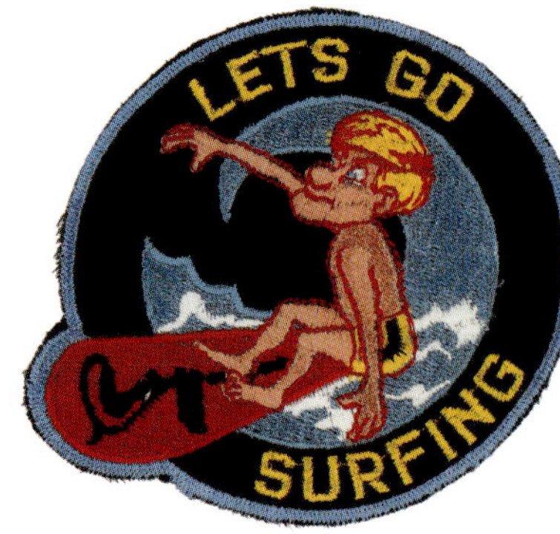
LETS GO
SURFING

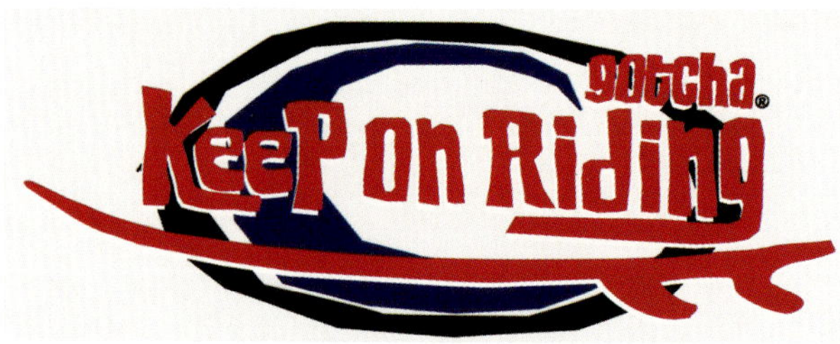
gotcha
Keep on Riding

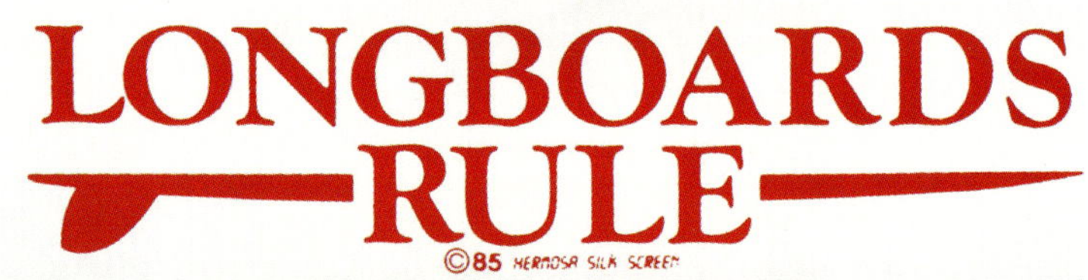
LONGBOARDS
RULE
©85 HERMOSA SILK SCREEN

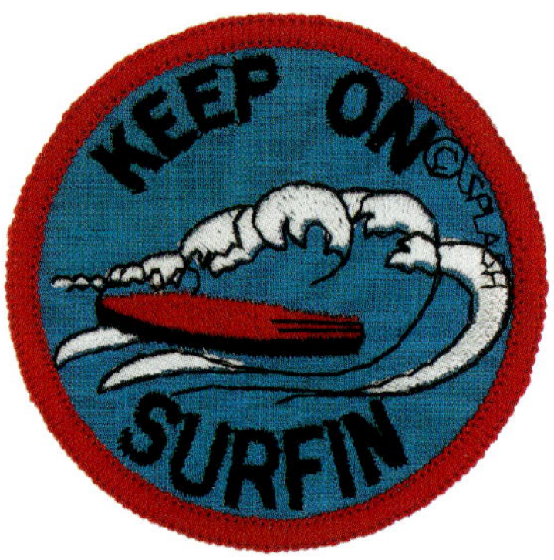
KEEP ON
SURFIN

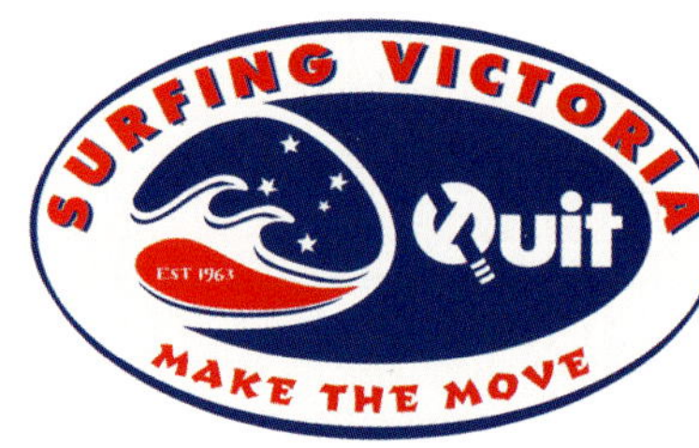
SURFING VICTORIA
EST 1963
Quit
MAKE THE MOVE

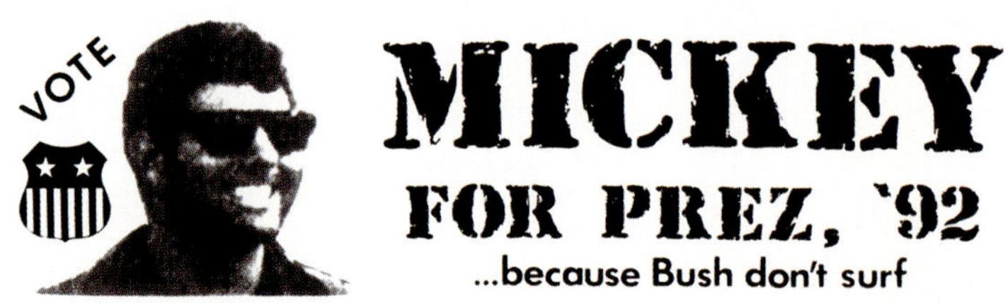
VOTE
MICKEY
FOR PREZ, '92
...because Bush don't surf

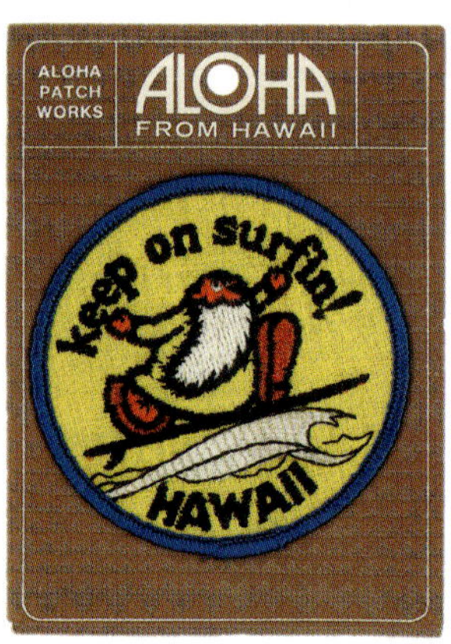
ALOHA PATCH WORKS
ALOHA
FROM HAWAII
keep on surfin!
HAWAII

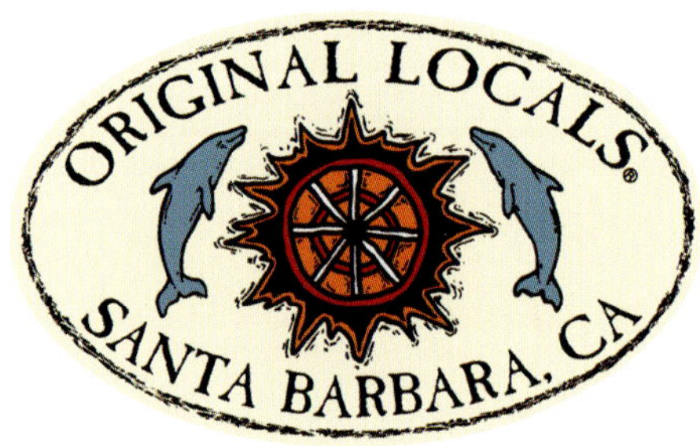
ORIGINAL LOCALS
SANTA BARBARA, CA

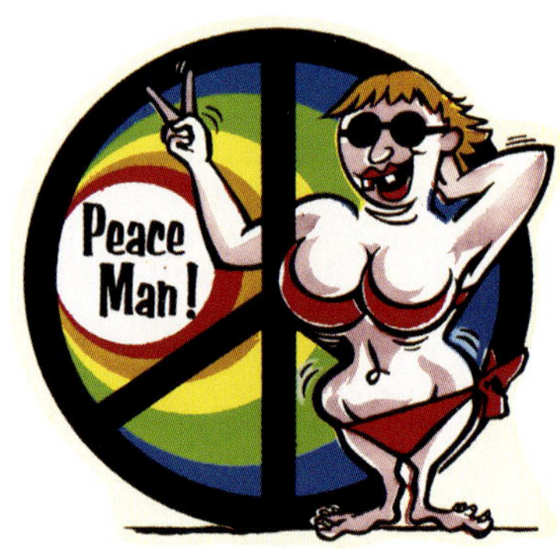
Peace Man!

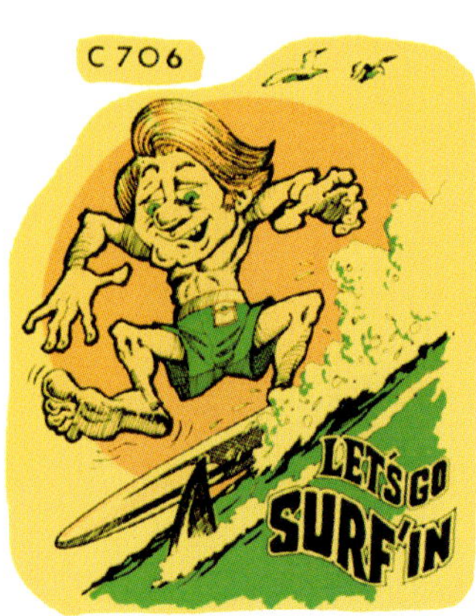
C706
LET'S GO
SURF'IN

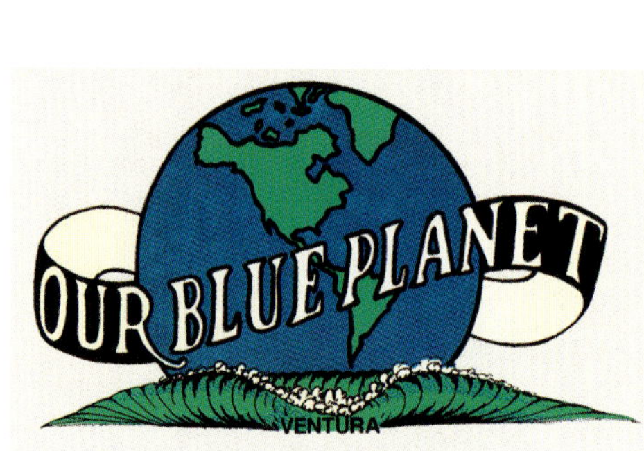
OUR BLUE PLANET
VENTURA

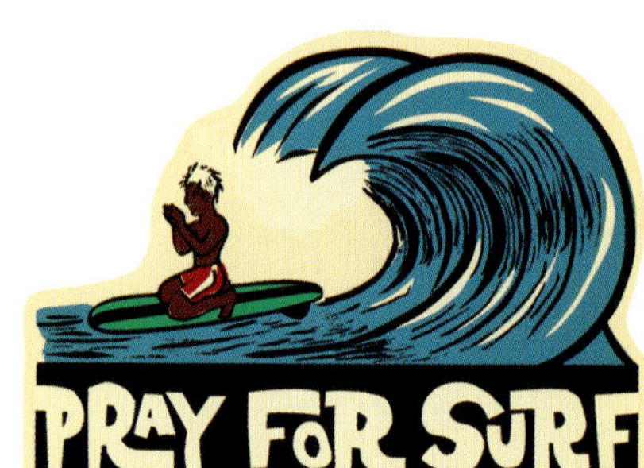
PRAY FOR SURF

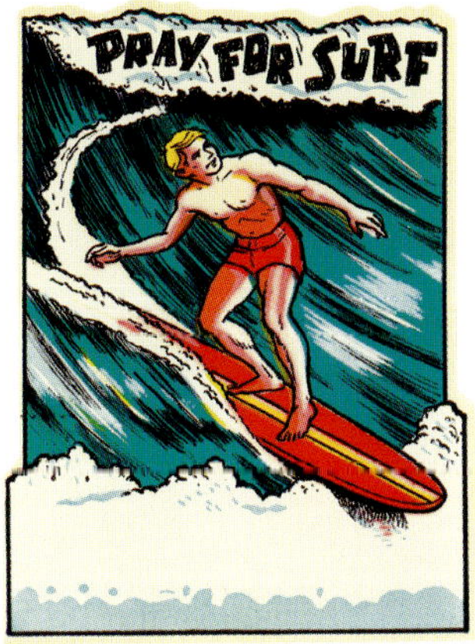
PRAY FOR SURF

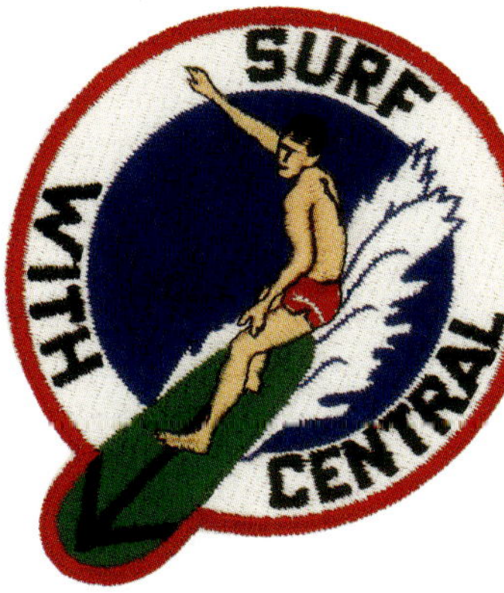
SURF
WITH
CENTRAL

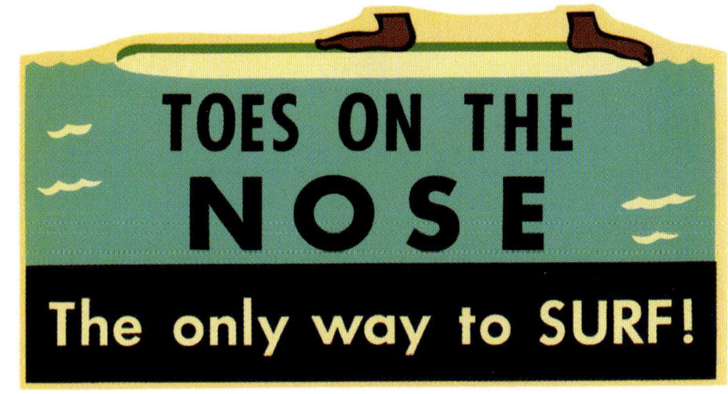
TOES ON THE
NOSE
The only way to SURF!

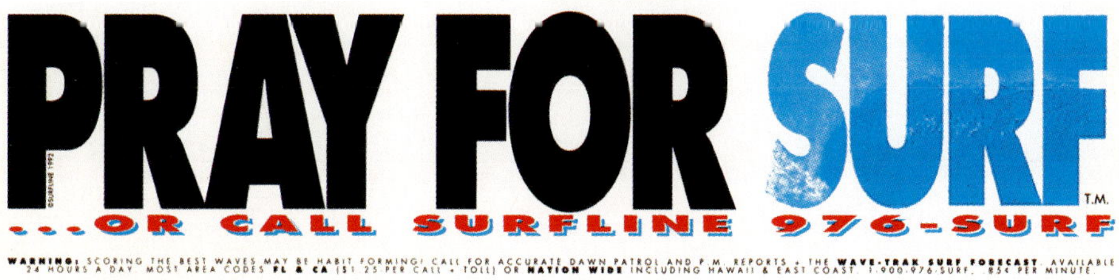
PRAY FOR SURF
T.M.
...OR CALL SURFLINE 976-SURF
WARNING: SCORING THE BEST WAVES MAY BE HABIT FORMING! CALL FOR ACCURATE DAWN PATROL AND P.M. REPORTS + THE WAVE-TRAK SURF FORECAST. AVAILABLE 24 HOURS A DAY. MOST AREA CODES FL & CA ($1.25 PER CALL + TOLL) OR NATION WIDE INCLUDING HAWAII & EAST COAST. 1-900-976-SURF. 85¢ PER MINUTE.

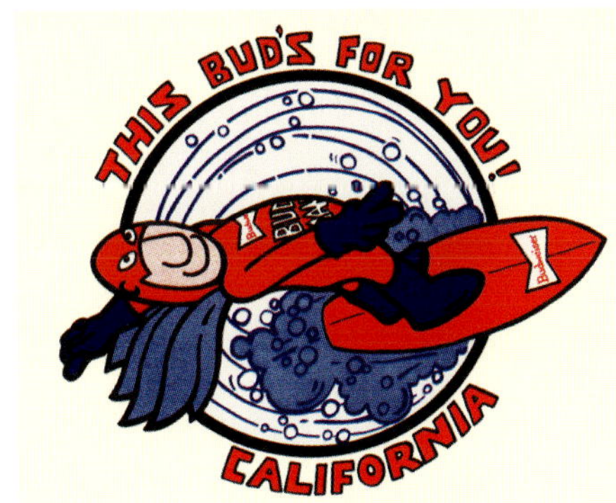
THIS BUD'S FOR YOU!
CALIFORNIA

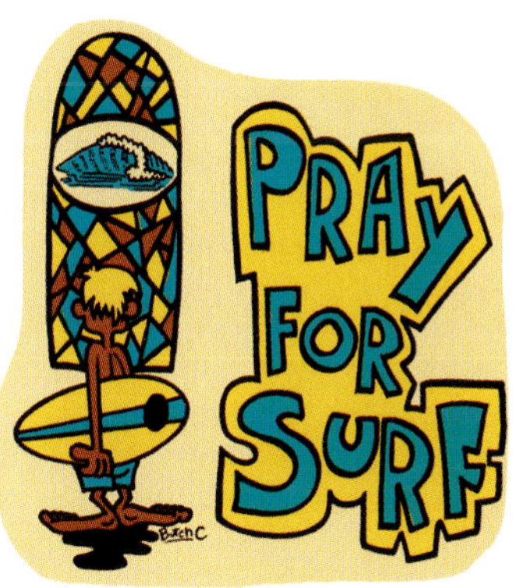
PRAY
FOR
SURF

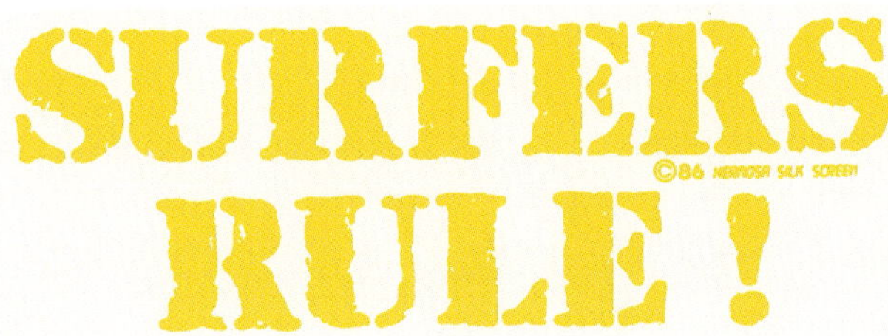
SURFERS
RULE!
©86 HERMOSA SILK SCREEN

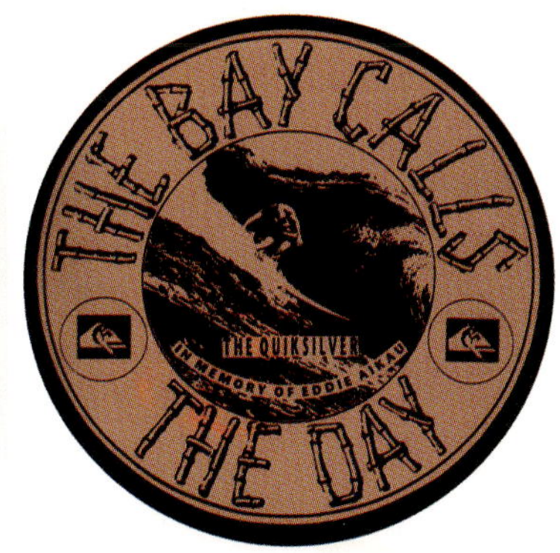
THE BAY CALLS
THE DAY
THE QUIKSILVER
IN MEMORY OF EDDIE AIKAU

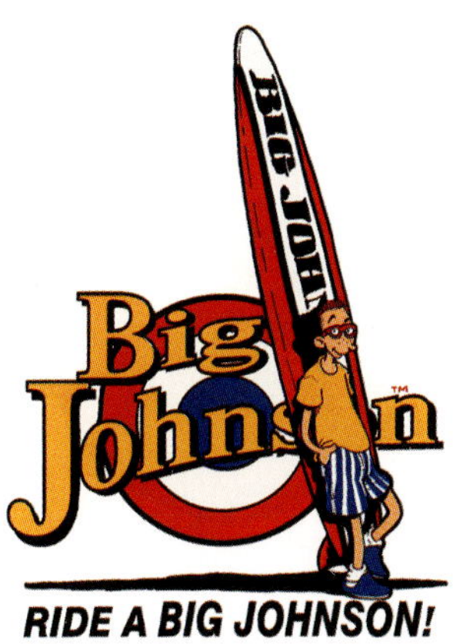
BIG JOHN
Big
Johnson
RIDE A BIG JOHNSON!

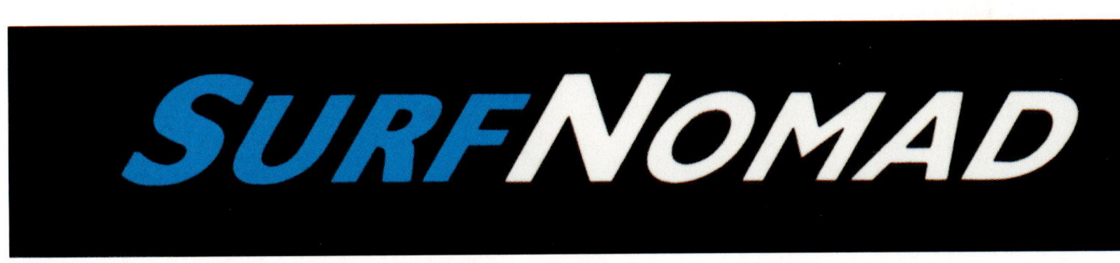
SURFNOMAD

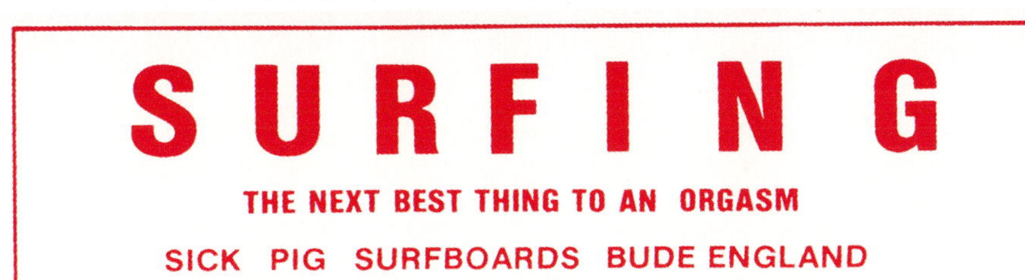
SURFING
THE NEXT BEST THING TO AN ORGASM
SICK PIG SURFBOARDS BUDE ENGLAND

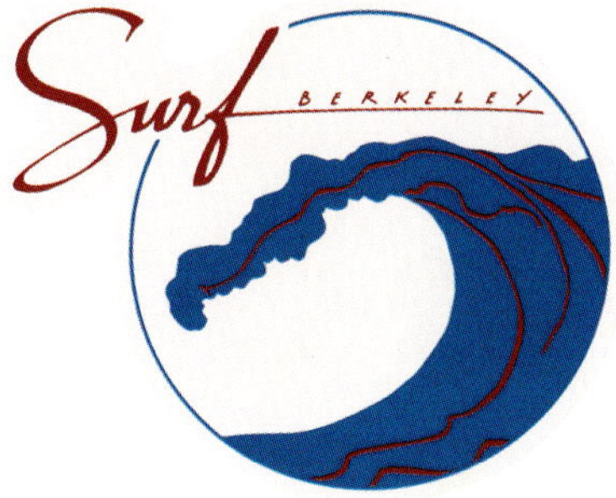
Surf
BERKELEY

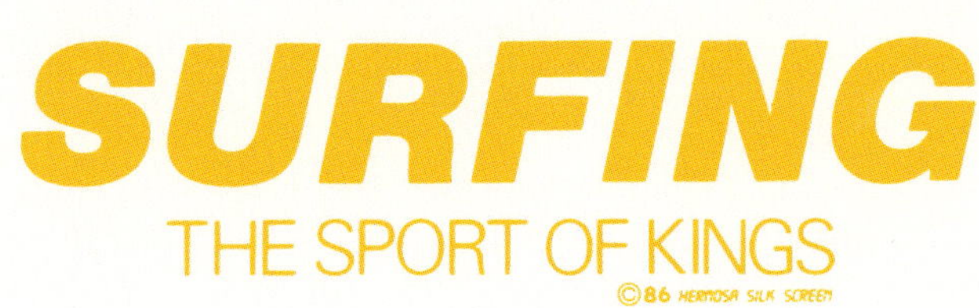
SURFING
THE SPORT OF KINGS
©86 HERMOSA SILK SCREEN

CHAPTER 8

POGS AND OTHER FOOD KINE STUFFS

POG stands for Passion, Orange, Guava, an alchemy of juices popular in Hawaii. POGs are also the popular name for milk and fruit juice bottlecaps, and also a kid's game in which collectors of POGs try to win their opponent's caps by hitting them with a slammer and turning them face up.

The game was first popular in Hawaii in the 1920s and 1930s, and a new mini-craze developed in the early 1990s. Here are some samples from the latest craze, along with some mainland stickers from A and W and Bob's Big Boy.

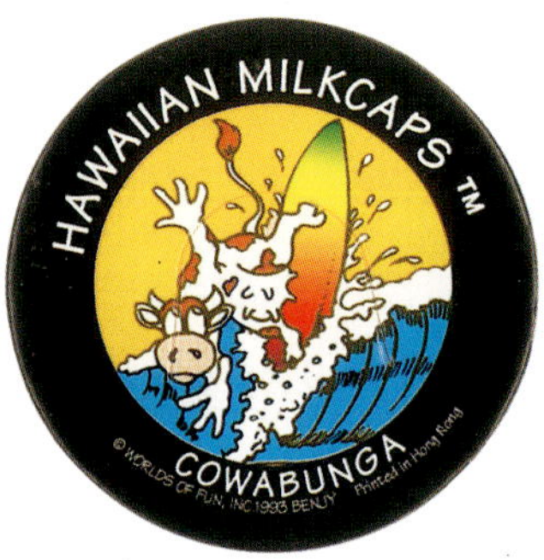

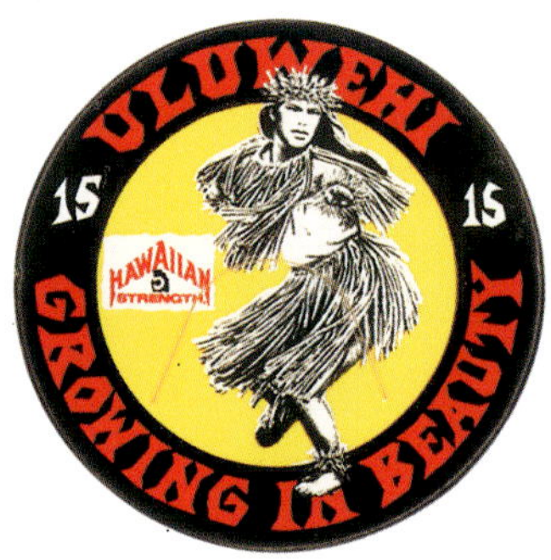

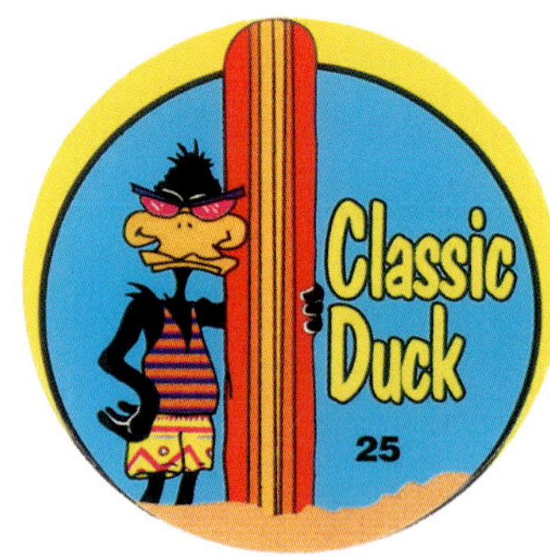

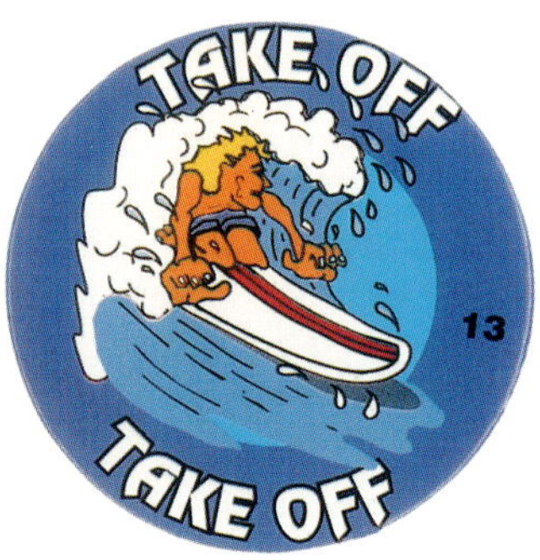

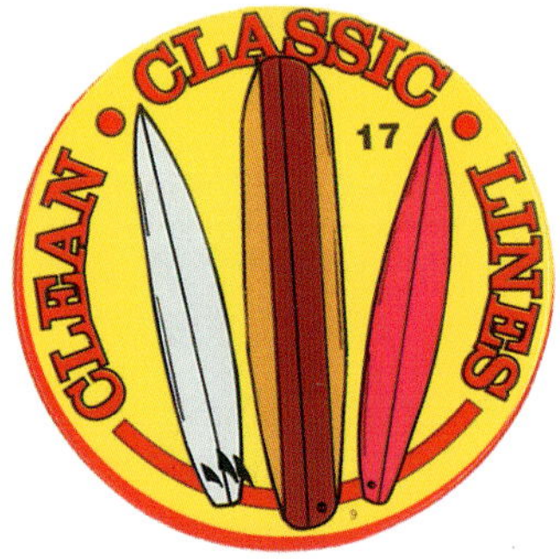

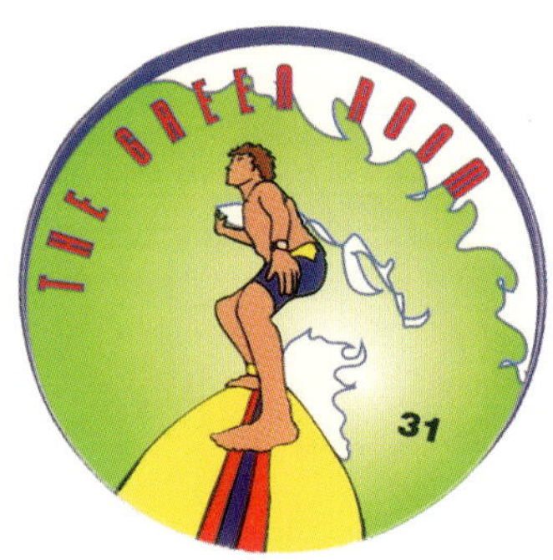

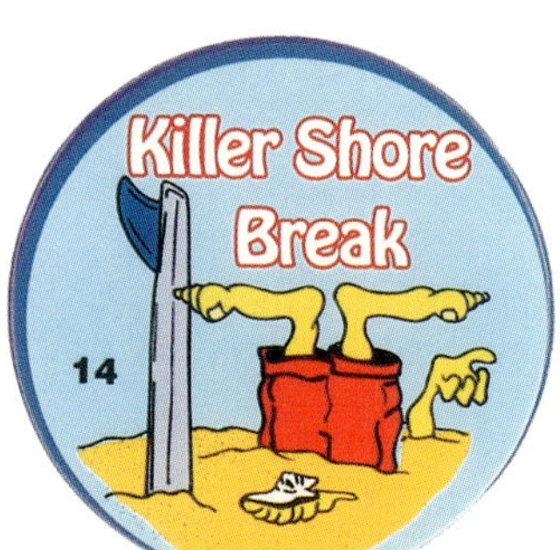

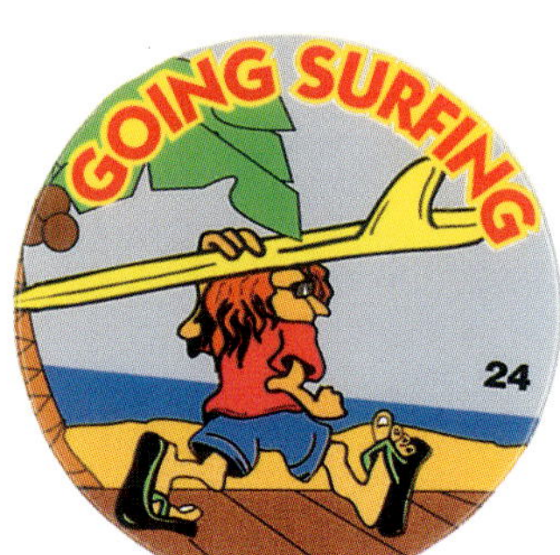

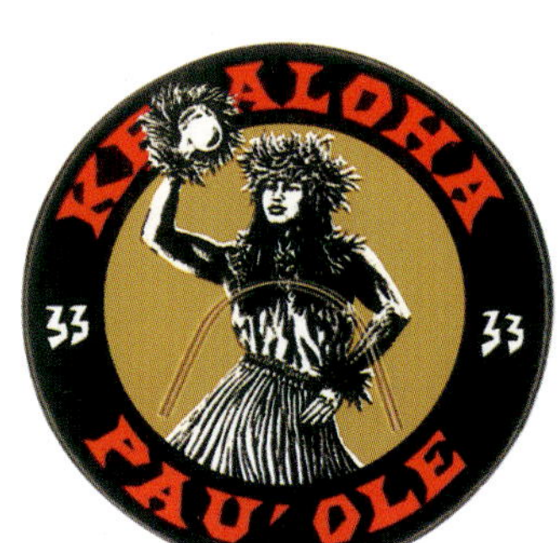

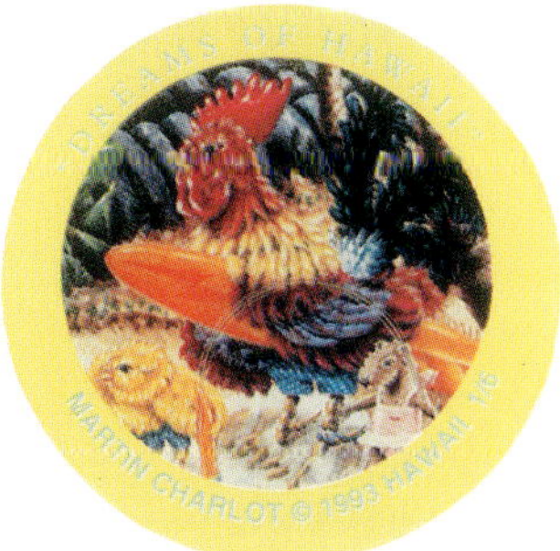
DREAMS OF HAWAII
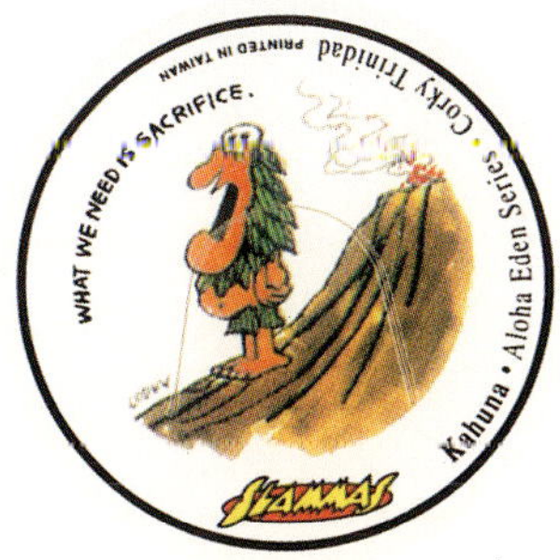
WHAT WE NEED IS SACRIFICE.
Corky Trinidad PRINTED IN TAIWAN
Kahuna • Aloha Eden Series
SLAMMAS
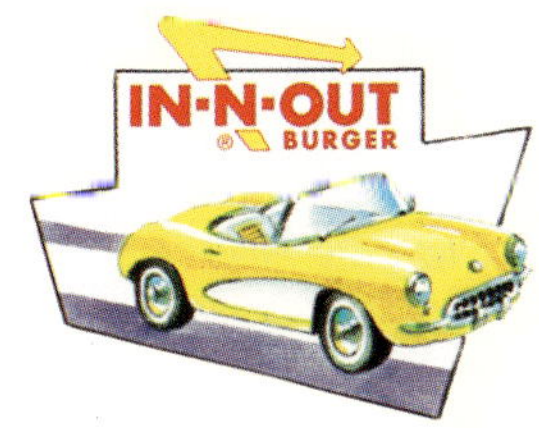
IN-N-OUT BURGER
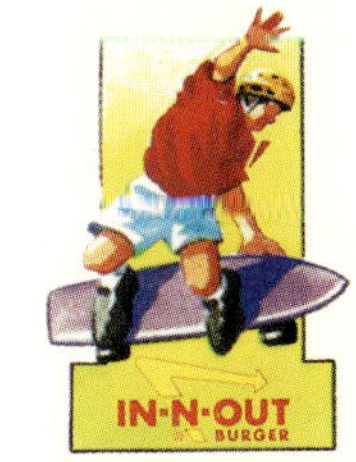
IN-N-OUT BURGER
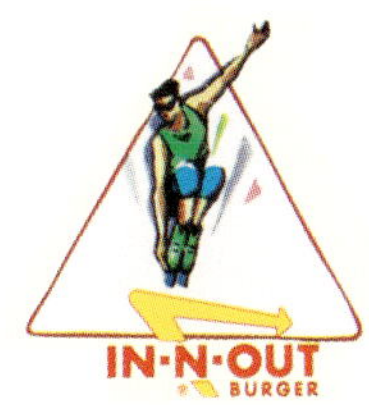
IN-N-OUT BURGER
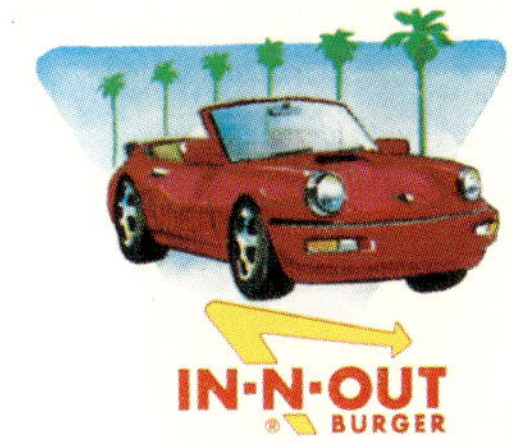
IN-N-OUT BURGER
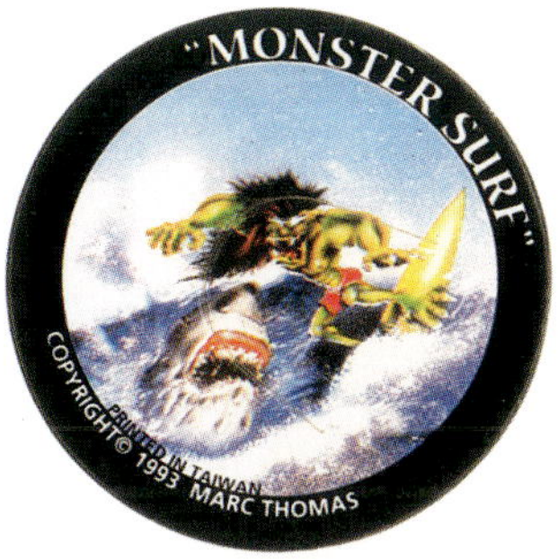
"MONSTER SURF"
PRINTED IN TAIWAN
COPYRIGHT © 1993 MARC THOMAS
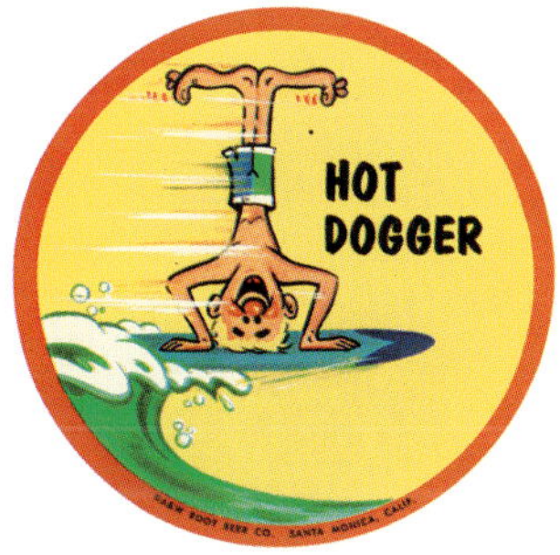
HOT DOGGER
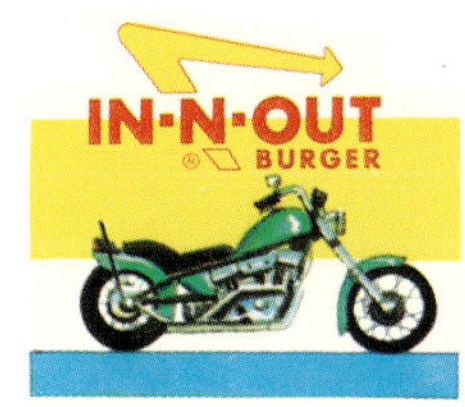
IN-N-OUT BURGER
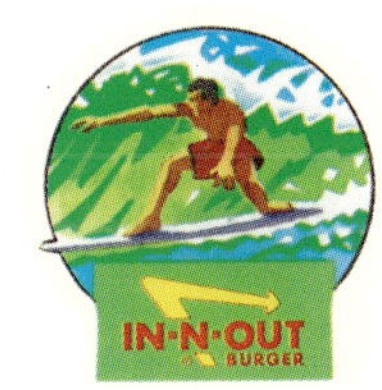
IN-N-OUT BURGER
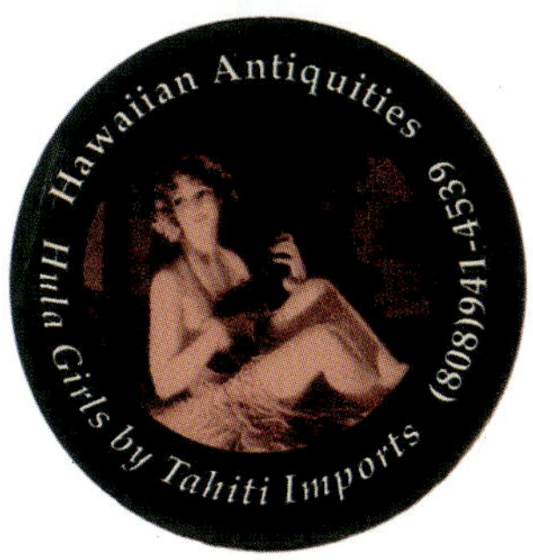
Hawaiian Antiquities
(808)941-4539
Hula Girls by Tahiti Imports
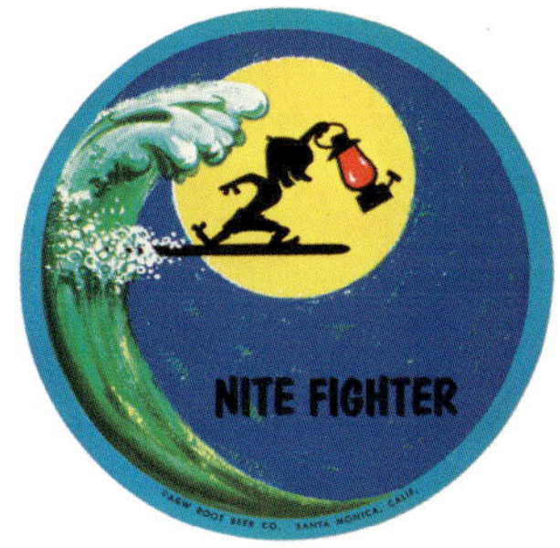
NITE FIGHTER
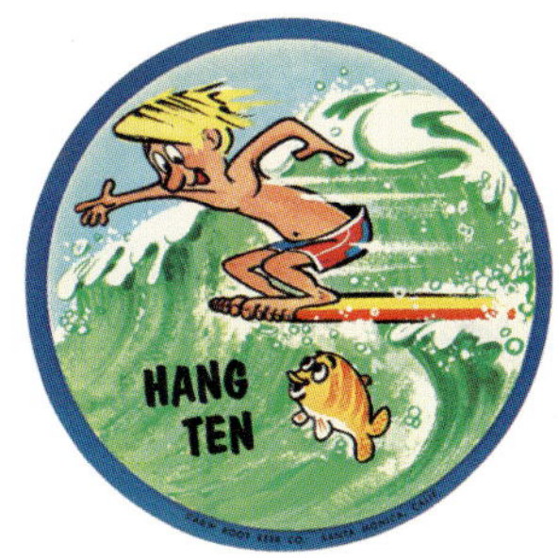
HANG TEN
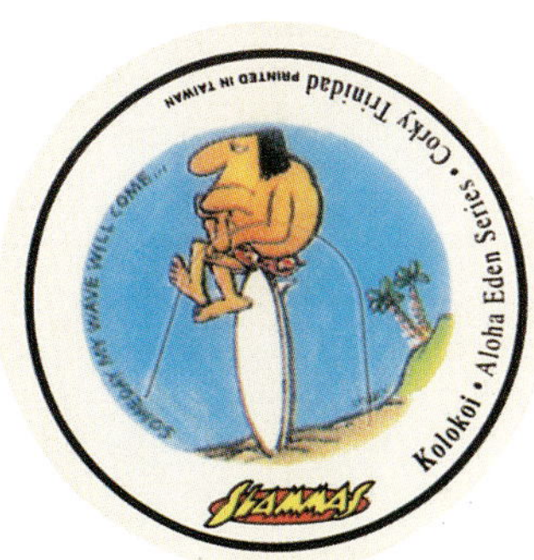
Corky Trinidad PRINTED IN TAIWAN
Kolokoi • Aloha Eden Series
SLAMMAS
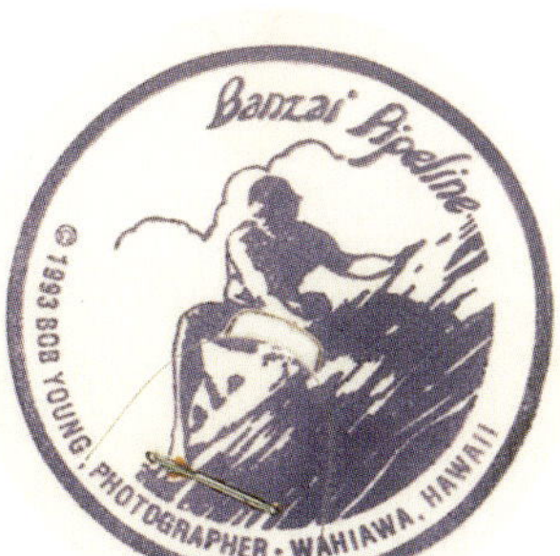
Banzai Pipeline
© 1993 BOB YOUNG, PHOTOGRAPHER • WAHIAWA, HAWAII
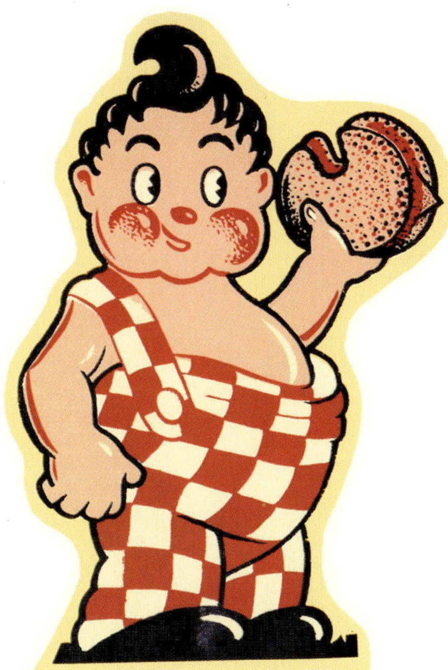
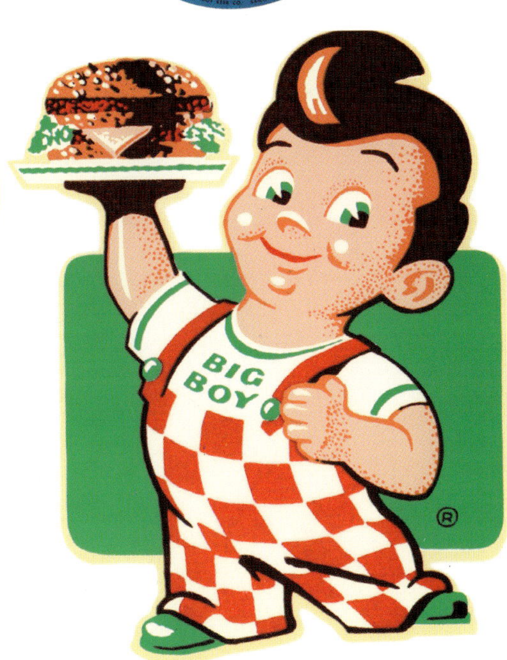
BIG BOY
®

CHAPTER 9

MISH MOSH AND MISCELLANY

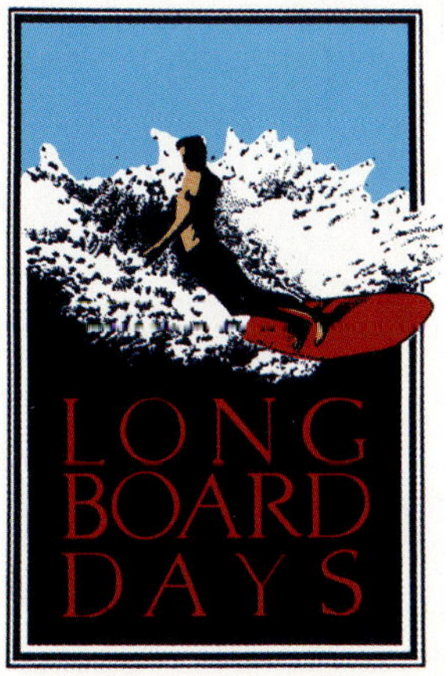
LONG
BOARD
DAYS

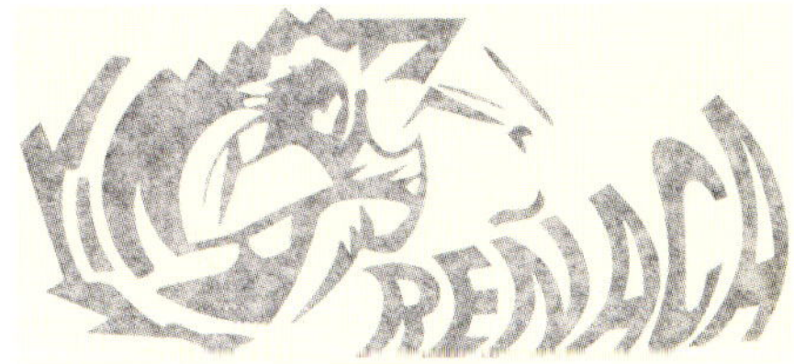
REÑACA

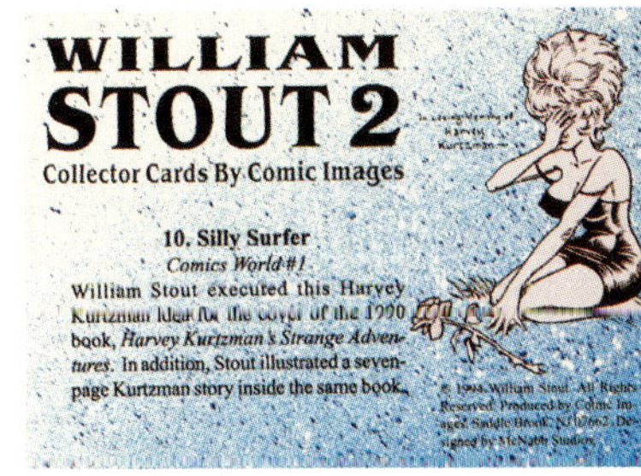
WILLIAM
STOUT 2
Collector Cards By Comic Images
10. Silly Surfer
Comics World #1
William Stout executed this Harvey Kurtzman idea for the cover of the 1990 book, Harvey Kurtzman's Strange Adventures. In addition, Stout illustrated a seven-page Kurtzman story inside the same book.

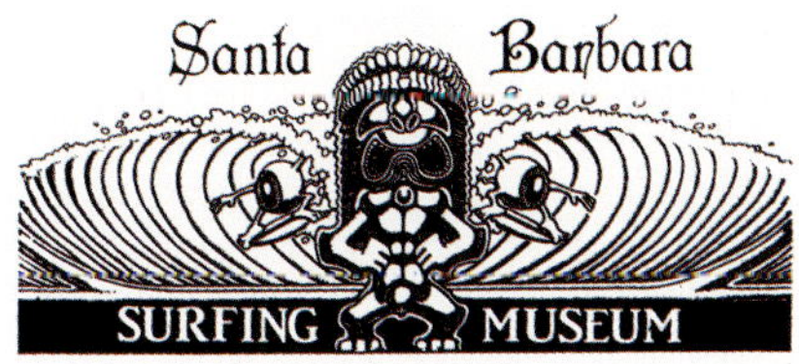
Santa Barbara
SURFING MUSEUM

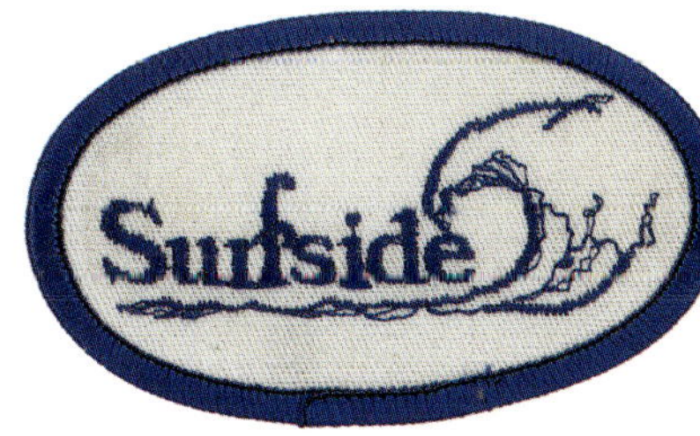
Surfside

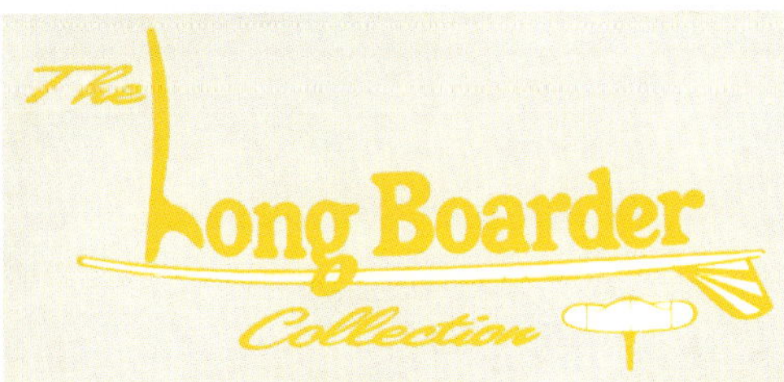
The
Long Boarder
Collection

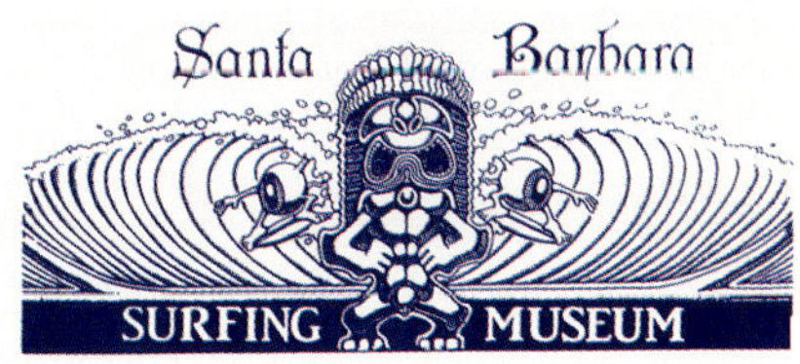
Santa Barbara
SURFING MUSEUM

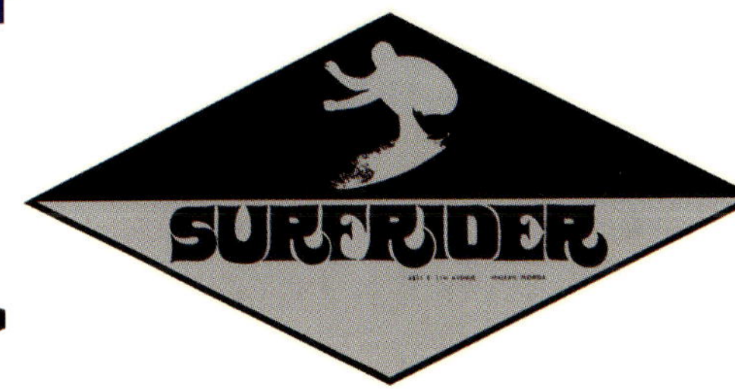
SURFRIDER

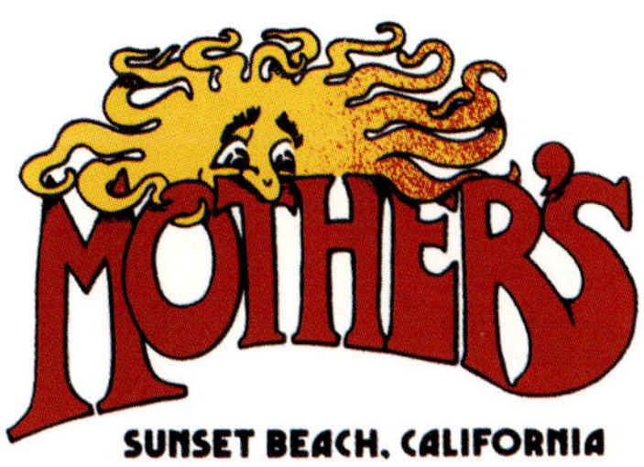
MOTHER'S
SUNSET BEACH, CALIFORNIA

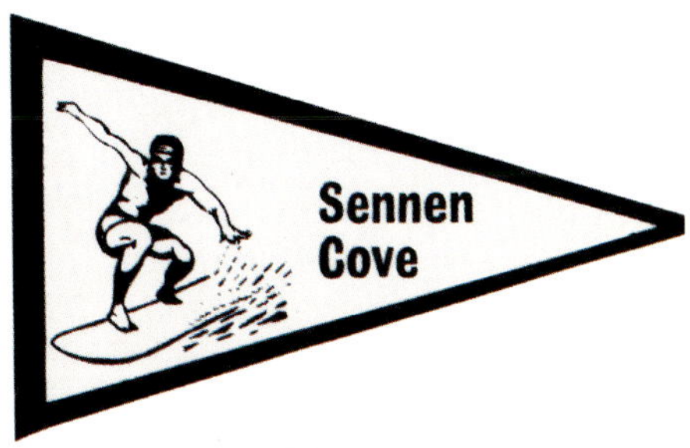
Sennen
Cove

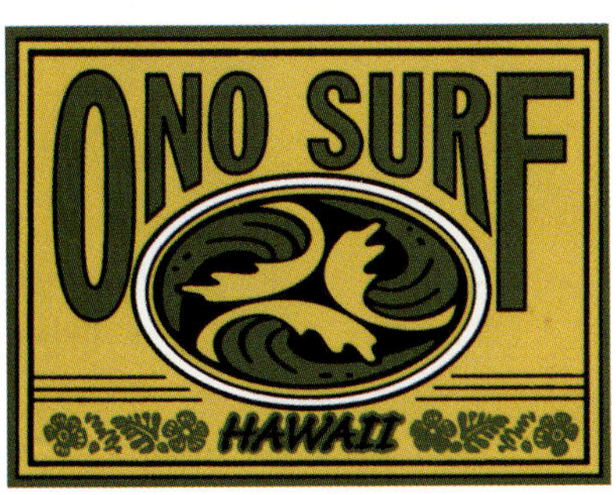
ONO SURF
HAWAII

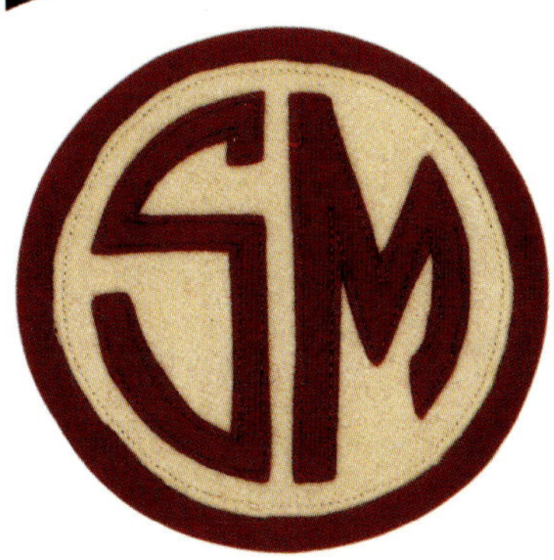
SM

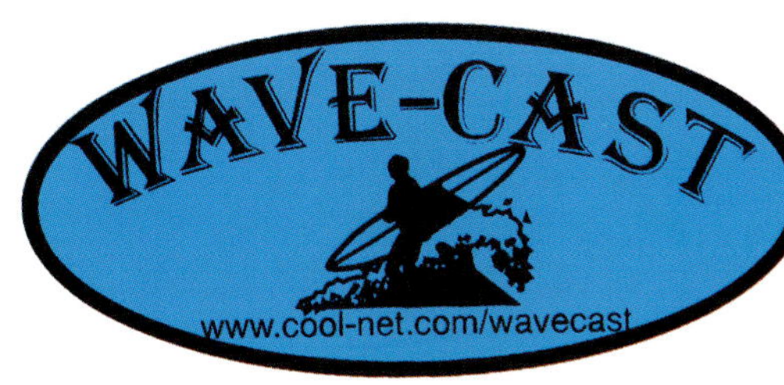
WAVE-CAST
www.cool-net.com/wavecast

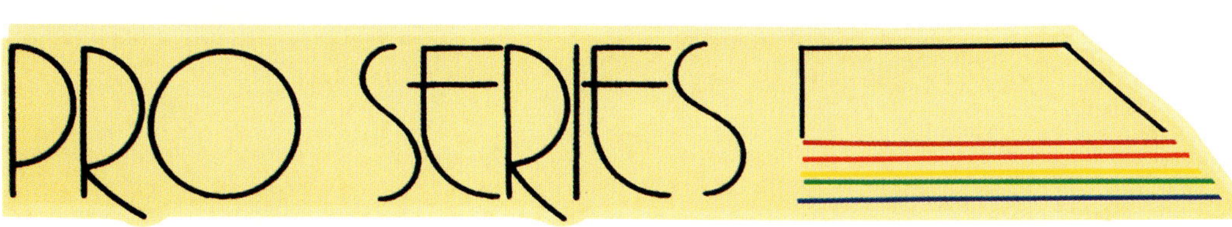
PRO SERIES

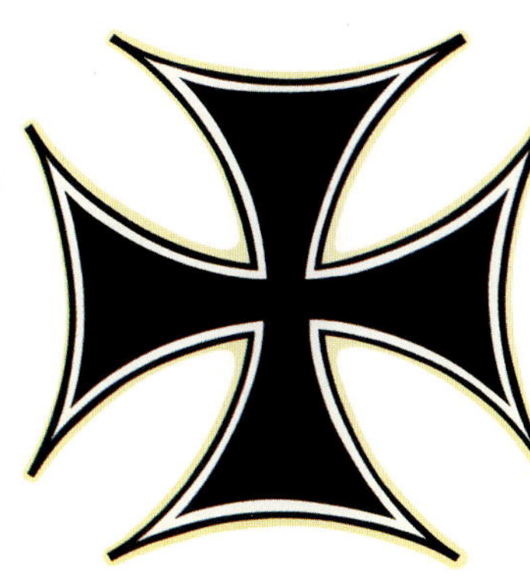

The Red Baron

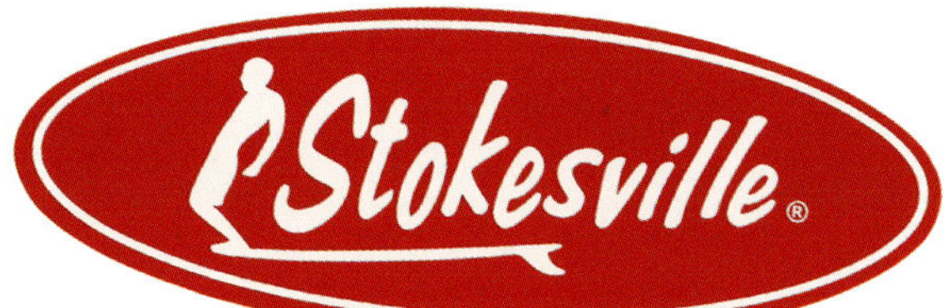
Stokesville®

ABOUT THE AUTHOR, & ACKNOWLEDGEMENTS

Although I produced this book for sticker collectors Pete Noble, Cary Weiss and Keith Eshelman, I too am a sticker collector. And I have produced a few myself.

Most of my sticker collection is displayed in and around my 1999 Ford Econoline van: on the back window, on the ceiling over the driver and passenger sides, everywhere. This van has 200,000 miles on it, many of them racked up on two trips to Alaska, up and down the California coast and to Montana and back several times; many of them reminders of places I have visited, foreign and domestic.

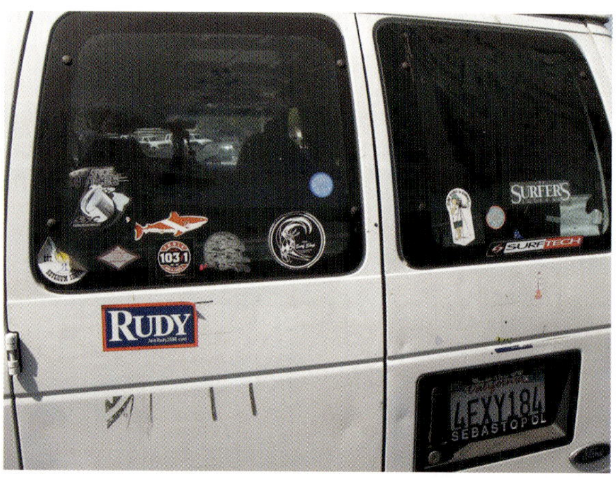

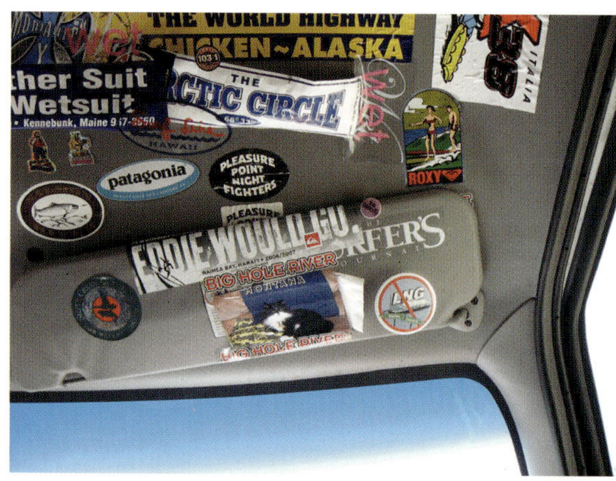

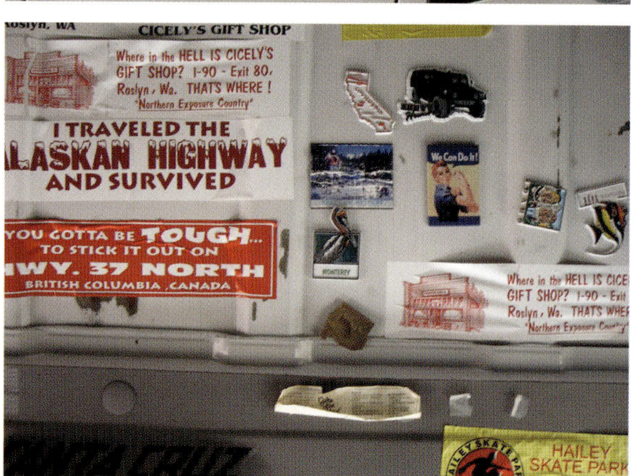

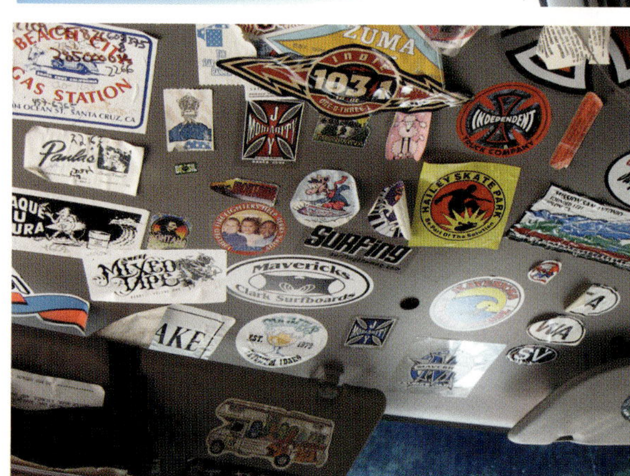

I also have produced some stickers. Most recently, I had a batch made up for a women's surf magazine I produced in 2006. The stickers were nice and so was the magazine, but advertisers weren't interested and WET Magazine didn't make it past the first issue. I still have about 5000 copies of the magazine, and a few handfuls of stickers.

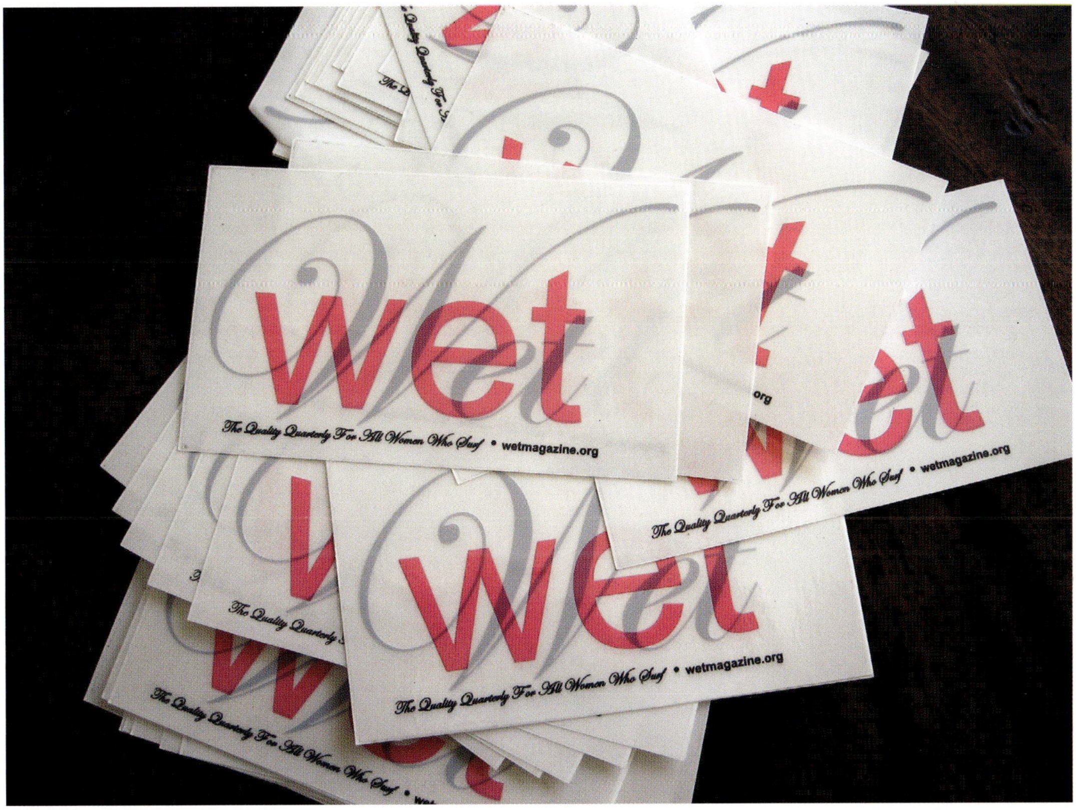

But that is what stickers are about: permanent reminders of memories that could fade. Pleasant experiences, lessons learned.

In 2004 I made up a bunch of political bumper stickers under the name Strange Bedfellows, mixing and matching political candidates. The stickers were funny and amused anyone stuck behind me in traffic, but they didn't sell either. Another lesson learned.

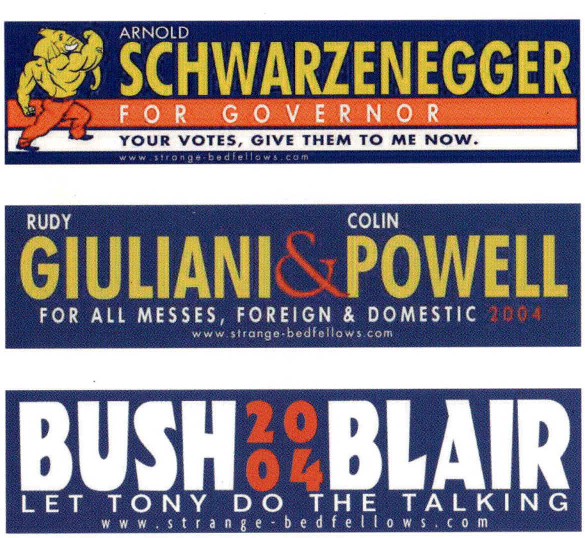

Some samples of Strange Bedfellows bumper stickers made by the author for the 2004 election.

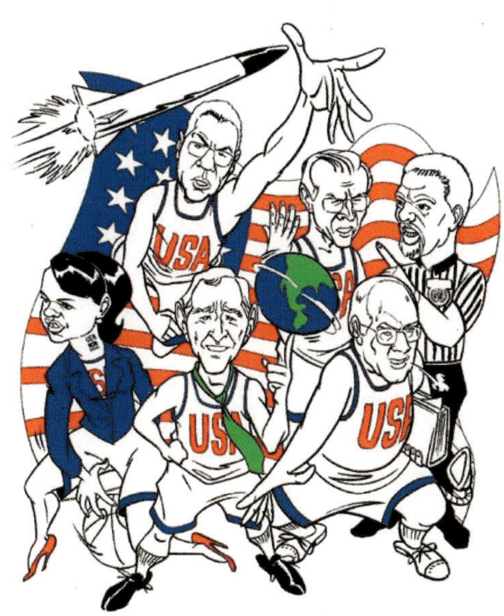

This book on collectible stickers took a long time to produce. I agreed to do it in the fall of 2004, I think. Pete Noble, Cary Weiss and Keith Eshelman all sent me their sticker collections, which I then sent to Schiffer books to be scanned.

Then I got sidetracked by six books in a row: *Surfing USA!, Surfing and the Meaning of Life* and *The Surfboard: Art, History, Stoke* for Voyageur Press. *The Surfing Guides to North, Central and Southern California* for Chronicle Books and *Surf Wax* for Schiffer Books.

I also launched that women's surf magazine and several other projects. The sticker book was always there in the corner of my desk and the corner of my mind, but I kept putting it off until the guilt consumed me.

I didn't get back to the sticker book until the spring and summer of 2007. I had about a thousand stickers to work with and took some time organizing them into categories. In a way it helped that I had done those six books before this one as I had a head full of surfing history and that helped me find a structure for this book, which I am hoping to mail to Schiffer tomorrow: Tuesday the 25th of June.

I would like to thank Tina Skinner and Doug Congdon-Martin at Schiffer Books for their patience and Pete Noble, Cary Weiss, and Keith Eshelman for their patience and input in getting this book done.

Also, Fernando Aguerre and Voyageur Press for letting us use the surfboard photos, The Surfing Heritage Foundation for access to their photo files, and Cary Weiss for coming in at the last minute and saving the day with his photo collection.

Ben Marcus
Malibu, California